Themes in
West Africa's History

16.95

Western African Studies

Lineages of State Fragility
Rural Civil Society in Guinea-Bissau
JOSHUA B. FORREST

Willing Migrants
Soninke Labor Diasporas, 1848–1960
FRANÇOIS MANCHUELLE

El Dorado in West Africa
The Gold-Mining Frontier,
African Labor & Colonial Capitalism
in the Gold Coast, 1875–1900
RAYMOND E. DUMETT

Nkrumah & the Chiefs
The Politics of Chieftaincy in Ghana, 1951–60
RICHARD RATHBONE

Ghanaian Popular Fiction
'Thrilling Discoveries in Conjugal Life'
& Other Tales
STEPHANIE NEWELL

Paths of Accommodation
Muslim Societies & French Colonial Authorities
in Senegal & Mauritania
1880–1920
DAVID ROBINSON

Slavery & Reform in West Africa
Toward Emancipation in Nineteenth
Century Senegal & the Gold Coast
TREVOR R. GETZ

Ouidah
The Social History of a West African
Slaving 'Port'
1727–1892
ROBIN LAW

Between the Sea & the Lagoon
An Eco-social History
of the Anlo of South-eastern Ghana,
c.1850 to Recent Times
EMMANUEL KWAKU AKYEAMPONG

West African Challenge to Empire
Culture & History
in the Volta-Bani Anticolonial War
MAHIR SAUL & PATRICK ROYER

'Civil Disorder is the Disease of Ibadan'
Chieftaincy & Civic Culture in a Yoruba City
RUTH WATSON

*Smugglers, Secessionists & Loyal Citizens
on the Ghana-Togo Frontier*
The Lie of the Borderlands since 1914
PAUL NUGENT

Eurafricans in Western Africa
Commerce, Social Status, Gender
& Religious Observance
from the 16th to the 18th Century
GEORGE E. BROOKS

'Koda is God's Gift'
Agricultural Production, Export Initiatives
& the Kola Industry of Asante & the Gold Coast
c.1820–1950
EDMUND ABAKA

Fighting the Slave Trade
West African Strategies
SYLVIANE A. DIOUF (ED.)

Themes in West Africa's History
EMMANUEL KWAKU AKYEAMPONG
(ED.)

Themes in
West Africa's History

Edited by

EMMANUEL KWAKU AKYEAMPONG

Professor of History, Harvard University

Ohio University Press
ATHENS

James Currey
OXFORD

Woeli Publishing Services
ACCRA

James Currey
73 Botley Road
Oxford OX2 0BS

Ohio University Press
The Ridges, Building 19
Athens, Ohio 45701

Woeli Publishing Services
P. O. Box NT 601
Accra New Town, Ghana

British Library Cataloguing in Publication Data
Themes in West Africa's history. — (Western African Studies)
1. Africa, West — History 2. Africa, West — Historiography
I. Akyeampong, Emmanuel Kwaku

ISBN 10: 0–85255–996–8 (James Currey cloth)
ISBN 13: 978–085255–996–3
ISBN 10: 0–85255–995–X (James Currey paper)
ISBN 13: 978–085255–995–6

Library of Congress Cataloging-in-Publication Data
Themes in West Africa's History/edited by Emmanuel Akyeampong
p. cm. — (Western African studies)
Includes bibliographical references and index
ISBN 0–8214–1640–5 (cloth : alk. paper)
ISBN 0–8214–1641–3 (pbk : alk. paper)
1. Africa, West — History, I. Akyeampong, Emmanuel Kwaku. II. Series

DT 475.T48 2006
966–dc22   2005044917

ISBN 0–8214–1640–5 (Ohio University Press cloth)
ISBN 0–8214–1641–3 (Ohio University Press paper)
ISBN 9988–626–56–8 (Woeli Publishing Services paper)

Typeset in 10˚/11˚ pt Book Antiqua
by Woeli Publishing Services, Ghana
Printed and bound in Britain by Woolnough, Irthlingborough

Contents

Contents

Contents

List of Maps & Figures

Maps

Figures

Acknowledgements & Notes on Contributors

I would like to express my gratitude to the thirteen contributors for their commitment to this volume, knowing the busy schedules they keep. I am also grateful to two of my graduate students, Harmony O'Rourke and Myles Osborne, for superb editorial assistance.

Emmanuel Kwaku Akyeampong is Professor of History and Harvard College Professor at Harvard University, where he also chairs the Committee on African Studies. His research interests include social history, religious interaction, environment, and disease in West Africa. He is the author of *Drink, Power and Cultural Change: A Social History of Alcohol in Ghana, c.1800 to Recent Times* (1996); and *Between the Sea and the Lagoon: An Eco-Social History of the Anlo of Southeastern Ghana, c.1850 to Recent Times* (2001).

David Conrad is Professor of History at the State University of New York in Oswego. He specializes in early West African kingdoms, oral tradition, indigenous religions and Islam, and African resistance to European imperialism. He is the author of several books including *A State of Intrigue: the Epic of Bamana Segu* (1990); and *Somono Bala of the Upper Niger* (2002).

Cyril K. Daddieh is Professor of Political Science and Director of the Black Studies Program at Providence College, Rhode Island. His research interests include state-civil society relations, ethnicity and conflict, and the nature of the state in Africa. His publications include a co-edited volume on *State Building and Democratization in Africa* (1999).

Mary Esther Kropp Dakubu is a Professor of Linguistics, and Head of Publications for the Institute of African Studies at the University of Ghana. An expert on Ga-Adangme language, history and culture, she is the author of *The Dangme Language: An Introductory Survey* (1987); and *Korle Meets the Sea: A Sociolinguistic History of Accra* (1997).

Acknowledgements & Notes on Contributors

Andreas Eckert is Professor of History at Hamburg University. He has conducted research on colonial rule and decolonization in Cameroon and Tanzania, and more recently on landed property and conflict in urban, colonial Cameroon. He is the author of *The Douala and Colonial Powers* (1991); and *Landed Property, Land Conflicts and Colonial Change: Douala 1880–1960* (1999).

Ogbu U. Kalu is Henry Winters Luce Professor of World History and Mission at McCormick Theological Seminary, Chicago. He is a leading expert on church history, world Christianity, and religious interaction in Africa. He is the author of numerous books including *Power, Poverty and Prayer: The Challenges of Poverty and Pluralism in African Christianity, 1960–1996* (2000); and *The Embattled Gods: Christianization of Igboland 1841–1991* (2003).

Brian Larkin is Assistant Professor in the Department of Anthropology at Barnard College, New York. His research focuses on the role of media technologies in the shaping of popular culture and of secular and Muslim modernities in northern Nigeria. He is the co-editor of *Media Worlds: Anthropology on New Terrain* (2002).

Patrick Manning is Professor of History and of African-American Studies, and the Director of the World History Centre at Northeastern University (Massachusetts). His research interests include the history of slavery and slave trade, the African diaspora, and colonial and post-colonial Francophone Africa. His numerous books include *Slavery and African Life: Occidental, Oriental and African Slave Trades* (1990); and *Francophone Sub-Saharan Africa, 1880–1995* (1999).

Susan Keech McIntosh is a Professor of Anthropology at Rice University, Texas. Her major interests are in the origins of complex societies, West African Iron Age, archaeology, human osteology and ceramic analysis. Her current research has been on early urbanism in West Africa, particularly in the Niger and Middle Senegal Valleys. She has written with Roderick McIntosh, *Prehistoric Investigations in the Region of Jenne, Mali* (1980); and is co-editor of *The Way the Wind Blows: Climate, History and Human Action* (2000).

Birgit Meyer is Senior Lecturer at the Research Centre on Religion and Society, Department of Sociology and Anthropology, University of Amsterdam. Her research has been on missions and local appropriations of Christianity, Pentecostalism, popular culture and video films in Ghana. She is the author of *Translating the Devil: Religion and Modernity among the Ewe in Ghana* (1999); and co-editor of *Globalization and Identity: Dialectics of Flow and Closure* (1999).

Célestin Monga is a Senior Economist at the World Bank, Washington D.C. One of the leading intellectuals of Cameroon, he left the country after his arrest in 1991 for criticizing the President in an article in *Le Messager*. He is the author of *The Anthropology of Anger: Civil Society and Democracy in Africa* (1998).

Pashington Obeng is Assistant Professor in Africana Studies at Wellesley College, Massachusetts and an adjunct faculty at Harvard University. He has written on African religions and cultures, and on the African diaspora. His recent research is on the cosmologies and life ways of African Indians in Karnataka in south India. He is the author of *Asante Catholicism: Religious and Cultural Reproduction among the Akan of Ghana* (1996).

Ismail Rashid is Assistant Professor of History at Vassar College, New York. His primary interests are slave and peasant resistance, Pan-Africanism, and social conflicts in contemporary Africa. He is the co-editor of *West Africa's Security Challenges: Building Peace in a Troubled Region* (2004).

James L. A. Webb Jr. is Professor of History at Colby College, Maine. He works on global ecological history, the ecological histories of Africa and South Asia, and historical epidemiology. He is the author of *Desert Frontier: Ecological and Economic Change along the Western Sahel, 1600–1850* (1995); and *Tropical Pioneers: Human Agency and Ecological Change in the Highlands of Sri Lanka* (2002).

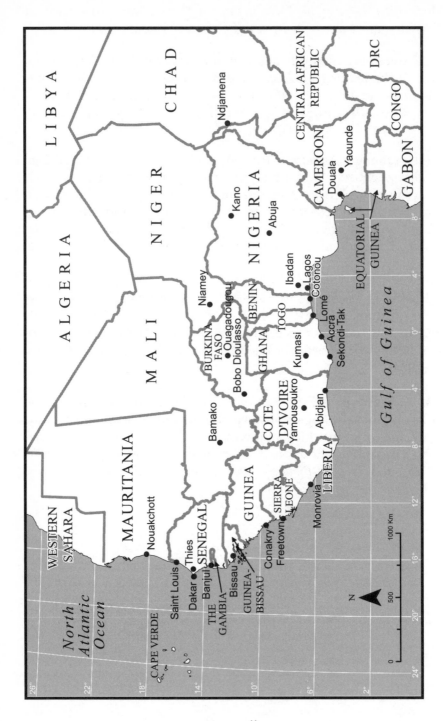

Map of West Africa
(Source: Patrick Florance, Harvard University Map Collections)

Introduction

EMMANUEL KWAKU AKYEAMPONG

This edited volume originated about three years ago in an invitation from James Currey Publishers to consider writing a textbook of West African history and a Historical Atlas of West Africa. I conceded the need for these texts, and after some hesitation opted to edit a volume of essays on West Africa's history and deferred the Historical Atlas for a later time. I chose to edit a volume on West Africa because I sought an easy way out. More importantly, reviewing my syllabi on West Africa over the past decade — cobbled from various sources — convinced me that a comprehensive textbook on West Africa's history needed to draw on different disciplines and expertise. I am grateful to James Currey Publishers for the invitation and their persistence and to the thirteen contributors of this volume who responded with enthusiasm to the prospectus for this textbook.

The volume is arranged thematically and chronologically, but not necessarily as a continuous historical narrative. It aims to bring together in about 300 pages key themes from West Africa's prehistory to the present. It is designed as a textbook for undergraduate and graduate levels, discussing various disciplinary approaches to West African history, providing overviews of the literature on major topics, and breaking new ground through the incorporation of original research. The goal was to write in an accessible style and with few footnotes, though I was the first to fall foul of that prescription in respect to the latter. At the end of each chapter is a short list of recommended reading. Though there is important overlap between the chapters, I made no attempt to harmonize the intellectual views expressed within them. As the chapters went through the review process, I shared drafts with other contributors to the volume in their areas of expertise. We therefore served as our own peer review system. For future editions, I hope to convene workshops at Harvard University that will enable contributors to deliberate over the text as a whole and how it should be reshaped, as well as their individual contributions.

Teaching West African history

The need for this volume arose from awareness of the limitations in existing texts for teaching West African history. In addition, most of these texts are out of print. The major text for teaching West African history remains J. F. A. Ajayi and Michael Crowder (eds) *History of West Africa*, which has been issued in three editions (1971, 1976 and 1985–7). This two-volume work constitutes an important landmark in West African historiography and remains my favorite text as a scholar. The mid-1980s edition includes some new chapters in Volume 1 that take cognizance of the emerging themes of ecology, disease, and maritime history. But the conceptual framework remains the same. Nevertheless, the two volumes provide comprehensive geographical and chronological coverage of West Africa's history, something that this volume does not attempt to do. The chapters in Volume 1 on ecology, early savanna kingdoms, and coastal societies between the Volta and the Niger remain 'state of the field' essays.

Volume 2 of Ajayi and Crowther, which covers the period between 1800 and about 1960, is equally impressive in its scholarly pool and geographic coverage. One limitation of Volume 2 is that too much has happened in post-colonial West Africa in spite of Richard Rathbone's efforts to extend the coverage to 1980 in the concluding chapter. Volume 2 in its third edition also comprises 21 chapters and is 833 pages long, an unwieldy textbook for classroom use, aside from being out of print. That undergraduate students who enroll in my West Africa since 1800 class are often drawn to the contemporary issues of religious ferment and creativity (Pentecostalism and Islamism), political conflicts, state-civil society relations, the elusiveness of economic development, the specter of disease, and the oppressive reality of poverty makes it impossible for the historian to take refuge behind the thirty-year rule and argue that historians do not examine contemporary issues. These are themes or developments that have come to shape life as it is lived and experienced in West Africa.

There is also a demand for scholarship on Africa to respond to Africa's myriad problems and challenges. In the 1986 edited volume on *African*

Historiographies, Congolese historians Mumbanza Mwa Bawele and Sabakinu Kivulu lament that 'our present discourse is foreign to the society of which we speak; it is ignored by the masses and by the intellectual, political, and economic elites. It is in fact history for the historians, for the specialists. And it lacks commitment.' Bawele and Kivulu called for a 'history for development'.[1] The contributors to this volume are scholars who have shown a keen interest in understanding the African past and present, as well as having their scholarship shed light on the African 'condition'.

There are several single-volume texts on West African history, and I have used many selectively in my courses over the years.[2] The utility of a historical atlas was clear when Kwamena-Poh et al., *African History in Maps* (1982) and Ajayi and Crowder (eds) *Historical Atlas of Africa* (1985) were in print and available.[3] For students without an Africa background, these were invaluable introductions to the study of the continent with a visual depiction of themes and geographical areas. Segments of Basil Davidson's documentary series, *Africa: A Voyage of Discovery* and Ali Mazrui's *The Africans* brought a sense of immediacy to my West Africa courses and to a younger generation very oriented towards multimedia. In terms of textbooks to be purchased by students of West Africa up to 1800, I have used Boahen's *Topics in West African History* (1986), Austen's *African Economic History* (1987), Manning's *Slavery and African Life* (1990), Mbiti's *African Religions and Philosophy* (1989), and *The Epic of Sunjata*, now available in various editions. Then comes the long list of other works as we examine sources and methods for the study of African history, ecology, climate change, agriculture, early states in Western and Central Sudan, the West African economy, religious interaction, the Atlantic trade and slavery, and case studies of forest and coastal kingdoms. And the students complain that I make them read too much, and that I need a course packet. They are also intrigued by the way I constantly revise the material in the texts during lectures with more current interpretations and evidence; the need for a new text was obvious.

---

[1] Mumbanza Mwa Bawele and Sabakinu Kivulu, 'Historical Research in Zaire: Present Status and Future Perspectives,' in Bogumil Jewsiewicki and David Newbury (eds), *African Historiographies: What History for Which Africa?* (Beverly Hills, CA: Sage Publications, 1986), p. 234.

[2] These include Michael Crowder, *West Africa: An Introduction to its History* (London: Longman, 1977); J. D. Fage, *A History of West Africa* (Cambridge: Cambridge University Press, 1969); and Basil Davidson, *West Africa before the Colonial Era: A History to 1850* (London: Longman, 1998).

[3] See also Brian Catchpole and I. A. Akinjogbin, *A History of West Africa in Maps and Diagrams* (London: Collins Educational, 1984).

Introduction

For my course 'West Africa since 1800' the students' favorite is Boahen and Webster, *The Revolutionary Years: West Africa Since 1800* (1980), which is now out of print. Textbooks purchased by students include Boahen's *African Perspectives on Colonialism* (1987), Echenberg's *Colonial Conscripts* (1991), and Manning's *Francophone Sub-Saharan Africa: 1880-1985* (1998). Another important recent text is Cooper's *Africa since 1940* (2002). Then comes, again, my long list of readings for lecture themes on nineteenth-century kingdoms, the abolition of the slave trade and its impact, Euro-African interaction (merchants, explorers and missionaries), the partition and conquest of Africa, colonial rule, the World Wars, African nationalism and independence. The last three weeks of the course deal with post-colonial Africa, and here Manning's *Francophone Sub-Saharan Africa* and Cooper's *Africa since 1940* have become crucial to the continuation of the historical narrative. There were years when I divided the class into groups to research on the various aspects of post-colonial West Africa — economic performance, regionalism and ECOWAS, ethnicity and political conflict, Pentecostalism and Islamism, military intervention, the burden of disease — and make short presentations with handouts for the class. In short, we created our own materials and I guided discussions after brief introductions of relevant issues. The abundance of rich African novels for the post-1800 history enlivens the course: Achebe's *Things Fall Apart*, Armah's *The Beautyful Ones are not yet Born*, Oyono's *Houseboy*, and Beti's *Remember Ruben* being a select few.[4]

Structure and content of the book

This textbook is designed to be used with other valuable texts, particularly since it does not aim to present a narrative history of West Africa. The book is divided into three parts, retroactively, in my desire to provide large organizing categories. But there are important connections and overlaps, and some of these are highlighted in the following discussion. Part One: Paths to a West African Past comprises the first four chapters, which provide perspectives on West Africa's history from archaeology (McIntosh), ecology and culture (Webb), linguistics (Dakubu), and oral traditions (Conrad).

Part Two provides *longue durée* perspectives on the environment, society, agency and historical change in West Africa. There is important

---

[4] For a good overview of some of these novels, see Margaret Jean Hay (ed.), *African Novels in the Classroom* (Boulder, CO: Lynne Rienner Publishers, 2000).

overlap between Manning's chapter on slavery and the slave trade in West Africa from 1450 to 1930 and Rashid's chapter on castes, pawns and social inequality in West Africa. Indeed, Rashid's chapter has a sub-section that examines slavery, as he conceptualizes kinship, caste, pawnship and slavery in a relational schema. Obeng's chapter on religious interaction (African religions, Islam, and Christianity) in pre-twentieth-century West Africa also provides an important context for the contemporary discussion of Pentecostalism and Islamism by Larkin and Meyer in Part Three. Kalu's chapter on poverty in colonial West Africa explores indigenous meanings of wealth and poverty, with the Igbo serving as a detailed case study. The chapter dovetails with the discussion of social inequality in both Manning and Rashid. Akyeampong's chapter on disease in West African history builds on the context provided in Webb's review of ecology and culture, as he discusses diseases rooted in the African environment and others that were externally introduced. There is also important overlap with Eckert's examination of urbanization in colonial and post-colonial Africa, especially with regard to disease in colonial towns.

Part Three has three chapters: Monga on West African economic history with special attention to structural adjustment in the post-1980s; Daddieh on ethnicity, conflict and the state in contemporary West Africa; and Larkin and Meyer on Pentecostalism, Islam and culture. Economic and political developments have shaped religious expression and identity in significant ways, and some see the current Pentecostal and Islamist fervor as a response to the changing political economy. Monga's chapter, which also seeks to provide an alternative economic model to structural adjustment, resonates with Kalu's call for Africa-centered approaches to poverty reduction.

Part One: Paths to a West African Past

In Chapter 1, McIntosh gives an excellent overview of what we know of the West African past from about 10,000–1,000 BP. The chapter examines climate changes and their impact on migrations and settlements, pastoralism and farming. It sheds important light on indigenous innovations in pastoralism, agriculture, and metal technology (copper and iron), as well as external influences on these spheres. The chapter builds on McIntosh's work in the Middle Niger Valley, particularly at Jenne-jeno, and how this revises our understanding of early subsistence specialization, exchange, and urbanization before Arab influence. There is important dialogue between McIntosh's chapter and Webb's. In Chapter 2, the external influence in West Africa's history is etched more firmly, situating West Africa within global networks. Webb does an excellent job extending his analysis of ecology and culture into the last two centuries.

Dakubu in Chapter 3 examines the contribution of linguistics to West African history. She points out that linguistics can be useful to historians in the reconstruction of West African history, even if they lack linguistic skills. The chapter discusses different approaches to linguistics: historical and comparative linguistics and contact studies. Dakubu uses several historical examples to illustrate these approaches. Particularly revealing is the case study of maize in West Africa, where linguistic studies have shown that for Nigeria maize was introduced through northern trade routes and not from the south, as is expected of a New World crop during the era of Atlantic trade. This underscores the continued relevance of the north in cultural innovation in West Africa even after the European arrival. In Chapter 4 Conrad demonstrates the divide between Manding understanding of history and European historiographical traditions, as the Manding view epic narratives like *Sunjata* as a literal Magna Carta of clan identity. The chapter also shows how oral traditions are a rich source of cultural information. The genealogical engineering that characterizes some traditions, such as the incorporation of Muslim ancestors into Manding traditions, is revealing of the growing importance of Islam and how this was inserted into the Manding worldview and historical narratives.

Part Two: Perspectives on Environment, Society, Agency and Historical Change

Manning in Chapter 5 presents an excellent review of the history and historiography of slavery and slave trade in West Africa, examining the changing contours of enslavement through the interaction of the Occidental, Oriental and African slave trades. The chapter also provides an important discussion of the political, economic, and social impact of slavery and the slave trade on West African societies. Rashid (Chapter 6) expands the scope of social inequality in West Africa to include kinship, caste and pawnship. He views kinship as a cultural ideology that organizes blood, marital, and fictive relations; pawnship as the operating of political economy, particularly in the realm of accumulation; and caste as the complex interaction of culture and political economy with different historical configurations in space and time. He situates these various social categories in a relational schema and uses case studies to illustrate how they cannot be understood in isolation.

Obeng in Chapter 7 argues against the common interpretation that African indigenous religions lacked internal dynamism and a missionary or evangelical component. Moreover, the chapter shows that the interaction of African religions with Islam or Christianity did not always result in African conversion or religious subordination. Indeed, the examples of *Santa Mariafo* and *Ntona Buw* show how African indigenous religions emerge or can be recharged through contact with non-African religions. Both religions appropriated elements of Christianity and redirected them in ways that responded to local needs and had nothing to do with the Christian faith. In Chapter 8 Kalu interrogates the nature of poverty in pre-colonial West Africa and its transformation during the colonial era. He argues that poverty is not just an economic condition, but also a cultural fact. Hence, its meaning is specific to local cultures. He demonstrates this in a compelling way with the Igbo of southeastern Nigeria, advocating that measures to redress poverty must take cognizance of this cultural dimension if they are to succeed.

Akyeampong in Chapter 9 uses disease as a lens to review continuity and change in West Africa's history from the medieval time to the present. The chapter examines the context of the environment and disease, and the impact of the Atlantic trade on epidemiology in West Africa. The changing disease environment during colonial rule and the responses of Western biomedicine, as well as the continuing reality of medical pluralism in the post-colonial era, conclude the chapter. Akyeampong also incorporates a discussion of African maladies and therapies from the extant sources, especially for the pre-colonial period. In Chapter 10 Eckert examines urbanization in the colonial and post-colonial eras. The chapter reviews key themes in the field — such as rural immiseration and rural-urban migration, the trend towards urban agriculture, urban planning and architecture as an instrument of colonial hegemony — and some of the pertinent historiography. It breaks new ground through Eckert's own work on urban land ownership in Cameroon. There is important overlap with Akyeampong's chapter on disease in Eckert's discussion of health in the colonial city, urban planning and the advent of segregation.

Part Three: Understanding Contemporary Africa through Religion and Political Economy

In Chapter 11 Monga reviews the economic history of West Africa with special emphasis on the post-1980s and the introduction of Structural Adjustment Programmes (SAPs) by the World Bank and the International Monetary Fund. Monga provides an illuminating

7

discussion of the historiography and theoretical debates on Africa's development and underdevelopment. The chapter presents a lucid explanation of why SAPs have failed to achieve their objectives. Daddieh in Chapter 12 raises several issues pertinent to understanding the nature of the post-colonial state and contemporary West African conflicts. Early in this chapter, Daddieh notes that the omnibus nature of West African nationalism papered over ethnic pluralism in the march to independence. At independence a social compact emerged that united charismatic nationalist leaders and their mass followers around a developmental agenda. At independence, West Africans inherited a 'weak' state, and economic decline vitiated the ability of states to deliver on development. The result was a crisis of legitimacy and a transition to autocratic rule. Violence became the mechanism for regime change. The recent civil wars in Liberia, Sierra Leone, and Côte d'Ivoire have demonstrated how destructive this avenue can be.

In Chapter 13 Larkin and Meyer review new religious movements in West Africa with a focus on Pentecostalism and Islamism. A declining political economy is crucial to understanding these religious trends, and the preceding chapters by Monga and Daddieh provide an important context in this respect. Strikingly, their discussion of Pentecostalism and Islamism reveal how much these movements have in common — despite the opposing rhetoric — in terms of the political economy that spawned them, their *modus operandi*, and how both represent important strategies in a new 'religious imaginary' which affirms a distinctly religious conception of the moral order of society.

PART I

Paths to a West African Past

1

The Holocene Prehistory of West Africa
10,000–1000 BP

SUSAN KEECH McINTOSH

Introduction

Over the past thirty years, most archaeological research in West Africa has focused on the record of human activities since 10,000 BP.[1] Although the coverage is spotty and huge areas remain inadequately understood and documented, this research has transformed earlier notions of a West African past that was largely static until stimulus or intervention from the north transformed Iron Age societies. Furthermore, the sequences of change through time that this research documents indicate some unexpected and possibly unique historical trajectories.

Current evidence suggests that West African food production was indigenous and followed a different pattern from the familiar sequences of the temperate Old World (the Near East, Europe, and China) in which domesticated plants were an important element of the earliest food-producing economies. The earliest food-producing economies in West Africa were pastoral, based on cattle that were domesticated indigenously in northeast Africa, it appears, several millennia before the first domesticated plants appear in the archaeological record.

As archaeological research has shifted from a focus on isolated single sites, where data from one excavation were extrapolated and assumed to apply to a broad set of sites with nominally similar material culture, to the investigation of many sites within a region, our understanding

---

[1] The convention used here for dates is as follows: BP is used for radiocarbon dates 'before present', which must be calibrated before their correspondence to calendar years is known; YA (years ago), CE ('Common era') and BCE ('before Common era') refer to dates in calendar years.

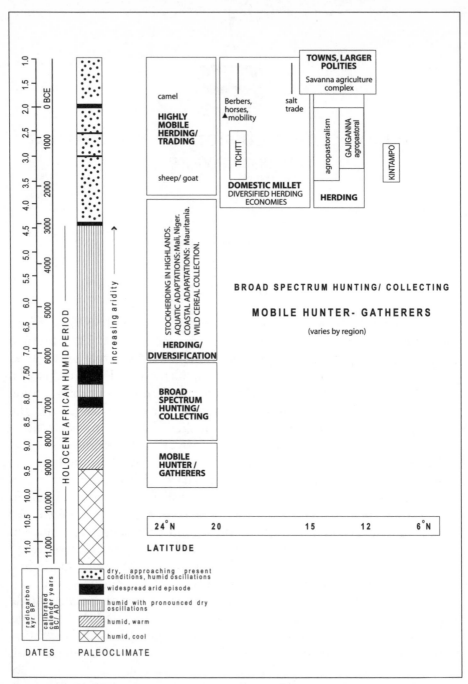

Fig. 1.1 Table showing major economic changes in West Africa, along with recognized archaeological traditions, arranged by latitude against changing climate trends through the Holocene.

of the complexity and diversity of the West African past has grown. In the temperate Old World, economic specialization, an early sign of growing social complexity, most frequently involved craft activities; in West Africa, an equally important aspect was subsistence specialization. By 4000 BP when the earliest documented domestic plants appeared, there was a concomitant development of specialized fishing economies that probably interacted with food-producing economies within the same region by means of subsistence exchange, creating a complex web of interdependent communities.

Upon the important bases of cattle (with varying percentages of sheep and goats), domestic cereals (millet, rice) from 4000 BP, and ecologically based subsistence exchange, complex societies emerged in favored locales in West Africa. These were areas of low rainfall (where the tsetse fly that carried sleeping sickness so frequently fatal to cattle and humans could not thrive) and abundant water. The Middle Niger floodplain, where the Niger flows north through arid grass- and scrubland thereby seasonally flooding the vast flat expanse of the Inland Niger delta, is one such locale. Here, the domestication of African rice reduced population mobility to the extent that settlement mounds began to form in the floodplain. From investigation of these highly visible sites in various regions of the Middle Niger, we can begin to trace the emergence of extensive multi-settlement systems and their increase in scale and complexity.

Urban thresholds were reached at Jenne-jeno by 800 CE, and may have been reached earlier at Ja, the source of Jenne's founding population, according to oral tradition. Undoubtedly, in the vast, undocumented regions elsewhere in West Africa, similar transformations occurred. Much research remains to be done, but enough has been accomplished to make it clear that many earlier assumptions about the trajectory of West Africa's past were wrong.

The Pleistocene/Holocene transition

There is abundant evidence for human occupation in West Africa during the Pleistocene (1.7 million years to 10,000 years ago). The discovery of hominid fossils in the Lake Chad Basin confirms that hominids were present in West Africa much earlier, extending back as far as six or seven million years ago. Unlike East Africa, however, the record of hominid fossils and undisturbed archaeological sites is extremely sparse. Fossil discoveries depend on two geological processes: sedimentation to preserve and fossilize the skeleton after death, and

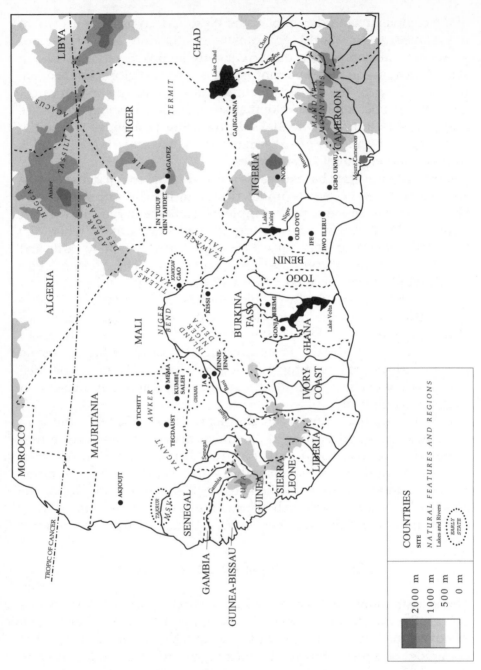

Fig. 1.2 West Africa: natural features and regions
(Source: based on map p.27, The Atlas of Africa, *Règine Van Chi-Bonnardel, New York: Free Press, 1973, editions 'Jeune Afrique')*

exposure of the ancient fossil-bearing sediments through tectonic uplift, erosion, or both. Much of West Africa is relatively flat and geologically ancient. There is little topographic variation south of the Sahara to generate robust sedimentation, and even less recent faulting and uplift. Therefore, discovery of hominid fossils will probably remain a rare event. Many of the more recent Pleistocene deposits containing not just fossils, but artifactual evidence of human activities, have long ago been scoured away and reworked by water and wind. Sometimes, the artifacts have been transported to new locations by rapidly moving water and redeposited. Surface materials of the Lower Paleolithic/Early Stone Age (chopper tools, 'Acheulian' hand axes and cleavers) are especially common north of 16° N latitude. Middle Stone Age artifacts (a variety of flake and core industries dating presumptively to 120,000–20,000 BP) are also quite widespread, but rarely found in primary contexts (i.e., original contexts of use and deposition). For these reasons, our discussion focuses on the last 10,000 years, for which evidence of human society and activity can be found in its original context.

The end of the Pleistocene involved a dramatic change in vegetation communities and their distribution in West Africa. For much of the last glacial maximum 20,000–14,000 BP, West Africa was exceptionally dry and substantially cooler. The desert margin lay 500 km south of its present position. Equatorial forest was restricted to a few refuge areas along the southern coast. Small bands of hunter-gatherers were sparsely distributed in the south. Approximately 12,500 years ago (10,500 BP) the rapid onset of much wetter conditions transformed the landscape of West Africa. The humid forest zone expanded 350 km north of its present limits, and the desert effectively disappeared from West Africa. Closed lake basins all over northern West Africa reached Holocene high stands between 9500 and 8500 BP. Lake Chad, for example, became Megachad, over fifteen times its present size and 40 m deeper. The Sahara became a land of lakes, grassy plains, and forested uplands.

The fauna of northern Mali, Mauritania and Niger included elephant, giraffe, hippo, crocodile, and Nile perch plus many varieties of catfish. Hunter-gatherers expanded into this newly verdant zone. In the Aïr Mountains of Niger, hunters seasonally occupied base camps in the mountains as well as specialized, hunting/processing sites on lakeshores in the adjacent lowlands. Armed with small blades, geometric microliths, and a variety of arrow points, these groups hunted wild buffalo, antelope and gazelle, and also fished. By the tenth millennium BP, Saharan groups were making pottery, among the earliest anywhere in the world. After 9000 BP, grinding stones became common at

15

northern sites, indicating intensive processing of plant foods, especially wild cereals.

What accounted for such a rapid change in climate? Climate in West Africa is proximally produced by the seasonal migration and pulsation of two air masses — the dry tropical and the humid maritime continental masses. Where these air masses meet and interact (a front known as the Intertropical Convergence Zone — ITCZ) monsoonal rainfall occurs.[2] The ICTZ annual migration cycle proceeds from the desert margin in the north to the equatorial forest in the south, producing ever more prodigious rains as it moves southwards, and these are repeated as the ITCZ moves northwards again. To the north, the dry season between the two passages of the ITCZ is nine to eleven months long. The migration of the ITCZ, along with the relatively flat topography of West Africa, produces the familiar West African latitudinal zoning of vegetation, from equatorial forest to Guinean forest and savanna, to dry, Sudanic savanna, sahel and desert. The zones shift latitudinally in response to the changes in the displacement of the ITCZ migration. During the early Holocene, the northern front of the ITCZ was displaced 500-700 km or more northwards.

This dramatic shift in vegetation zones and water budget was only one — although certainly the most extensive — of many changes in climate during the Holocene in West Africa. Some of these lasted for hundreds of years and were pan-African or even global in scale. Others were shorter and more regional or local in effect. Many variables could affect climate and mediate how its effects were experienced locally. Unlike in temperate zones, where temperature is the major factor affecting the rhythm of the seasons, moisture dictates the pattern of growth cycles in the tropics. Particularly in the sahel and dry savanna zones, even minor shifts in the availability of water can have major effects on human societies. During the Holocene, human groups faced the challenge of climatic oscillations occurring on scales ranging from millennia to decades.

Human response to this challenge involved interaction between the physical world of plants, animals, soils and climate and the human domain of culture, experience and action. The African milieu has been

[2] Ultimately, the position of the ITCZ is affected by heating patterns influenced by the intensity of sunlight falling on the earth. Important factors here are the changing tilt of the earth's axis to the sun, and the timing of the earth's closest passage to the sun (perihelion). In 9000 BP, for example, the earth's axis was more strongly tilted than today, and perihelion occurred in July. It takes place in January today. The longer exposure of the northern Hemisphere to heating just when earth was closest to the sun affected the heating and position of these air masses over West Africa.

characterized as hostile, with its inhabitants engaged in continual struggle. Some suggest that African innovation in the face of the challenge was infinite. This probably overstates the case. The West African environment posed constraints on innovation; one finite subset of responses was more viable than another. At the same time, what was a disaster to one group was a potential opportunity to another. The farmer, the fisher and the nomad view the world very differently! All, however, developed strategies to address effectively an environment where moisture fluctuations represent substantial risks to life and health. Looking across the Holocene, we can see several recurring patterns in the response of West African societies to risk over time: mobility, which kept population densities generally low (aided by disease vectors) and labor at a premium; and exchange and alliances across ecological boundaries.

The Holocene Humid Period and the appearance of cattle herding

The early Holocene Humid Period that began 11,000 years ago was punctuated by at least one abrupt, widespread desiccation phase between 8000 and 7000 BP. Soon after this, pottery-using pastoralist groups with domestic cattle and some sheep and goats became widespread in West Africa between 20 and 24° N. They exploited wild plants, and also hunted and fished to varying degrees. Analysis of cattle DNA indicates that indigenous, wild African cattle were domesticated as early as 9000 years ago in northern Africa. Dung, dried plant fodder, and the bones of Barbary sheep (*Ammotragus lervia*) dating between 9000 and 8000 BP in caves in the Acacus highlands of Libya indicate that hunter-collectors were penning and controlling these animals. These behaviors did not, however, lead to domestication, defined as genetic changes indicating dependence on humans. The only domesticated caprines documented in Africa were sheep and goat introduced from the Near East 7000–8000 years ago.

Ammotragus is but one of the 86 species of artiodactyls (grazing animals with an even number of functional toes) in Africa that were not domesticated. What accounts for the successful domestication of cattle alone among this rich diversity of ungulates? Wild cattle had a package of characteristics that made them particularly suited for control by humans: they live in herds with a hierarchical social structure (the human herder usurped the role of the lead male), are relatively slow and easy to pen without inducing panic and shock, and will tolerate

17

being penned with individuals from different herds. Human cultural preference and behavior probably also played a role. Fiona Marshall has suggested that wild cattle may have initially been brought under control in order to assure predictable access to meat for important rituals and feast occasions, when gifts of meat were essential. This would have been of particular concern during dry periods, when grazing prey became more mobile. Although we commonly think of domestication as producing a more abundant food supply, perhaps predictability was the goal of the North African hunter/collectors who started herding cattle as well.

Plants were not domesticated for several millennia after herding economies were widely established. Elsewhere in the world, plants were domesticated before animals (New World, New Guinea), or contemporaneously with animals (temperate Old World). Why was the African pattern different? Marshall suggests that for hunter/collectors in the fluctuating environments of the early Holocene Sahara, herding mobile animals seasonally through several different environments was a less risky strategy than having to stay in one place for several months to cultivate plants. Wild cereals were seasonally available for harvesting without cultivation in the great sahelian grasslands of the Sahara in the early- to mid-Holocene. A mixed strategy of herding, collecting, fishing, and hunting provided a maximum of options in the face of unpredictable conditions.

From Mali and Niger especially, we have abundant archaeological evidence for the expansion of these herder/hunter/collectors into the grassland zone between 19° and 24° N, as Saharan lakes refilled after the severe dry episode c. 7500 BP. Cattle pose two constraints: they must be watered at least once every day, and they must stay away from the high grass and bushy savanna that harbor the tsetse fly. This noxious insect carries the trypanosome parasites that cause sleeping sickness, which is frequently fatal to domestic livestock, especially cattle. Herding economies were thus restricted to areas with less than 500-700 mm rainfall annually. Between 6500 and 4500 BP, this was north of 19° N latitude. This zone included a wide variety of landscapes and features, from areas with limited topographic variation that had seasonal or permanent lakes in vast depressions and seasonal rivers in wadis (northern Mali), to regions with important highlands and mountains (Aïr, Hoggar, Adrar des Ifoghas), where permanent lakes and rivers were present at high and low altitudes. These offered a range of opportunities for seasonal exploitation. While early pastoral economies are often discussed in terms of an assumed similarity to present-day nomadic African pastoralists, most living pastoralists do not have unhindered access to both grasslands and water in the way these mid-Holocene herders did. There were no farmers competing for these same resources! Specialized nomadic pastoralism, which involves extensive seasonal movements of the entire social group and their herds as exemplified by the Fulani today, probably arose only when agriculture became established and herders were forced into more marginal zones.

At the present time, it is not clear how rapidly domestic stock spread. Initially, it appears that domestic stock was added to the existing hunting/collecting economy. Between 7000 and 5500 BP, most of the dated evidence for herding/hunting/collecting economies comes from the Saharan highlands and adjacent lowland water-catchment areas. These are regions where the exploitation of diverse resource zones at different altitudes was possible. In the highland regions, livestock-based economies are attested to not only by remains of cattle bones but also in rock art. The best known rock art comes from the Tassili n'Ajjer and Tadrart Acacus of South-East Algeria/South-West Libya. Here, human groups and their livestock, along with wild fauna and hunting weapons, are depicted in naturalistic paintings. In some cases, substantial herds are shown. In others, what appear to be rituals involving cattle are depicted. Rock engravings are also present, and their distribution extends further south, into the Hoggar of Algeria, the Adrar des Ifoghas of Mali, and the Aïr of Niger.

Further west and south, hunter/collectors probably persisted in areas not conducive to herding. In northern Mali, there are sites from the period 7000-5500 BP with substantial numbers of heavy grindstones used for processing wild cereals. There are also sites with bone harpoons and other specialized equipment for fishing and hunting aquatic species. Further south, the extraordinary discovery of an 8.5 meter dugout canoe buried in the old shoreline of Megachad in northern Nigeria and dated to over 8000 years ago (7500 BP) suggests that technologies for lacustrine exploitation were well developed. On the Mauritanian coast, middens from this period indicate that some groups had begun to process large numbers of shellfish. In all of these cases, domestic stock seem to have been absent, but caution is warranted. Where people maintained very small herds that were conserved or exploited for milk or blood rather than meat, the archaeological record would show only wild animals. Or consumption of stock may have been seasonal, associated with particular rituals, in which case, bones of domesticates might be present only on sites occupied during that season.

As dry oscillations increased in severity and duration after 5000 BP, it is easy to imagine that herders were increasingly affected by boom-and-bust cycles similar to those experienced by present-day pastoralists. When herds are lost to drought or disease, herders rely on social networks and relations of obligation, reciprocity and mutual assistance to replenish their stock. During boom periods, when herd numbers swell, social and kin networks facilitate the mobilization of additional labor to manage the herds. Such social technologies are a key element of risk management. So, too, is mobility to access a wider range of essential resources. Both are likely to have expanded after 5000 BP, linking increasingly larger areas. The mid-Holocene humid period came to an abrupt end c. 4000 BP. There is evidence that this onset of arid conditions was dramatic. Precipitation fell, summer temperatures rose, and vegetation thinned to the extent that most available moisture was lost to evaporation. Herders were obliged to move to more reliable sources of water, many of which lay farther south. Herders of domestic cattle during the period 4000-2500 BP became concentrated between 20° and 13° N. latitude, as the tsetse zone retracted southwards.

Late Holocene climate oscillations and the expansion of food production

The disruption to human society as a consequence of this arid onset must have been massive, probably exceeding the effects on pastoralists of the sahelian drought of the 1970s. Long-occupied areas, such as the northern Aïr, were abandoned by pastoralists; new sites were colonized further south, in river valleys (Tilemsi, Azawagh), on the shores of lakes (Tichitt and Chad), and in seasonally inundated regions (the Mema). Several important innovations and trends were associated with this period: a domesticated cereal, pearl millet (*Pennisetum glaucum*), came into widespread use; sites were larger and more densely occupied than earlier in the Holocene; specialized subsistence economies became elaborated; increased population density and diversity in favored locales seem to have been associated with the first potential evidence for social differentiation and ranking. All of these were undoubtedly interrelated.

Wild cereals had been collected and processed for much of the Holocene. Many continue to be collected today in the sahel and are sold in the markets alongside domestic cereals. But between 4000 and 3500 BP, one of the most drought-tolerant cereals in the sahel — pearl, or bulrush, millet — was apparently the first to be domesticated, probably in Mauritania, based on DNA analysis. Pearl millet can be grown where there is as little as 200 (and up to 1000) mm of rain. The earliest direct dates on millet seeds are c. 3500 BP from the Awker region of Mauritania and Birimi, on the Gambaga plateau in northern Ghana, over 1000 km to the south.

In the Awker, along the curved escarpments (*dhar*) running between Tichitt and Néma, a distinctive early agropastoral society emerged and flourished between at least 3500 and 2600 BP. Initially, permanent lakes existed at the base of the escarpment, and extensive village settlements flanked their shores. On the escarpment itself, people used the naturally exfoliating sandstone as building material, creating stone-walled compounds that presumably had thatch or mat houses, as no stone house foundations have been found. Grindstones are exceptionally numerous, and upright stone plinths within compounds have been interpreted as supports for granaries. This is the earliest evidence for such storage facilities in West Africa.

The original sequence outlined by Munson thirty years ago suggested that domesticated millet appeared after 3000 BP, as the lakes dried up and people abandoned the lake villages and shifted to the escarpment. Yet more recent dates on grains of domestic millet demonstrate that it was present on escarpment sites by 3500 BP. Along the lakeshore at that time, herders with cattle and goats hunted, fished and processed wild cereals (mainly the large, fat-rich seed of the sand-burr, *Cenchris bifloris*, to judge by the seed impressions on the pottery). The relationship of these lake-dwellers to the groups with stone architecture and domesticated millet on the escarpment and, in a few cases, at its base, is not fully understood. Were these contemporaneous, interacting groups? Or do the differences in material culture between the lake and *dhar* settlements indicate occupation at different time periods?

In any event, the escarpment sites are spectacular, with many small sites and a handful of larger settlements covering 20–95 hectares and possessing 200–600 large, stone-walled compounds. They appear to have been occupied seasonally by agropastoralists who also hunted and collected wild plants. If all the compounds in these few, very large sites were contemporaneously occupied (something which has never been investigated), then this number of people would certainly require a more complex form of social organization — either hierarchical (chiefs) or heterarchical (for example, a council of lineage heads, plus leaders with ritual authority). The research needed to investigate the question of sociopolitical change on *dhar* Tichitt is, unfortunately, hindered by the fact that much of the soil matrix of the archaeological deposits on the escarpment has been eroded away by the wind. Artifacts are now jumbled on the surface, making studies of change through time very challenging. There is still a great deal that we do not understand about the society that built the stone enclosures on *dhar* Tichitt.

Pottery assemblages similar to those from the Tichitt area extend all along the *dhars* of south-eastern Mauritania down to Néma, where relatively small agropastoral sites have been documented dating to at least 3500 BP. Just over the Malian border, similar pottery appears in the seasonally inundated Mema region of the Niger basin by 3100 BP on small (<1.5 ha) sites located mainly on the edge of the then-active floodplain. These have been interpreted as the southern, dry season camps of (agro?) pastoralists who spent the rainy season along the seasonally filled depressions at the base of the *dhars*. Their material culture included types of stone (a fine-grained siltstone and chert) unavailable locally but present in the *dhars*. Also present in the Mema floodplain were herder/fisher/hunter/collector groups that made pottery quite different from the *dhar*-affiliated pottery. These groups may also have had cattle, but occupied the area much more intensively, creating large middens of fish bone and freshwater oyster shell within the Mema floodplain during the period 3500–2600 BP. We do not yet know whether these people also had domestic millet. The agropastoral sites with *dhar*-related pottery tended to be smaller and located on the edge of the floodplain. Did these two groups occupy the Mema simultaneously after 3100 BP? Although the relationship of these two groups through time needs much more clarification, it is possible that we are seeing in the Mema the emergence of subsistence specialization, allowing more efficient and intensive exploitation of particular resources by two or more interacting groups linked by subsistence exchange. In this case, fish may have been exchanged for grain. This is the pattern that characterizes the middle Niger floodplain historically.

Further east, in Niger, agropastoralists established settlements in the Azawagh Valley between 4000 and 3300 BP. Some of these, such as Chin Tafidet and In Tuduf, were substantial villages that were occupied for several centuries. The inhabitants fished abundantly, hunted, and probably cultivated millet. But most of the mammal bones recovered were from cattle and sheep or goats. The central ritual significance of stock is indicated by several deliberate burials of sacrificed cattle and caprines in specific areas of the site. Hundreds of human burials eroding from the surface of these sites have also been mapped and investigated. Generally people were buried in simple pit graves with their knees flexed, accompanied by very few grave goods (a pot or two, several ivory beads), if any. These riverbank settlements were abandoned c. 3300 BP, when the river no longer flowed throughout the year.

The period 3300–3000 BP was one of increased climate stress for herding populations south of the Aïr mountains. New opportunities opened up farther south as Lake Chad receded. Between 3500 and 3200 BP, short-term camps of herder/fisher/hunter/collectors were established in the Gajiganna region west of Lake Chad. Only wild cereals, including rice, were exploited. After 3200 BP, larger mounds with more intensive occupation developed, apparently related to the appearance of domestic millet.

Several important patterns characterized the grassland zone between 4000 and 3000 BP as climate deterioration became more pronounced:

a. Herding economies were diversified. Fish, wild animals, and wild cereals were important components of the subsistence economy, in addition to domestic stock.
b. Between 3500 and 2700 BP, domestic millet became an important subsistence element in these economies from southern Mauritania to the Lake Chad basin. Fisher/hunter/collector economies undoubtedly persisted in areas less suited to herding or agriculture.
c. Intensified, sedentary occupation of larger settlements was associated with agropastoral economies in favored areas.
d. Specialized subsistence economies linked by exchange (fishing, agropastoral) may have emerged in some areas.

The rapid spread and expansionist momentum of agropastoral economies is not surprising. At about the same time that early millet was first documented at Tichitt (3500 BP), it was also present one thousand kilometers to the south, at Birimi on the Gambaga escarpment of northern Ghana, associated with artifacts of the Kintampo complex. The distribution of Kintampo sites extends throughout central and northern Ghana and includes both open-air sites with architectural features (wattle and daub houses) and rock shelter sites. The reduced residential mobility signified by Kintampo village sites is presumably related to the appearance of domesticates and represents the earliest known instance of both south of 13° N latitude. Although the Birimi inhabitants were heavily reliant on domestic millet, wild plant foods dominated subsistence at Kintampo sites further south, and wild animals associated with cleared areas far outnumbered domestic sheep or goats in the bones recovered from excavation.

In various intervening areas in Burkina Faso and Mali, as well as coastal Mauritania and Senegal, hunter/collectors persisted for centuries longer. Thus, despite the expansionist tendencies of food production, it did not spread smoothly along a broad wave of advance. Rather, it spread in fits and starts in a more mosaic pattern. In certain regions, hunting/collecting remained more efficient and advantageous until iron tools were available and the diverse 'savanna complex' of domesticates — including African rice, sorghum, fonio, Bambara nut, bottle gourd, and watermelon — had been fully developed, perhaps as late as the first millennium AD. South of the 500-700 mm rainfall isohyet, domestic cattle could not penetrate until varieties that were able to tolerate trypanosome infection were developed. When these emerged is not known. So far, however, the earliest animal domesticates found in the southern savanna and forest margin are sheep and goats, in economies that are heavily reliant on hunting and the collection of giant landsnails.

Little is known about the chronology for the domestication of plants of the forest margin complex: yam, Hausa potato, cowpea, African groundnut, okra, and oil palm. Recently, banana phytoliths recovered from a trash pit in a southern Cameroon archaeological site were dated to 2500 BP. Bananas are native to southeast Asia/Oceania and may have moved inland from the East African coast at a much earlier date than previously imagined. Some researchers suggest that the extremely dry episode of 3000 BP caused disruption, population movement, and subsistence innovation across a broad area of Africa, including the equatorial zone. The expansion of Bantu speakers from the core area in south-eastern Nigeria and Cameroon may have been related to this.

In general, the risk profile for subsistence during the period 4000–3000 BP skyrocketed due to climate oscillations and a dramatic period of aridity. Human groups in the sahel, a zone now located further south than in previous millennia, appear to have responded by both intensifying food production through the addition of millet agriculture where possible, and maintaining diversity through hunting and collecting. Settlements along permanent rivers and lakes were sometimes quite large and clearly involved considerable sedentism. There is evidence from these favored areas that groups with different economies co-existed and perhaps exchanged subsistence products. Pastoralism probably became increasingly mobile, linking large areas through movement, social and kin alliances, and gift exchange. This pattern persisted and became substantially elaborated over the following millennium.

3000–2000 BP: crisis and change

Between 3000 and 2000 BP, West African populations faced continuing climate oscillations with major arid episodes at around 3000, 2500 and

2000 BP. This was a period of population movement, increased mobility in the zone between 18° and 22° N, penetration of northern Berber-speaking horse nomads, and technological change involving the smelting of copper and iron. The main difficulty for archaeological reconstructions of the sequence of events during this period is the fact that radiocarbon dates of 2600–2400 BP, when transformed into calendar years by applying the necessary calibration curve, become hugely imprecise.[3] A carbon-14 date of 2500 BP, for example, has a ratio of carbon-14 to carbon-12 (taking into account a statistical error factor) that has been found in tree rings of known dates ranging from 800 to 400 BCE. The calibration curve essentially stands still for 400 years. Radiocarbon dating is largely useless as a tool for discerning the order in which events occurred in different areas or even on different sites in the mid-first millennium BCE. Without additional, independent chronological evidence (from stratigraphic sequencing in excavations, or the presence of imports of known historical date, for example) it simply is not possible to know whether an event with a 14C date of 2500 BP was closer in calendar years to 800 or 400 BCE. Furthermore, dates of 2600 BP cannot automatically be assumed to be older than dates of 2400 BP, because their calibrated ranges in calendar years overlap substantially. The middle of the third millennium BP (2600-2400 BP) is a muddle.

At Tichitt, as seasonal lakes became less reliable after 3000 BP, sites were smaller, less numerous, and defensively positioned in nearly inaccessible areas. Rock art of cattle from the previous millennium was replaced by depictions of horses and riders and inscriptions in tifinagh, an alphabet related to Phoenician and used by Berbers into recent times. Further east, rock art from the Malian Adrar east to the Ennedi in Chad depicts warriors with feathered headresses or turbans carrying ogival lances and shields. Increased mobility and conflict characterized the arid north during this period. The occupants of the Sahara developed their historical aspect as mobile traders, raiders and herders of camels and goats.

---

[3] The element carbon is present in every living thing, as well as the upper atmosphere. Each living organism contains several isotopes of radioactive carbon; radiocarbon dating works by measuring the ratio of carbon-14 to carbon-12 in an organism. This is possible because when an organism dies, the ratio of carbon-14 to carbon-12 changes as radioactivity decays; the extent to which it has changed tells us the radiocarbon date. Yet because the amount of carbon-14 in the atmosphere has also changed over time, the system must be calibrated against a known source for dating. This is done through trees. Scientists take samples of tree rings with known dates and then measure the ratio of carbon-14 to carbon-12 in them; this enables the calibration of the dating system.

Further south, populations clustered and settlements grew in the well-watered basins of Lake Chad and the Middle Niger, among others. Here, as elsewhere in West Africa, a relatively narrow range of domestic plants and animals were present in subsistence economies that still relied to varying degrees on wild species. In most areas, seasonal mobility was still an important aspect of economic strategies geared toward flexibility in the face of erratic rainfall and recurrent drought. With increasing dryness after 2500 BP, people were displaced from certain areas that became too dry to support cattle (the old lakeshore of Lake Chad, for example). There is emerging evidence that larger villages (ten hectares) with defensive enclosures and large storage structures were established a few centuries later on the lakeshore, perhaps reflecting a new organizational strategy to cope with competition and resource stress in an uncertain environment.

Between 800 and 200 BCE, metals and metalworking became widely, but not continuously, distributed in West Africa. Copper ores were smelted in the Agadez region of Niger and near the copper mines at Akjoujt in Mauritania, beginning sometime between 800 and 400 BCE and ceasing around the start of our era. The copper artifacts found in both areas include a variety of small tools (arrow points, spear and lance heads, knives, harpoons, simple pointed rods), bar or rod ingots, and decorative items (rings, bracelets, earrings), which appeared alongside stone tools.[4] The sites in both areas were seasonally occupied by (agro?) pastoral groups who also hunted and fished. Coppersmiths may have been itinerant, given the highly localized sources of copper and the extended distribution of copper artifacts — a 400 km radius in both cases.

Although there is no evidence for any direct contact between the copper-making and copper-using groups of Mauritania and Niger, the many general similarities between them, and their common chronology plausibly point to a common origin for copper smelting. Mediterranean contact is demonstrated at Akjoujt by bronze jewelry in a North African style dated to the sixth century BCE. A distinctive style of copper earring has been found in graves from Morocco to southern Mauritania. Years ago, it was suggested that Saharan Libyco-Berbers who worked the copper mines of southern Morocco for the Phoenicians, as Herodotus mentioned, may have introduced the technology to the south.

Elsewhere in the Old World, iron smelting was preceded by an extensive period of experimentation with other types of metallurgy,

---

[4] Earlier claims that copper metallurgy in Niger occurred as early as the second or even third millennium BCE have been largely discredited by later research.

especially copper. This does not seem to be the case in West Africa. In Niger, iron smelting first appears at around the same time as copper smelting (2600-2500 BP), according to dates on charcoal from smelting furnaces.[5] Iron smelting is well documented in the Nok Valley of central Nigeria and at Nsukka from 2500-2200 BP (i.e., between 800 and 200 BCE). Recently, iron artifacts were recovered from an early agropastoral settlement along the Middle Senegal Valley first occupied between 800 and 500 BCE, and with abundant smelting activity attested between 500 and 200 BCE, at which time copper from Akjoujt was also used. Interestingly, a Mauritanian iron smelting industry contemporaneous with the Akjoujt copper industry has not yet been found. The fact that the malachite ores of Akjoujt occur in a matrix of iron ores (magnetite, hematite) which were broken up to extract the copper ore, then left as fill in the mining pits, suggests that the copper smelters either did not know how to smelt iron, or chose not to do so.

Other early evidence of iron smelting is found in the Agadez and Termit regions of Niger between 2600 and 2400 BP, the Inland Niger Delta of Mali by 2100 BP, the Tagant of Mauritania by 2000 BP, the Mandara mountains of northern Cameroon and the Lake Chad basin by 2600/2500 BP, and the Gonja region of Ghana by 2300 BP. In other areas, particularly in rock shelters excavated in Liberia and Sierra Leone, iron seems to have arrived a millennium later. Documenting the absence of iron after 2500 BP is much more difficult than documenting its presence, however (the absence of evidence is not necessarily evidence of absence). A great deal more work is needed before the chronology of the spread of iron-using and -working throughout West Africa can be reliably understood. The usefulness of iron in relation to its cost (in production time or exchange goods) probably varied depending on subsistence (hunter/collectors may have found stone tools perfectly adequate, while farmers derived a big advantage from iron tools in tillage and reaping) and other factors.

A notable increase in site size and settlement intensity correlates generally with the advent of iron. Certain new environments, including the heavy clay alluvium of the present Inland Niger Delta and the firki clay plains of Lake Chad, could be more intensively exploited with iron agricultural tools. And there is growing evidence that the domestic

---

[5] There is considerable controversy over the evidence for iron from the Termit region of Niger, because surface pottery radiocarbon-dated to the second millennium BCE has been assumed to be contemporary with iron artifacts also on the surface. Most archaeologists put more confidence in the dates directly on smelting furnaces, all of which are in the first millennium BCE.

plant assemblage was substantially expanded and diversified by iron-using farmers. Domestic sorghum, its tough stalks more effectively harvested by iron sickles than stone, was added to the plant assemblage perhaps as late as the first millennium CE.

Iron metallurgy provided an important stimulus for the rise of social differentiation because it involved specialist producers. The chain of production is lengthy, involving a large number of tasks, from mining and preparing the ore to gathering clay and firing bellows pipes, even before the furnace is constructed. Everywhere in Africa, historically, iron smelting was regarded as a very powerful transformation that could be safely and successfully achieved only by observing essential rituals. We do not know how far into antiquity the role of smith as a ritual specialist extends, but there are suggestions that the rise of political power in early West African states was linked to the blacksmith's occult knowledge and power to transform iron. Smiths also had economic power, because they controlled a desirable material and kept the knowledge of how to produce it secret. Smiths were undoubtedly important links in trade systems that were especially crucial for areas lacking ore deposits (for example, many alluvial zones).

The first millennium AD: trade polities and urban growth

The Inland Niger Delta of Mali was one such area that was involved since its initial settlement c. 200 BCE in trade and exchange for items lacking on the floodplain — most importantly, iron, stone, and salt. At sites such as Ja and Jenne-jeno, the productive capacity of the floodplain presumably permitted the export of food surpluses, including rice and dried fish, to neighbouring regions in exchange for these resources. Settlement growth appears to correlate with the expansion of trade networks: copper from Saharan sources was present at Jenne-jeno from 400 CE, a time of rapid site expansion. By 800 CE, the settlement had reached its maximum size of 33 hectares and was the centre of a tight cluster of over forty mounds. The functional interdependence of these mounds is suggested by surface distributions of ironsmithing debris and fishing equipment that were restricted to only a few of the sites within the cluster. The population of the entire urban cluster is estimated to have been between 10,000 and 25,000 people.

Large, clustered mounds dating to the first millennium CE have also been investigated in the Mema region to the northwest of the Inland Delta, where there is some evidence that this pattern may extend back into the first millennium BCE or even earlier. This clustered pattern appears to be characteristic of the Middle Niger 'urban zone' within the floodplain. Commonly, a cluster comprises a large, central settlement mound of up to ten meters in height and 20–80 hectares in area, which is surrounded by intermediate and smaller size mounds at distances of 100–1000m. R. McIntosh has suggested that clustered, functionally integrated settlements such as these may have been a common form of early urbanism in Africa (as well as early Bronze Age China) in cases where a powerful centralized authority had not yet emerged. The consolidation of political power may be thwarted by cultural strategies that successfully counterpoise multiple sources of power, and limit the ability of a single individual to hold great wealth (economic power), military control, ritual power, and political control all at the same time. This may account for the unusual spatial patterning of clustered urbanism, so different from the dispersed Central Place geometry of state-based urbanism.

In the Inland Niger Delta, then, the early emergence of complex urban forms of organization was indigenous and tied to expanding networks of trade and exchange. This finding overturned decades of historiography based on Arabic sources that viewed towns and long-distance trade as late developments prompted by contact with traders from the Mediterranean zone. It is now clear that complex societies in the Inland Niger Delta did not arise as a consequence of incorporation into the 'golden trade of the Moors', as was initially thought. Rather, the rapid consolidation of the trans-Saharan trade grid after the ninth century CE was possible only because extensive long-distance trade networks and highly organized societies were already in existence in West Africa. This, of course, is one of archaeology's great strengths: it can interrogate the propositions made by historians and even the claims made by historical sources.

This is not to say, however, that West Africa had no trade links to North Africa. Throughout the first millennium CE, the lines of contact linking West African societies stretched both north-south and east-west. Cattle herders, now living well south of the salt-rich soils of the Sahara, required access to salt to keep their herds healthy. Today, cattle in West Africa are herded primarily by specialized pastoralists, the Fulani, who have vast herds of hardy zebu hybrids capable of moving long distances to pasture and salt. Two thousand years ago, however, zebu from India had not yet penetrated West Africa, and the suitability of the small Inland Niger Delta cattle for long-distance travel is unknown. Nomadic camel herders in the southern Sahara may have transported salt to herders in the Inland Niger Delta and Lake Chad basin, providing an important link between savanna and Sahara. In addition to salt, did they also transport gold to Roman and Byzantine mints in North Africa?

Although Tim Garrard made a strong argument on the basis of mint outputs that this was so from the fourth century CE, recent work on chemical fingerprints of different gold sources indicates that the West African fingerprint is absent from coins struck before the eighth century CE. So while there is no evidence currently for a pre-Arab gold trade across the Sahara, there is definite evidence for interaction between Saharan and sub-Saharan groups. Of particular interest is the recent discovery of warrior graves at Kissi in Burkina Faso, dated to the sixth and seventh centuries CE. Huge curved swords and knives, armband daggers, and arrow bundles were found in graves of males wearing iron bracelets and brass anklets. The presence of wool fabric (fortuitously preserved by contact with copper) and brass, plus cowries, glass and carnelian beads indicates trade connections with the north as far as the Mediterranean or possibly east to the Indian Ocean.

East-west connections linked people throughout the great sahelian grassland belt. Ibn Hawkal recounted in the mid-tenth century that an earlier east-west trade route from Egypt to Ghana had been abandoned. Of particular relevance to the question of east-west contact and interaction in the grasslands is the horse, attested archaeologically from the sixth/seventh century onward. A late first millennium statuette from the Gurma region of the Niger Bend shows a horseman riding bareback. Horses were probably introduced to the sahel from North Africa by Berbers in the later first millennium BCE, based on rock art depictions. But horse-breeding cultures may not have become significant until the first millennium CE. Without riding equipment such as bitted bridles and stirrups, introduced in the thirteenth/fourteenth century, horses were of limited use for cavalry warfare. Yet even ridden bareback, horses extended the catchment range of societies by reducing transport time and increasing raiding capacity.

In the seventh to tenth centuries CE, Arab chroniclers mention the early development of the trade polities of Takrur, Ghana, and Kawkaw. Is their development in the grasslands related to the breeding and use of horses to expand political reach? Al-Bakri described small ponies at the Ghana court in the eleventh century. Despite their small size, they offered a way to move raiders quickly to targets, making warfare and booty collection more efficient. They also would have facilitated collection of trade levies and the patrolling of trade routes. Finally, horses could be used as gifts to enhance a ruler's prestige and wealth. Future research will, I believe, demonstrate how essential the development of horse breeding was to the emergence of the early sahelian trade polities and the spread of peoples and ideas.

The early association of horses with authority is further reinforced by the cast bronze horse and rider figure on a fly-whisk handle from a rich burial at Igbo Ukwu, deep in the Nigerian forest. Horses would have quickly sickened and died from sleeping sickness there. Dated to as early as the ninth century CE, Igbo Ukwu illustrates the combination of indigenous innovation and complexity plus long-distance connections that characterized a number of West African societies in the later first millennium CE. The stunning array of bronze objects discovered by Thurstan Shaw in the burial and a nearby household shrine displays astounding technical and artistic virtuosity. Initially assumed to have been the product of metals and technology introduced from the north, the sources of the copper and tin used have been definitively pinpointed to a location further south in Nigeria. The lost-wax casting technology used also appears to be indigenous. Yet the vast numbers of glass and carnelian beads (perhaps of Indian manufacture) found in the burial suggest international connections through trade.

Unfortunately, the state of archaeological research in West Africa is such that the history of societies in the forest and forest margins during the first millennium CE is largely unknown, except for brief, brilliant flashes such as Igbo Ukwu. The picture between 800 and 1000 CE is much clearer in the savanna and sahel. At this time, several patterns are clear: monumental burial traditions, such as tumuli, became widespread, from the Niger Bend to central and western Senegal; new trade goods and systems of value were introduced as Arabo-Berber trading towns were established in the southern Sahara at Tegdaoust and Kumbi Saleh; political competition for trade, followers and status was intense at sahelian centres on the Senegal (Takrur), and Niger Rivers (Gao/Kawkaw), in the Awker (Ghana) and around Lake Chad (Kanem-Bornu); earthworks and walls that can be interpreted as defensive appeared at Jenne-jeno and in the Nigerian savanna at Old Oyo and perhaps Ife.

But the Arab chroniclers tell us only about gold trade, Berber levies on trade goods, slave-raiding, and gift exchange among West African rulers of unequal status. If we want robust developmental histories that transcend these few details for the period prior to 1000 CE, only archaeology can provide the necessary information. West Africa still has plenty of Jenne-jeno's and Igbo Ukwu's hidden beneath its surface. If we can find this archaeological evidence and excavate the sites properly before development and looting destroy them, we have many additional surprises in store, and many future re-writings of West Africa's past to anticipate.

Recommended Reading

Breunig, P. and K. Neumann (2002) 'From Hunters and Gatherers to Food Producers: New Archaeological and Archaeobotanical Evidence from the West African Sahel', in Fekri A. Hassan (ed.) *Droughts, Food and Culture* (New York: Kluwer Academic/Plenum), pp. 123–55.

Connah, G. (2001) *African Civilizations: An Archaeological Perspective* (Cambridge: Cambridge University Press).

Grove, A. T. (1993) 'Africa's Climate in the Holocene', in C. T. Shaw, P. Sinclair, B. Andah and A. Okpoko (eds) *The Archaeology of Africa: Foods, Metals and Towns* (London: Routledge), pp. 32–42.

Haour, A. (2003) 'One Hundred Years of Archaeology in Niger', *Journal of World Prehistory* 17(2), pp. 181–234.

Killick, D. (2004) 'What do we know about African iron working? Review Essay', *Journal of African Archaeology* 2(1), pp. 97–112.

MacDonald, K. C. (1997) 'The Late Stone Age and Neolithic Cultures of West Africa and the Sahara', in J. Vogel (ed.) *Encyclopedia of Precolonial Africa* (Walnut Creek, CA: Altamira Press), pp. 394–8.

Marshall, F. and E. Hildebrand (2002) 'Cattle before Crops: The Beginnings of Food Production in Africa', *Journal of World Prehistory* 16(2), pp. 99–143.

McIntosh, S. (2000) 'West African Neolithic', in P. Peregrine and M. Ember (eds) *Encyclopedia of Prehistory: Africa*. Human Relations Area Files (New York: Kluwer Academic/Plenum), pp. 323–38.

McIntosh, S. (1994) 'Changing Perceptions of West Africa's Past: Archaeological Research Since 1988', *Journal of Archaeological Research* 2(2), pp. 165–98.

McIntosh, S. and R. (1988) 'From Stone to Metal: New Perspectives on the Later Prehistory of West Africa', *Journal of World Prehistory* 2(1), pp. 89–133.

Smith, A. (1992) *Pastoralism in Africa: Origins and Development Ecology* (London: Hurst & Co.)

Stahl, A. (1994) 'Innovation, Diffusion and Culture Contact: The Holocene Archaeology of Ghana', *Journal of World Prehistory* 8(1), pp. 51–112.

Stahl, A. (ed.) (2004) *African Archaeology: A Critical Introduction* (London: Blackwell).

2

Ecology & Culture in West Africa

J A M E S L. A. W E B B Jr

For tens of thousands of years, human communities in West Africa grappled with some of the most varied and challenging environments in the world. The members of these communities evolved strategies for living on the arid grasslands of the Saharan edge, in the savanna woodlands to the south, and even down in the wet green rainforests north of the Gulf of Guinea. Like the successful Stone Age pioneers elsewhere in the African and Eurasian tropics, early West Africans drew upon a shared cultural tradition of tool-making to fashion clothing, shelter, storage containers and weapons. They used fire to shape their immediate domestic and natural environments. They cooked meat, fish and plants, transforming the yields from their hunting, fishing and gathering. In order to improve their hunting prospects, they burned patches in the grasslands and woodlands to draw wild game to the resulting fresh plant growth. In the rainforests, where lightning and natural tree fall had already torn holes in the green canopies, they charred out biologically productive edge environments, or ecotones,[1] that likewise enhanced their opportunities to harvest wild game.

The ecological zones in which early West African pioneers struggled can be depicted on a map as long and narrow bands that extend from east to west across the region. These ecological bands are characterized by distinctively different annual rainfall profiles as well as different plant and animal populations. Over a mere 2000 kilometers, a succession of highly diverse ecological zones begins at the southern edge of the Sahara, known as the sahel, where only plants and animals that have adapted to very arid conditions are able to survive. Below the sahel

[1]An ecotone is a transitional zone between two biotic communities — such as forest and field.

33

begins the vast and open grasslands known as the savanna, and then, at the southern edge of these grasslands, begins an ecological zone with an even denser distribution of trees, known as the woodlands. These open forests in turn merge into the nearly full humidity of the tropical rainforests and lagoons along the Gulf of Guinea.

For the countless generations of early pioneers, travel within and across one or more of these ecological zones was a common experience, building up an ecological knowledge of plants, animals, insects, water supplies and mineral resources. Newly arriving groups from neighboring regions had extensive contacts with hunting and gathering communities already familiar with the local flora and fauna in the different ecological zones, and this knowledge was critical to the success of the immigrants.

The mobility and interactions of small communities of hunters, gatherers, and fishers in the early epochs of West African history also established a common linguistic framework throughout the entire region, and this helped to forge a common West African cultural identity. Indeed even today, West Africans south of the Sahara speak West African languages that are closely related and are thus considered by scholars to belong to a single West African language family.[2]

To understand historical change in more recent eras, the diversity among these ecological zones presents special challenges for interpreting the evolving relationships between ecology and culture in West Africa. Social and natural scientists now understand that these ecological zones have been shaped in part by human activities and, in turn, that the lifestyles, which have developed in the different zones, have been fundamentally constrained by a fluid set of ecological realities. Human beings in West Africa, as in other parts of the world, were not so much living in balance with nature as they were actively shaping environments that permitted more intensive human use. From these findings, social scientists have jettisoned outdated views that the 'environment' *determined* ways of life. Put another way, the realities of ecological adaptation and human inventiveness were far more complex and more interesting than simple environmental determinism would allow.

From the natural sciences has come new knowledge about the patterns of historical climate that has led social scientists to abandon the idea that the peoples of West Africa were rooted in stable environments. Over the early ages of human colonization, the rhythms of natural climate change forced humans living in certain ecological bands to shift

---

[2] With the principal exception of the Hausa speakers of northern Nigeria, whose linguistic ancestors were relatively recent arrivals.

their survival strategies and relocate to areas that offered relief from ecological stress. These ongoing movements, in combination with the fact that early West Africans lived and built with natural materials that broke down without much trace, have meant that archaeological evidence of very early communities (with the exception of those using stone tools) has been impossible to recover. But even if the early human footprints in West Africa's tropical ecological zones were ephemeral, the early accomplishments and ecological knowledge gained in these difficult tropical environments were of great significance. They laid the foundations upon which later West African communities would develop.

Ecological zones and constraints

The aforementioned pattern of elongated ecological bands is created by the interaction of a global system of wind currents. Every year, a system of humid air circulation picks up moisture over the Gulf of Guinea, and with the rotation of the earth on its axis over the course of the year, this moist wind system moves slowly north and then retreats. A countering circulation of arid continental wind blows from the Mediterranean across the Sahara.[3] This annual pattern of wind circulation results in a marked gradient of humidity that is highest near the Gulf of Guinea, where rain falls all year long, and that then tapers to a short season (at best) of intermittent summer rainfalls in the southern Sahara. Over the course of the annual cycle, variations in total rainfall are most dramatic in the northern, arid regions. The sahelian and savanna zones are thus the most susceptible to drought.

Climatological research has also uncovered the existence of long phases of arid and humid conditions in the deep past, as well as more fine-grained understandings of fluctuations in climate in more recent millennia. These natural variations forced the migrations of human communities and changed the natural conditions under which they struggled. During drier phases, such as the period 6,000-5000 BCE, the ecological bands were compressed towards the south; during wetter phases, such as the period 4,000-2,500 BCE, this compression was reversed, and the vegetation bands migrated northward.[4] Because all

---

[3] The interface between these wind systems is known at the Inter-Tropical Convergence Zone. For further information on West African climate, see Derek F. Hayward and Julius S. Oguntoyinbo, *Climatology of West Africa* (London, 1987).

[4] See A.S. Brooks and P.T. Robertshaw, 'The Glacial Maxima in Tropical Africa: 22,000-12,000 BP', in O. Soffer and C. Gamble (eds), *The World at 18,000 BP, Vol. 2: Low Latitudes*

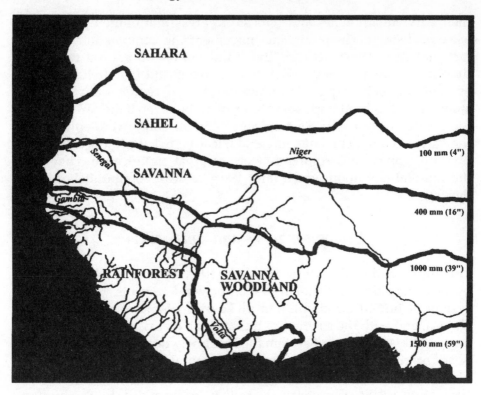

Fig. 2.1 Ecological zones of West Africa
(Source: adapted from Map 1.2 'Rainfall Patterns and Ecological Zones', in George E. Brooks, Eurafricans in Western Africa, Athens, OH: Ohio University Press, p. 3, with the permission of Ohio University Press)

of West Africa is situated within the tropics and receives considerable warmth from solar radiation during the year, rainfall, rather than warmth, was the principal limiting determinant of the different ecological zones' floral and faunal productivity. Biological productivity was lowest in the arid areas and increased progressively into the rainforest zones.

These zones of diverse vegetal and animal biodiversity stretched across broad plains at three different general elevations. Along the Atlantic coast, much of the terrain is below 200 meters elevation; one set of the interior plains extends at elevations between 200 and 350 meters, and another set at between 350 and 900 meters. From the highland areas of the southwest are found the sources of the Gambia and Senegal Rivers that drift north and west to the Atlantic Ocean, and the Niger and Volta Rivers that flow in arcs north and east, and then south to the Gulf of Guinea. These rivers pass through vast flatlands, endowed with shallow top-soils and with the generally poor sub-soils that are characteristic of the entire region.

Beyond the visible and complex worlds of flora and fauna, West Africa — like the rest of tropical Africa — also harbored a lethal universe of microparasites. Two particular diseases — trypanosomiasis (also known as African sleeping sickness) and malaria — became the most significant of the microparasitic infections that influenced human settlement patterns and culture. The indigenous mammals of West Africa had developed, over evolutionary time, a relationship with the trypanosomes; this allowed the mammals to serve as carriers of the parasite without suffering from the symptoms of the disease. Human beings, however, had evolved in a much more recent era and had not achieved this symbiosis. Sleeping sickness for human beings was the classic disease of the West African frontier, endemic throughout the rainforest, woodland, and grasslands. Pioneering settlers succeeded in reducing the disease threat through the extensive burning of the bush habitat required by the tsetse fly, the carrier of the disease.[5]

Malaria was a fundamental challenge to West African pioneers across all of the ecological zones, from the sahel south to the rainforest. It imposed high burdens of morbidity and mortality. To counter malaria, however, human communities evolved genetic defenses. An early

(London, 1990), 121–69; Susan K. McIntosh and Roderick J. McIntosh, 'West African Prehistory (from c. 10,000 to A.D. 1000)', *American Scientist*, 69 (1981): 602–13; George E. Brooks, *Landlords & Strangers: Ecology, Society, and Trade in Western Africa, 1000–1630* (Boulder, CO, 1993), pp. 7–9.

[5] The classic work on this is John Ford, *The Role of the Trypanosomiases in African History* (Oxford, 1972).

mutation known as Duffy antigen negativity became common at some point after 50,000 BCE and provided immunity to *vivax* malaria, a type of malaria that caused general debilitation. So successful was this genetic defense that *vivax* almost disappeared from West Africa. A second mutation known as sickle-cell afforded some members of these early communities limited immunity to the *falciparum* malaria, the deadliest and most recently evolved type of malaria that is endemic to West Africa. West Africans still died in appallingly large numbers, particularly from *falciparum* infections in childhood, but they did not die in the numbers they would have done without sickle-cell. The downside to this imperfect form of ecological adaptation was that a minority of West Africans with the sickle-cell mutation suffered from the complications of sickle-cell anaemia.[6] Furthermore, malaria and sleeping sickness were only two — although the most important — of an array of formidable, deadly challenges to human settlement in the region. The struggles and successes of West African societies in the distant past stand out boldly when one considers that they were forged in the most difficult human- and animal-disease environment in the world.[7]

The first era

Throughout the micro-regions that were settled across all ecological zones, the most important cultural advances in early West African history were those that allowed human communities to increase dramatically the number of calories they consumed. These advances allowed for a more rapid increase in human populations, which in turn brought about rapid transformations within the West African biomes.[8] One of the most significant of these early developments was agricultural innovation, which is thought to have progressed earliest in the transition zones between the rainforest and woodland biomes.

Tens of thousands of years ago, early pioneers dug up tubers that flourished naturally in moist ecotones with partial sunlight — in woodland and rainforest clearings. Some tubers were richer in calories than others, and over thousands of years the pioneers' selection of the better tubers eventually began to develop two varieties of genetically

---

[6] Georges C. Benjamin, 'Sickle-Cell Anemia', in Kenneth Kiple (ed.), *The Cambridge World History of Human Disease* (Cambridge, 1993), pp. 1006–8.
[7] See Emmanuel Akyeampong, 'Disease in West African History', this volume for more information on this subject.
[8] A biome is a term that refers to a major ecological zone and the organisms that live in it.

modified yams.[9] At some much later era — perhaps at approximately 6000 BCE — human communities began to plant these yams, rather than simply gather them. And at a later period still—perhaps during the first millennium BCE — the white and yellow Guinea yams became staple food crops.[10] This was momentous; the settlement of the rainforest zone — and the extensive rainforest clearance that made it possible — was predicated upon the domestication of these two yam varieties that flourished in the wet forest environment and stored well after harvest. This horticultural revolution that began in the rainforest openings may have preceded the agricultural revolution in the more arid zones. It should be noted, however, that the horticultural revolution is not possible to date with exactness. Moist conditions do not permit the survival of plant evidence.

In the sahel and savanna, another process of agricultural innovation unfolded. Over tens of thousands of years, communities had gathered wild grasses in the floodplains and along the banks of the Senegal and Niger Rivers and their tributaries. They had also fished and hunted in the aquatic environments. In the fourth or third millennium BCE, a long era of ongoing experimentation with wild grasses culminated in the development of millets, sorghums and wild rice. As communities began to plant these newly domesticated grains, this incipient agriculture allowed for denser human settlements along the riverbanks in the savanna and sahelian regions. Population growth was, however, very slow. The agronomic systems were adapted to the unpredictable rainfall and flood patterns, and even in good years produced very low yields by contemporary standards.

Compelling evidence of these now all but unrecoverable early ecological accommodations can be found, however, in the linguistic record. The vast array of West African languages, all related yet distinct, is testimony to the demographic impact of the horticultural and agricultural revolutions, which offered positive inducements to settlement and ultimately allowed for denser human populations and the emergence of new languages.

Even before the horticultural and agricultural revolutions had unfolded in West Africa, human communities in what are today the Sudan and Turkey began to develop their own cultural breakthroughs in the domestication of cereal grains and livestock.[11] By the sixth

---

[9] *Dioscorea cayensis, Dioscorea rotundata:* the white and yellow Guinea yams, respectively.

[10] Patricia J. O'Brien, 'Sweet Potatoes and Yams' in Kenneth F. Kiple and Kriemhild Coneè Ornelas (eds), *The Cambridge World History of Food* (Cambridge, 2000), vol. I, pp. 207–18, especially pp. 212–15.

[11] The relative timing of these breakthroughs is not agreed upon by experts. Christopher Ehret

millennium BCE, the vast grasslands of the western and central Sahara — to the north of West Africa — had become a far frontier of these Anatolian and Nilotic centres of human innovation. A virtual continent unto itself, these grasslands were home to groups of cattle and horse pastoralists, who lived from their animals, gathered, and hunted. Some of these pastoral peoples may well have drifted west from environments along the Nile River. They spoke languages that were branches of the large Afro-Asiatic language family of northern Africa and southwest Asia.

Over time, the northern developments of animal domestication and grain production percolated into the sahelian and savanna regions of West Africa. Owing to the limitations of the evidence, it is not possible to date exactly when agriculture and livestock herding began to be incorporated into the West African lifestyles. It probably happened long before the dramatic climate shift that began in the middle of the third millennium BCE, when the Saharan grassland pastoralists were driven south during a period of marked aridity.

As the Sahara became drier, the central grasslands withered and pastoralists were forced to the margins of the desert. This resulted in a larger pastoral presence across the sahel and the northern reaches of the savanna. Over time, the practice of herding cattle, goats and sheep became widely adopted throughout the region. Although some villagers incorporated livestock directly into their agricultural systems, the major pattern to emerge was the formation of new social groups that specialized in livestock herding to the exclusion of agriculture. This development came about as people needed to move the herd animals in order to take advantage of seasonal grazing lands. The specialization of the pastoralists meant, however, that they were dependent upon settled communities for grain and other goods and services. The symbiotic relationship between livestock-herding peoples and agricultural peoples remains a prominent cultural pattern in the sahelian and savanna regions into the twenty-first century.[12] The

has recently weighed the evidence and suggested that the complex of early human achievements in food-gathering, planting, and iron-making took place in the Sudanic region of Eastern Africa as well as in the southwestern region of Eurasia. For new historical perspectives on early Africa, see Christopher Ehret, *The Civilizations of Africa. A History to 1800* (Charlottesville, VA; Oxford, 2002).

[12] Some of the most detailed and influential work has been done on the ancient communities in the Niger Bend region, where the Niger River flows north into the desert edge, before turning east to empty into the Bight of Benin. In the Niger Bend, the fluctuations in historical climate were significant enough to force populations out of settled areas and into the pastoral livestock-herding sector. This 'pulse model' of historical change might be extended to unveil new understandings of cultural identity in West Africa. Boundaries of all types — ecological

domesticated animals were slow to find a niche below the savanna, due to the hostile disease environment. The trypanosome-carrying tsetse fly in particular injected sickness and death into domesticated livestock. The best defense against the trypanosomiasis threat to livestock — burning out the tsetse fly habitats in order to keep the fly some distance from the villages — was less practicable south of the savanna grasslands. In the first millennium BCE, a new revolutionary technology that allowed for the smelting of iron came to West Africa.[13] The new furnace designs that were capable of generating the higher temperatures that allowed for iron smelting had a profound influence on the evolution of West African history. The ability to make iron agricultural implements, land-clearing tools, and weapons of war gave dramatic advantages to those who mastered the new technologies.[14]

Continuing along the time line, which must remain highly uncertain owing to the limitations of the surviving evidence, larger human communities began to form in the southern rainforests in the first millennium BCE. This growth was possible because the ancient knowledge of fire could be harnessed to the iron-working technology, and because settled communities of good size had been able to form when the productive capacity of the cleared forest-land had been greatly increased through yam cultivation. These changes, in turn, made it possible to clear large spaces in the rainforest, although only with truly enormous investments of labor. One scholar has estimated that the clearing of a *single hectare* of mature rainforest — approximately 2.5 acres and 1400 tons of plant material — required 500 man-days.[15]

The process of Iron Age rainforest conversion, once launched, proceeded to run its course. Communities learned to draw upon the iron deposits of highly variable quality that occur throughout much of West Africa. Yet relatively dense populations took root only in a few rainforest areas. The growth of social and political complexity was principally constrained by the disease environment, the nutritional

and cultural — were porous and changed over time. Roderick J. McIntosh, 'Pulse Model: Genesis and Accommodation of Specialization in the Middle Niger', *Journal of African History*, 34(2) (1993): 181–200.

[13] Iron smelting is believed to have originated in Turkey or perhaps in Sudan.

[14] Nok culture on the great Jos plateau in what is today central Nigeria may mark the southernmost extension of large-scale settled community life in the first millennium BCE, and it is in Nok culture that one finds the earliest evidence of smelting iron in West Africa. On the importance of metallurgy in African history, see John Iliffe, *Africans: The History of a Continent* (Cambridge, 1995), pp. 18–36.

[15] Ivor Wilks, 'Land, Labor, Gold, and the Forest Kingdom of Asante: A Model of Early Change', in Ivor Wilks (ed.), *Forests of Gold: Essays on the Akan and the Kingdom of Asante* (Athens, OH, 1993), pp. 58–9.

limitations of the yam-based diet, and the scarcity of people to carry out the necessary labour of forest clearance.

By the beginning of the first millennium CE, West African settled communities, which were more complex than hunting and gathering societies, were well ensconced in all of the various ecological zones. These successes were built upon a deeply rooted knowledge of the local ecologies. Yet, despite this knowledge, West African societies were engaged in an ongoing struggle to achieve social and political stability in the face of a difficult environment. They developed new ways of organizing their societies. For example, in the northern regions, the communities developed the institution of endogamous caste, which allowed for individual and small-group mobility and supported the transmission of advanced technical knowledge within specialist sub-groups. In the woodlands and rainforests, the communities organized themselves around the institution of the clan, which allowed for those in authority to control access to and to assign responsibility for the agricultural fields, which had been cleared through prodigious effort. Furthermore, across all regions, people developed new cosmological systems that linked their own struggles to those which had come before them. Their artisans worked with local materials and achieved impressive artistic successes.

Over time, this more intensive human settlement generated a wealth of new ecological knowledge about regional flora, fauna, climate, and mineral resources that the growing communities could put to use. Through fire, hunting, gathering, land clearance for agriculture and horticulture, and the introduction of domesticated animals, West African communities, like other Iron Age communities elsewhere in the world, began to have a great impact on their local environments and to generate more significant environmental change. Livestock herds grazed selectively and began to modify their environments. Agriculturalists and horticulturalists burned and simplified their local biotic environments, thereby producing more biologically productive edge environments for smaller animals and birds. West Africans, like other Iron Age communities, worked to reduce their own exposure to dangerous wild animals, pushing them away from villages and their environs. Some of these initiatives were strikingly successful. To cite only one example, the elephant, once a capstone species prominent across West Africa's ecological zones, was pushed close to regional extinction.[16]

---

[16] One of the most striking results of these initiatives is the virtual disappearance of the elephant from West Africa. See Jonathan Kingdon, *Island Africa. The Evolution of Africa's Rare*

James L. A. Webb Jr

New northern influences

In the millennia before the common era, the introduction of domesticated animals and iron-making technology had profound impacts on the course of West African history. In the last centuries of the first millennium CE, new northern influences had helped to redirect the course of West African historical change. Camels came to replace horses and oxen as the principal beasts of burden in North Africa c. 300–600 CE, and by c. 800 CE camel caravans were regularly traveling across the Sahara.[17]

The more regular contact between West and North Africa had important repercussions. The complex changes taking place in the societies of the Mediterranean region, including more intensive market exchange, began to stimulate new forms of economic activity in West Africa. The demand for West African export goods was highly specialized, and because the distances from West Africa to the Mediterranean markets were great, only export goods that, in economic terms, had a high value-to-bulk ratio could bear the cost of transport. The two principal goods that met this requirement were gold and captives.[18]

Local political authorities near the sahelian gold fields built more elaborate political structures both to organize gold mining and to raise and maintain military forces capable of protecting the high-value exports. Ultimately, these military forces were bolstered by the availability of new steel weapons and cavalry horses imported from North Africa. In brief, this meant that the cultural and political implications of the export of West African gold and captives were highly significant, because the long-distance trade across the Sahara underwrote the successive growth and elaboration of the celebrated empires of Ghana (c. 800–1240 CE), Mali (1240–1464 CE), and Songhai (1464–1591 CE). This would not be the last time that international trade would prove to be a 'double-edged' sword; although the export of gold itself does not seem to have had a deleterious effect on West Africa's path of development, the political violence that generated slaves for export produced immense suffering among the societies of the sahel and savanna that found themselves under assault. The growth of empire

---

Animals and Plants (Princeton, 1989), p. 94.

[17] The one-humped camel, the dromedary, was first domesticated in Arabia c. 1200 BCE.

[18] Arabic texts are the principal sources for our understanding of the early trans-Saharan trade. See Nehemiah Levtzion and J. F. P. Hopkins (eds), *Corpus of Early Arabic Sources for West African History*, trans. J. F. P. Hopkins (Cambridge, 1981).

meant that even those communities which were not raided, but which lay within the imperial sphere, were forced to give up some of their agricultural product to augment state coffers.

Even beyond the arid zones of the sahel and savanna, the influence of international economic demand was considerable. In the case of Asante, for example, which was the largest precolonial polity carved out of the West African rainforest, the export of gold to international bullion markets produced an inflow of slaves, rather than an outflow.[19] Asante's gold sales allowed for the massive importation of workers both from the savanna and from coastal lands along the Gulf of Guinea into Asante, whose labor could be committed to a truly massive clearance of rainforest. The result was the elaboration of the kingdom of Asante, a polity that replaced earlier hunting and gathering communities with the great matriclan system. These political and cultural institutions evolved along with the massive ecological transformation of the rainforest in the course of the fifteenth, sixteenth, and seventeenth centuries.[20]

The introduction of Islam was also fundamental in redrawing the cultural map of West Africa. Islam percolated south into and across the Sahara in the course of the seventh and eighth centuries and very gradually began to produce a new line of cultural demarcation between the sahel and savanna to the north, and the forest regions to the south. The Islamic worldview was conducive to trade; it also brought with it literacy, and insisted upon a code of conduct and belief that was consistent with practices of the great intercultural Muslim zone of the Mediterranean and southwest Asia. Over time, Islamic and non-Islamic societies in West Africa grew increasingly distinct; indeed, one eminent historian held that these divisions between Islamic and non-Islamic West African societies were so fundamental that one might dispense altogether with the idea of a West African cultural zone.[21] Yet from other perspectives, such as that of state building in the arid zones that were later Islamized, the case for grand cultural continuities — both before and after Islam — is very strong. The empires of Ghana, Mali, and Songhai flourished with the same general basis of political economy before, during, and after the conversion to Islam. The cultural impact

---

[19] On slaves in early Asante history, see A. Norman Klein, 'Slavery and Akan Origins', *Ethnohistory*, 41(4) (1994): 627–56 and Ivor Wilks, 'Slavery and Akan Origins? A Reply', *Ethnohistory*, vol. 41(4) (1994): pp. 657–65.

[20] Wilks, 'Land, Labor, Gold, and the Forest Kingdom of Asante', pp. 41–90.

[21] Philip Curtin, 'Africa North of the Forest' in Philip Curtin et al., (eds) *African History* (Boston, MA, 1978), especially pp. 79–81.

of Islamization, however, was without doubt broad and far-reaching. Islamic conversion brought with it some familiarity with the ethos and worldview of Muslims in northern Africa. Cultural influences from West Africa also flowed north across the Sahara, although at terrible cost. Muslim merchants and raiders funneled Africans who were captured in West African warfare into the Saharan and trans-Saharan slave trade, and in this manner brought about a further mixing of cultural influences.

Atlantic influences

One of the staples of international trade in the period before c. 1500 CE was the export of captives across the Sahara. This might at first appear surprising because in West African communities, owing to the difficult disease environment and to the low caloric yields from the principal grain crops, labor was in chronically short supply. Indeed, because an agricultural surplus was so hard won from the generally poor soils of West Africa, virtually all West African societies across all ecological zones developed cultural mechanisms for the control of labor, including distinctive social identities for dependants and slaves.[22] Yet beyond the need for an agricultural surplus, an elite ruling class required the services of a powerful military to support its political dominance. For this reason, West African political authorities were generally willing to sell captives in exchange for military goods.

The slave trades imposed high costs in human suffering. The economic logic of the slave trade into and across the Sahara was cold: captives were sold to import war horses and steel weaponry that in turn were used to collect taxes and gather more slaves.[23] This was also the fundamental economic logic upon which the Atlantic slave trade was built. West African political authorities purchased iron bars (that could be transformed into weapons and agricultural implements) and guns, in addition to consumable goods, in exchange for captives.[24] As in the case of international trade with North Africa, the result was the growth of larger and more complex political structures among the more

---

[22] See Ismail Rashid, 'Class, Caste, and Social Inequality in West African History', this volume for more information on this subject.

[23] James L.A. Webb, Jr, *Desert Frontier: Ecological and Economic Change along the Western Sahel, 1600–1850* (Madison, WI, 1995); Robin Law, *The Horse in West African History* (Oxford, 1980).

[24] John K. Thornton, *Africa and Africans in the Making of the Atlantic World, 1400–1680* (Cambridge, 1992).

powerful state participants in the trade, and a general increase in the level of insecurity and suffering for those outside the umbrella of state protection. Beyond the political and military realms, the consequences of the Atlantic slave trade for West African societies were complex and varied. From an ecological point of view, one large benefit during the course of the Atlantic slave trade was the transfer of several New World crops with very high caloric yields — particularly corn (maize), cassava (manioc), and to a lesser extent the peanut (groundnut) and potato — which set off rapid demographic growth, perhaps as significant as that caused in earlier millennia by the agricultural and horticultural revolutions and the introduction of iron technology.

From the 1830s, following the abolition of the Atlantic slave trade, communities in or near the coastal zones began to specialize in the production of vegetable oil crops such as the peanut, palm kernel, and palm oil.[25] The reallocation of labor and productive terrain along the coast had significant consequences for West African societies, because the new opportunities for production of agricultural goods for export created pressures to create a new gendered division of labour. Often, men took charge of the vegetable oil 'cash crops'; women came to specialize increasingly in the grain 'food crops'. Later these new opportunities (and in some cases, colonial requirements) for the production of other cash crops were extended into zones far from the coast in the interior by the construction of railways, and in the second quarter of the twentieth century by the construction of roads for long-distance truck transport.

This new orientation towards export agriculture thus began well before the establishment of European colonial rule and continued throughout the twentieth century and into the twenty-first. In conjunction with rapid population growth, this export orientation brought about the conversion of rainforest and savanna to agricultural fields. The ecological consequences of this conversion were a complex set of costs and benefits, depending in part upon the characteristics of the export crop, the soil endowment, and the style of cultivation. On the cost side was damage to the soil; in the sahel and savanna, the cultivation of cotton and peanuts was notorious for impoverishing the soil. In the rainforest and woodlands zones, export crops could wreak similar damage; in the cocoa regions of Ghana, for example, the soils became depleted and degraded.[26] Another cost was the fact that

---

[25] Oceanic transport costs dropped sharply beginning in the 1830s, owing to the use of the steam engine on ever larger ships.

[26] Kojo Sebastian Amanor, *The New Frontier: Farmers' Response to Land Degradation. A West African Study* (London, 1994).

planting large fields of a single crop ('mono-cropping') could dramatically increase the opportunities for insect infestation and fungal blight. These difficulties, of course, had also plagued the simple fields of millets, sorghum, and rice; the difference was one of scale and the extent of vulnerability. When the root-borer struck the cocoa plantations in the Gold Coast (Ghana) in the 1930s, the entire colonial economy — and that of the local producers — was threatened.

On the benefit side, at least potentially, lay opportunities for West African farmers to increase the flow of income to their families and communities, and to improve health and future prospects. According to liberal economic theory, this new export orientation would produce an economic stimulus towards general development, as well as providing a financial foundation for the colonial state; however, the real effects were less salubrious than those imagined by the theorists, and the colonial authorities made sure that their state revenue bases were secure before passing on revenue from export sales to producers. But the increase in export trade brought larger numbers of West Africans into the margins of a rapidly evolving international commercial culture. Among the more significant cultural transformations that took place over the colonial period was an increasing familiarity with the European-style paper and metal coin currencies, which replaced the cowry shell and brass manila currencies. With the general acceptance of 'modern' European-style currencies, West Africans came to embrace a new, and increasingly global, ethos of consumerism.

Other forms of ecological change within West Africa were initiated directly by European colonialists who were guided by cultural values that were profoundly different from those of their African subjects. Late nineteenth-century and early twentieth-century Europeans in colonial service were, in general, unfavorably impressed by the low productivity of West African agricultural systems, which they understood to be a function of less advanced technology, a lack of initiative, and primitive ecological practices. They identified the agronomic practice of 'shifting cultivation' (that allowed for long fallow periods) as responsible for environmental degradation. Thus the colonialists, presuming that they had ecological knowledge superior to that of West Africans with centuries of accumulated experience, prescribed an intensification of agricultural production, to be led either by market forces or by coercion. These beliefs may seem irrational today, but they were a 'logical' extension of the hodgepodge of ideas known as 'pseudo-scientific racism' that insisted on the general inferiority of Africans. These beliefs were to prove remarkably resilient.

Colonial and post-colonial interventions

One of the principal colonial ecological beliefs was that the Sahara was expanding as a result of destructive human land-use practices. Europeans believed that the ongoing process of desertification was caused principally by the misuse of grasslands at the desert edge by pastoralists, and by the destruction of trees by villagers. Taken together, these deleterious practices were thought by European colonizers to have allowed the arid landscape to expand and thereby to threaten the viability of local economies. In this view, sahelian ecological practices were directly responsible for poverty and food scarcity. The idea that there could be dramatic shifts in regional climate that were generated by broader natural forces was not considered, and nor was there an appreciation that the historical record was closer to one of short and medium shifts in climate than to long-term equilibrium. In fact, as noted above, climate shifts were one of the fundamental forces for ecological and cultural change in earlier epochs.

The belief that West Africans were responsible for environmental degradation, combined with the general frustration the colonial masters felt with the low level of wealth creation from small-farmer export-oriented agriculture, led colonial regimes before and after the Second World War to begin planning for large-scale ecological interventions, particularly in arid regions. One French colonial project — to bring in African workers to the floodplains of the Niger River in order to develop new 'rational' models of irrigated agriculture — was a dismal failure.[27] In the post-war period, the emphasis shifted from the control of labor to more overtly technological solutions. In the second half of the twentieth century, both the French and the British, and later their international partners, joined forces to construct large storage dams on the major West African rivers (the Senegal, Niger, and Volta) to make impounded water available for irrigation and to produce hydroelectricity.

The rationale for these interventions appeared logical and purposeful to its designers, who worked 'from the top down' and did not attempt to elicit responses, reactions, and suggestions from the villagers who would be most directly affected by the interference. The building of dams dramatically reversed ancient patterns of the floodplains and

---

[27] Monica van Beusekom, *Negotiating Development: African Farmers and Colonial Experts at the Office du Niger, 1920-1960* (Portsmouth, NH, 2002).

rain-fed agriculture, and involved the uprooting of communities. With massive capital investments, West African watershed ecologies were reworked to an international model with mixed success. A parallel development took place in the dryland farming systems where the agricultural practices of West African farmers began to be reshaped by the ideas of international scientific agronomy. The denigration of the indigenous ecological knowledge of West African communities by outside 'development experts' has proved remarkably persistent, although in the small-farmer sector today there is an increasing appreciation of local wisdom.[28]

Another major set of ecological interventions emerged from professional ecologists' concerns about the loss of global wildlife habitat. By the 1980s, the ongoing conversion of the rainforest biome to agriculture (under the aegis of European-owned plantation agriculture as well as that of West Africans) began to cause alarm in Western conservationist circles. West Africans were once again blamed for environmental degradation, and chief among the charges was that of profligate deforestation. The empirical reality of deforestation in West Africa is extremely complex, and it is indeed certain that rainforest habitat was shrinking. The forces responsible were numerous: multinational corporations cut rainforest timber, as did West African entrepreneurs; population growth generated political pressure to open up new lands; and the net result was a loss of wildlife habitat.[29] With the rise of non-governmental organizations (NGOs) in the last decades of the twentieth century, and with the global environmental ideal of biodiversity protection honored at least in word in the agenda of the World Bank, some NGOs such as the World Wildlife Fund for Nature moved in aggressively to protect wildlife habitat. In the Central African Republic, they did this by creating a small military force to keep forest peoples away from protected areas, justifying their policies in the belief that forest peoples were ecologically destructive.[30]

In the late twentieth and early twenty-first centuries one of the most significant transformations in West African ecology and culture has come about as a result of the growth of urban centres. The roots of this recent urbanization stretch back into the early colonial period, when railroads and roads were built to facilitate the evacuation of cash crops to the ports. Over time, large numbers of West Africans left their rural

---

[28] Michael Mortimore, *Roots in the African Dust* (Cambridge, 1998).

[29] James Fairhead and Melissa Leach, *Reframing Deforestation. Global Analysis and Local Realities: Studies in West Africa* (London, 1998).

[30] Tamara Giles-Vernick, *Cutting the Vines of the Past: Environmental Histories of the Central African Rain Forest* (Charlottesville, VA, 2002).

communities in search of better life prospects in the dense and sprawling urban environments. These migrants, who often initially traveled to urban areas with the intention of returning ultimately to the countryside, have generally not returned. This rural-urban movement has been particularly pronounced since the 1960s, when West African governments began to subsidize the importation of staple foods for urban populations. These policies had the effect of reducing the incentives for farmers to grow food for the urban market, thereby encouraging more rural-urban migration.

In the cities, the children of first-generation urban settlers have grown up without an unbroken, intimate knowledge of rural ways of life and ecology. This cultural transformation is part of a broader pattern of increasing globalization. In urban West Africa, rice flows in from Southeast Asia; city-dwellers wear clothes woven on looms in Europe, East Asia, and North America; and families watch television shows that flood their compounds with new socio-cultural messages. These influences also spill, to a lesser extent, into the rural towns and villages of West Africa. Globalization has created new desires for participation in the culture of consumerism. Yet incomes in West Africa remain very low by global standards, and most individuals are still unable to embrace a Westernized lifestyle devoted to consumerism.

At least since the mid-twentieth century, population growth has been rapid in both the burgeoning urban centres and in the countryside. The expansion of West African population — even under the constraints of the HIV/AIDS epidemic and the continuing burden of malaria — constitutes the single most important force for ecological change today.[31] It exerts ongoing pressure to open up new lands for agriculture, livestock herding, mining, and logging, as well as urban settlement. The net result is an accelerated process of biome conversion that is part of a global pattern throughout the tropics.

Recommended Reading

Akyeampong, Emmanuel (2000) *Between the Sea and the Lagoon: An Eco-social History of the Anlo of Southeastern Ghana c. 1850 to Recent Times* (Athens, OH: Ohio University Press; Oxford: James Currey).

Amanor, Kojo Sebastian (1994) *The New Frontier: Farmers' Response to Land Degradation. A West African Study* (London: Zed Books).

---

[31] See Emmanuel Akyeampong, 'Disease in West African History', this volume for more information on this subject.

Brooks, George E. (1993) *Landlords & Strangers: Ecology, Society, and Trade in Western Africa, 1000-1630* (Boulder, CO: Westview Press).

Fairhead, James and Melissa Leach (1995) *Misreading the African Landscape: Society and Ecology in a Forest-Savanna Mosaic* (Cambridge: Cambridge University Press).

McIntosh, Roderick J. (1998) *The Peoples of the Middle Niger* (Oxford and Malden, MA: Blackwell Publishers).

Richards, Paul (1985) *Indigenous Agricultural Revolution: Ecology and Food Production in West Africa* (London: Hutchison).

Webb, Jr, James L. A. (1995) *Desert Frontier: Ecological and Economic Change along the Western Sahel, 1600–1850* (Madison, WI: University of Wisconsin).

3

Linguistics & History in West Africa

M. E. KROPP DAKUBU

Introduction: language and the historian of West Africa

This essay examines the contribution of one discipline, linguistics, to the work of another discipline, history. But disciplinary contributions aside, it is worth noting that language is always important to the historian, for the simple reason that by far the most important sources of historical knowledge are those transmitted through languages, whether as written documents or as oral testimony. A language is, among other things, a highly sophisticated cultural artifact, which is extremely sensitive to the social, psychological and political environment in which it is used. It therefore behoves the historian to be sensitive to the language in which sources are couched. There is also the practical problem, that sources for the history of a given area in West Africa may be in any of several European languages or Arabic, and first-hand control of oral sources may require familiarity with one or more African languages. It is not always possible for the individual historian to master all the languages required. One must then resort to translations, but problems of interpretation are almost inevitable.

Textual criticism: J. O. Hunwick

The critical study of the language of older written texts has not been a prominent feature of recent West African historical practice, no doubt because, for most areas, written texts are of fairly recent origin (within the past two hundred years). Outstanding have been J. O. Hunwick's assessments both linguistic and historical of mediaeval Arabic sources.[1]

[1] J. O. Hunwick, 'The influence of Arabic in West Africa', *Transactions of the Historical Society of*

52

His article, 'The term "Zanj" and its derivatives in a West African chronicle', is a model of its kind, carefully unpacking the possible meanings and nuances of a politically and ethnographically charged term that is no longer used in the sense in which it appears in the text (*Ta'rîkh al-Fattâsh*, a chronicle of the Songhay Empire), but is important to proper interpretation of that text.

The historical significance of language studies: P. E. H. Hair

Hunwick is a historian, not a linguist, albeit a historian who is an expert on the Arabic language. Another historian writing in English who took a close interest in language but from a rather different perspective was the late P. E. H. Hair.[2] He was interested in the study of West African languages from the point of view of social history, particularly the circumstances under which the languages were first documented. As he points out in his introduction to the 1963 edition of S. W. Koelle's *Polyglotta Africana*,[3] African language study as we know it today has its roots in the activities of Christian missions. No doubt the linguistic goals of many missionaries went no farther than the requirements of practical evangelizing, but a major aim of the British Church Missionary Society's linguistic activity in the mid-nineteenth century was also to 'demonstrate the essential humanity of Africa's tongues, . . . and thus serve as a final argument in the humanitarian campaign against the African Slave Trade';[4] that is, language study was an important weapon in the political and moral battles of the nineteenth century. The missionary Koelle himself said that 'the genuine humanity of the Negroes can be proved in various ways: and one of them is philological'.[5]

Ghana 7 (1964), pp. 24–41; J. O. Hunwick, 'The term "Zanj" and its derivatives in a West African chronicle', in David Dalby (ed.), *Language and History in Africa* (London: Frank Cass & Co. Ltd., 1970), pp. 102–8; J. O. Hunwick, 'African language material in Arabic sources — the case of Songhay (Sonrai)', *African Language Review* 15 (1973), pp. 51–73.

[2] P. E. H. Hair, *The Early Study of Nigerian Languages*, West African Language Monographs 7 (Cambridge: Cambridge University Press, 1967); P. E. H. Hair, 'The contribution of early linguistic material to the history of West Africa', in David Dalby (ed.), *Language and History*, pp. 50–63. See also David Dalby and P. E. H. Hair, ' "Le Langaige de Guynee": a sixteenth century vocabulary from the Pepper Coast', *African Language Studies* 5 (1964), pp. 174–91; David Dalby and P. E. H. Hair, 'A West African word of 1456', *Journal of West African Languages* 4 (1967), pp. 13–14.

[3] Sigismund Wilhelm Koelle, *Polyglotta Africana* (London: Church Missionary Society, 1854). Reprinted (1963) by the University of Sierra Leone, with a historical introduction by P. E. H. Hair.

[4] Koelle, *Polyglotta Africana*, p. 7.

[5] Koelle, *Polyglotta Africana*, p.10.

One aspect of the history of any language is the history of the external circumstances of its use: at the most basic level, where it has been spoken, when, and by what kind of community. Another focus of Hair's interest in language and language study was to use the earliest records of West African languages to answer these questions, thereby contributing to an understanding of population distribution in earlier times and especially the impact on it of European contact. To continue with the case of the *Polyglotta*, Hair's interest was not aroused merely by the fact that a German missionary working in mid-nineteenth-century Freetown took the trouble to compile a list of almost 300 words in more than 190 languages from all over West Africa.[6] Koelle not only performed this linguistic task with remarkable success, but he obtained detailed information on each speaker's place of origin, other names for the language and its speakers, the names of its neighbours, the distances separating them, and how long ago the speaker had left home and by what route (many of the speakers were former slaves or captives who had been released in Freetown). The result is a remarkable compilation of evidence concerning the geographical distribution of languages, peoples and settlements throughout West Africa in the first half of the nineteenth century. The re-publication of the *Polyglotta Africana* in 1963 was followed by a series of papers, published mainly in the *Sierra Leone Language Review* and in *African Language Studies*, a periodical of London University's School of Oriental and African Studies, in which linguistic specialists identified the various languages and discussed the linguistic and historical significance of the material.

Identification of a language can have more historical significance than one might expect. Hair[7] considered how early records of West African languages, even the briefest and most inadequate, can provide important evidence for the presence of a community at a particular time and place. He points out, for example, that the French Africanist scholar Delafosse concluded in 1914 that material on the Soninke, Malinke, Songhay and Fula languages found in mediaeval Arabic texts indicates that these languages were recorded in places where they are still spoken today. Dalby and Hair[8] considered one isolated African word occurring in a Portuguese traveler's description of a voyage to the west coast in 1456, in an attempt to determine just how far along the coast he may have reached. They did this by identifying the language

---

[6] He recorded many of them for the first time and in several cases provided the only documentation available until very recently.

[7] Hair, 'The contribution of early linguistic material to the history of West Africa'.

[8] Dalby and Hair, ' "Le Langaige de Guynee".'

or at least the group of similar languages the word came from, and concluded that it was probably the word for 'elephant' in a language of the Atlantic language family spoken on the northern shore of the Rio Jeba estuary. Rather more successful was the identification by the same authors of a list of more than 80 words in a 1540s French manuscript as a Kru language, probably Kra. The identification provides evidence that Kra was spoken at that time on the coast of Liberia, where it or a language very like it is still spoken today.

Lest it be thought that these conclusions are only to be expected, sometimes the results of such a study are quite different. Farther east along the coast and a few hundred years later, T. E. Bowdich[9] provided a considerable amount of information about languages on the Gold Coast in the early years of the nineteenth century, including a short wordlist of a language which he labelled 'Adampe', spoken at Ningo, a few miles east of Accra. The spelling 'Adampe' in European writings generally refers to the people and language called Adangme (or Dangme). Ningo is Adangme-speaking today and probably has been since its foundation several hundred years ago. However, Bowdich's list is not from that language at all, but from a Guang language similar to those now spoken in Larteh and Abiriw, hill towns some miles north of Ningo, or in the Awutu area west of Accra.[10] This is best explained by reference to the tradition that Guang-speaking people from Akuapem were active in trading with Europeans through Ningo. It may be evidence of their prominence in this trade relative to the Adangme-speaking locals.

Occasionally, someone has collected words from a language that is no longer spoken at all. Debrunner[11] found traces of languages once spoken in the hill area in the Ghana-Togo border region, that by mid-twentieth century were remembered by only a few people. The communities speaking these languages were apparently destroyed by local wars that scattered their populations. This area today has a large number of languages spoken by communities of only a few thousand. This evidence of extinct, vaguely remembered languages reinforces other evidence that the region went through turbulent times in the nineteenth century.

Old wordlists also provide evidence concerning the economic activity

[9] T. E. Bowdich [1819], *Mission from Cape Coast Castle to Ashantee,* Third Edition (London: Frank Cass & Co., 1966).

[10] M. E. Kropp Dakubu, 'Bowdich's "Adampe" word list', *Research Review* (Legon) 5(3) (1969), pp. 45–9.

[11] Hans W. Debrunner, 'Vergessene Sprachen und Trick-Sprachen bei den Togorestvölkern', *Afrika und Übersee* 46 (1962), pp. 109–18.

of the people who spoke the language. The mere fact that a language was recorded is significant; Dalby and Hair[12] point out that Kra words were written down because the language happened to be spoken in the part of the coast most important to the European pepper trade. It was therefore useful for visiting traders, and a significant proportion of the words recorded are related to that trade. One could make similar observations elsewhere on the coast. It is thus no accident that the early vocabularies from the Gold Coast are of Akan (Fante dialect), the commercial language of Elmina and other centers of the gold trade.[13]

Historians of West Africa have thus been interested in language as the medium of historical sources, and in recorded language because it can indicate whether or not a political and economic community has existed continuously in a particular place. They have also been interested in language as a phenomenon in cultural history. The historian may tackle these linguistic problems either directly or in co-operation with a linguist, as in the joint work of Dalby and Hair.

Both textual criticism and the consideration of old wordlists require a combination of linguistic and historical skills, but do not depend heavily on the more specialized techniques of linguistics, although they may be helped by them. The discipline of linguistics, particularly the sub-discipline known as 'historical linguistics', studies how languages change over time. It does this through close examination of a language's internal structure, and by comparing it to other languages. The findings of such studies, especially when associated with evidence from other disciplines (such as botany or archaeology) expand the resources available to the historian in any field, but are potentially crucial for historians working in areas where written records are limited. Jan Vansina, writing on Central Africa, regarded modern vocabulary studies as the most historically revealing of linguistic contributions,[14] and the third chapter of his *Paths in the Rainforest* consists of social reconstruction based mainly on this kind of evidence. In West Africa, however, the potential of this line of thought has so far been mainly attractive to linguists and anthropologists, whose work we review later in this chapter.

The contribution of linguistics to our knowledge of the past in West

---

[12] Dalby and Hair, ' "Le Langaige de Guynee",' pp. 189–90.

[13] See, for example, Denis Escudier (ed.) *Voyage d'Eustache Delafosse sur la côte de Guinée, au Portugal et en Espagne (1479–1481)*, Transcription du manuscrit de Valenciennes, traduction et présentation de Denis Escudier, (Paris: Editions Chandeigne, 1992); also Pieter de Marees, *Description and Historical Account of the Gold Kingdom of Guine (1602)*, trans. and ed. Albert Van Dantzig and Adam Jones (Oxford: Oxford University Press, 1987).

[14] Jan Vansina, *Paths in the Rainforest* (Madison, WI: University of Wisconsin Press, 1990), p. 11.

Africa may often seem to fall into the domain of pre-history, rather than history, if pre-history is taken to signify the study of the past before textual documentation (written or oral) is available. But the dividing line is neither clear nor constant, and the general thrust is to push back the beginnings of what can be considered 'historical'. We now turn to the main focus of this chapter, the contribution of 'linguistics proper' to history.

The methods of historical linguistics

The historian does not need to be an expert in linguistics, any more than an archaeologist needs to be a chemist in order to use C14 or thermo-luminescence techniques for dating. But in both cases, some basic understanding of the principles involved is required if a student of the past is to use the findings of another discipline intelligently. This includes understanding the limitations of these findings. Each topic will therefore be introduced with a short review of the linguistic principles involved. The linguistic sub-disciplines most relevant to historical problems can be divided into two categories: (i) *historical comparative linguistics*, or the reconstruction of past forms of related languages and the classification of these languages according to their most recent shared form, giving their 'genetic classification';[15] and (ii) *contact studies*, or study of the ways in which languages have influenced each other. Particularly important is the study of the distribution of names for cultural goods among languages, regardless of their genetic classification.

The historical problems on which these techniques can shed light include principally pre-historic settlement, prehistoric migration patterns, and certain aspects of culture history and pre-history, particularly the sources and spread of diffused cultural items and practices. Less directly, such studies shed light on past power relations, since the weak are usually influenced by the powerful, and not vice versa. If the linguistic criticism of documents, indeed of sources generally, is an old tradition in historical studies and has been carried out as much by historians themselves as by linguists, the use of the findings of linguistics proper to reconstruct various aspects of cultural and political history has mainly been the province of linguists with a historical bent, or of historians using linguists' interpretations. Africanists in particular have been very conscious of the value of inter-disciplinary collaboration

---

[15] Note that 'genetic' here refers to genesis, common origins, not genetics and genes!

in this area, as witnessed by the volumes edited by Dalby[16] and by Ehret and Posnansky[17], and by Nurse's article,[18] that explain one discipline to another. We shall consider first the significance of diachronically oriented linguistic classification, and then the application of contact studies.

The comparative method and genetic classification

Briefly, the 'comparative method' technique in linguistics is to compare words of the same or very similar meaning across languages. If a pair of languages turns out to have a number of words that are clearly related in *both* sound and meaning, the set of similar words is further investigated to see whether the sound structures of the pairs of words differ from each other in a systematic manner. Systematic difference means that there should be several pairs of words with the same meaning that show the same difference in sound. For example, the Ga and Adangme languages of Ghana have numerous words that are virtually identical in sound and meaning except that wherever Ga words have the sound *f*, Adangme words have *p* (for example, Ga *fee* = Adangme *pee* meaning 'do, make'; Ga *fo* = Adangme *po* meaning 'cut'; Ga *fu* = Adangme *pu* meaning 'bury'). Where this situation of systematic differentiation exists, we think that the only reasonable explanation is that the words of both languages are derived from a common source. If a number of such 'comparative series' can be detected, especially if they involve most of the languages' sounds, and the words include what might be called the basic vocabulary of both languages, we deduce that the languages as a whole are derived from a common source: an 'ancestor language' spoken at some time in the past and which lives on in the modern languages. The technique excludes as evidence words that are similar in sound but not meaning, and vice versa. It also excludes words that are very similar in sound and meaning but unique. For example, the fact that the English pronoun *me* strongly resembles a pronoun with the same meaning and almost identical sound in several Ghanaian languages is not proof of a common source for English and these languages, because no other words can be found that show the same kind of resemblance in sound, that is, with *m* as the first consonant, and meaning.[19] Such occasional resemblances can easily be due to

---

[16] Dalby, *Language and History in Africa*.

[17] Christopher Ehret and Merrick Posnansky (eds), *The Archaeological and Linguistic Reconstruction of African History* (Los Angeles: University of California Press, 1982).

[18] Derek Nurse, 'The contribution of linguistics to the study of history in Africa', *Journal of African History* 38 (1997), pp. 359–91.

[19] In this case there is also *ma* or *mami* as an address term for 'mother', but this is certainly a recent borrowing.

chance or borrowing from other languages, but it is very unlikely that systematic correspondence involving many sounds and words of the languages could be accidental.

The implication of the ancestor language hypothesis is that one or normally both of the 'daughter' languages, the languages compared, have introduced their own changes into the common ancestral language. To take the example above, either Ga has changed p to f, or Adangme has changed f to p, or the ancestral precursor of both of them (the 'proto-language') used another sound in these words and they have both changed it. Classification is possible when at least three languages are related by such systematic differentiation, and it is determined that two languages but not the third have made the same alteration in the ancestral language. This 'same alteration' is referred to as a *common innovation*. Again referring to the Ga-Adangme case, Ga has changed the ancestral p to f while Adangme has not. On the other hand, all the Adangme dialects (the major ones are Ada and Krobo) have made the common innovation of shortening words with double vowels to one vowel, so that, for example, the word for 'woman' is *yo* in Adangme but *yoo* in Ga, and 'river' is *pa* in Adangme but *faa* in Ga. Within Adangme, however, the Ada dialect has made its own unique changes to the tone system, with repercussions in the grammar, while the Krobo dialect has not. This allows us to draw the following diagram, a 'family tree' of the Ga-Adangme language group.

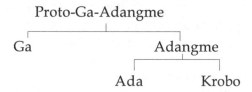

The branching process may be repeated ad infinitum, and there may be not just two but three or more branches at the same level. This in essence is the foundation of the genetic classification of languages. Note also that the principle of common (and exclusive) innovation closely resembles the principle of cladistic classification used in biology, which is no accident since they both arise out of theories of evolution established during the past 200 years. In both disciplines, the principle results in an either-or, bi-unique classification: a language belongs either to the Ga group or the Adangme group (or neither) but it cannot belong to both, or to one for some purposes and the other for other purposes. The principles of systematic differentiation and common innovation together distinguish scientific, historically oriented language comparison from linguistically uninformed speculation about language origins and relationships.[20]

Of course, the correct application of these principles is not always straightforward. In West Africa in particular, scanty and often inaccurate data mean that much is still to be learned about the classification of many languages. Nevertheless, the general outlines are known. The work of J. H. Greenberg in the 1950s and '60s led to a major breakthrough in the overall classification of African languages, and the synthesis he outlined[21] is broadly accepted, although corrections continue to be made. Greenberg classified all the thousand and more languages of Africa (except those originating from Europe and the Austronesian languages of Madagascar) into four super-families or 'phyla': Khoisan, Nilo-Saharan, Niger-Congo, and Afroasiatic. In West Africa we find members of all the phyla except Khoisan, although Nilo-Saharan is represented only by Songhay, whose classification, moreover, is still disputed, and by Kanuri at the far eastern edge of the region. The great majority of West Africans speak a language belonging to one or another branch of Niger-Congo, although one of the largest West African languages, Hausa, belongs to the Chadic branch of Afroasiatic.[22]

Historical applications

These purely linguistic findings provide historians with food for thought in two related spheres: migrations of peoples and the dating of these migrations. But theorizing on these topics rests on a further set of postulates having to do with the relationship between a language and its speakers. It can normally be assumed that a language may be identified with a community that speaks it, and vice versa. From a historical perspective, it tends to be assumed that just as a language is a continuation of a proto-language, its community of speakers is also

---

[20] For fuller discussion and exemplification of genetic classification see M. E. Kropp Dakubu, 'Genetic Classification', *The Oxford International Encyclopaedia of Linguistics* Vol. 2 (New York/ Oxford: Oxford University Press, 1992), pp. 53–7; Bruce Connell and Kojo Maison, 'A Cameroun homeland for the Lower Cross languages?', *Sprache und Geschichte in Afrika* 15 (1994), pp. 47–90; or any general textbook of historical linguistics, e.g. Terry Crowley, *An Introduction to Historical Linguistics* (Auckland, NZ: Oxford University Press, 1992); or Winfred P. Lehmann, *Historical Linguistics: an Introduction* (New York and Chicago: Holt, Rinehart and Winston, 1962).

[21] Joseph H. Greenberg, *The Languages of Africa*, Second revised edition (Bloomington, IN: Indiana University Press, 1966).

[22] Arabic belongs to the Semitic branch of Afroasiatic, and the Berber languages and Ancient Egyptian constitute additional branches.

descended from the community that spoke that proto-language. When the proto-language divided into two or more languages, the community that spoke it must have divided, each new community speaking one of the 'daughter' languages. Thus one sometimes sees references to 'the Proto-Akan' or 'the Proto-Gur', signifying a community whose members were the ancestors, both linguistic and biological, of the Akan or Gur language speakers of today.

Actually, we know that, to a considerable extent, the hypothesis of a former unified community composed of the direct ancestors of a corresponding modern linguistic community is a fiction. Large numbers of people, including communities that today speak English or Spanish, have recent ancestors who certainly did not speak those languages, but belonged to different language communities. Even in situations where many individual ancestors of a community spoke the same language, it is unlikely that all of them did. The reason why this is unlikely is that individual human beings are capable of learning new languages, and whole communities can undergo *language shift*, in other words, give up one language in favor of another.

Languages spread therefore in two ways: by assimilation of groups that originally spoke other languages, and by migration, when speakers of a language move to occupy a wider (or different) area. Blench[23] cites Hausa as an example of the former, Fulfulde as an example of the latter. Quite often the two modes combine; if speakers of one language spread through and settle in a populated area, eventually outnumbering the previous inhabitants, the latter may eventually be linguistically assimilated, that is, shift to the new language. This seems to be the pattern, for example, in parts of the Akan-speaking area of Ghana, and also accounts for the spread of Ga eastwards along the Ghanaian coast.[24] On the other hand, when the earliest Niger-Congo dispersions occurred, for example when the speakers of proto-Mande first appeared in West Africa and eventually divided into western and eastern communities, it is quite likely that they were spreading into and populating virtually uninhabited lands, which makes it much more likely that these were indeed migrations of small communities.

Relevant to geographical language spread is the economy principle in migration theory.[25] If we look at a map of linguistic distribution,

---

[23] Roger M. Blench, 'The westward wanderings of Cushitic pastoralists', in Catherine Baroin and Jean Boutrais (eds), *L'homme et l'animal dans le bassin du lac Tchad*, Actes du colloque du Réseau Méga-Tchad, Orléans 1997, (Paris: Editions IRD, 1999), pp. 39-89.

[24] M. E. Kropp Dakubu, *Korle Meets the Sea, a sociolinguistic history of Accra* (New York and London: Oxford University Press, 1997), p. 110.

[25] The classic exposition is by Isidore Dyen, 'Language distribution and migration theory', *Language* 32 (1956), pp. 611-26.

such as is found in Greenberg,[26] it is evident that a family of related languages generally occupies a continuous area, and that neighbours tend to be classificatory relatives. When a language spreads and eventually divides, barring some special circumstance, it usually does so over a continuous area. Therefore, if we are interested in where a particular language community or group of communities might originally have come from, we look for the location of the closest linguistic relatives. The case of Fulfulde (Fulani) provides a striking instance of the importance of this principle. As Greenberg pointed out,[27] this language was long classified as Hamitic (an earlier name for Afroasiatic), for reasons that had more to do with racial and cultural stereotyping than with any linguistic evidence. The language is also spoken in communities spread over a huge area, from the Atlantic to the Nile, usually among neighbors speaking entirely different languages. Greenberg made a major contribution to the destruction of racism in both linguistics and history by conclusively establishing that Fulfulde is closely related to Serer-Sin and Wolof, and belongs to the same northern subgroup of West Atlantic (now called simply Atlantic), the most western branch of Niger-Congo. Its homeland is therefore to be found in the west, probably in Senegal, from which it spread eastwards, in nomadic migrations associated with a pastoralist culture, apparently reaching present-day northern Nigeria in the eighteenth century.[28]

The case of Fulfulde is especially dramatic. On a more local scale, if close linguistic relatives are generally also neighbors, this tends to support theories of the gradual process of division into separate communities, where migrants do not migrate very far. Boahen[29] applied this principle of gradual division to the work of linguists such as Stewart[30] and Painter[31] to propose that communities speaking Akan dialects are the modern representatives of a proto-community that arose and then spread within its present area in south-central Ghana. Using

[26] Greenberg, *Languages of Africa*.

[27] Greenberg, *Languages of Africa*, p. 24.

[28] See also W. A. A. Wilson, 'Atlantic', in John Bendor-Samuel (ed.), *The Niger-Congo Languages* (Lanham, MD and London: University Press of America, 1989), pp. 81–104. Wilson points out that the older attitude to the classification of Fulfulde dies very hard among non-linguists, including African scholars.

[29] Adu Boahen, 'The origins of the Akan', *Ghana Notes and Queries*, 9 (1966), pp. 4–10.

[30] J. M. Stewart, 'Akan history: some linguistic evidence', *Ghana Notes and Queries*, 9 (1966), pp. 54–8.

[31] Colin Painter, 'The Guang and West African historical reconstruction', *Ghana Notes and Queries* 9 (1966), pp. 58–66.

the same basic principle, Owens[32], in a detailed dialect study, traces the spread of Arabic into Nigeria from southern Egypt via the central Sudan, and examines the implications of this spread for population movements in the area.

A corollary of the above principle is that the more uniform a linguistic area is, the more recent the spread of the language or language group. It is noticeable, for instance, that there is far less dialect variation in the eastern part of the Akan-speaking area than in the western. This supports other kinds of evidence that the Akan, with their language and particularly speakers of the Ashanti dialect, spread eastwards with the expansion of the Ashanti empire, for example into Kwahu and across the Volta. The Chadic languages are extremely diverse, but the Hausa language extends comparatively uniformly over a very large area lying west of all its relatives. This is a sign that Hausa has expanded relatively recently into areas where no Chadic language was spoken before.

When a language is *not* adjacent to its closest relatives, it is clear that there has been a real population movement, although it may not always be clear what kind of community moved. The Anufo language (also known as Chakosi) is spoken in and near Sansanne Mango in northern Togo and across the border into Ghana, and is surrounded by languages belonging to the Gur branch of Niger-Congo's closest relative. However, it is clearly Anyi, a language of the southern border area of Ghana and Ivory Coast where it borders its very close relatives Nzema and Bawule, and the slightly more distant Akan, all of which are part of the Kwa branch of Niger-Congo.[33] It is therefore not surprising to find that Chakosi speakers have a tradition of arrival in their present area from the southwest, in the service of a Mamprusi king.

The actual words compared to reach a genetic classification may provide important clues as to where the proto-language was originally spoken and thus the area from which its daughters and their speakers dispersed, as well as about the culture of those speakers, and may even indicate an approximate dating for the dispersal. If it can be shown, for instance, that the proto-language, on the evidence of its descendent languages, must have had words for 'slave' and 'market', then we can deduce that these social phenomena must have been known to the

---

[32] Jonathan Owens, 'Nigerian Arabic in comparative perspective', *Sprache und Geschichte in Afrika* 14 (1993), pp. 85–176.

[33] For the composition of the Kwa group of languages see J. M. Stewart, 'Kwa', in Bendor-Samuel, *Niger-Congo Languages*, pp. 217–45.

speakers of the proto-language. Similarly, if the vocabulary of the proto-language had words for savanna animals and plants, but not forest animals and plants, it is more likely that the language was spoken in savanna country than in the forest. On this principle, Manessy[34] points out that the vocabulary of Proto-Central Gur reflects a neolithic agricultural society located in a wooded savanna country containing a large river and that used the bow and arrow, made pottery, cultivated rice and okra, brewed beer, and raised small cattle. The Oti-Volta branch of Central Gur, a branch that includes such languages as Moore (the language of the Mosi of Burkina Faso) and Dagbani (of the Dagomba of Ghana), retains more of this ancient vocabulary in the northeastern part of the present area in which Oti-Volta languages are found than in other areas. Since this is also the area that best matches the flora and fauna named in this vocabulary, Manessy suggests that Proto-Oti-Volta was most probably spoken there, in the northwest of the present Republic of Benin in the upper basin of the Oti River.

At the Proto-Central Gur stage metallurgy was unknown; that is, no vocabulary for it can be reconstructed. Saddle horses were not known either, nor kings apparently, at least the type of kings historically identified with these cultures. By the time of Proto-Oti-Volta, however, all these cultural 'items' were known to its speakers.[35] Since the first archaeological evidence of iron working in West Africa dates from about 250 BC at Nok in northern Nigeria, Manessy further suggests that Proto-Oti-Volta must have become a language distinct from other Central Gur proto-languages after the arrival of the conquering horsemen who founded the Mosi-Dagomba states, which were in existence well before the early fourteenth century when the Mosi (or Moshie) sacked Timbuktu. Manessy thus arrives at an approximate earliest period for the westward movement of the groups speaking Oti-Volta languages. The date of the Mosi invasion of Timbuktu (1333) gives an approximate latest date, putting the Oti-Volta dispersion and westward movement rather firmly into the mediaeval period.

Dating is, of course, a major problem in West African mediaeval history and pre-history. Genetic classification of a group of languages may allow us to infer a relative chronology of the geographical and social differentiation of the speaker population, but it rarely provides dates of any precision. The most ambitious attempt at a linguistically

[34] Gabriel Manessy, 'Langues et histoire des peuples voltaïques: signification et limites de la comparaison historique', *Gur Papers/Cahiers Voltaïques* 4 (1999), pp. 3-18.

[35] For a thorough discussion of the historical and cultural significance of this vocabulary see Klaus Beyer, *Pferde, Schwerter und Macht, eine historische-vergleichende Studie zu Kulturwortfeldern in den Oti-Volta-Sprachen*, Gur Monographs Vol. 2 (Cologne: Rüdiger Koppe Verlag, 1998).

based dating method is known as lexicostatistical glottochronology:[36] 'lexicostatistical' because it is based on statistical manipulation of comparative wordlists, that in some ways is similar to the traditional comparative method of historical linguistics; 'glottochronology' because it purports to deduce from these manipulations the number of centuries that have elapsed since any two languages diverged from their common ancestor. Glottochronology claims empirically that after one hundred years a language will retain an average of 74 per cent of its 'core' vocabulary, the core vocabulary consisting of about 200 basic, supposedly culturally neutral words.

This method enjoyed considerable vogue in the 1960s[37] but is now largely in disfavour, at least as a method for dating the break-up of a proto-language. Statistical problems apart, there seems to be no way of establishing that the 74 per cent retention of core vocabulary per century is valid for West Africa, especially since the standard wordlist used for the purpose is itself problematic. The method continues to be used for producing approximate genetic classifications, but dating of linguistic divisions must rest on non-linguistic evidence.[38]

In their model paper, Connell and Maison[39] show how several kinds of linguistic evidence can be used to evaluate oral history in a case where related oral histories make incompatible claims. The time depth of the divisions that must be accounted for is considerably less than in the case of either Proto-Gur or even Proto-Oti-Volta, where the time of split is much too far in the past to be reflected in oral history. The particular problem concerns the likely homeland of the Lower Cross group of languages and their speakers. The Lower Cross languages, which include Efik (the language of Calabar) and Ibibio, are spoken in south-eastern Nigeria at the mouth of the Cross River close to the ocean and the Cameroon border, and are a division of the Cross River languages. The Cross River languages in turn are a branch of Benue-Congo, one of the major branches of Niger-Congo. The oral histories of the area indicate arrival from the north towards Igbo country, from the west near the Niger delta, or from the east, across the Cameroon

---

[36] The theory is explained and illustrated in Mauricio Swadesh and Evangelina Arana with J.T. Bendor-Samuel and W.A.A. Wilson, 'A preliminary glottochronology of the Gur languages', *Journal of West African Languages* 3(2), (1966), pp. 27–66.

[37] R. G. Armstrong, 'Glottochronology and African linguistics', *Journal of African History* 3 (1962), pp. 283–90; Heine, Bernd, *Die Verbreitung und Gliederung der Togorestsprachen* (Berlin: Dietrich Reimer Verlag, 1968); Painter, 'The Guang and West African historical reconstruction'.

[38] See, for additional discussion, including on uses of lexicostatistics for historical purposes distinct from glottochronology, Bruce Connell and Kojo Maison 'A Cameroun homeland for the Lower Cross languages?' *Sprache und Geschichte in Afrika* 15 (1994), pp. 47–90.

[39] Connell and Maison, 'A Cameroun homeland for the Lower Cross languages?'

border. These histories cannot all be true, and the authors are concerned to decide among them.

First, the languages of the particular area are all Lower Cross languages, thus each other's closest relatives. Second, there is no linguistic evidence that any of the communities speaking Lower Cross languages have undergone language shift. This negative evidence consists of the fact that if there had been shift, at least some of the languages would be expected to show traces of the languages the people had shifted from, but they do not. Therefore, it is likely that they all emigrated from a single homeland. Third, the closest relatives of the Lower Cross languages are the Upper Cross languages, spoken immediately to the north, and not languages spoken to the east in Cameroon. Finally, the vocabulary that can be reconstructed for Proto-Lower Cross includes words for 'forest', 'yam', 'palm oil', and 'hoe' but not 'sea', 'swamp', or names of salt water fishes, as would be expected of a language that developed inland. However, words for 'river', 'canoe', and 'swim' can be reconstructed. The ancient vocabulary therefore points to an inland, riverine environment, such as exists just to the north of their present habitat. The authors therefore conclude that the cradle of the Lower Cross languages can be posited as north of their present location, that an origin on the coast to the east is highly unlikely, and that some group members probably came from the west in their migration from the north. They also suggest that lexicostatistical vocabulary retention rates (as discussed above) may be used to establish a relative chronology of migration, so that the language with the lowest percentage of the common vocabulary (namely Obolo) probably left the homeland first.[40] However, actual dating depends on documentation and hypotheses concerning what impelled the people to move in the first place. If this migration was precipitated by Igbo expansion, then it may have begun in the fourteenth or fifteenth century. Early European documentation indicates that some Lower Cross people were in their present location by the beginning of the fifteenth century, although the migrations were not complete. For example, the Efik did not move into the Calabar area until the sixteenth century or even later.

Languages in contact: the spread of words and things

The studies examined so far have been based on data derived from internal developments in the languages. Yet a large part of the vocabulary and structure of any language does not come from its

[40] Connell and Maison, 'A Cameroun homeland for the Lower Cross languages?', p. 82.

ancestral forms, but has been added in later times. Very often, structural modifications and vocabulary additions take place under the influence of other languages. The most obvious result is loanwords or borrowed words, when a language acquires new words by adopting them from another language. This can only happen if the languages are in contact, and languages, being immaterial things, can only be in contact when someone speaks two or more of them.

Bilingualism implies contact between persons of different communities. As a general rule, contact between communities that results in one group affecting another in important ways is not symmetrical. If one community has influenced the political system or the agricultural practices of another, the chances are that the influencing community had a more elaborate, or more successful, at least more powerful political or agricultural system than the groups that received the influence. These differences have consequences for vocabulary acquisition; people learn the language and borrow the words of people who are more powerful than themselves. To take an English example, the words 'cow' and 'sheep' are old common Germanic words inherited through Old English, but 'beef' and 'mutton' were taken from French in late mediaeval times. Those words refer to the animals strictly as prepared for eating, and reflect the influence of French culture in culinary matters, and indirectly its political and military power as well.

Historical applications

In recent years a number of studies have used linguistic contact phenomena, especially loanwords, to trace patterns of cultural diffusion in West Africa that often have implications for political, social, and cultural history.[41] Such studies often combine documented history with the findings of linguistics. Greenberg[42] used both written and oral sources to examine the social historical implications of Arabic loans in major languages of northern Nigeria. An early historical essay was Wilks' 1962 examination of Mande words in Akan as a way of showing that the Akan polities had been influenced by Mande at an early stage.[43]

---

[41] For a general discussion of methodology see Christopher Ehret, 'Historical inference from transformations in culture vocabularies', *Sprache und Geschichte in Afrika* 2 (1980), pp. 189–218.

[42] Joseph Greenberg, 'Linguistic evidence for the influence of the Kanuri on the Hausa', *Journal of African History* 1(2) (1960), pp. 205–12; 'Arabic loan-words in Hausa', *Word* 3(1) (1945), pp. 35–97.

[43] Ivor Wilks, 'The Mande loan element in Twi', *Ghana Notes and Queries* 4 (1962), pp. 26–8.

Wilks' suggestions are reviewed and extended by Dakubu[44] in a paper that confirms that Mande cultural influence must indeed have been far reaching.

More recently, Reichmuth[45] examined Songhay loanwords in Yoruba. He concluded that the nature of these loanwords, which include both political and cultural terms related to war, horses, trade and Islam, reflects intensive social interaction and confirms the importance of Songhay contact for the Yoruba area at an early stage in its political development. These words, moreover, point to the Dendi variety of Songhay as the main dialect involved in the contact. Dendi was a trade language of the Borgu area, which in turn functioned as a centre for the eastern diffusion of Mande cultural influence. Reichmuth attributes these loanwords, and thus the political and social influences they reflect, to the period of the rise of Oyo after the sixteenth century.

The combining of documentary and oral data in word studies that incorporate linguistic data with those of other disciplines is particularly evident in a number of recent studies of plant and animal names. One vexed question has been the path of the introduction of maize into Africa, especially West Africa. It is a given that the ultimate source is the New World, but a number of its local names, like *masar*,[46] point to the north and east, including Egypt, and not directly to the Atlantic coast. Pasch[47] considered the names for maize over the whole of Africa, and concluded that it appeared in different places at different times and by various routes, and that it was introduced into the lower Nile valley from North Africa and then spread westwards into the western savannah, and south from Lake Chad, although it was introduced independently into Nigeria and Cameroon from the coast. She also points out that crop names often reflect cultural associations that do not necessarily match actual geographical sources. Much of Pasch's data is derived from historical accounts.

Blench, Williamson and Connell[48] discuss the same problem with specific reference to Nigeria, and take the argument a considerable step further. They point out that there is remarkably little early mention

[44] M. E. Kropp Dakubu, 'The Mande loan element in Twi revisited', *Sprache und Geschichte in Afrika* 16/17 (2001), pp. 273-91.

[45] Stephan Reichmuth, 'Songhay-Lehnwörter in Yoruba und ihre Historischen Kontext', *Sprache und Geschichte in Afrika* 9 (1988), pp. 269-99.

[46] In some European languages it is known as 'Turkish wheat'.

[47] Helma Pasch, 'Zur Geschichte der Verbreitung des Maises in Afrika', *Sprache und Geschichte in Afrika* 5 (1983), pp. 177-218.

[48] Roger M. Blench, Kay Williamson and Bruce Connell, 'The diffusion of maize in Nigeria: a historical and linguistic investigation', *Sprache und Geschichte in Afrika* 15 (1994), pp. 9-46.

of maize on the West African coast, even though the Portuguese would seem to be the logical intermediary with the Americas. They consider the historical and anthropological documentation, and make a detailed comparison of the names for maize in several hundred Nigerian languages, reducing them to twenty base forms. They come to the conclusion that, 'In the south of Nigeria, there is almost no trace of a Portuguese introduction . . .',[49] and that, 'Excluding the single case of Isekiri, all names for "maize", even those on the sea-coast, refer directly or indirectly to a northern origin.'[50] The names reflect diffusion from farmer to farmer, and also spread through trade. The most important route through which maize arrived in Nigeria was from the north via Borno (consonant with Pasch's findings), although it also spread along the Niger River, and in some places arrived from the east (Cameroon) or west (Benin). It reached the sea coast from northern Yorubaland and then spread eastward. We may note (the authors do not) that it is commonly assumed that the establishment of trade with Europe on the coast of West Africa meant that the northern link was completely overshadowed as a source of major cultural innovation, which from then onwards came from Europe. The saga of maize in southern Nigeria demonstrates that the assumption is mistaken.

In a series of papers published together, Blench uses a wide range of evidence, including linguistic, to reconstruct the history of animal husbandry in Africa. Even though he rates the value and precision of linguistic data for this purpose rather low,[51] it nevertheless makes an important contribution in some areas. For example, on the basis of the spread of the Hausa term for 'pigeon', which is probably ultimately borrowed from Tuareg (a Berber language), he suggests that the practice of pigeon keeping was brought across the Sahara.[52] The terms for 'donkey' are particularly revealing. The donkey was domesticated in Africa from the wild ass that was once common across North Africa and the Horn. Names of ancient origin are found in the languages of those regions (Berber, Cushitic, Omotic), as well as Chadic and Semitic, thus all branches of Afroasiatic. The implication is that these names may well extend back to Proto-Berber and Proto-Cushitic, for example,

---

[49] *Ibid.*, p. 38.

[50] *Ibid.*, p. 39.

[51] Roger M. Blench, 'A survey of ethnographic and linguistic evidence for the history of livestock in Africa', in Roger Blench and Kevin C. MacDonald (eds), *The Origins and Development of African Livestock: Archaeology, Genetics, Linguistics and Ethnography* (London, New York: UCL Press, 2000), p. 19.

[52] Roger M. Blench, 'African minor livestock species', in Blench and MacDonald, *Origins and Development*, p. 329.

which makes them very ancient indeed, but not as far back as Proto-Afroasiatic itself, since each branch has a distinctive term. This suggests that different peoples in the areas where the wild ass existed domesticated it separately.[53] However, the Chadic branch is an exception: it shares a name for 'donkey' with the Cushitic languages and a number of Nilo-Saharan languages (Mbay, Kanuri) that are spoken on the southern edge of the Sahara, between the Chadic and Cushitic areas. The wild ass was never indigenous to the southern edge of the Sahara, only the north. This suggests that the donkey arrived in the Chadic-speaking area from the east, perhaps brought by Cushitic speakers, although in other more western parts of the Sahel it was introduced across the Sahara from the Berber north.[54]

Whether the pig was domesticated in Africa or introduced as domesticated is debatable, according to Blench,[55] who points out that the Portuguese terms that have led some to regard it as entirely a Portuguese introduction are of very limited geographical distribution. The most widespread name by far[56] points to an 'early spread of the [small black] domestic pig, from the Nile to other regions of Africa both east and west', to the west at least as far as Burkina Faso and northern Ghana. These data suggest that pig-keeping culture in West Africa is probably ancient to a degree not previously suspected.

One of the interesting outcomes of these linguistic investigations is that they seem to underline the long-standing importance of what Blench[57] calls the 'inter-Saharan corridor'. Movement from east to west, from Ethiopia and the Sudan into the Lake Chad basin, seems to have been a major route for the introduction of innovative cultural goods into West Africa from ancient times,[58] through the mediaeval period[59] and into recent historical times.[60] The feeling among many linguists is that an east-to-west pattern accounts for the distribution of the major Niger-Congo families across West Africa. As the Mande family is the

---

[53] Roger Blench, 'A history of donkeys, wild asses and mules in Africa', in Blench and MacDonald, *Origins and Development*, p. 447.

[54] *Ibid.*, p. 351.

[55] Roger Blench, 'A history of pigs in Africa', in Blench and MacDonald, *Origins and Development*, p. 355.

[56] *-kutu. This is a summary formula for various manifestations of the name in a wide variety of languages.

[57] Roger Blench, 'The westward wanderings of Cushitic pastoralists', in Catherine Baroin and Jean Boutrais (eds), *L'homme et l'animal dans bassin du lac Tchad*, Actes du colloque du Réseau Méga-Tchad, Orléans 1997 (Paris: Editions IRD), p. 47.

[58] Blench, 'The westward wanderings of Cushitic pastoralists', p. 48. Blench, 'A survey of ethnographic and linguistic evidence for the history of livestock in Africa', in Blench and MacDonald, *Origins and Development*.

[59] Owens, 'Nigerian Arabic in comparative perspective'.

[60] Blench, Williamson and Connell, 'The diffusion of maize in Nigeria: a historical and linguistic investigation'.

most distantly related of the Niger-Congo languages, Welmers[61] put forward the idea that it moved westwards first. Manessy, as we have seen, posits a cradle to the east of the present areas in Burkina Faso, Côte d'Ivoire and Ghana for both Gur as a whole and for a later descendant, Proto-Oti-Volta. An ultimate eastern point of origin for the Kwa languages also seems reasonable, although there have certainly been reverse movements more recently, for example the probable eastward spread of Akan already mentioned.[62]

We have seen that linguistics can provide evidence related to the migration of people and to the migration of objects used by people. The evidence may support broad hypotheses reaching far back to ancient times, but it may also provide valuable evidence concerning small-scale movements and developments of the more recent past. It must be emphasized that the possibilities have by no means been fully exploited. The area is vast, and it is linguistically extremely complex. As linguistic knowledge becomes more precise and detailed, and the documentation of individual languages improves, there is every reason to expect that the contribution of linguistics to African history will grow.

[61] William E. Welmers, 'Niger-Congo, Mande', in T. Sebeok (ed.), *Current Trends in Linguistics Vol. 7: Sub-Saharan Africa*, (Bloomington, IN: Indiana University Press, 1971), pp. 113–40.
[62] It must be said that considerable doubt has recently been voiced (but not as yet published) on the validity of the hypothesis of common origin for the group of languages known as 'Kwa' of south-eastern Côte d'Ivoire and the southern halves of Ghana, Togo and the Republic of Benin (but not Nigeria, see Stewart, 'Kwa', in Bendor-Samuel, *The Niger-Congo Languages*). It may well be that there is no 'point of origin' to be determined. This, however, only pushes the question of the diffusion of languages into the area back in time and makes it more complicated. Many would still regard an ancient movement from east to west as likely.

Recommended Reading

Bendor-Samuel, John (ed.) (1989) *The Niger-Congo Languages* (Lanham, MD and London: University Press of America).

Blench, R. M. and Kevin C. MacDonald (eds) (2000) *The Origins and Development of African Livestock: Archaeology, Genetics, Linguistics and Ethnography* (London and New York: UCL Press).

Crowley, Terry (1992) *An Introduction to Historical Linguistics* (Auckland, N. Z.: Oxford University Press).

Dakubu, M. E. Kropp (1992) 'Genetic Classification', in *The Oxford International Encyclopaedia of Linguistics* Vol. 2 (New York and Oxford: Oxford University Press), pp. 53-7.

Dakubu, M. E. Kropp (1997) *Korle Meets the Sea, a Sociolinguistic History of Accra* (New York and London: Oxford University Press).

Dalby, David (ed.) (1970) *Language and History in Africa* (London: Frank Cass & Co. Ltd).

Ehret, Christopher and Merrick Posnansky (eds) (1982) *The Archaeological and Linguistic Reconstruction of African History* (Los Angeles: University of California Press).

Greenberg, Joseph H. (1966) *The Languages of Africa*, Second Edition (Bloomington, IN: Indiana University Press).

Nurse, Derek (1997) 'The contribution of linguistics to the study of history in Africa', *Journal of African History* 38, pp. 359–91.

Vansina, Jan (1990) *Paths in the Rainforest* (Madison, WI: University of Wisconsin Press; London: James Currey).

4

Oral Tradition & Perceptions of History from the Manding Peoples of West Africa

DAVID C. CONRAD

The past in the present: living with the ancestors

Who are the Kanté around here?
Are there any Kanté here?

These questions were asked by a bard (*jeli*) of the Maninka people of Northeastern Guinea. Performing away from home in a village where he was unable to recognize everybody in the audience, the *jeli* was being careful not to embarrass or offend anyone whose family name was Kanté. The epic narrative on which the *jeli* was basing his performance describes events that are alleged to have occurred in the first half of the thirteenth century, but the people of Manding[1] societies still identify closely with characters of that era whom they believe to be their ancestors. The *jeli* asked if there were any Kanté present, because in Manding epic tradition the king of Soso, Sumaworo Kanté, was defeated in a climactic battle that led to the foundation of the Mali Empire. Prior to asking these questions, the *jeli* had been describing the battle but suddenly said,

I will stop here.
I cannot describe the rest.

---

[1] Within the broad Mande family of languages, the branch called 'Manding' includes, among others, the Maninka (Guinea and Mali), Bamana (Mali), Dyula (Côte d'Ivoire), and Mandinka (Gambia). These terms describe both the people and their languages, which have a high degree of inter-intelligibility. The core area or 'heartland' of the Manding peoples which lies in southern Mali and northeastern Guinea, is called 'Manden'.

He then went on to talk about how the Kanté ancestors' weapons and clothing were captured, but stressed that no harm came to the Soso king. It was at this point that he asked if there were any Kanté in the audience or living in the village, and when he was told there were none, he expressed his relief by saying 'Praise God, His blessings are upon us'.[2] The *jeli* had not wanted to describe the rest of the story involving Sumaworo's fate, out of concern that if he were to dwell on the defeat and death of the Soso king, it would be humiliating for any local people named Kanté. Most Manding *jeliw* who describe Sumaworo's defeat avoid stating that this king was actually killed.[3] Our primary goal in this chapter will be to explore how legendary West African ancestors, whose very existence has been questioned according to strict Eurocentric standards of historiography, can remain so vital in Manding village society more than 700 years after the era that is attributed to them.

Manding *jeli* perceptions of what is important in the distant past do not always correspond to those of European historians. Moreover, the *jeliw's* methods for recalling the people and events of long ago do not adhere to European standards of scholarship. Historians from outside Manding society are very cautious in their use of oral tradition as a source of information, and this is a fundamental difference between the local African point of view and the perspectives of foreign academics. On the most fundamental level, foreign scholars question the usefulness of Manding epic as a reliable source of historical evidence simply because stories that have been passed on by word of mouth for several generations are bound to be problematic according to European ideas of historical accuracy. Manding epic as narrated by the *jeliw* includes detailed dialogue between characters that were conversing centuries before there was any way of recording their words. The *jeliw* also employ raw folklore, supernatural beings, improbable feats of magic, and mythological elements in ways that provide insight into their beliefs and values, but which clearly defy scientific credibility. Some historians labor to analyse Manding oral sources in the belief that they can yield evidence that has at least a reasonable degree of historical probability, with many years spent scrutinizing every available version of the

---

[2] Mamadi Condé in David C. Conrad (ed.) *Epic Ancestors of the Sunjata Era: Oral Tradition from the Maninka of Guinea.* (Madison, WI: African Studies Program, University of Wisconsin Press, 1999) p.147.

[3] Djibril Tamsir Niane, *Sundiata: An Epic of Old Mali* (London: Longman, 1965), pp. 67, 94; Gordon Innes, *Sunjata: Three Mandinka Versions* (London: School of Oriental and African Studies, 1974), p. 79; John W. Johnson, *The Epic of Son-Jara: A West African Tradition* (Bloomington, IN: Indiana University Press, 1986) p. 176.

tradition in search of useful clues. Such endeavors require thorough knowledge of all aspects of the culture, including the social and spiritual values underlying the deeply ingrained sense of a shared history expressed through oral epic.

In many rural West African communities, traditional social values and customs have not been submerged by foreign influence, as has been the case in capital cities and other urban centers. In agricultural villages and market towns of the countryside, notions of what happened in the distant past are still expressed through oral traditions that provide part of the framework for the way people live from day to day. The deeds of ancestral heroines and heroes are described in narratives that are passed down from one generation to the next in chains of oral communication that can be measured in periods of time ranging from several generations to many centuries. In some cases, the discourse rises to the level of epic that is filled with rich and colorful imagery in both narrative and song, reflecting the values of the cultures that produced them. Epic narratives vary in length, content and complexity depending on the desires and composition of the audience, and on the knowledge, purpose, and momentary whim of the performer. They tell the stories of village communities, kingdoms and empires that were peopled by charismatic leaders both male and female, who founded family lineages and accomplished momentous deeds during periods that are recalled as defining moments of the past. Here is the way one of the great *jeliw* of Mali expressed his feelings about those glorious times:

In those days the world was not like it is now.
They bent the world like a scythe and unrolled it like a road,
They walked the four directions of the world and settled at its center.
In those days the word of every human being could be relied upon.
There was nobility then.[4]

In this chapter we explore the importance of oral tradition in West Africa's Manding culture, where musicians and narrative specialists are responsible for preserving and performing oral narratives that have evolved through many generations. We shall examine prominent themes that demonstrate which aspects of life are most valued by the people of the culture in question, how genres of oral tradition function

[4] Tayiru Banbera of Ngoin, Mali in David C. Conrad (ed.), *A State of Intrigue: The Epic of Bamana Segu According to Tayiru Banbera*, Union Académique Internationale, Fontes Historiae Africanae, Series Varia VI (Oxford and New York: Oxford University Press for the British Academy, 1990), p. 63.

as the voices of the people who created them, and how these texts provide avenues to understanding the rich fabric of the brilliantly creative cultures from which the traditions emerge. West African oral tradition rarely reveals facts about the past that can be accepted according to strict European historiographical standards, because the past existence of people and events that is described in the narratives usually cannot be confirmed by independent evidence such as written documentation involving contemporary eyewitnesses. Nevertheless, oral tradition does convey useful information, both literally and metaphorically, about African perceptions of the past and how those perceptions affect today's cultural values.

The bards of Manding culture

One of the most impressive bodies of oral tradition in all of sub-Saharan Africa has emerged from the heartland of the vast West African Mande cultural complex which includes the Bamana of Mali, the Maninka of northeastern Guinea, the Mandinka of Senegambia and Guinea-Bissau, the Dyula of northern Côte d'Ivoire, and many other groups located between southern Mauritania, western Burkina Faso, northern Liberia, and the Atlantic coast of Senegambia. The seat of the Mali Empire that flourished from the mid-thirteenth to the fifteenth century was located in present-day northeastern Guinea and southern Mali. Among the Bamana, Maninka and related peoples of the Mande heartland, oral tradition is the domain of *jeliw* that were born into specialized occupational groups collectively known as *nyamakalaw*.[5] The *nyamakalaw* are blacksmiths and potters (*numuw*), leatherworkers (*garankéw*), *jeliw* specializing in Islamic texts (*funéw* or *finaw*),[6] and *jeliw* who are musicans, oral traditionists and public speakers. The *jeli* occupation is most closely associated with music and the oral arts, but any *nyamakala* with verbal or musical gifts and the opportunity to profit by them could and would engage in those activities. For example, some of the greatest musicians who specialize in singing the praises of hunters have come from blacksmith (*numuw*) families.

---

[5] David C. Conrad and Barbara E. Frank (eds), *Status and Identity in West Africa: Nyamakalaw of Mande* (Bloomington: Indiana University Press, 1995).
[6] For details on the *funé* occupation see David C. Conrad, 'Blind Man Meets Prophet: Oral Tradition, Islam, and funé Identity', in David C. Conrad and Barbara E. Frank (eds), *Status and Identity in West Africa: Nyamakalaw of Mande* , pp. 86–7.

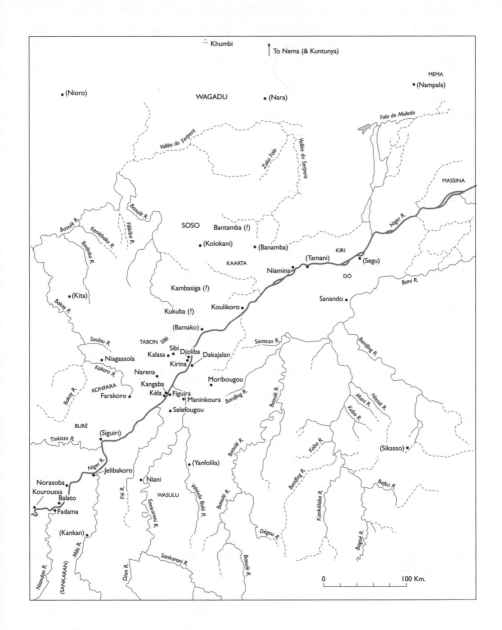

Fig 4.1 The Mande heartland and related *Jamanaw* according
to oral tradition

*(Source: David C. Conrad, ed., Sunjata: A West African Epic of the Mande People,
Cambridge and Indianapolis: Hackett Publishing Company, 2004, pp. xl–xli. Reprinted
by permission of Hackett Publishing Company, Inc. All rights reserved)*

The *jeliw* that we shall focus on here are the *jeliw*, who are popularly known by the generic term 'griot'.[7] For many centuries the *jeliw* have served as genealogists, musicians, praise-singers, spokespersons and diplomats.[8] As the principal narrators of oral tradition, they have been responsible for preserving the cultural record of what Manding peoples believe to have happened in the distant past. The spoken word is their domain, and they are famous for the manner in which they use metaphorical language to express the attitudes and values of the Manding peoples, using proverbs such as:

If you live at a time when roosters are used as horses,
You must attach the saddle to your own thighs.[9]

Individual *jeli* families were traditionally attached to patron families in mutually beneficial relationships, which in some cases endured for centuries. In return for their services as spokesmen, advisers, entertainers, family historians, and political negotiators, the *jeliw* lived with the patron family and were provided with food, clothing, shelter, and other basic living requirements. In cases where leading *jeliw* served powerful rulers in prosperous states like the Mali Empire or Bamana Segu, they were very richly rewarded. Therefore it was naturally to a *jeli*'s advantage to do everything possible to promote his patron's reputation and success. In ordinary day-to-day life this could mean performing duties like helping to settle a dispute with a neighboring farmer or negotiating an advantageous marriage for one of the family's sons or daughters. More dramatic examples include known instances where the patron conquered a neighboring people or was otherwise elevated to a position of political leadership to which he had no legitimate claim, according to local standards of authority. In these

[7] The Mande-specific term *jeli* (var. *jali*) is preferred to the very broadly used 'griot' (pronounced 'gree-oh'), which describes bards of many cultures from the Senegambian coast to the Republic of Niger. For a discussion of the origin of this word see Eric Charry, *Mande Music: Traditional and Modern Music of the Maninka and Mandinka of Western Africa* (Chicago and London: University of Chicago Press, 2000), pp. 105–14.

[8] During a visit to the Mali Empire in the years 1352–3, the North African traveler Ibn Battuta described *jeliw* at the court of Mansa Sulayman; see Nehemia Levtzion and J.F.P. Hopkins, *Corpus of Early Arabic Sources for West African History* (Cambridge: Cambridge University Press, 1981), p.293.

[9] Demba Kouyaté of Dinli in Conrad, *Epic Ancestors of the Sunjata Era*, p.163. This proverb reminds people that they must live according to the customs of their day, and make do with what they have. An American equivalent would be the expression, 'play with the hand you're dealt'. For a large collection of Bamana proverbs see Kassim Koné, *Mande Zana ni Ntalen Wa ni kò: Bamanankan ni Angilèkan na* (*More than a thousand Mande Proverbs in Bambara and English*) (West Newbury, MA: Mother Tongue Editions, 1995).

cases the *jeli* might well fabricate a genealogy or alter the narrative to legitimize his patron's claim to authority. If parts of the legend of Sunjata and his contemporaries have at least some basis in historical fact, most of it will have inevitably experienced great distortion through centuries of oral transmission so that what survives may have little resemblance to the original. The intentional embellishment of patrons' reputations and the exaggeration of their accomplishments by the *jeliw* have undoubtedly contributed to the distortions.

Clearly, the Manding peoples' ideas of what is important in the past are quite different from the kinds of history that are studied and appreciated by people of European descent. In Manding society where matters involving kinship are of supreme importance, people are identified by their *jamu*, which is the family name or patronymic associated with one or more famous ancestors who are remembered for important deeds that are alleged to have occurred in the first half of the thirteenth century. There are no written records from that time, though in the following century the respected Arab historian Ibn Khaldun collected informative oral historical traditions from Malian scholars.[10] A general awareness of the heroes and heroines of ancient times enters the people's consciousness in childhood and remains there throughout their lives. This occurs because the ancestors are constantly evoked in praise songs and narrative episodes that professional *jeliw* sing or recite on virtually any occasion that calls for entertainment.

In the customary elaborate greetings that are tendered during social encounters, friends, acquaintances, and strangers alike salute each other with reference to their respective *jamuw*, that is to say, family names extending back to distinguished ancestors of the heroic past. In the case of strangers meeting, they quickly learn each other's *jamuw* or patronymics, thus establishing their relative places in the cultural landscape. Travelers meeting far from home soon establish relationships through their *jamuw* because of links that were formed between their ancestors during encounters that are described in the epic narrative. Strangers arriving in distant towns or villages form immediate connections with 'related' families and find comfort and security with their hosts. When elders meet in village council, the ancestral spirits are felt to be present because, according to tradition, it was they who established the relative statuses of everyone present, as well as the administrative protocols to be followed and the values underpinning every decision. It is no exaggeration to say that, regardless of gender, the ancestors described in *kuma koro*, or 'ancient speech', define the

---

[10] Levtzion and Hopkins, *Corpus of Early Arabic Sources*, pp. 317, 333.

identity of virtually everyone of Manding origin.

The most gifted and popular *jeliw* are often invited to private homes to entertain the host's invited guests. On these special family occasions, a *jeli* might appear alone, personally performing the instrumental accompaniment to his narrative. Most public ceremonies such as marriages, circumcision feasts, funerals, and seasonal celebrations will include *jeli* performances involving music, praising, and fragments of narrative performances. On these larger occasions, the principal artist will often arrive with a supporting cast of other musicians and one or more female vocalists, depending on the size of the event. One of the accompanists will probably function as a *naamu*-sayer,[11] encouraging the performer with approving sounds or comments like 'yes!', 'we hear you!' and 'it's the truth!'. In any gathering, whether private or public, the host will usually be the first to hear himself praised through references to his ancestors in song or narrative.[12] However, the *jeliw* take pains to know the names of everybody attending the event, so they can maximize their profits by structuring the performance according to the identities of the people in the audience. As the performance progresses and various members of the audience hear their *jamu* mentioned, they come forward to reward the *jeli* with gifts of cash.

The substance of Manding discourse

The Bamana Empire of Segu, which flourished from the late seventeenth century to the middle of the nineteenth century, is the subject of one Manding epic tradition.[13] The nineteenth-century empire builders Al-Hajj 'Umar Tal and Almami Samori Touré have epic narratives devoted to their memory.[14] However, the epic narrative that provides the fundamental framework for Mande cultural values and social organization is the one that is popularly known by the name of one of

---

[11] More specifically, *naamu namina,* or *naamutigiw* (*naamu* 'owner'). The term probably originates from the Arabic *na'am.*

[12] For an example see Conrad, *Epic Ancestors of the Sunjata Era,* p. 57.

[13] See Conrad, *A State of Intrigue.*

[14] For Al-Hajj 'Umar Tal, see Samba Diop (ed.), *The Epic of El Hadj Umar Taal of Fuuta* (Madison, WI: University of Wisconsin African Studies Program, 2000); and the definitive historical study by David Robinson, *The Holy War of Umar Tal: The Western Sudan in the mid-Nineteenth Century* (Oxford: Clarendon Press, 1985). Epic traditions of Almami Samori Touré are collected in David C. Conrad, *Almami Samori: Nineteenth-Century West African Conquest in Maninka Epic Tradition* (Madison, WI: University of Wisconsin African Studies Program, forthcoming).

its principal heroes, Sunjata. The longer versions of that tradition can run to many thousands of lines, and virtually all of the most prominent old family names or *jamuw* of Manden are represented by a charismatic ancestor who appears somewhere in the story.

The Sunjata epic comprises a series of episodes, some of which form the core of the narrative and are the most frequently performed. These are more or less familiar to most people of traditional Manding societies, and the basic storyline and characters have become known to the outside world through both popular and scholarly publications. Other, less familiar episodes of the epic are known to relatively few of even the most knowledgeable *jeliw*, and these are rarely performed publicly. In any case, depending on the type of occasion, the time available and the make-up of the audience, most performances mention only a few of the episodes. At one end of the spectrum, in the course of a brief street performance for example, a female *jeli* (*jelimuso*) might simply evoke the name of Sunjata, Fakoli, or another of the epic heroes in one of her songs. At the other extreme, *jeliw* have been known to narrate one episode after another for five hours or more without stopping, and to continue at that rate for several days.[15]

As the occupational specialists who preserved these traditions, the *jeliw* have had enormous influence in establishing the identities or *jamuw* of each of the descent groups. In village society, people and events described in the epic are accepted as fundamental elements of the historical record, as they explain kinship patterns and the social relationships of today. For example, popular etymologies abound, wherein statements made on particular occasions are said to have become people's names. One of the best-known examples of this occurs in the Sunjata epic's buffalo episode that will be described below: just after the younger brother, Danmansa Wulanni, kills the great beast, his excited older brother begins to praise him, thereby recognizing the courageous younger sibling's superiority. This is believed to have resulted in two descent groups of different status: descendants of the brother who killed the buffalo are said to be of the 'noble' Traoré *jamu*, while the offspring of the hunter who sang his brother's praises became *jeliw* who go by the name of Diabaté.

It was partly through stories like these that *jeliw* exercised the power of 'the word', and part of that power accounts for the ancient speech

---

[15] In the author's experience such *jeliw* include the late Tayiru Banbera, see Conrad, *A State of Intrigue*, and the late Djanka Tassey Condé, in David C. Conrad (ed.), *Sunjata: A West African Epic of the Mande People* (Indianapolis, IN and Cambridge, MA: Hackett Publishing Company Inc., 2004).

known as *kuma koro*. The basis of this power lies in the Manding peoples' perceptions that *jeliw* know the secrets of the past. Esoteric knowledge gives them the ability to create or destroy the reputations of key people through public performance of praise songs and narrated texts. The best thing that could happen to a political leader, and by extension to his descendants, was to have a praise song composed specifically for him. Following the death of a popular *mansa* (king) of memorable accomplishments, poetic praises would lament his passing and contribute to the glory of his memory, as in the following lines that metaphorically describe a troubled and confused world left behind by Monzon Diarra of Segu (c. 1787–1808):

> The goat is sick,
> The goat owner is ailing.
> The knife is dull,
> The goat's throat is tough.
> The day is drawing to a close,
> The ground is hot.
> We have no basket to sit on,
> While we tell our troubles to the angels of God.[16]

Praise songs and glory

An incident that occurs in a variant of the epic of Almami Samori Touré illustrates how seriously praise songs were regarded, both by the *jeliw* who composed them and by those who were honored by them. Almami Samori Touré was a Maninka conqueror who, between 1861 and the 1890s, established an empire in what are today Guinea, Mali, and Côte d'Ivoire. Although Samori is a historic figure whose deeds are well documented through eyewitness descriptions and even a few photographs, he is also a legendary figure in his own society, and versions of his story are told in traditional narrative form by Maninka *jeliw* of Guinea. One of the episodes in this narrative is about a praise song, which Samori sends to his brother Kèmè Brèma, who is one of his best commanders, on a military campaign. Along with the troops, Kèmè Brèma is accompanied by many *jeliw*, including some who are from Samori's household. According to the Mande system of power and authority, the entire contingent is meant to represent Almami Samori, performing all deeds in his name. However, during the course

---

[16] Tayiru Banbera in Conrad, *A State of Intrigue*, p. 171.

of the campaign, the accompanying *jeliw* collaborate in composing a song to praise Kèmè Brèma. This behavior was condemned by Mamadi Condé, the *jeli* who told the story in the late 1980s. He stresses that all the troops including Kèmè Brèma owe total allegiance to Samori because it is 'his war', and all praise songs should be for him: 'The song was bad', says Mamadi Condé, 'because Kèmè Brèma was carrying firewood for his brother, not for himself'. Indeed, to celebrate the success as if it were Kèmè Brèma's campaign instead of Samori's is regarded as an act of treachery. When Kèmè Brèma returns to his brother's headquarters, Samori expresses outrage that his brother has accepted the *jeliw's* praise as his own:

> The *jeliw* sang that this was your war.
> You never said, 'It is my brother's war'.
> Do you have a war?

Samori then strips Kèmè Brèma of his horse and weapons and sends him home to work on the family farm, and it takes an emotional intervention by their father to eventually reconcile the two great men. Even so, once the quarrel is ended, Samori makes a final demand on the *jeliw*:

> Sing a song for me that will never be sung to anybody else.
> I do not want to hear anybody else's name in that song.
> Sing a song for me like the one you made for Kèmè Brèma.
> You will not go home until you sing my song.[17]

The *jeliw* then realize that all the great praise songs they know are for other heroes, and they are finally forced to compose a new song, 'Almami Bolo', for Samori. Nevertheless, to this day in Mali, Guinea, Gambia, and other parts of the Mande world, the song 'Kèmè Brèma' is one of the most famous in the *jeli* repertoire. Relatively few great praise songs were ever composed, and in those cases it guaranteed the fame of those they honored, and brought ongoing distinction to people claiming to be their descendants.

The spiritual dimension

In Manding societies there are still people who follow the old, pre-Islamic spiritual practices of the ancestors, involving sacrifice and other

---

[17] Mamadi Condé in Conrad, *Almami Samori*.

forms of ritualized communication with a variety of spirits believed to inhabit secluded groves, rock formations, or bodies of water found everywhere in the countryside. However, the majority of the Manding peoples are either Muslims or they practice a mixture of the Islamic faith and the indigenous system of belief. Thus, the oral performances sometimes begin with a blessing in the local manner of speaking Arabic, such as:

> May God bless our master Muhammad,
> Grant peace to him and his family,
> Peace to our master Muhammad.[18]

Some peoples of the broader Mande cultural family have been exposed to Islam since at least the tenth century when Muslim traders crossed the Sahara desert to conduct trade with the Soninke of the Ghana Empire, which was locally known as Wagadu.[19] At some point the Soninke and other Mande branches, including the Manding, began to conceive of Islam as a source of significant spiritual power that could be added to the indigenous power sources that they already possessed. During the centuries when Islam was being integrated into Manding societies and becoming an African religion, Manding *jeliw* assimilated elements of Islamic tradition. Pilgrims returning from Mecca told stories that appealed to Manding audiences, and some of these were borrowed by the *jeliw* and woven into the fabric of previously existing narratives. Among the Islamic ideals that were absorbed by Manding peoples was the notion that direct ancestral links to the prophet Muhammed and his followers were especially desirable sources of prestige, and therefore Islamic forebears began to appear in family descent lists.

Creating identities and establishing values

Performances of the Sunjata epic often include genealogies of some of the most prominent characters. As noted earlier, one of the main occupational responsibilities of the *jeli* was to establish or maintain his patron's status by recalling the latter's ancestors in song and story and praising the most distinguished among them. If, on occasion, genealogies were completely fabricated for political leaders needing to

---

[18] Tayiru Banbera in Conrad, *A State of Intrigue*, p. 43.

[19] The Soninke are a northern branch of the Mande peoples. Their ancient empire was Wagadu, but it was known to the Arabs as Ghana, a name that might be derived from the Soninke ruler's title.

have their claims to authority legitimized, there were also instances where previously established lines of descent were adjusted to accommodate changes in the culture's socio-political needs, or its religious values. In the Soninke legend of Wagadu, the great snake Bida that protects the kingdom against all evil and guarantees its prosperity is included in some versions of the royal genealogy.[20] In the traditional genealogy of the Keita lineage of ancient Mali's founding hero Sunjata, most of the names that *jeliw* recite clearly stem from non-Islamic times. However, when it became desirable to claim distinguished Muslim ancestors, some of them were borrowed from Islamic tradition and added to Sunjata's descent list. This is why a character that the *jeliw* call Bilali Bounama often appears in the lists of Sunjata's ancestors.

Bilali originates in Islamic tradition as Bilal ibn Rabah,[21] a black slave from Abyssinia and early convert to Islam who became the first muezzin (Ar. *mua'dhadhin*) or caller to prayer. Bilal is described as 'a faithful Muslim, pure of heart' whose master tortured him by forcing him to lie on his back under the sun during the hottest part of the day with a heavy stone on his chest, in a vain effort to make him renounce Islam. Ransomed and freed by Abu Bakr, a fellow-convert who was impressed by the strength of the slave's conviction, Bilal is said to have joined the company of Muhammad. According to tradition, when one of the other companions sees in a dream how the faithful should be called to prayer, Bilal is chosen as the first muezzin because of his penetrating voice. Bilal becomes Bilali in Manding tradition, where in one variant the *jeli* claims Bilali was born the day after Muhammad's birth, and that at the famous battle of Kaybara[22] he held the bridle of the prophet's camel and blew the trumpet to assemble the army. Other *jeliw* tell how one of Bilali's offspring wanders for many years until he settles in the ancient land of Manden and engenders the Keita lineage, eventually producing the epic hero Sunjata, who is credited with founding the Mali Empire in the early thirteenth century.

---

[20] David C. Conrad and Humphrey J. Fisher, 'The Conquest that Never Was: Ghana and the Almoravids, 1076, II. The Local Oral Sources', *History in Africa* 10 (1983), p. 63.

[21] Rabah was Bilal's father, but he was sometimes called Ibn Hamana after his mother, which is the case in Bamana tradition where he is known as Bilali Bounama, a shortened form of Bilali Boum Hamama, in David C. Conrad, 'Islam in the Oral Traditions of Mali: Bilali and Surakata', *Journal of African History* 26 (1985), p. 37. Local custom tends to identify the son with the mother rather than the father as in the case of Sunjata, whose name derives from Sogolon's Jara (*jara* = 'lion': So'olon Jara, Son-Jara).

[22] Kaybara is the Maninka pronunciation of 'Khaybar' which was the site of a battle remembered as one of the most important fought by Muhammad's supporters.

Some famous episodes

The most familiar or core episodes of the Sunjata epic include one about Kamissa, a shape-shifting sorceress of the land of Dò, also known as Buffalo Woman.[23] Her story illustrates the influence of hunters' lore and tradition in Manding discourse, as well as the importance of divination and the notion that physical deformity is a sign of great spiritual power. Kamissa is denied her share of the family legacy by her elder step-brother, the *mansa* of Dò. She seeks revenge by transforming herself into a buffalo that lays waste to the countryside and kills every hunter who tries to stop her. Two brothers, Danmansa Wulanba and Danmansa Wulanni, arrive from a distant land and befriend Kamissa in her human form. She reveals the secret of how to kill her buffalo wraith in exchange for a promise that they will deliver her younger sister Sogolon to Maghan Konfara (*mansa* or 'king' of Konfara), the man she is destined to marry. A diviner has prophesied that the Konfara *mansa*'s son, who is to be the future leader of an empire will be born to a wife he has not yet married. The younger of the two hunters kills the buffalo, and their reward is the choice of any unmarried girl of Dò. Keeping their promise to Kamissa, they choose the ugly, deformed Sogolon and after some misadventures finally deliver her to Maghan Konfara, who will be the father of the hero.

The next major episode familiar to most Manding illustrates the popular notion that a hero receives his power from his mother, and that both mother and son must endure various humiliating and painful ordeals on the road to eventual glory. In this story we learn of Sogolon's problems in giving birth to Sunjata, future founder of the Mali Empire. Sogolon and her co-wife Sansuma Bèrètè, mother of Sunjata's step-brother and rival Dankaran Tuman, are both characterized as powerful sorceresses, as are many female characters in the Sunjata epic.[24] Sansuma and the other co-wives conspire against Sogolon, using their sorcery to delay her son's birth by many months, and then causing him to be born lame. After years of suffering as a cripple, Sunjata eventually gains his feet and becomes an accomplished hunter along with his

[23] See Stephen Bulman, 'The Buffalo Woman Tale: Political Imperatives and Narrative Constraints in the Sunjata Epic' in Karin Barber and P. F. de Moraes Farias (eds), *Discourse and its Disguises: The Interpretation of African Oral Texts* (Birmingham: Birmingham University Centre of West African Studies, 1989).

[24] David C. Conrad, 'Mooning Armies and Mothering Heroes: Female Power in Mande Epic Tradition' in Ralph A. Austen (ed.), *In Search of Sunjata: The Mande Epic as History, Literature and Performance.* (Bloomington, IN: Indiana University Press, 1999), p. 195.

brother Manden Bori. However, the elder, rival step-brother Dankaran Tuman inherits their father's position of power, and it becomes clear that Sunjata's life is in danger. The hero's mother Sogolon leaves Manden for exile in the distant land of Nema (or Mema), accompanied by her sons and her daughter Kolonkan who is another of the epic's important female characters.

Another well-known episode involves the kingdom of Soso, ruled by the great sorcerer king Sumaworo[25] Kanté. This story reinforces the connection between music and the spirit world, and demonstrates the importance of master *jeliw* in the lives of powerful rulers. While Sogolon and Sunjata are in exile, Sumaworo conquers Manden and subjugates its people. Sunjata's *jeli*, Bala Fasaké Kouyaté, who had remained in Manden, goes on a diplomatic mission to Soso and is detained there by Sumaworo. One day, in the king's absence, Bala Fasaké enters the sacred grotto and sees for the first time a great *balafon* (traditional xylophone) called the Soso Bala, which Sumaworo had acquired from the king of the genies. It is taboo for anyone but the Soso *mansa* to touch the instrument, but Bala Fasaké finds it irresistible and sits down to play it. Sumaworo hears the music from a distance and returns intending to kill the trespasser, but is enchanted by Bala Fasaké's playing. Sumaworo takes such pleasure in hearing his own praises sung that he spares the *jeli*'s life and claims him as his own *jeli*.

One of the most famous and influential of the epic characters is Fakoli, who is claimed as the ancestor of several Mande blacksmith lineages, including both the Koroma and the Dumbia.[26] This man's story provides another example of the identification of physical flaws with spiritual power and also reflects the close relationship between blacksmithing and sorcery. Fakoli is recalled as one of the greatest of sorcerers and as one of the most important generals in Manden's war with Soso. He is usually described as being of dwarf-like stature and is praised as 'Big-headed Fakoli, big-mouthed Fakoli'. One of the most complex characters of the Sunjata epic, Fakoli is prominent in several episodes, two of which are better known than the rest. In one of these, Fakoli is ridiculed by other elders, because he stoops to enter the doorway of the council hall even though the top of the door-frame is far above his head. Reacting to the elders' ridicule, Fakoli proves to them that his small size is no indication of his power. Using his sorcery he causes the elders to flee

---

[25] This, or a variant of it, is how the name is pronounced by the Maninka of northeastern Guinea. The Bamana *jeliw* of Mali pronounce it as Sumanguru, or a variant thereof.

[26] David C. Conrad, 'Searching for History in the Sunjata Epic: The Case of Fakoli', *History in Africa* 19 (1992), pp. 174–5.

from the building as he inflates his size until he fills the entire council hall, towering above it and wearing the thatched roof as a hat.[27]

Both divination and filial devotion to a mother motivate the action in an episode where the people of Manden learn from a seer that the only man who can deliver their land from Soso oppression is Sunjata. The mission to find the hero and bring him back to liberate his homeland is so important that many *jeliw* still recite the names of the delegates who were sent. After a long search the delegates arrive at Kuntunya, the capital of Nema, and Sogolon hears that her eldest son is invited to return to Manden and take command. Sogolon realizes that she is too old to make the journey home, and she explains to her children that they must return without her. Sunjata refuses to leave before his mother dies, and she passes away before her frailty can delay their departure. Sunjata requests a burial plot from their host Faran Tunkara, the *mansa* of Nema, but the king rudely refuses. The hero sends Tunkara a message consisting of some broken pieces of pottery and calabash containing dust and a few bird feathers. A wise man correctly interprets this as a metaphor symbolizing the future ruins to which Kuntunya will be reduced if Sunjata is not given a burial plot for his mother, so Faran Tunkara grants the request.

In Manding epic narrative where warfare is concerned, one rarely encounters detailed descriptions of actual fighting. The *jeliw* and their audiences are more interested in the human relationships, political dynamics, and interaction with the spirit world that lead to conflict. Some *jeliw* do describe a series of battles between Manden and Soso that were fought in various locations,[28] but most variants emphasize a deciding battle at a place identified as either Kirina or Dakajalan, in which Manden defeats Soso and Sumaworo is finally vanquished by Sunjata's troops. As with all episodes of the Sunjata epic, details vary considerably depending on the performer, but the Dakajalan/Kirina battle episode often concludes with Sunjata pursuing Sumaworo as the sorcerer king disappears into the mountain at a place called Kulikoro, which is downriver from Bamako, the capital of present-day Mali. Some *jeliw* have been known to describe the death of Sumaworo, but the Kouyaté and Diabaté *jeliw* are normally quite careful not to say that Sumaworo was slain by Sunjata, Fakoli, or anybody else. As we saw at the beginning of this chapter, these things are taken seriously in modern times because Manding peoples identify with the ancestors whose names they carry. To give details of a humiliating defeat, even

[27] For details of this episode see Conrad, 'Searching for History in the Sunjata Epic', pp. 162–6.
[28] For example, Jeli Mori Kouyaté in Conrad, *Epic Ancestors of the Sunjata Era*, p. 631.

one alleged to have occurred more than seven centuries ago, could evoke bad feelings between the descendants of the victors and the vanquished.

Great heroines stand tall with the heroes

An important distinguishing feature of Manding epic tradition is that, along with recounting the deeds of great men from the past, it also describes the deeds of many important women. The same cannot be said of the conventional written documentation of the Mali Empire that is contained in Arabic sources. There, descriptions of prominent women who are actually identified by name are extremely rare. One instance where a woman is highlighted in the written sources is provided by the North African traveler Ibn Battuta, who visited the royal court of Mali in 1352–3. He describes an attempted coup d'état by Kasa, a wife of Mansa Sulayman. Kasa apparently believed that the army of Mali was prepared to abandon her unpopular emperor husband if she called on their backing for a government takeover. Unfortunately, we have only enough details to know that she must have been an extremely interesting person whose full story deserved to be told but was not.[29]

In contrast to such scarcity, Mande epic tradition from the era of Sunjata to stories of nineteenth-century heroes is greatly enhanced by descriptions of many powerful, independent women.[30] The epic that is generally identified with Sunjata, which has many prominent male heroes, is also particularly rich in colorful portrayals of mothers, sisters, and wives, who played pivotal roles in crucial events. The Condé identity or *jamu* is particularly well represented by three women who comprise a fountainhead of Mande social identity. The force of their combined impact on legendary events leading up to the foundation of the Mali Empire is enormous, and it all begins with Dò Kamissa the buffalo woman. She is responsible for the fate of her younger sister Sogolon Wulen Condé, who is destined to be Sunjata's mother. Sogolon is the best known of the three, but the third, Ma Tènènba, plays a very significant role in her own right. Her complete name is Sumansa Sona Tènènba, the first part of which, *sumansa*, praises her as a formidable sorceress.[31] The identification of Ma Tènènba with occult powers is appropriate, because she is both a sister of Dò Kamissa, the buffalo

---

[29] Levtzion and Hopkins, *Corpus of Early Arabic Sources*, pp. 295–6.
[30] Conrad, 'Mooning Armies and Mothering Heroes'.
[31] *Sumansa* is from *subaga* (*suba*) *mansa*, meaning 'sorcerer king'.

woman, and foster-mother of the great sorcerer and war leader Fakoli.

The episode describing Fakoli's early life offers a useful example of how extensive the network of powerful ancestral relationships can be, as manifested in the Mande epic. It also illustrates degrees of closeness within the nuclear family between co-wives, on the one hand, and brothers and sisters, on the other. These stand in contrast to stories of deadly step-brother rivalry which characterizes, for example, the relationship of Dankaran Tuman and Sunjata. Also demonstrated here is the characteristic Manding reverence for music and musical instruments, and perceptions of how the business of everyday life interacts with the spirit world.

Fakoli's father was Mansa Yèrèlenko of Nègèbòriya. The oral evidence indicates that Nègèbòriya was an important iron-producing region of Manden, which helps to account for the tradition of Fakoli being the ancestor of more than one blacksmith lineage.[32] Mansa Yèrèlenko's senior wife is Ma Tènènba Condé, sister of Sunjata's mother Sogolon and of Dò Kamissa, the buffalo woman. Ma Tènènba is childless, so she encourages her husband to get a second wife. He eventually marries Kosiya Kanté, sister of Sumaworo the *subamansa* (sorcerer king) of Soso. This marriage, which produces Fakoli, forms an alliance between the greatest blacksmith family of Manden and the Kanté blacksmith lineage that rules Soso. In the story of how Sumaworo acquires the Soso *bala* (xylophone) from Jinna Maghan, the king of the genies, Kosiya discovers that the genie *mansa* demanded that Sumaworo sacrifice a close family member in exchange for the Soso *bala*. Determined to have her brother acquire the Soso *bala*, Kosiya entrusts the infant Fakoli to her co-wife Tènènba Condé, and sacrifices herself to the genies. Fakoli remains with Tènènba Condé, who takes him on an initiation pilgrimage to all the great power sources of Manden to acquire his *dalilu* (occult power) and to prepare him for his role as spiritual 'ancestor' of all later sorcerers. On this pilgrimage the infant Fakoli receives protective medicine, magic, and instruction from the most powerful pre-imperial *mansaw* (kings) of Manden, including Kamanjan Kamara of Sibi, Tanan Mansa Konkon of Kirina, Faran Tunkara of Nema, and Nyèmogo Diarra of Dò and Kiri.[33] Thus, as virtual godson of all these powerful *mansaw*, as nephew of Sumaworo of Soso, and as one of Sunjata's most important military commanders, Fakoli stands at the core of the Mande power structure.

Great as Fakoli is, Sunjata is the hero consistently acknowledged as the leader who liberates Manden from Soso oppression and becomes

[32] Conrad, 'Searching for History in the Sunjata Epic', pp. 174-80.
[33] Conrad, 'Mooning Armies and Mothering Heroes', p. 205.

mansa of the unified chiefdoms that subsequently expand into the Mali Empire. For that reason, in today's Manding societies the Keita *jamu* carries special distinction, even for those not directly connected to village chiefs who base their claims to authority on direct descent from Sunjata's lineage. However, at modern-day *jeli* performances, members of many other families bask in the reflected glory of early kings, because the *jeliw* like to say that there were no less than seven *mansaw* who ruled individual chiefdoms in Manden during the period leading up to imperial unification. The *jeliw* do not always list the same *mansaw*, so more than seven are actually named, and this has the effect of extending the reflected glory to the alleged descendants of additional ruling ancestors.

Relationships real and imagined

For the Maninka, Bamana, and other peoples of traditional Manding culture, the epic's greatest importance clearly lies in the descriptions of how the ancestors behaved in relation to one another during the period that saw the Mali Empire in its infancy. Underlying the surface distinction of prominent names from Mande epic tradition is an ongoing awareness of significant relationships between different *jamuw* that charismatic ancestors of ancient times founded. Interactions between characters in the Sunjata epic still influence the social relations between people of today, establishing the boundaries of their behavior towards one another. Joking relationships or *senankuya* are based on popular notions of what happened between ancestors, with perhaps only vague awareness of what actually led to the customary jokes. For example, when people named Traoré and Condé are introduced to each other, one of them will almost invariably announce that the other is his 'slave'. This will be followed by humorous banter about whose ancestor enslaved the other, but the chances are that neither of the two can explain how this custom began.

Sibling rivalries, marriages and political alliances, individual adventures, spiritual power, humiliating experiences and heroic deeds of ancestors both male and female, are what establish the identities of all later generations of the core families of Mande society right up to the present time. Clearly, everybody named Keita cannot actually be descended from Sunjata or his brother Manden Bori; not all Traoré are legitimate descendants of Tiramakan; and the same applies to the relationship of Kamara people to Kamanjan Kamara, the Koroma and Dumbia to Fakoli, the Condé to Sogolon Wulen, the Tunkara to Faran of Nema, and so forth. There are certain branches of the Keita lineage that are regarded as having the most legitimate claim to descent from the Mali Empire's founder or members of his family. They remain in positions of authority as chiefs of historically significant towns like Kita and Nana-Kènièba in Mali, and Niagassola, Niani, and the Hamana region in Guinea.[34] Nevertheless, anybody of the Keita *jamu* enjoys at least a faint aura of distinction owing to their nominal association with Sunjata.

The same is true of anybody named Traoré and their nominal association with Tiramakan, the general who insisted on leading the campaign against Jolofin Mansa. Anybody named Koroma or Dumbia, among others, will be praised in *jeliw* performances by being called 'Fakoli', the legendary hero recalled as ancestor of sorcerers and several blacksmith lineages. When anybody with these and other names associated with ancestors of the Sunjata epic hear the praise music specially dedicated to their ancestral heroes, they clearly appreciate the public distinction as they step forward to hand money to the performer. When performing a narrative that includes recitation of a descent list, a *jeli* will acknowledge the 'honored lineage' believed to be the branch that genuinely produced the charismatic ancestor in question. However, on these occasions social convention allows all people of that name to share in the glory.

The musical dimension

If the deeds of Sunjata and his contemporaries as described in epic tradition are deeply woven into the Maninka social fabric, how is this apparent in day-to-day life? One area in which the modern consciousness of the ancestors is most evident, is in the extremely rich music of Manden. Many of the oldest and most famous songs that are played on the *bala* are associated with specific ancestors of Manding oral tradition. One of the oldest, 'Janjon', is often associated with Fakoli, 'Tiramakan' praises the hero of that name, 'Boloba' is dedicated to Sumaworo Kanté, and several songs including 'Sunjata fasa' and 'I bara kala ta', praise Sunjata. Some famous musical pieces are dedicated to more than one subject, as in the case of 'Dugha', which honors both

---

[34] According to one tradition, the Keita were late-comers to power in Kita. It is said that after the defeat of Soso, Sunjata's army marched on Kita though it should not have done so, because it was ruled by Kamara and Tunkara from leading families of Wagadu who had sent troops to aid in the war against Soso. The Kouyaté *jeliw* who serve the Keita of Nana-Kènièba now live in Niagassola (Cheick M. Chérif Keita, pers. comm. 5/6/01).

the Kamara and Condé ancestors. Some heroes of nineteenth-century Manding history are among ancestors who are honored with songs. We saw earlier that 'Kèmè Brèma' is sung for the brother of the famous conqueror Almami Samori Touré, and Samori's own song is 'Almami Bolo'. 'Taara' is dedicated to the great Tukulor conqueror Al-Hajj 'Umar Tal, and 'Tutu Jara' is dedicated to a king of the Bamana Empire of Segu.[35] Many of these pieces are played in both traditional and modern musical repertoires, so Manding audiences are constantly reminded of the ancestors associated with them.

Certain indigenous musical instruments form direct links with the past, not just by the music played on them, but also through stories of their association with charismatic ancestors. This is especially true of the famous xylophone known as the Soso *bala*, which is said to have been originally acquired from the king of the genies by Sumaworo Kanté. According to the legend, when Sumaworo was finally vanquished, the Soso *bala* became the possession of Sunjata's *jeli*, Bala Fasaké Kouyaté. Bala Fasaké's direct descendants are said to be the Kouyaté *jeliw* of the town of Niagassola in northern Guinea. This branch of the Kouyaté is still the offical *jeliw* of a branch of the Keita family that claims direct descent from Sunjata. The eldest male member of that branch of the Kouyaté patrilineage is still the official guardian of the Soso *bala*, which is now regarded as a sacred relic, symbol of the great days of the Mali Empire. An unusually large old *bala* that is claimed to be the original one, stands today preserved under a white shroud, enshrined in its own special building in Niagassola.[36]

Ancestral influence today

One of the best examples of how the Sunjata tradition plays out in today's world derives from the more detailed variants of the episode in which the exiled Sunjata is asked to return to lead his people in the struggle against Soso. After Sunjata's sister Kolonkan encounters the delegation from Manden in the market and brings them to her mother Sogolon, she finds that there is no meat in the house for the stranger's

---

[35] See Charry, *Mande Music*, pp. 152–5.

[36] It seems unlikely that the instrument currently in the shrine at Niagassola has actually survived from the thirteenth century, because wooden objects in West Africa are extremely vulnerable to termite damage and are eventually destroyed. Whatever the true provenance of the present-day Soso *bala*, it is proudly regarded with sincere veneration and is a genuine symbol of the glorious days of ancient Mali. In fact, in 2001 it received official UNESCO designation as a relic of the world cultural heritage.

welcoming meal, which it is her responsibility to prepare. Sunjata and his brothers Jamori and Manden Bori are away in the bush hunting, so Kolonkan goes into the bush and finds a slain antelope that the brothers have left to collect later. Using her powers as a sorceress she removes the heart and liver without leaving a mark on the carcass, and as she cooks the visitors' meal, her brothers return from the hunt. In the Manding value system, sisters are expected to have great influence over the fate of their brothers, and to be respected by them. However, the hotheaded brother Manden Bori violates this custom by angrily accusing Kolonkan of showing off for the visitors. Apparently upset that in practicing her sorcery she has diminished the impact of his hunting accomplishments, he denounces her for removing parts of their kill before they can bring it home. Manden Bori humiliates Kolonkan by chasing her and handling her roughly, causing her wrapper to come off in front of the guests. Kolonkan then pronounces a curse on Manden Bori, a deed that has far-reaching consequences. Kolonkan reacts to Manden Bori's behavior by condemning him and his branch of the Keita royal lineage with a curse that is said to explain the troubles of later generations, and whose effects remain evident in today's Manden:

> Because you have done this to me,   (Naamu)
> The *mansaya* will be passed on to you,   (Naamu)
> But your descendants will never agree on one *mansa* until the trumpet is blown.[37]

In local society this kind of curse from a woman is still taken very seriously. As one researcher explains it, 'a woman can damn a man forever by removing her *pagne* [wrap-around skirt] pointing to her sex, and cursing the offender with its power'.[38] A man who is cursed in this way is said to be ostracized forever by both men and women unless he begs forgiveness and persuades the offended woman to revoke her oath.[39] There is no tradition that Kolonkan's brother ever begged for forgiveness, and men of today's Manden continue to discuss the effects of her curse on the Mansaré lineage that is descended from Manden Bori. The *jeli* is emphatic on this point, and his audience replies enthusiastically:

---

[37] Conrad, 'Mooning Armies and Mothering Heroes', pp. 211–12. The excerpt is from Djanka Tassey Condé in Conrad, *Sunjata*.

[38] Sarah Brett-Smith, *The Making of Bamana Sculpture: Creativity and Gender* (Cambridge: Cambridge University Press, 1994), p. 122. This has been confirmed by Kassim Koné in Conrad, *Epic Ancestors of the Sunjata Era*, p. 213 (n. 22).

[39] Brett-Smith, *The Making of Bamana Sculpture*, p. 123.

Even up to tomorrow   (The curse will be there!)
The curse will be there.   (It's true!)[40]

Rural (and many urban) Maninka of Upper Guinea retain the traditional world view, and the curse leveled by Kolonkan on Manden Bori serves as a convincing explanation for the lack of continuity in Mande royal succession from the fourteenth century to the post-colonial era. In conversation resulting from this performance, the learned elders of Fadama mentioned that results of Kolonkan's curse are manifest in the cases of weakness among *mansaw* of the Mali Empire. The consequences they remember correspond in kind to various thirteenth- and fourteenth-century disruptions mentioned in the Arabic sources, including various usurpations, the insanity of one Malian emperor, and the tyranny of another.[41] For modern times, the elders cite the 1968 overthrow of the Republic of Mali's first President Modibo Keita, as well as recent power struggles among candidates and regimes of other countries containing large Mande populations.

Conclusion

In this chapter we have seen that the West African Manding peoples' collective view of what is worth remembering from the distant past is considerably different from European notions of historically significant events. According to European academic standards, the very existence of ancestors who, according to Manding perceptions, performed empire-building deeds is scarcely credible. Nevertheless, owing to the richly textured imagery and poetically narrated stories of ancient heroes and heroines passed along by generations of specialists in the oral arts, the ancestors maintain an ongoing presence in the everyday consciousness and affairs of local villagers and townspeople. Indeed, all people who are known by the ancient family names derive their fundamental identities from characters described in the epic traditions. The legendary deeds performed by larger than life forebears interacting with formidable denizens of the spirit world provide an idealized paradigm for social relationships and behavior in today's Manding societies.

[40] Conrad, 'Mooning Armies and Mothering Heroes', p. 214.
[41] Ibn Khaldun in Levtzion and Hopkins, *Corpus of Early Arabic Sources,* pp. 333–5.

Recommended Reading

Austen, Ralph A. (ed.) (1999) *In Search of Sunjata: The Mande Epic as History, Literature and Performance* (Bloomington, IN: Indiana University Press).

Brett-Smith, Sarah (1994) *The Making of Bamana Sculpture: Creativity and Gender* (Cambridge: Cambridge University Press).

Barber, Karin and P.F. de Moraes Farias (eds) (1989) *Discourse and its Disguises: The Interpretation of African Oral Texts* (Birmingham: Birmingham University Centre of West African Studies).

Charry, Eric (2000) *Mande Music: Traditional and Modern Music of the Maninka and Mandinka of Western Africa* (Chicago and London: University of Chicago Press).

Conrad, David C. (ed.) (1999) *Epic Ancestors of the Sunjata Era: Oral Tradition from the Maninka of Guinea* (Madison, WI: University of Wisconsin, African Studies Program).

Conrad, David C. (1985) 'Islam in the Oral Traditions of Mali: Bilali and Surakata', *Journal of African History* 26, pp. 33–49.

Conrad, David C. (ed.) (1990) *A State of Intrigue: The Epic of Bamana Segu According to Tayiru Banbera*, Union Académique Internationale, Fontes Historiae Africanae, Series Varia VI (Oxford and New York: Oxford University Press for the British Academy).

Conrad, David C. (ed.) (2004) *Sunjata: A West African Epic of the Mande People* (Indianapolis, IN and Cambridge, MA: Hackett Publishing Company, Inc.).

Conrad, David C. and Humphrey J. Fisher (1983) 'The Conquest that Never Was: Ghana and the Almoravids, 1076, II. The Local Oral Sources', *History in Africa* 10, pp. 53–78.

Conrad, David C. and Barbara E. Frank (eds) (1995) *Status and Identity in West Africa: Nyamakalaw of Mande* (Bloomington, IN: Indiana University Press).

Diop, Samba (ed.) (2000) *The Epic of El Hadj Umar Taal of Fuuta* (Madison, WI: University of Wisconsin African Studies Program).

Johnson, John W. (1986) *The Epic of Son-Jara: A West African Tradition* (Bloomington, IN: Indiana University Press).

Levtzion, Nehemia and J. F. P. Hopkins (eds) trans. J.F.P. Hopkins (1981) *Corpus of Early Arabic Sources for West African History* (Cambridge: Cambridge University Press).

Robinson, David (1985) *The Holy War of Umar Tal: The Western Sudan in the mid-Nineteenth Century* (Oxford: Clarendon Press).

PART II

Perspectives on Environment, Society, Agency & Historical Change

5

Slavery & Slave Trade in West Africa
1450–1930

PATRICK MANNING

Slavery and slave trade, 1450–1650

In 1450, approximately 20 to 25 million persons lived in relative stability in West Africa. This population, while divided into numerous ethnic, linguistic and political communities, was at the same time interconnected with ties of trade, migration and religious affiliation. For thousands of years, West African populations had developed their societies in the overlapping zones of forest, savanna and desert edge; and among their many social institutions and structures existed some that could be called 'slavery', in that war captives, pawns and other dependants were held in subservience by individuals, families and states. While historians have little direct evidence for these early antecedents of West African slavery, it is clear that the small scale of slavery in West Africa contrasted with the far more developed systems of slavery in the regions of the Mediterranean, the Black Sea, and the Middle East. Holding people in captivity could succeed only if the captors had substantial resources and substantial incentives to carry out this oppression. Slavery could expand only if connected to significant demand for captive labor — brought about by the ability of a monarchy to extract servile labor, or by the existence of markets for slave-produced goods, or through purchasers who would carry captives a distance to where these conditions could be obtained.

In 1450 all three of these conditions arose along the Sahara fringe. The declining kingdom of Mali and the rising kingdom of Borno gathered, exploited and exported captives, as is documented in Arabic-language records. For the rest of West Africa, slavery became a major

99

factor only after 1550, when trans-Atlantic encounters brought collapse of Amerindian populations and a resulting demand for African labor.

Europeans voyaging to the West African littoral found that they were able to seize and purchase captives, and gradually increased the number of their purchases. An estimated 600 persons per year were taken from the West African coast between 1450 and 1500, and this number grew steadily for three centuries. By 1650 the European purchases of enslaved West Africans had risen to about 4,000 per year, a number more than six times greater than maritime slave exports in 1500, and which equaled the number of captives sent from West Africa across the Sahara in 1650.[1] By 1780 the number of trans-Atlantic slave exports from West Africa had multiplied by another factor of more than ten, to 50,000 per year. (In the same period, slave exports across the Sahara rose from about 2,800 per year in the late fifteenth century to about 7,000 per year in the late eighteenth century.) These figures indicate that, to explain the expansion of slavery and slave trade in West Africa, one must concentrate on studying the interactions between Europeans and West Africans, far more than on the earlier patterns of life among West Africans alone.

For the period from 1450 to 1650, we shall focus on the beginnings of the processes that could later deliver many more slaves in trade across the Atlantic. These initial patterns of trade and exploitation, replicated and reinforced over the following four centuries, ultimately brought dramatic and unfortunate changes to the population and society of West Africa.

Well-informed West Africans in 1450 knew about the Mediterranean Sea and the Europeans living to the north of it. But it was different to have Europeans on African shores in advanced ships, opening new routes of communication. The Europeans had known, similarly, of the trade across the Sahara: this exchange in West African captives, linked to trade in gold, salt, and cowries, had been in existence for centuries. The majority of West African captives went through Mali to Morocco as domestics and to desert stations as laborers in oasis agriculture and salt mines. A smaller number crossed the desert from Borno and the

---

[1] On the volume of slave exports before 1650, see Philip D. Curtin, *The Atlantic Slave Trade: A Census* (Madison, WI: University of Wisconsin Press, 1969); Ivana Elbl, 'The Volume of the Early Atlantic Slave Trade, 1450–1521', *Journal of African History* 38 (1997), pp. 31–75; and Ralph A. Austen, 'The Trans-Saharan Slave Trade: A Tentative Census', in Henry A. Gemery and Jan S. Hogendorn (eds), *The Uncommon Market: Essays in the Economic History of the Atlantic Slave Trade* (New York: Academic Press, 1979), pp. 23–76. See also Nehemia Levtzion and J. F. P. Hopkins (eds) trans. J. F. P. Hopkins *Corpus of Early Arabic Sources for West African History* (Cambridge: Cambridge University Press, 1981).

Central Sudan to Fezzan and then to the Eastern Mediterranean. European visitors to West Africa sought to undercut the trans-Saharan trade, and to some degree they succeeded. But in other ways the trans-Saharan trade expanded along with that of the Atlantic.

In the days before Columbus, the Portuguese focused their attention on four areas of the West African coast — Senegambia, Upper Guinea, Gold Coast, and Benin — and these remained the principal points for West African contact with the Atlantic until 1650. The first Portuguese slave trade was the transportation of captives to Portugal as well as to the Atlantic islands — the Azores, Madeira and, later, the Cape Verde islands.[2] This trade, lasting from 1450 until it contracted sharply by 1550, brought West African slaves into the production process of wheat in Portugal and the islands. Slaves from the Upper Guinea coast were most numerous in Cape Verde; slaves from Senegambia were most numerous in Portugal.

Between the Senegal and Gambia rivers, Portuguese merchants purchased gold brought from the mining areas in Bambuk and Bure, and purchased slaves, mostly Wolof-speaking. The wealth brought by slave sales enriched local and provincial leaders, but undermined the monarchy of the Jolof kingdom, which by 1500 had broken up into smaller kingdoms, each seeking to benefit from the growing Atlantic trade. The Portuguese, unable to establish a firm base on the mainland, established a base in the Cape Verde islands. From there, merchants led voyages to the Upper Guinea coast in particular, to purchase captives who had been seized in the region's expanding slave trade. The Portuguese did establish a firm base on the Gold Coast, with the construction of Elmina castle in 1480–82, which served as a centre for gold trade for several centuries, drawing gold for export from the Akan hinterland and further afield. Portuguese mariners set up commercial ties with the kingdom of Benin, buying slaves and beads to sell for gold at Elmina, and buying pepper to send to Portugal.

In the years following 1500, enslavement of peoples in West Africa began to expand in several ways.[3] Portuguese merchants returned from

---

[2] On Portuguese slave trade to 1550, see Elbl, 'The Volume of the Early Atlantic Slave Trade'; Boubacar Barry, *Senegambia and the Atlantic Slave Trade,* trans. Ayi Kwei Armah (Cambridge: Cambridge University Press, 1998); John William Blake (ed.) *Europeans in West Africa 1450–1560,* vol. 1 (London: Hakluyt Society, 1942); and A. F. C. Ryder, *Benin and the Europeans, 1485–1897* (New York: Humanities Press, 1969).

[3] On expansion of the slave economy, see Jan S. Hogendorn and Marion Johnson, *The Shell Money of the Slave Trade* (Cambridge: Cambridge University Press, 1986); Manuel Lobo Cabrera, *La Esclavitúd en las Canarias Orientales en el Siglo XVI (Negros, Moros y Moriscos)* (Santa Cruz de Tenerifia: Cabildo Insular de Gran Canaria, 1982.); and J. P. Olivier de

the Indian Ocean with cowries, and sold them in West Africa; Spain built up a substantial system of enslaved labor in the sixteenth century on the Canary Islands, with slaves purchased from the Portuguese; and Morocco too expanded its production of sugar. At the desert edge, the rising empire of Songhai (more than its predecessor and neighbor Mali) relied on slavery and slave trade as a pillar of its economy. Ottoman demand for slaves may have also encouraged more trans-Saharan slave trade through Libya. The total of all these exports from West Africa reached about 6,500 persons per year in 1500.

Only after 1550 did West African captives travel in large numbers to the Americas. Small numbers of Africans participated in the early voyages of discovery and conquest, and an early effort at creating a sugar plantation on Hispaniola in the 1520s relied upon African slave labor. Spanish and Portuguese conquest of mainland territories in the Americas took decades, and the conquerors sought first to obtain laborers by enslaving local Amerindian populations. After 1550, however, it became clear that the Amerindian population was declining because of disease, and both the Spanish and Portuguese turned to African slave labor. The Spanish, ill-equipped to collect slaves directly, awarded a contract known as the *asiento* to merchants of other nations: Portuguese merchants dominated these *asiento* contracts from 1580 to 1660. Three main centers of slave population in the Americas grew up in the late sixteenth and early seventeenth centuries. The first two were Peru and Mexico, which acquired captives from West Africa. Slave populations were concentrated mainly in the urban centres of Lima in Peru, as well as Mexico City and Vera Cruz in Mexico. Urban slaves served especially as artisans and as domestics; rural slaves worked as field labourers, artisans, and as miners. As Bowser and Palmer have shown, these slaves came especially from Senegambia, Upper Guinea, and the Bight of Benin.[4] They were brought to the Americas via the Portuguese *asiento*.

For the third center of African population in the Americas, Brazil, the slaves came from Central Africa rather than West Africa. From 1480 Portuguese merchants had taken slaves from Kongo to the island of São Thomé, and made it the main center of sugar production in the sixteenth century. Thereafter, sugar production in Brazil began to grow,

Sardan, 'Captifs ruraux et esclaves impériaux du Songhay', in Claude Meillassoux (ed.) *L'Esclavage en Afrique précoloniale* (Paris: F. Maspero, 1975), pp. 99–134.

[4] On American slavery 1550–1650, see Frederick Bowser, *The African Slave in Colonial Peru, 1524–1650* (Stanford, CA: Stanford University Press, 1973); and Colin W. Palmer, *Slaves of the White God: Blacks in Mexico, 1570–1650* (Cambridge, MA: Harvard University Press, 1976).

and by 1600 had exceeded that of São Thomé. Slaves from Kongo and then from Angola went mainly to the plantation settlements of Brazil's northeast coast, especially in Bahia and Pernambuco. A few captives from West Africa went to Brazil.

We should not exaggerate the impact of slavery and slave trade in the era up to 1650. Some of the important changes of that time resulted not from slavery in particular but more generally from new connections in maritime and land-based trade. These included expansions in West African exports of gold, pepper and gum Arabic, as well as imports of such commodities as cowries, metals and textiles. There was also expanded trade between West African ports.

But slave trade did grow, and the initial lineaments of the West African system of slavery and slave trade were in place by 1650. The quantity of captives exported from West Africa almost tripled from 1450 to 1650, and most of the increase came from regions bordering the Atlantic. The expansion of enslavement generated improved techniques for seizing captives: armed raids, kidnapping and judicial enslavement. Individual regions underwent cycles of expansion and contraction in slave trade. In the peak export years, men came to be in short supply, and populations declined. Walter Rodney has argued, for the Upper Guinea region, that the first century of contact with the Portuguese resulted in an expansion of slavery where it had not previously been prevalent, and John Thornton has shown, for the same region, the social change brought about by the shortage of men. The developments up to 1650 in Senegambia, Upper Guinea, Songhai, Gold Coast and Benin served to foreshadow the elements of the larger system that was later to emerge.[5] The local and episodic impact of enslavement had yet to become broad and general, but the writing was on the wall.

Slaves from West Africa also became involved on a large scale in sugar cultivation beginning in about 1650, as the global economy entered a period of growth. Since 1500, many regions of the world had been put in contact by maritime transport. The initial connections, however, had brought more devastation than fortunes — cycles of war and disease, plus the difficulty of making new acquaintances, meant that the early days of the world economy were difficult. For West Africa, as for the world, global connections grew, but local societies did not prosper.

With time, however, commercial and political systems began to fit

---

[5] For slave trade from West Africa 1550–1650, see Walter Rodney, *A History of the Upper Guinea Coast 1545–1800* (Oxford: Clarendon Press, 1970); and Barry, *Senegambia and the Atlantic Slave Trade*.

more closely with global realities. From the 1570s, the silver mines of Mexico and Peru had begun to provide coins that circulated throughout the world. A growing system of global trade now encompassed Africa and its labor. For instance, Europeans used Mexican silver to purchase textiles in India and cowries in the Maldives. These commodities, after passing through Europe, went to West Africa in exchange for slaves; some of the slaves became mine workers in the Americas.

Hints of changing times that would draw West Africans into the sugar-and-slavery nexus came from new military and commercial ventures. The Dutch, seeking to develop their own commercial power and to break free from Spain, launched expeditions all over the world from 1580, and by 1650 had established themselves as the greatest commercial power in Europe. The Sa'dian dynasty in Morocco, seeking also to build up commercial and military strength in opposition to the Iberian powers, defeated Portugal in 1578 and destroyed Songhai in 1591. While sugar production declined in seventeenth-century Morocco, the import of slaves from the Niger and Senegal valleys expanded. These and other changes opened up the era in which slave trade dominated the Atlantic economy, when West Africa paid the price for that economic growth.

Sugar and slavery, 1650–1800

Senegambia, the Bight of Benin, and the Gold Coast were the first regions to feel the impact of expanding slave trade in the mid-seventeenth century. Dutch, English and French merchants came to West Africa as part of a trend towards world-wide commercial expansion. In the early seventeenth century these northern European adventurers each seized West Indian islands and North American territories (as well as ports in the Indian Ocean) and from mid-century they searched for West African slaves to work on the Caribbean sugar plantations. The Dutch East Indies Company (VOC), founded in 1602, focused its efforts on the Indian Ocean.[6] The West Indies Company (WIC), founded in 1621, took as its objective the conquest of Brazil from the Portuguese and the expansion of a slave colony supplied from Angola, although that venture had failed by 1650. Once expelled from Brazil, the Dutch retreated to islands they had seized in the Caribbean, especially Curaçao, and became merchants rather than planters. In 1663 the Dutch WIC, replacing Portuguese shippers, gained the *asiento* contract for

---

[6] On Dutch slave trade from 1650, see Johannes Menne Postma, *The Dutch in the Atlantic Slave Trade 1600–1815* (Cambridge: Cambridge University Press, 1990).

supplying slaves from West Africa to Mexico and Peru through the Caribbean. Dutch seizure of Elmina castle in 1637 gave them control over gold exports, and strengthened their base in West Africa.

In Senegambia, the expansion in volume of slave exports soon ran into problems.[7] The Dutch had established a fort on the island of Gorée from 1621, French merchants had established a base on the island of Saint-Louis in the mouth of the Senegal (where they built a fort in 1659), and Afro-Portuguese merchants from the Cape Verde islands had also purchased Senegambian slaves. The numbers of slave purchases increased, but opposition to slave trade arose, especially among Moors north of the Senegal River. In the war of the marabouts, which lasted from 1657 to 1679, Islamic leaders gained wide popular support in their attempt to halt the enslavement of Muslims and create a theocratic state. The effort failed after initial success, as French aid to the embattled Wolof kings enabled them to regain their thrones and continue slave exports. Yet Senegambia, while its slave exports expanded, was not able to satisfy the demand for slaves in the Caribbean. In part, this was because Senegambia and the upper Niger valley also sent slaves to Morocco during the seventeenth century. In Morocco, the large free and slave population of Africans was organized into the royal military force. Alawite sultan Mawlay Isma'il (son of the previous sultan and a concubine enslaved in West Africa), began his fifty-year reign in 1672 by impressing all black men into his army. This corps, known as the 'Abid, grew to a reported 150,000 by the 1720s and maintained the strength of the monarchy.

In the Bight of Benin, in contrast to Senegambia, Atlantic slave exports grew rapidly.[8] The kingdom of Ardra, composed of Gbe-speaking people in what is today the Benin Republic, was a polity that experienced the growing linkages of the global economy. In the late sixteenth century, Ardra opened ties with Portuguese merchants from São Thomé, who purchased slaves for work on the island and for

---

[7] For slavery and slaves from 1650 to 1800 in Senegambia, the Niger Valley, and Morocco, see Barry, *Senegambia;* Philip D. Curtin, *Economic Change in Precolonial Africa: Senegambia in the Era of the Slave Trade,* and supplement (Madison, WI: University of Wisconsin Press, 1975); James Searing, *West African Slavery and Atlantic Commerce: The Senegal River Valley, 1700–1860* (Cambridge: Cambridge University Press, 1993); Richard L. Roberts, *Warriors, Merchants and Slaves: The State and the Economy in the Middle Niger Valley, 1700–1914* (Stanford, CA: Stanford University Press, 1987); and Jamil M. Abun-Nasr, *A History of the Maghrib in the Islamic Period* (Cambridge: Cambridge University Press, 1987).

[8] On the Bight of Benin, 1650–1800, see Patrick Manning, *Slavery, Colonialism, and Economic Growth in Dahomey, 1640–1960* (Cambridge: Cambridge University Press, 1982); and Robin Law, *The Slave Coast of West Africa 1550-1750: The Impact of the Atlantic Slave Trade on an African Society* (Oxford: Clarendon Press, 1991).

dispatch to Brazil. By the mid-seventeenth century this region encountered, in addition, a trickle of Dutch, English, and French merchants, and a pair of Spanish priests who wrote a catechism in the Gbe language that came to be widely used in Spanish America. In this densely populated area, the kings and merchants of Ardra and the surrounding states were willing to sell slaves to Europeans. Dutch merchants set up lodges for the purchase of slaves in Savi, Ardra, and Grand Popo, and delivered them to the Caribbean – to the Spanish through the *asiento*, and to Dutch, English and French buyers on Caribbean islands. The English Royal African Company, founded in 1672, took up trade in slaves to supply the expanding English colonies of the Caribbean and North America. Both Dutch and English merchants imported substantial quantities of cowries as money for the purchase of slaves, and contributed to the expansion of the region's money supply.

Also imported to West Africa were firearms and gunpowder, and military forces in the region became reliant on musketry and cannon. Slave trade and gun trade reinforced one another as warfare and slave exports both grew in the Bight of Benin. Savi and Ardra positioned themselves against each other in the slave trade, and each set up rituals in which Europeans provided gifts to open trade and became allies of the states in regional wars.

Parallel processes developed at much the same time on the Gold Coast, though the number of slave exports was somewhat smaller.[9] The rise of the kingdom of Akwamu, which spread from the interior of the Volta valley to seize the coastal Ga kingdom in 1680 and then areas to its east, brought sales of slaves to the Danes at Accra and to the Dutch along the coast of modern Togo. Ga refugees fled eastwards along the coast to settle in Little Popo, and there the rise of military leaders such as Foli Bebe launched a series of wars among neighboring Gbe-speaking peoples that continued to the 1730s. From the 1690s, slave exports from the region reached 5,000–6,000 per year — a rate of loss sufficient to bring about population decline in the region — but the wars and the slave trade continued.

These events in the Bight of Benin and the Gold Coast at the end of the seventeenth century brought about the largest impact of slave trade on West Africa to that date. Warfare expanded, population declined

---

[9] On the Gold Coast, including its overlap with Bight of Benin, 1650-1800, see Ray A. Kea, *Settlements, Trade, and Polities in the Seventeenth-Century Gold Coast* (Baltimore, MD: Johns Hopkins University Press, 1982); and Kwame Yeboa Daaku, *Trade and Politics on the Gold Coast, 1600–1720* (Oxford: Clarendon Press, 1970).

across a substantial coastal belt, monarchy and elite families became heavily dependent on revenue from slave exports, government was transformed, residential patterns changed, and the holding as well as the selling of slaves expanded. The most clearly documented aspect of these changes was the sharp increase in the selling price of slaves to European merchants, which rose by a factor of from three to six from the 1690s to the 1720s. During this era of conflict and transition, the gold trade continued, but slave exports grew as prices rose. For a while, the Gold Coast imported gold (from the newly opened mines of Brazil) as well as exporting it. Prices for slaves were so high that slaves were sold for cash, much as the cowries which came to the Bight of Benin. Perhaps more socially significant, but more difficult to document, was the holding of numerous women in slavery throughout the region, and the expanding requirements for their labor, especially as men were in short supply. In a pattern that was to be repeated up and down the coast, the Bight of Benin, after decades of heavy involvement in slave trade, found itself with declining numbers of slaves to deliver, and prices that became so high as to be uncompetitive.

In response to these changes, two powerful states arose, conquering much of the region. The great expansions of Asante (1701–7) and of Dahomey (1724–7) were in large part a response to the crisis created by the expanded slave trade. But if the two states were similar in their expansion, they differed sharply in their subsequent histories. In 1701 the Asante confederation defeated Denkyera and soon gained control of most of the Akan-speaking area. Asante control of this region reduced slave raiding within its realm, but maintained the capture of slaves from its periphery. As a result, the population of the Gold Coast as a whole declined for much of the eighteenth century. To the east, the impact of the slave trade was to be more severe. The kingdom of Dahomey, which expanded as an efficient machine for warfare and enslavement, conquered Ardra in 1724 and Savi in 1727, and was poised for a regional dominance parallel to that of Asante. But repeated cavalry invasions from Oyo, combined with long-term resistance from Savi and Grand Popo, left the coastal Bight of Benin to experience perpetual warfare accompanied by enslavement and population decline into the 1780s. The Akwamu kingdom, located between Asante and Dahomey, was destroyed in 1730 by a coalition of its enemies and its rebellious subjects.

As the Atlantic slave trade from West Africa expanded in the early eighteenth century, the balance among European merchants changed.[10]

---

[10] For data on the English, French and Dutch slave trades, see David Eltis, Stephen Behrendt,

Merchants from Brazil arrived in the Gold Coast and the Bight of Benin, so that by the 1720s a substantial export of slaves from the Bight of Benin to Brazil had opened up, continuing to 1850. By the early eighteenth century, the English were able to establish primacy over the Dutch in many areas of commerce. The English colonies in the West Indies expanded their sugar output, and English merchants in India gained access to the cottons that were so important for the purchase of slaves. (Despite all their wars against each other, the Dutch and English also co-operated widely in Europe in organizing African voyages.) English success in acquiring slaves won for them the *asiento* in 1713, after which the English delivered slaves to the Spanish for the rest of the eighteenth century.

With the sharp increase in slave prices in the early eighteenth century, region after region expanded its slave exports: in chronological order, the Niger Valley, the Bight of Biafra, and Upper Guinea. In the Niger Valley, a band of marauding warriors under the leadership of Mamari Kulibali developed by 1712 into the leaders of the Bambara kingdom of Segu, and their captives went to Senegal as well as across the desert. The Wolof and Bambara slaves from Senegal became important in settling the new French colony of Louisiana.

The Bight of Biafra entered the export of slaves on a large scale in the early eighteenth century.[11] The system of collecting slaves that evolved there was sharply different from that of the Gold Coast or Bight of Benin; rather than large-scale war, it focused on individual kidnappings and seizure of individuals through court proceedings. The Ijo port of Bonny and the Efik port of Calabar became the main entrepôts. The Aro clan among the Ibo, relying on its dominance of the widely respected oracle at Arochukwu, built up a network for channeling captives of kidnappings and judicial procedures to the ports of Bonny and Calabar. By the mid-eighteenth century, the Bight of Biafra too was experiencing population decline. For Upper Guinea, slave exports remained at a low level in the early eighteenth century, expanding modestly as both Portuguese and French merchants collected cargoes. After 1750, exports rose to a peak of over 15,000 captives per year, and initiated a fifty-year period of regional population decline.[12]

Resistance to enslavement now became more general and easier to

David Richardson, and Herbert S. Klein (eds), *The Trans-Atlantic Slave Trade: A Database on CD-ROM* (Cambridge: Cambridge University Press, 1999).

[11] On the Bight of Biafra, 1650–1800, see David Northrup, *Trade without Rulers: Pre-Colonial Economic Development in South-Eastern Nigeria* (Oxford: Clarendon Press, 1978).

[12] On Upper Guinea, 1650–1800, see Rodney, *History of the Upper Guinea Coast.*

document. Some groups organized themselves to fight off attacks, as with the Mahi populations caught between Dahomey and Oyo. Others moved to hills or swamps to escape raids: the Dogon moved up the escarpments east of the middle Niger and the Dasha moved to the hills north of Dahomey, while the Weme and Holli escaped Dahomey by moving to swampy regions. Settlements of escaped slaves are documented for Senegambia, and captives on board ships crossing the Atlantic rebelled with regularity.

For West Africa in general, the number of captives sent across the Atlantic increased steadily, from about 4,000 per year in 1650 to about 50,000 per year in 1800. During this time the trade in slaves across the Sahara from West Africa remained roughly constant at about 8,000 per year.[13] The overall patterns were that population declined, in general, in West Africa from 1730, and the decline continued well into the nineteenth century. Enough women were lost for the remaining population to be unable to replace them or their children. In addition, the loss of many more men than women left West Africa with a substantial shortage of men. Of the women who remained, many were in slavery. The result was the development of a new social system in which women were held in slavery within families. This system reinforced multiple marriage, concubinage, and sent women to work in areas beyond those that had earlier been their occupations. The women who went overseas in slavery were overwhelmingly from the coastal regions of West Africa. In ethnicity and language, they were Wolof, Kisi, Mandingo, Akan, Gbe-speaking, and Ibo-speaking. The men, in contrast, came from these groups and from all other groups, such as Bambara, Gur-speaking, Hausa and Songhai.

In sum, slavery expanded to create a global system of forced labor.[14] The European trading powers grew in influence on the African coast and especially in their American colonies. The volume of Atlantic commerce grew, and that growth included the expansion in African exports and in the quantity of the money supply (in cowries and other commodities). But the loss of population and the social disruption of enslavement caused an economic shrinkage for West Africa. Slavery brought growth to the Atlantic economy as a whole, but not to West Africa.

---

[13] For regional volumes of slave exports, 1650-1800, see Patrick Manning, *Slavery and African Life: Occidental, Oriental, and African Slave Trades* (Cambridge: Cambridge University Press, 1990).

[14] On social change, 1650–1800, see Manning, *Slavery and African Life*; and David Geggus, 'Sex Ratio, Age and Ethnicity in the Atlantic Slave Trade: Data from French Shipping and Plantation Records', *Journal of African History* 30 (1989), pp. 23–44.

Yet when the slave trade is explored region by region within West Africa, a far more complex pattern comes to light. Some regions exported almost no slaves in the seventeenth century; for each region there was a period of rapid expansion in slave exports, usually followed by a decline in slave exports in a cycle of about 40 years, though in some cases exports continued at a high level. The effects on West African regions varied greatly: sometimes there were expansions of great states, sometimes there was social and political devastation; sometimes a large number of slaves was exported without apparent transformation of the region.

The Atlantic system of slavery, as it reached its peak in the late eighteenth century, began to reveal significant weaknesses. The anti-slavery movement began the moment enslavement began, in the minds of those enslaved, and was revealed in acts of rebellion in the barracoons, on board ship and on slave plantations. Among writers in Europe and the Americas, anti-slavery began during the eighteenth century. The movement rose to a crescendo at the end of the century with the abolition of slavery in several American territories, and with an active anti-slavery movement in Europe and North America. More than anything, however, the uprising of slaves in Haiti and their assertion of freedom and, eventually, independence, created an anti-slavery movement that led ultimately to the emancipation of almost all those held in slavery.

Slavery and anti-slavery, 1800–1900

In the course of the nineteenth century, slavery and slave trade in West Africa were at once challenged, reaffirmed, and transformed. By the end of the century, the capture and export of slaves had been greatly curtailed, but the number of West Africans living in slave status was larger than at the opening of the century. Along with its expansion, the system of enslavement was transformed from reliance on female slaves held within households to the development of systems of slave villages, with links to production for markets in Africa and overseas.

Throughout the world, the complexity of slavery in the nineteenth century matched that in West Africa.[15] For British, American and eventually French territories in the Americas, slave resistance and the anti-slavery movement brought a decline in slave imports from West Africa. But imports to Cuba expanded and those to Brazil continued.

---

[15] David Patrick Geggus, *Haitian Revolutionary Studies* (Bloomington, IN: Indiana University Press, 2002).

Trans-Saharan demand for slaves also expanded. Slave exports from Central Africa expanded in the early nineteenth century; from the 1820s, slave exports from Central Africa (and also from East Africa) exceeded those from West Africa, though the number of people enslaved within Central Africa never reached that of West Africa. The Haitian revolution of 1791–1804 launched the most memorable signal to threaten the system of slavery. In those tumultuous events, slaves overthrew the system of their oppression and joined with free people of color to defeat numerous invaders and establish an independent nation. Yet emancipation and abolition, though now announced as inevitable, were to be slow in reaching their completion throughout the world.

In West Africa, at the moment when the Haitian revolution was unfolding, another revolution exploded in the Central Sudan, linked in part to the issue of slavery. This revolution promised for a while to reduce enslavement but ended up expanding it.[16] The jihad pronounced by Usuman dan Fodio, which overthrew one after another of the Hausa kingdoms and replaced them with the expanding Sokoto Caliphate, began with a critique of the enslavement of Muslims by Muslim raiders. It ended up with the establishment of a powerful regime that enslaved few Muslims but many others. In the wars of the Caliphate, combatants on both sides were captured and sold, so that the number of Muslims among captives sent to the Americas rose sharply at the end of the eighteenth century.

Before the launching of these holy wars, the empire of Oyo to the south had embarked on an active program of slave raiding in the 1780s, and this brought the expansion in the number of Yoruba, Nupe, and Igala captives sent to the Americas. The wars of Oyo became connected with those of the Hausa and Fulani to the north, and further expanded the exports of captives from the region. Ultimately, Oyo collapsed in c. 1830, and in the abandonment of its capital and the dispersal of its factions, civil wars developed among the Yoruba peoples, resulting in still more exports of slaves. In sum, the era from 1780 to 1850 brought a great expansion of slavery throughout modern Nigeria, and expansion in exports of slaves of Yoruba, Hausa and other ethnicities of the region. The exception was Eastern Nigeria where, for the Ibo slaves sent out from Efik and Ijo ports, slave exports came virtually to an end in the 1830s.

The British and American governments declared the Atlantic slave trade to be illegal as of 1808, and the British gradually began enforcing

---

[16] For slavery and slave trade in the Sokoto Caliphate, the Oyo Empire and its successors, 1800–1900, see H. A. S. Johnston, *The Fulani Empire of Sokoto* (London: Oxford University Press, 1967); Robin Law, *The Oyo Empire, c. 1600–c.1836* (Oxford: Clarendon Press, 1977).

the abolition of the slave trade on other European powers and on African states and merchants. Anti-slave trade measures were effective almost immediately for British and American vessels, but did not become effective for vessels of other nations until about 1820. The British anti-slavery fleet was established and, especially at the conclusion of the Napoleonic wars, began to take effect in cutting back slave exports. As a result, a new sort of settlement developed on the West African coast, in which liberated slaves built communities under the protection of the navies of the great powers. Freetown in Sierra Leone was the earliest and most substantial such community, but others grew up on the island of Fernando Po, at Monrovia in Liberia, and at Libreville in Gabon; emancipated Brazilians settled along the Bight of Benin without external protection. British anti-slavery treaties with African states became effective in the Gold Coast in the 1820s, in the Bight of Biafra in the 1830s, and in other areas after 1850.

The era from the 1830s to the 1880s brought a complex mix of expansion and contraction in slavery. In the United States, slavery expanded, even without the import of many new captives, as cotton production replaced the earlier emphasis on tobacco. Similarly in Brazil, the expansion of coffee production in São Paulo led to the migration of a million slaves from sugar fields in Bahia to coffee plantations. While sugar production declined in Brazil, slave production of sugar expanded dramatically in Cuba, with the import of thousands of African slaves up to 1850. For the mainland territories that gained independence from Spain, slavery was abolished in stages — by 1828 in Mexico, but not until the 1850s in Venezuela or Peru. In the British territories, slavery was formally limited in 1832, but the slaves were forced to work in indenture until their liberation in 1838. Slavery expanded rapidly in Egypt under Muhammad Ali, but the parallel expansion of slavery in North Africa was halted after France, newly converted to anti-slavery in 1848, restricted the slave trade in Algeria and then in Tunisia. For both West Africa and Central Africa, the export of slaves to the Americas had virtually ended by 1850, and with that change almost all ties between Africa and the Americas were interrupted for a century.

Quantities of West African slave exports declined in the 1790s but remained steady from then to the 1830s, with about 30,000 captives sent across the Atlantic and with trans-Saharan exports rising to over 10,000 per year. Thereafter the Atlantic trade dropped almost to zero after 1850, while the Saharan trade continued at nearly 10,000 per year until late in the nineteenth century.[17] (Central African exports of

[17] For quantities of slave exports 1800-1900, see David Eltis, *Economic Growth and the Ending of*

captives across the Atlantic, meanwhile, reached a plateau at about 30,000 per year from 1800 to 1850.)

The global combination of abolitionism, industrialization, and expanding trade brought a wave of transformation in West African slavery. [18] Sugar was no longer produced by slave labor, and other crops entered the market in Africa as well as overseas. Coffee, cotton, palm oil and peanuts became major export crops, each relying on slave labor. New markets arose for African products, within and beyond the continent. From the 1830s, prices of slaves along the West African coast began to fall, as purchases by Europeans decreased. At mid-century, when the export of slaves across the Atlantic had almost ceased, prices of slaves had declined by roughly 50 per cent from their peak at the beginning of the century. This brought the purchase of slaves into the realm of possibility for a larger number of Africans, and slave ownership therefore increased. In particular, the male slave population of West Africa rose, as males ceased to be exported to the Americas.

As the nineteenth century continued, a thriving system of slavery and slave trade developed in the West African savanna, especially in the Sokoto Caliphate, but also in the middle Niger and in Borno. Now the system came to depend as much on local as on external demand. Slave labor was used for grain production, for textiles and for leather work. Control of slave women and children became the prerogative of wealthy men throughout the region. Thus a new social system developed, as substantial numbers of males were held in slavery. Slave families also changed. Now slave households developed, and they constructed lineages subordinate to those of the masters.

One measure of the expansion of slavery in West Africa was the wave of slave uprisings in the mid-nineteenth century. Best documented of these was the set of demonstrations of slaves near Calabar c. 1850, who protested against their liability to be executed at the funerals of their owners, and won this and other concessions on their status. Within the next couple of years, the recently captured Yoruba slaves of the King of Dahomey rose in rebellion on the palm-oil plantations of the Abomey plateau. They were put down firmly, but the masters were careful thereafter about collecting such large numbers of slaves in one place.

the Transatlantic Slave Trade (New York: Oxford University Press, 1987); and Manning, *Slavery and African Life.*

[18] For social change 1800–1900, see Manning, *Slavery and African Life;* Paul E. Lovejoy, *Transformations in Slavery: A History of Slavery in Africa* (Cambridge: Cambridge University Press, 1983); A. J. H. Latham, *Old Calabar, 1600–1891: The Impact of the International Economy upon a Traditional Society* (Oxford: Clarendon Press, 1973).

As the nineteenth century progressed, the European powers became steadily more aggressive. At mid-century, they controlled small segments of the African coastline, in a modest expansion of the enclaves they had dominated for centuries. Then after 1880 the French, Germans and British claimed larger territories, and by 1900 had sent armies to ensure the submission of almost all of West Africa to the expanded European empires. This sudden expansion of European empire in West Africa brought dramatic changes for the institution of slavery, but it did not bring immediate emancipation for most of those held in subjugation.

The campaign against African slavery, from the 1880s, provided the ideological prop for the European advance. France, which had itself not abolished slavery until 1848, justified its advance up the Senegal River during the 1860s and 1870s as being, in part, to abolish slavery. Yet as the wars with Al-Hajj 'Umar and later with Samori Touré became problematic, the French regimes turned to holding captured slaves in bondage rather than liberating them. As late as 1905, the French regime held thousands of men, women, and children in captivity along the middle Niger and required them to grow grain for the French army and administration.

Aftermath: slavery under colonial rule

European regimes in West Africa gave high priority to halting the slave trade, but low priority to emancipating the slaves. The French conquerors of Senegambia and Dahomey announced that slavery was abolished, but made no systematic effort to enforce the announcements. In these and other areas, the arrival of European-led armies enabled slaves to escape and attempt to make their way home. The new administrations gained a monopoly of armed force, and thus rapidly ended most new acts of enslavement. The colonial regimes stopped short, however, of formally declaring the emancipation of all slaves, and made almost no attempt to free the slaves or to guide them to their homes or to places of safety.

As a detailed report from colonial Dahomey made clear, it was far more difficult for enslaved women to take their freedom than for men. Many of the women had children by their masters or other free men, and the children belonged by law to the men — a law that the colonial regimes declined to alter. Women could take their freedom only by abandoning their children, and commonly refused to do so. Instead, these women and the men who chose to remain with their masters sought to renegotiate terms. In some cases they were able to gain control of land; in other cases they became subordinate lineages within the master's lineage.

In addition, the colonial regimes turned to justifying slavery in West Africa. In a striking change of attitude, the imperial agents of the European powers changed their approach to slavery once they had gained power. Even E. D. Morel, later known for his courageous criticism of King Leopold's violent regime in Congo, underwent a sudden change from his 1895 condemnation of slavery in the Sokoto Caliphate to his 1900 justification of slavery as a natural and benign institution in African society.

Slavery did indeed undergo major reform with the colonial conquest.[19] The establishment of European rule meant that it was virtually impossible to conduct raids to enslave new captives. For those already enslaved, however, their captivity was recognized as legal, and they could still be bought and sold. Slave owners, unable to obtain large numbers of new captives, turned to better treatment of adult male slaves and especially of women and children. Thus 'slavery without slave trade', whether in the Americas or Africa, urged owners to treat their slaves more generously, as they could no longer be replaced with a cheap captive. African slavery in the post-slave-raiding days of the twentieth century therefore became comparable to that in the Americas after the abolition of the slave trade: that is, it was similar to 'antebellum' US slavery from 1808 to 1865, to slavery in British territories from 1808 to 1838, to French territories from the 1820s to 1848, and to Cuba and Brazil from 1850 to the 1880s.

For each West African territory, the laws leading to the end of slavery differed. In several territories, laws approved in the first decade of the twentieth century specified that all children born after a certain date would be free — or would be free once they reached their majority. Sierra Leone — with its capital in Freetown, the haven of freed slaves — nonetheless did not adopt an ordinance ending slavery throughout the colony until 1928. In Northern Nigeria, the slave population remained at the level of perhaps 3 million persons even in the mid-1920s. There were no holidays or emancipation proclamations to

---

[19] For slavery in colonial Africa, see Paul E. Lovejoy and Jan S. Hogendorn, *Slow Death for Slavery: The Course of Abolition in Northern Nigeria, 1897–1936* (Cambridge: Cambridge University Press, 1993); Suzanne Miers and Richard Roberts (eds), *The End of Slavery in Africa* (Madison, WI: University of Wisconsin Press, 1988); Martin A. Klein, *Slavery and Colonial Rule in French West Africa* (Cambridge: Cambridge University Press, 1998); Claire C. Robertson and Martin A. Klein (eds), *Women and Slavery in Africa* (Madison, WI: University of Wisconsin Press, 1983).

celebrate the return of slaves to citizenship, only a slow and individual accumulation of the rights and privileges of ordinary life.

It was under these circumstances of life in the early colonial period, the era from 1900 to 1930, that European ethnologists and colonial officials wrote up their descriptions of West African society and slavery. This was at a time when the violence of precolonial slave raids had been halted by the might of colonial armies, and when slaves, though not yet freed, nonetheless had begun to make demands for fair treatment. Linking their current observations to a belief that African societies were static and unchanging, these authors wrote that slaves were treated benignly as subordinate members of the master's family, and that they had almost enough advantages in their situation to balance the disadvantages of enslavement. These descriptions, usually written in the form of a social balance sheet, provided the data from which later analysts of African slavery developed their interpretations.

Slavery has left a complex residue in West Africa today. A historical approach to slavery in West Africa — recognizing its early origins but tracing its expansion and transformation through the impact of external demand for servile labor — helps explain the complexity. Following the impact of market demand, another sort of external force, the power of imperial armies and administration, halted the expansion of slavery and initiated its decline. Yet the colonial regimes were more devoted to social hierarchy than to social equality, and prevented the full elimination of slavery. With independence, the new republics of West Africa inherited the inequalities of slavery along with the inequalities of colonialism.

Recommended Reading

Barry, Boubacar (1998) *Senegambia and the Atlantic Slave Trade*, trans. Ayi Kwei Armah (Cambridge: Cambridge University Press).

Eltis, David (1987) *Economic Growth and the Ending of the Transatlantic Slave Trade* (New York: Oxford University Press).

Law, Robin (1991) *The Slave Coast of West Africa 1550–1750: The Impact of the Atlantic Slave Trade on an African Society* (Oxford: Clarendon Press).

Lovejoy, Paul E. (2000) *Transformations in Slavery: A History of Slavery in Africa*, 2nd edn (Cambridge: Cambridge University Press).

Lovejoy, Paul E. and Jan S. Hogendorn (1993) *Slow Death for Slavery: The Course of Abolition in Northern Nigeria, 1897–1936* (Cambridge: Cambridge University Press).

Manning, Patrick (1990) *Slavery and African Life: Occidental, Oriental, and African Slave Trades* (Cambridge: Cambridge University Press, 1990).

Meillassoux, Claude (1991) *The Anthropology of Slavery: The Womb of Iron and Gold,* trans. Alide Dasnois (Chicago: University of Chicago Press).

Miers, Suzanne and Richard Roberts (eds) (1988) *The End of Slavery in Africa* (Madison, WI: University of Wisconsin Press).

6

Class, Caste & Social Inequality in West African History

ISMAIL RASHID

Over the last millennium, a number of factors, namely, kinship, migration, settlement, economics, war and colonial conquest, have intersected to produce a wide variety of social and political arrangements in West Africa. These arrangements varied from so-called acephalous (stateless) societies, to the sprawling sahelian empires, and in contemporary times, 'modern' nation-states. The different political arrangements usually reflect specific power, as well as social and cultural relations between different groups of peoples. This chapter is mainly concerned with different forms of inequalities of power, social hierarchy and exploitation expressed by those social and cultural relations. Its major focus will be on different forms of 'unfree labor' and 'bonded labor', namely, caste, enslaved and pawned peoples. It looks at how these forms are defined, produced and transformed, as well as the relationships that occurred between them.

This chapter primarily utilizes a conceptual framework that encompasses kinship, class and caste. Kinship offers a cultural framework for the construction of identity and citizenship, and for determining social exclusion. Class offers the opportunity to capture the status of people, especially unfree and bonded individuals, in the process of acquisition and distribution of economic resources and political power in different societies. In West Africa, class becomes increasingly significant with the expansion of mercantilist systems during the last five hundred years. Finally, caste provides insight into situations in which culture and political economy combine to produce unique forms of social bondage among certain West African groups. Historical examples are drawn very broadly from all over West Africa;

Ismail Rashid

however, there is greater emphasis on those societies in the upper Niger, Senegambian and Guinea coastal regions.

Kinsmen, minors and outsiders

Despite the tendency of anthropology to treat 'kinship' ahistorically, it nevertheless remains a valuable starting point for the discussion of culture, politics and social stratification in West African societies. Kinship exists in all human societies, though its use in political, economic and social affairs has waned in many parts of the world. In West Africa, kinship expressed a set of affective blood, matrimonial or fictive relations within a family, household, lineage or even an ethnic group. It was usually the prime determinant of a person's social identity. The kinship idiom provided the fundamental basis of social solidarity and collective action, patterns of family inheritance and succession, definitions of corporate citizenship or outsider status as well as the political unit of competition for power. In many West African societies, however, the initiation into, and membership of, 'secret' societies based on age-sets, religious beliefs, gender, profession, and even wealth, gave individuals broader social identities and created communal solidarity beyond the kinship group.

The precise relationships between members of a kinship group are shaped primarily by genealogical claims, descent patterns, age and gender. Together, these factors determined a person's standing, rights and access to resources within a kinship group or larger society. Over time, some West African groups like the Mande, Fulbe and Yoruba adopted patrilineage, giving precedence to male inheritance and acquisition of rights and resources through males. Others, such as the Asante, Wollof and Tuareg, adopted matrilineage, stressing inheritance through females. In general, many African groups ascribed wisdom, respect and authority to older members of societies. Through descent patterns and age, 'senior' members of kinship groups acquired certain decision-making powers, including control of group resources, organization of work, ritual and religious processes, and marriage arrangements. Among the Yoruba and Igbo, 'seniority' was attainable not only through ancestry and age, but also through worldly success.[1] Even though women usually became 'senior members' of lineages, the system generally tended to be patriarchal, with older men exercising

[1] See Ife Amadiume, *Male Daughters, Female Husbands* (London: Zed Press, 1994); Oyèrónké Oyewùmí, *The Invention of Women: Making an African Sense of Western Gender Discourses.* (Minneapolis, MN: University of Minnesota Press, 1997).

power over women, young men and children, who were regarded as 'junior' members. This domestic inequality of power and status produced a constant source of tension within kinship groups between 'senior' and 'junior' members of the lineage; it also formed the basis of patriarchical and gerontocratic forms of power that became common in different precolonial societies in the region, even in the so-called acephalous groups.[2]

Kinship groups and relationships were dynamic and constructed by different societies to suit different historical circumstances. The social and political standing of a kinship group was shaped by several factors. Groups which first established a settlement acquired rights over the distribution of land, rituals, and titles of 'landlords', thereby relegating subsequent immigrants to the subordinate position of 'strangers' and tenants. Kinship groups with more members, more access to markets, and more wealth were sometimes able to successfully defend or extend their claims to political, social or religious precedence. These groups became the 'recognized' or 'ruling' lineages, while smaller and poorer ones became subordinate. Within similar ethnic groups, and across the region, kinship dynamics gave rise to vastly different forms of political leadership and socio-political organization.

The concept which perhaps adequately captures the unequal relationships within, and between, different kinship groups in kinship-based political systems, is 'rank and status' rather than class. The system of rank, underlined by specific titles and privileges, highlighted a person's or lineage's social standing and political role in society in relationship to others. Acquiring certain status in this system enabled individuals and lineages to gain social recognition and political authority by ascription or achievement. Different forms of political authority also enabled certain persons or lineages to access economic and social resources by virtue of their political standing. While status could be transferred to subsequent generations, opportunities also existed for others who distinguished themselves in the acquisition of wealth, war and service to the societies, to move up in the ranking system.

Subsistence strategy or occupational choice has played an important role in kinship dynamics, power relations, identities and the kinds of societies that have evolved in West Africa. West African groups have engaged in hunting, fishing, farming, animal husbandry and mineral extraction, but over the last one thousand years, some groups have

---

[2] Claude Meillassoux, *The Anthropology of Slavery: The Womb of Iron and Gold* (London: Athlone Press; Chicago: University of Chicago Press, 1991), pp. 23–35.

become more closely associated with specific occupations. Bozo, Fante, Ewe and Ijo peoples, for example, have been closely linked with fishing or maritime occupations while Fulbe and Tuareg have been regarded as predominantly pastoralists. Fishing societies have been generally small and loosely structured. Pastoral societies have been mostly non-centralized and more egalitarian, because of their mobility and minimal control over land. The main subsistence strategy of the majority of West African groups in the savanna and forest regions since the second millenium BC has been farming. Farming entailed spatial control, mobilization of labor, and the understanding of climatic conditions. Farming communities tended to have more clearly defined communal leadership, laws and rituals, and hierarchy.

Craftsmen, trade and urbanization

The adoption of farming by West African groups may have provided the catalyst for the emergence of new secondary skills, crafts and technology. Potters and woodcarvers have produced utilitarian and ritual objects in different West African societies for thousands of years. From around 1000 BC, smiths, who transformed iron ore into weapons, farming implements, ritual objects and other useful items, became part of the region's occupational landscape. In Nok, in present-day northern Nigeria, and Jenne-jeno, in Mali, iron-smithing assumed 'industrial'proportions around 500 BC to 200 BC. Gold miners and smiths also emerged in gold-rich regions like Bambuk and Boure along the middle Senegal River and upper Niger River, and later in the Asante region of present-day Ghana.

The mastery of iron-smithing became a new source of social power as well as anxiety. Among the Mande and Wollof, ironsmiths were associated with the mastery of supernatural knowledge, and linked with specific deities. In pre-Islamic Wollof and Mande religious systems, smiths acted as diviners and priests. Linguists, oral traditionalists, musicians and singers, who also emerged to provide political or social services for different societies, were also seen as having certain supernatural skills. From the earliest periods, and even up to contemporary times, many of these artisans also worked as farmers, cattle-herders or fishermen. In Mande, Wollof and Soninke societies, however, these practitioners emerged as distinct 'professional' groups defined by their products and services. Over time, the distinct identities and the perceived supernatural powers of professional groups were reinforced through endogamous marriage, ritualism and membership in certain secret societies like the *Komo* and *Poro* among the Mande.

The manufactured goods, and specialized skills of artisanal groups, as well as the surplus products of their primary occupational groups, contributed to the development of trade among different groups and areas in West Africa. Trade engendered the rise of new social groups as well as political competition and conflict. Merchants, a social group which derived their livelihood and status primarily from being the key brokers in the process of commercial exchange, facilitated trade. Over time, the Diakhanke (Dyula) and Hausa fashioned a reputation for long-distance trading in West Africa. Along with Berber and Arab traders, Diakhanke and Hausa merchants moved salt, gold, spices, religious texts and people between different population centers within and outside the region. Different cultural ideas, as well as new religious movements like Islam, moved through the different trade networks. By the eighth century, an intricate web of commercial routes linking western and northern African communities, known as the trans-Saharan trade, had emerged.

The expansion of trade networks increased urbanization in West Africa and made it possible for certain groups to concentrate wealth and power. Kumbi Saleh, Timbuktu, Gao, Jenne and Walata grew into larger cities and became major commercial, cultural and religious hubs in the trans-Saharan trade network. These hubs became magnets for empire builders and political adventurers over the centuries. From the Soninke of Ghana in the fifth century to the Mande of Mali in the fourteenth century, and from the Kanuri of Kanem-Bornu in the eleventh century to the people of Songhai in the sixteenth century, the dominant ruling lineages of successive West African groups endeavoured to capture and maintain control over different regional trading centers. The competition to control the trading centres and networks resulted in the development of larger and more sophisticated armies. The capture and control of the centers and networks gave successful lineages wealth and power over other lineages and social groups in their societies, as well as those of newly conquered ones. It is not surprising therefore that some of the earliest evidence of deep social stratification and disempowerment, especially those of caste and enslavement, are found in these urban spaces and empires.

Caste people and aristocrats

The emergence of 'caste people', as a distinct subordinate social group in between 'free' noble groups — namely rulers, farmers and pastoralists

— and enslaved people in West Africa, has been associated with the trans-Saharan trade and urbanization. Caste typically delineated the status of a person, family or group, their designated occupations, their assigned political and religious positions and roles, marriage options and choices, socio-religious status and taboos, as well as their social rights and privileges. It implied that persons or groups lacked the ability, whether inscribed or practical, to transcend or change their social designation at birth. However, the term 'caste' should be applied guardedly to the discussion of social hierarchy in West Africa. It bears little resemblance to the Hindi caste system with its rigid *varna*. Tal Tamari provides a short, specific, but useful working definition of caste in West Africa. She defines caste as 'endogamous ranked specialist group(s)' of blacksmiths, potters, leatherworkers and bards, found mainly among Wollof, Manding (Mande) and Fulfude (Fulbe)-speaking peoples in West Africa.[3]

The origins of caste peoples in West Africa are difficult to trace but some plausible theories have been suggested. Roderick McIntosh locates the origins of caste groups far back in time, to at least the first millennium BCE, and attributes their emergence to three interrelated processes, namely, (i) the early development of Mande cosmological notions of *Nyama*, the natural force that animated and regularly revitalized the world; (ii) the development of iron technology and artisanal groups; and (iii) the subsequent rise of urbanization.[4] The combination of these processes, he maintains, led to the exclusivity, endogamy and cultural traits that are characteristic of caste groups, especially among the Mande.

Tamari, however, contends that development of caste is fairly recent, appearing by 1300 among the Malinke and no earlier than 1500 among Wollof, Soninke, Songhai and Fulbe peoples. She offers three arguments in support of her position. The first argument is that collective terminologies for caste people exist in only four West African languages, namely Manding (*nyamakalaw*), Soninke (*ñaxanala*), Wollof (*ñeeño*) and

---

[3] According to Tamari, 'caste' people have been found among some fifteen West African groups, including the Manding (Bamana, Malinke, Dyula and Khasonke), Soninke, Wollof, Tukulor, Dogon, Senufo, Songhai, Fulbe, Tuareg, Moorish, Dan, Minianka, Serer, and the Soso in eastern Ghana. See Tal Tamari, 'The Development of Caste Systems in West Africa', *Journal of African History* 32(2) (1991), p. 223.

[4] Roderick McIntosh, *The Peoples of the Middle Niger: The Island of Gold* (Malden, MA: Blackwell Publishers, 1998). For further discussion of the notion of *Nyama*, see Patrick R. MacNaughton, *The Mande Black Smiths: Knowledge, Power and Art in West Africa* (Bloomington, IN: Indiana University Press, 1988); Tal Tamari 'Linguistic Evidence for the History of Western African "castes" ', in David C. Conrad and Barbara E. Frank (eds), *Status and Identity in West Africa: Nyamakalaw of Mande.* (Bloomington, IN: Indiana University Press, 1995), pp. 61–85.

Fulbe *(Nyeenyo)*. She concludes that the sources of these words, and therefore of caste formation, were Manding and Wollof. The second is that Arab travelers to Ghana in the eleventh and twelfth centuries did not notice castes, but those who traveled to Old Mali from the thirteenth century onwards, the most famous of whom was Ibn Battuta, did mention them. The third argument states that European and Arabic sources frequently referred to the terms *jeliw* (Manding), *gesere* (Songhai), *gewel* (Wollof), and *maabo* (Fulbe), denoting bards among different groups after the fifteenth century.[5] Tamari posits that the caste system among the Mande may have taken concrete shape after the epic struggle between the founder of the Malian Empire, Sundiata, and the Soso King, Sumanguru, in 1235. The battle sealed the fate of the Soso Empire and ushered in the rise of the Malian Empire. Tamari suggests that though Sumanguru was not a blacksmith-king, such as those found in the Central African kingdoms, he had powerful associations with the deities and occult forces associated with them. She maintains that after Sumanguru's defeat, Sundiata and his successors incorporated, but also subordinated, smiths and bards within the new imperial edifice so that they could no longer pose a threat to Mande power.

Tamari's ideas of 'caste' and the historical reconstruction of the subordination of caste people have been criticized by some scholars. In *Status and Identity in West Africa: Nyamakalaw of Mande* (1995), an anthology edited by David C. Conrad and Barbara E. Frank, different scholars challenge the concept of caste and class by critically exploring notions of status, identity and power in Mande society. They argue broadly that notions of power and hierarchy among the Mande should be regarded suspiciously, since French colonialists produced the distorting notions of 'caste' and 'class' in the nineteenth and twentieth centuries to fit their imperial ambitions. Many of the contributors to the anthology look particularly at the linguistic constructions of the different terms describing 'caste people' *(nyamakalaw)* as well as perspectives and agency of caste people vis-à-vis the free and noble classes *(horonw)*. They contend generally that term *'nyamakalaw'* lacks linguistic precision, and that its usage was regionally and contextually determined. They also point out that the study of the different names of the component professions within 'caste' groups reveals a diversity of origins, fluidity of usage and considerable change in meaning over time. The scholars also show that there was much transmission of

---

[5] See Tamari 'The Development of Caste Systems in West Africa', pp. 221–50; Conrad and Frank, *Status and Identity in West Africa*, pp. 1–23.

different caste professions, and that cultural exchange between the different ethnic groups occurred consistently. In sum, they challenge the
orthodox, rigid tripartite division of Mande society and Mande
aristocratic and colonial notions of *nyamakalaw* social 'inferiority' and
'powerlessness'. Instead, they reinterpret the Mande caste system as a
much more 'flexible, ever-changing structure that enables rather than
prevents individual agency'.[6] This reinterpretation gives recognition to
the interdependence of different social groups and the agency of
'powerful individuals' in the construction of their own identity.

The difference between the ideas of caste origins and dynamics put
forward by McIntosh, Tamari and the contributors to Conrad and
Frank's anthology is due to differences in disciplinary approaches,
evidentiary bases and scholarly foci. Instead of interpreting
archaeological remains like McIntosh, Tamari relies on the evidence of
language, written documents and oral tradition. McIntosh looks more
at urban centers while Tamari is decidedly 'Malicentric'. The
contributors to the Conrad and Frank anthology adopted a broader
regional scope but, like Tamari, relied on essentially similar linguistic,
anthropological and documentary evidence. The strength of the
anthology lies mainly in highlighting the agency of the people normally
designated as 'caste people'. However, the anthology's attempt to
repudiate the historical disempowerment of 'caste' people vis-à-vis other
social groups remains unconvincing.

From the different scholarly suggestions it is indeed difficult to agree
on the precise nature and moment of 'caste' development. Yet, taken
together, the various views do reveal insights into a number of key
processes that should be considered in order to understand the
emergence of this phenomenon. The first process was that of labour
specialization, which produced different kinds of artisan and artistic
professions around the manufacture of leather, wood, iron and words.
The second involved the development of religious and cultural ideas
associated with different types of occupations in ancient West African
societies. The third is related to political and linguistic processes, which
led to the ranking of professions and groups according to their social
and political importance. The fourth is the adoption, transference, or
diffusion of caste culture between different groups in the region. The
fifth process pertains to the self-perception of caste people, and how

---

[6] Conrad and Frank, *Status and Identity*, p. 5. James Searing also makes a similar argument
about the dynamism and transformation of social structures in Wollof societies. See James
Searing, 'Aristocrats, Slaves, and Peasants: Power and Dependency in the Wollof States,
1700–1850', *International Journal of African Historical Studies*, 21 (1988), pp. 475–503.

they have historically negotiated their identities, roles and places in different societies over time.

Despite their differences, scholars generally regard the Malian Empire and the Mande people as crucial to understanding the dispersal of caste people in West Africa. The consolidation, expansion, and decline of the Malian Empire led to the spread of caste people among other groups. The Mande — the chief people to make up the Malian Empire — had captured and expanded the trade networks that had been developed earlier by the Soninke of Old Ghana. These networks generated tremendous wealth and power for the Mande elite. They also became conduits through which traders, clerics, soldiers and caste people transmitted Mande religious beliefs (Islamic and non-Islamic), cultural ideas and political institutions to other West African groups. The Soninke became 'Mandiganized', leading to the appearance of new ethnic identities like Marka of mid-Niger, Jakhanke (Diakhanke) in the west, and Dyula in the south. The collapse of the Malian Empire by the sixteenth century led to the further dispersal of Mande peoples. By the late eighteenth and nineteenth centuries, caste people, especially leatherworkers, were present in Upper Niger, Bamana (Kaarta), Segu, Guinea, Sierra Leone and northern Gold Coast.[7] The demographic size of caste people among these different groups varied greatly, ranging from about 5 per cent to 20 per cent of the population. As caste people moved into other societies, their social and political status was modified. Societies like the Temne of Sierra Leone lacked the social rigidity of the Mande groups, and caste people like leatherworkers (*garankew*) became free commoners. In other societies, caste people abandoned or changed their professions and took on new group identities.[8]

Historically, caste people elicited ambivalent attitudes and responses from the 'noble' (free) classes. Caste people were crucial in the production and reproduction of material, political, social and ritual life in the different societies. Blacksmiths produced weapons, tools and ritual wooden objects, and their wives worked as potters. Leatherworkers transformed animal hides into dress, war objects and regalia, pouches, and protective cases for ritual objects. Bards acted as genealogists, linguists, oral traditionalists, poets and musicians. Smiths and bards also acted as political counselors, spiritual guides, mediators

---

[7] Richard L. Roberts, *Warriors, Merchants and Slaves: The State and the Economy in the Middle Niger Valley, 1700-1914* (Stanford, CA: Stanford University Press, 1987), pp. 26-7; Sundiata A. Djata, *Bamana Empire by the Niger: Kingdom, Jihad and Colonization, 1712–1920* (Princeton, NJ: Markus Weiner, 1997), pp. 2-3.

[8] Barbara E. Frank, 'Soninke *garankéw* and Bamana-Malinke *jeliw*: Mande leatherworkers, identity, and the Diaspora', in Conrad and Frank, *Status and Identity*, pp. 133-50.

and negotiators. They were usually admired, but at the same time were feared for their skills and perceived mastery of occult forces. The consequence was that they could command substantial payment and gratitude for their skills from the 'noble' classes, even though these same noble classes made great efforts to underline their political subordination and social alienation. While there were exceptions, caste people could not generally participate in farming, herding or trading, which were regarded as the 'noble' professions. Perceived as 'outsiders' and belonging to non-autochthonous lineages, they were forbidden from participating in politics as well as from holding political and religious offices. They were also forbidden from marrying outside their endogamous groups, under penalty of losing their status in the society. No other caste group had its subordination and social exclusion underlined more severely than bards, who were buried in the trunks of baobab trees rather than in the earth for fear of pollution.

The relationship between caste and enslaved people was equally complex. The presence of enslaved people enabled caste people to occupy the ambiguous middle position between enslaved and free. Though caste people generally had higher status than enslaved people, certain caste groups were perceived as possessing lower status than slaves. In several ways, caste people shared some of the enslaved population's disabilities. Though the labor of caste people was 'free', like enslaved people they were generally not considered full members of the society. Both groups had specific cultural and religious sanctions underlining their social inferiority and restricting their mobility. Although there were exceptions, enslaved and caste peoples were generally excluded from holding key political and religious offices or participating in certain religious rituals.

Enslaved people and merchant economies

The most extreme and complex form of social disempowerment to have emerged in Africa was enslavement. The origins, meaning, character, and impact of enslavement in Africa have generated many scholarly debates. The debates have revealed that definitions, processes, institutions and cultures surrounding enslavement varied vastly from region to region, and over time. Nonetheless, enslavement has been seen variously as having several common characteristics, in which a person was subjugated labor, commodified property, unfree and kinless (or lacking corporate citizenship).

One method by which historians have sought to capture the

complexity of enslavement in Africa is to divide enslavement into three systems, namely 'domestic' or 'indigenous', 'Oriental' and 'Occidental' or 'Atlantic'. Domestic enslavement referred to people who were enslaved within Africa. This system had ancient origins, and there are historians who have argued that it was the oldest form of slavery in Africa. Its impact and importance were, however, widely felt in the nineteenth and early twentieth centuries after the abolition of Occidental enslavement. Oriental enslavement, which drew captives mainly through the trans-Saharan and Indian Ocean networks to Asia, was usually associated with Arab traders who made their way into the continent with the expansion of Islam after the seventh century CE. Occidental slavery was linked to the expansion of Europe, the rise of capitalism and European colonization of the Americas. It began around 1444 and lasted for a little over 400 years. Of the three systems, it led to the enslavement of the greatest number of Africans and had the greatest consequences on the continent. While the different systems of enslavement have certain distinctive characteristics, they overlapped and reinforced one another over time, especially between the fifteenth and nineteenth centuries.

The European intrusion into West Africa began with the last great cycle of trans-Saharan imperial and economic expansion. Europeans first appeared in the region in the mid-fifteenth century during the dying throes of the Malian Empire. They became a fixture in the region by the time the Songhai people had arisen and imposed their will on the remnants of the Malian Empire. The Atlantic trading network Europeans established gradually took over, and eventually subordinated the different pre-existing trading networks in the region. The eventual triumph of the European-centred Atlantic trading network had arguably more far-reaching consequences for social stratification than the trans-Saharan network. It expanded or created new processes of economic production and exchange as well as new political and social institutions under the hegemony of different European powers. In its most aggressive stage, colonialism, the European presence produced new forms of power, subjugation, culture and citizenship.

For over three centuries, Africans became the dominant 'commodity' in the Atlantic trade network and economy, especially after the Europeans 'discovered' the Americas. By the nineteenth century, almost every West African society had to deal with enslavement, either as producer, trader or holder of enslaved people. About 10 million West Africans ended up in the Americas as enslaved people, and about three times that number probably died in the enslavement process. The majority of people transported into slavery were young men; women were usually retained within Africa as slaves, and slave traders rejected the old and the very young. This had tremendous implications for the construction of social identity, the structure of society and politics, and relationships between different peoples. For groups which held enslaved people, the challenge still remained the same: how to identify, use and integrate enslaved people within the dominant societies. The result was a range of strategies, depending on the size of the group and their internal social structure, culture, economic strategies and needs, geographical location, relationship with others groups, and the extent of their contact with Europeans and participation in the Atlantic trading system.

The social and political picture of the region remained complex and dynamic over the long period of Occidental trade and enslavement. No state or society remained static. Nonetheless, it is generally agreed that enslavement produced new forms of political power and reinforced social inequality. In the savanna and Senegambian sub-regions, the old 'medieval' political formations like the Songhai Empire and Wollof confederacy gave way to a series of militaristic regimes like the Wollof and Serer states of Waalo, Kajoor, Baol, Siin and Saloum, and the Soninke kingdoms of Gajaaja and Kaabu by the end of the sixteenth century. These states competed for regional hegemony as well as for the enslavement and sale of people in the region. The Fulbe, inspired by Islam and opposed to the violence of these *ceddo* states (states dependent on slave soldiers), also constructed a number of theocratic states stretching from Futa Toro and Bundu in the Senegambian area to Futa Jallon in the Upper Guinea coast in the seventeenth and eighteenth centuries. The new Fulbe theocracies, however, became part of the system of enslavement and violence that they had opposed.[9] Even though the violent processes of political centralization produced some of the captives for the Atlantic trade, many of the victims came from the systematic raiding of smaller and less centralized organized groups like the Bwa, Manianka, Bainuk, Joola, Landuma and Baga. Some like the Joola initially resisted participation in the enslavement system but eventually become slaveholders and traders themselves.[10]

The *ceddo* regimes had their counterparts in the Sudanic belt, the savanna and the eastern coastal areas of the region. In the middle Niger valley, the Bambara state of Segu became a militaristic entity, which

---

[9] Boubacar Barry, *Senegambia and the Atlantic Slave Trade* (Cambridge: Cambridge University Press, 1998), pp. 94–125.

[10] Martin Klein, *Slavery and Colonial Rule in French West Africa* (Cambridge: Cambridge University Press, 1998), p. 41.

produced enslaved people for internal use as well as for the regional markets. Akwamu, Asante, Allada, Hueda, Dahomey and Oyo developed along the same lines in the seventeenth and eighteenth centuries. Enslavement was not the original reason for the creation of these centralized states; yet with the rise of sugar production in the West Indies and the increased demand for enslaved labor, the fortunes of these states became almost inextricably tied to the Atlantic system. The ruling classes and armies of these states preyed on their weaker neighbours and became producers, traders and users of enslaved people.

Rulers and merchants of centralized and militaristic states were not the only groups drawn into participation in the Atlantic slave trade. In the Bight of Biafra, where no centralized state of significance emerged, groups of merchants from the loose networks of towns and villages established control over the local markets and trade networks. At Arochukwu, the Aro controlled the local markets by manipulating the prestige of the oracle *(ibinukpabi)*, while Bonny, Elem and Kalabari merchants monopolized the river transport and coastal exchange with Europeans through their ownership of large and heavily armed riverboats. The Niger Delta river merchants provided a significant historical exception to the general perspective that large-scale enslavement and trading of peoples depended on the presence of a strong militaristic state in a region.

The mosaic of small polities and loosely organized societies among the Temne, Soso, Mende, Vai, Sherbro, Gbandi and Bete in the lower Guinea area (from Sierra Leone to Liberia) was also drawn into the Occidental trading system. These groups, however, never produced enslaved people for the market on the same scale as the groups in the Niger Delta region. Two significant events stand out in the annals of enslavement in this zone. The Portuguese mentioned the Sapes Confederacy, which disintegrated in the early sixteenth century; the collapse of this confederacy has been attributed to the appearance on the coast of a group called the Manes. The Manes, probably a Mande offshoot, briefly became a major producer of enslaved people in the sixteenth century for the Atlantic trade before they were absorbed into the different local populations.[11] The next major increase in the production of enslaved people came during the Futa Jallon jihad of the mid-eighteenth century and the Samorian revolution of the nineteenth century. Nonetheless, the area never rivaled the Bight of Benin or even Senegambia in the production of enslaved people. The main slave traders

---

[11] Walter Rodney, *A History of the Upper Guinea Coast, 1545–1800* (Oxford: Clarendon Press, 1970), pp. 39–70.

in the region tended to be Afro-Europeans and the Mandingo, Soso and Fulbe elite.

The expansion of enslavement in the different areas of West Africa affected the social constitution and structures of society. The most obvious effect was in the determination of individual, family and corporate identity. All enslaved people, as the authors in the Miers and Kopytoff anthology, *Slavery in Africa: Historical and Anthropological Perspectives* (1977) argue, entered the societies of their captors and holders as outsiders, marginals and people without socially meaningful identities.[12] This fact was highlighted in the various labels attached to them. The precise moment at which these labels emerged in different societies is very unclear, but by the nineteenth century almost every West African society had words denoting unfree status, 'kinlessness' and lack of corporate citizenship. Among the Wollof, the enslaved were called *jaam*, and they belonged to the *gor*, a collective term that denoted foreignness. The same term was used for caste people. The term *odonko* among the Asante carried essentially the same meaning; it was a term applied loosely to Asante's northern neighbors, who were seen as liable to enslavement.[13] Among other peoples, it was the lack of freedom that was emphasized in the label. Enslaved people were called *jiyaado* (unfree) as opposed to the *ndimu* (freeborn) among the Fulbe. The Sherbro also labeled enslaved people *wono*, in contrast to the *mano*, who were free. On the whole, the different labels marked enslaved peoples as unfree, foreign and kinless.

The identity and status of enslaved people were further shaped by the roles they were assigned in the dominant society. Enslaved people served as wives, concubines, soldiers, administrators, trading agents, artisans, agricultural laborers and porters. Of these roles, enslaved soldiers and administrators tended to wield the most power and influence, and usually had the most access to privilege and wealth. Throughout the region, a pattern of using enslaved soldiers to buttress the wealth and power of ruling aristocracies emerged by the late eighteenth century. In the Wollof states, the power of the rulers became dependent on the *ceddo*. The *ceddo* became effective instruments of royal enslavement, tax and tribute collection, and suppression of popular discontent. They were non-Muslims and were regarded as hard drinkers in these Islamic (and therefore non-drinking) societies. Unlike other enslaved people, the *ceddo* maintained their distinctive

---

[12] Suzanne Miers and Igor Kopytoff (eds), *Slavery in Africa: Historical and Anthropological Perspectives*, (Madison, WI: University of Wisconsin Press, 1977).

[13] *Ibid.*; Robert S. Rattray, *Ashanti Law and Constitution* (Oxford: Clarendon Press, 1929).

slave status and did not integrate into mainstream Wollof society.

The Alafin (king) of Oyo in present-day Nigeria also used enslaved retainers in the security and administration of the royal palace and the state. Enslaved eunuchs guarded royal wives and children and participated in religious and judicial affairs. The *ilari*, distinguished by their shaven heads and tattooed bodies, served as elite royal guards, messengers and tax collectors. Enslaved soldiers also dominated the cavalry of the Oyo army. Enslaved people served in numerous other capacities within the royal household and were also involved in provincial administration in the empire. Enslaved soldiers, who were in most cases Muslims, were not assimilated into the dominant population. In Dahomey, enslaved people were usually among the military levies raised by the various vassals of the King. Perhaps the most famous slave soldiers were the 'Amazon women' who formed the royal guard of the Dahomean king.

In nearly all of the centralized states in the region, enslaved soldiers contributed greatly to the concentration of political power and authority in the hands of monarchs, the undermining of checks and balances with regard to royal authority, and the increasing oppression of commoners. For monarchs and the political elite, they provided alternative means of mobilizing wealth, political support and maintaining control over the population. People captured by soldiers could be traded for armaments and other goods, or used in agricultural estates. Enslaved soldiers made perfect political instruments because of their foreign status, lack of organic ties to the dominant society, and total dependence on royal patronage. In these centralized states, enslaved people exercised considerable power and authority over free people, and in many instances actually determined the direction of political succession. In centralized societies during the Atlantic enslavement period, the military became the site where state power and enslavement of new captives and soldiers were reproduced. It is at this level, perhaps, that one may argue that certain states in West Africa can be called slave societies.[14]

---

[14] Here, the term 'slave societies', is applied guardedly. M. I. Finley draws a clear distinction between *societies with slaves* and *true slave societies*. *Societies with slaves*, which have existed in nearly all regions and at different historical times, held and utilized enslaved people, but they were never the dominant factor in economics and politics. *Slave societies* were those societies in which the labor and production of enslaved people in large-scale plantations formed the core of economic production. The slaveholders were the dominant, and perhaps, sole ruling class. Enslavement penetrated the entire fabric of the society and left no part of it untouched. According to Finley, the examples of such true slave societies have been ancient

Enslaved women were regarded as valuable from the point of view of social and economic production and reproduction in the societies of West Africa, much more so than men. In the majority of West African societies, the children of enslaved women and free men inherited their fathers' status. This was the case in both Wollof and Fulbe societies, though the stigma of enslavement might have lingered for several generations. Among the matrilineal Asante, enslaved women, because they were kinless, enabled free Asante men to circumvent matrilineal inheritance rules and control.

Arguably women — whether through marriage or concubinage to free men — provided the quickest route through which some of the stigma and disadvantages of enslavement could be minimized in the next generation. In general, nearly all West African societies progressively improved the condition and increased the entitlements of enslaved people. Thus, centralized as well as non-centralized societies made distinctions between newly enslaved people and those who were long-serving or born in captivity. Among the Fulbe, a long-serving *jiyaado* became an *ndima* (client), and by the third generation, the enslaved person would become an *ndima nduka* (trusted client). Long-serving or second-generation captives were known as *olisos* or *wolisos* among the Soso and Temne. These long-serving and house-born (domestic) enslaved persons were in some respect considered a branch of the family. In Muslim societies, they might be converted to Islam and instructed in the reading of the Koran. In other societies, for example among the Mende, Temne and Sherbro, they were initiated into *poro* or *bundu* societies. As fictive kin, enslaved females worked alongside other women in the household, while the males were usually hired out to Europeans as wage laborers and sailors. Customarily, long-serving and house-born enslaved persons could not be sold except in cases of serious crime. In the late eighteenth and early nineteenth centuries, however, frequent accusations of witchcraft meant that they remained vulnerable to sale.

Ordinarily, enslaved persons were newly bought or captured males and females. They were used mainly in agriculture, the transportation of goods and other laborious tasks. Unlike the house-born or long-serving captives, they were regarded as 'outsiders' with no affinity or attachment to their owners' families and communities, and therefore could be readily sold. By the late eighteenth century and the beginning of the nineteenth century, the expansion of enslavement in the region

Greece, Rome, the United States, Brazil and the Caribbean. See M. I. Finley, *Ancient Slavery and Modern Ideology* (New York: Viking Press, 1980), p. 9.

had made it difficult for the more centralized states from Cayor to Futa Jallon, to the Hausa states of northern Nigeria, to absorb large numbers of enslaved people into mainstream society. The curtailment of the export market for enslaved people in the nineteenth century also compounded the problem. The aristocratic slaveholders increasingly placed newly enslaved people in separate villages. The idea of separate villages for enslaved peoples was not new and dated as far back as the Songhai Empire, where rulers had maintained special slave estates. By the nineteenth century, such villages had multiplied. From short-term holding areas for slaveholders and traders, they became new agricultural frontiers for large-scale production for internal and external markets.

As in the Americas, the general treatment of enslaved Africans in the Upper Guinea Coast varied from benign paternalism to naked brutality, depending on their length of servitude, status, employment and value, and the attitude of the enslavers. Islamic and indigenous laws minimized wanton murder, excessive abuse and cruelty towards enslaved persons. Throughout the era of Atlantic slavery, enslaved Africans tried to counter the dehumanization and loss of freedom and identity inherent in the system. Their strategies ranged from resisting capture and refusal to work, to escape and violent rebellion against slaveholders and slaveholding societies. They fought against African as well as European enslavers. Contemporary eyewitness accounts mention frequent revolts of captive and enslaved peoples from Futa Jallon to Cape Mount in the mid- to late eighteenth century. In many instances, these rebels established liberated zones and communities, which became magnets for other fugitives and rebellious enslaved persons. In the process of resistance and countering the impact of enslavement, people sometimes created new identities and cultural expressions for themselves. An example of this process of new identity creation was evident among the Hubbus of Futa Jallon.[15]

Pawned people

In many parts of West Africa, enslavement co-existed with another form of bondage known as pawnship. The institution of pawnship raises the same vexing questions as enslavement, as to its origins, definition, types, relationships between pawned people and other social

---

[15] Ismail Rashid, 'Escape, Revolt and Marronage in 18th and 19th Century Sierra Leone Hinterland', *Canadian Journal of African Studies* 34 (3) (2000), pp. 656–83.

groups in society, as well as the agency of 'pawns' themselves. Falola and Lovejoy define pawnship as a 'legal category of social and economic dependency' akin to debt bondage in parts of Asia and Latin America. It involved the momentary transfer of a person's labor power, partly as 'interest for the duration of the debt'. The pawn was a pledge, like natural or economic assets, given as collateral or security for a loan or debt. The pawn might be the debtor, a close relative or a dependant. Pawns might be free or enslaved.[16]

Scholars like Lovejoy and Richardson have suggested that pawnship is indigenous to the region, and was present before the arrival of Europeans and the institution of the Atlantic slave system. They base their argument on shaky linguistic deductions, namely the presence of indigenous terms in African languages like Akan and Yoruba (*Awowa* or *Ahoba*, respectively) to denote pawn peoples as distinct from enslaved peoples.[17] Meillassoux adopts a contrary view to that of Lovejoy and Richardson, asserting that the institution is not indigenous but a product of merchant economies. He argues, '[t]he existence of a debt presupposes a hierarchization of lineages based on the acquisition of wealth, and thus the disappearance of the principles of equality and solidarity between families; this can only take place through contamination by the merchant economy, if not by slavery itself'.[18] Indeed, it is this very 'contamination' and almost inextricable association with enslavement, which is evident even in the works of scholars of pawnship, which makes it difficult to discuss the institution exclusively. The pawnship institution is thus usually discussed in tandem with slavery, especially Atlantic slavery, in most of the literature.

Pawnship, however, was not enslavement, although it entailed similar forms of bondage and disabilities inherent in that institution. First, pawned people were not 'outsiders', as they were usually freeborn (even if their status may have been low), drawn from the society in which they were held as collateral. Consequently, they did not lose their kinship status when 'pawned'. Secondly, pawned people were not necessarily property, and there were expectations that they would be redeemed. In nearly all West African societies, pawned people only

---

[16] See entry by Paul Lovejoy on 'pawnship', in Seymour Drescher and Stanley L. Engermann (eds), *Historical Guide to World Slavery* (New York: Oxford University Press, 1998), pp. 308–12.

[17] Paul E. Lovejoy and David Richardson, 'Trust, Pawnship and Atlantic History: The Institutional Foundations of the Old Calabar Slave Trade', *American Historical Review* 104 (2) (1994), pp. 333–55; Toyin Falola and Paul Lovejoy, *Pawnship in Africa: Debt Bondage in Historical Perspective* (Boulder, CO: Westview Press, 1995).

[18] Meillassoux, *The Anthropology of Slavery*, p. 40.

temporarily lost their freedom and rights; they were restored upon the repayment of debt.[19] The loss of rights also did not imply the loss of kinship ties or citizenship status within the larger corporate society, nor the prerogatives attached to them. Unlike enslaved people (and very much like contemporary felons), their status was potentially reversible once the debt was cleared. Thirdly, in nearly all West African societies, pawned people (except where they were already enslaved persons) had higher social status and protection than enslaved persons. Fourthly, the distinction in status and entitlements between enslaved and pawned peoples was underlined by the fact that the names assigned to pawned persons did not denote 'foreign-ness'. Among the Akan, for example, they were known as *'awowa'* as distinct from *'odonko'*, the latter being the term assigned to enslaved people of foreign origin.

On the other hand, pawnship, especially of freeborn persons, did entail disability similar to those of enslavement. For pawned persons who were already enslaved, it added more layers of disabilities. Marriage did not liquidate the debt embodied by pawn status. Children of pawned people were liable to be shared with, or wholly acquired by, the holders of the pawned persons. Death did not erase the debt; other people were expected to take the place of the dead pawn. Unco-operative pawns, like enslaved people, were punished, and their families forced to repay the debt quickly. Furthermore, the fine theoretical distinctions between pawnship and enslavement usually broke down in practice. Inability of debtors to pay their debts, economic misfortunes of creditors, and the attitude and disposition of creditors sometimes led to the enslavement and sale of pawned people.

The presence and prevalence of pawnship in West Africa seems to be connected with two related developments. The first is the intensification of the Atlantic enslavement system. Since pawnship was one of the credit mechanisms employed by Africans and Europeans to facilitate trade transactions, it grew as the trade expanded. The use and growth of pawning varied in the region, with peoples in the Gold Coast and Bights of Benin and Biafra utilizing the institution far more than those in the Senegambia or sahelian zones. The second development is the deepening of social inequalities within West African societies. The creditors were usually the wealthiest members of society and the pawned peoples came from the lowest rungs. Pawning reinforced class and social differences, and exposed women and children to exploitation and unwanted marriages. It occurred as a

---

[19] Philip A. Igbafe, 'Slavery and Emancipation in Benin, 1945', *Journal of African History* 16 (3) (1975), pp. 409–29.

consequence of impoverishment due to famine, war, disease, economic misfortune, or expensive social obligations.

Just as the prevalence of pawnship had paralleled the expansion of the Atlantic enslavement economy, so did its decline. The shift from trading in peoples to trading in other commodities led to changes in the commercial arrangements of the Atlantic economic system. The pawnship-based credit arrangements that had helped fuel the Atlantic slave trade became obsolete. Pawned people became undesirable as collateral, interest, or guarantees against commercial credit. African traders, who had depended on the use of pawned people in their commercial transactions, became unable to participate effectively in the Atlantic economy. The changes in the Atlantic economy did not bring immediate relief to pawned people; their condition got worse in some instances. They became liable to longer and more permanent forms of servitude, as well as sale.

Colonialism and new forms of bondage

The European presence in West Africa changed by the end of the nineteenth century, with tremendous implications for power and social hierarchy in the region. The most obvious change was the European ascendance from 'strangers' and 'tenants' of African groups to supreme rulers over nearly all territories and peoples (except Liberia) in West Africa. In the process of imposing and consolidating European power, the different systems of enslavement, pawnship, and 'caste' gradually lost their relevance. Colonialism represented a shift in the Atlantic economic system. Though the European colonial project was primarily political and economic in orientation, it also produced vast social and cultural changes in Africa. Europeans conquered and partitioned the continent into different production estates. This bound African economies and societies more tightly into the wider Atlantic capitalist system and, in the process, further expanded the external markets available to Africans.

Over its duration, the colonial process transformed the social landscape unevenly, but almost irrevocably. It grafted older African production modes on to the new capitalist system to create new conditions of prosperity as well as poverty. The process thus reinforced certain older forms of power and social stratification, and destroyed others. It also created new classes as well as new forms of social inequality and marginality. Reinforcement of older structures of power came mainly within the rubric of 'indirect' rule and the codification of 'customary' law. Through indirect rule and customary law, European colonialists conceded to certain pre-existing power arrangements and cultural practices to ensure the stability of the colonial system. These concessions sometimes involved European acceptance, and even use, of 'forced' and 'domestic slave' labor, especially in the period before the First World War. On the other hand, European colonialism facilitated the gradual disappearance of some social classes and forms of social inequality. Different forms of enslavement, pawnship and caste were rendered illegal, and they disappeared as meaningful social categories. Colonial governments passed anti-slavery and pawnship laws in all West African colonies by the 1930s. However, these laws were sometimes rendered ineffective, as holders of enslaved and anti-pawned peoples found ingenious means of subverting and circumventing them. Chiefs and pawnholders frequently claimed that enslaved and pawned peoples were their servants, wards or wives.

The European onslaught against what they deemed as outdated forms of bondage, and the cultural constructions surrounding these forms, was waged not only by military and legal compulsion, but also with new religious (Christian) and political (paternalistic liberalism) ideas and institutions. Christian and liberal ideas and institutions provided alternative political and religious frameworks for definitions of identity, community and freedom. The new frameworks enabled enslaved and caste peoples to rise above some of the restrictions of kinship, ethnicity, culture and locale, and to find new modes of empowerment, success and self-realization.

Yet even as West African societies were being reconstituted in the aftermath of enslavement and caste, two other processes were also taking place. First, the memories and cultural codes based on systems of enslavement and caste lingered. They still continue to influence relationships between the descendants of 'bonded' groups and their former social 'superiors'. The second process was the development of new forms of disempowerment and 'bondage'. Those who could not find a niche in colonial and postcolonial structures, who were ill-equipped to function within society or who lacked the necessary kinship and social networks, became a new generation of rural and urban poor and social transients.[20] Consisting of beggars, transient laborers, the chronically unemployed, petty criminals, the mentally ill, the disabled and the incurably sick, these people are not 'bonded', or subjugated, but rather 'stigmatized', 'marginalized' and 'excluded'

---

[20] See Kalu's chapter in this volume for a detailed discussion of poverty and the poor in colonial West Africa.

from mainstream societies in ways that were similar to some categories of enslaved and caste peoples. In the blighted economic and social climate of the twentieth century's last decades in West Africa, their number increased tremendously, and no doubt contributed to the widespread outbreak of violent conflicts in the region.

Conclusion

In the last millennium, different forms of power, subjugation and social exclusion based on kinship, occupation and trade emerged in West Africa. The conceptualization of these forms of power and social exclusion continues to challenge scholars of the African past. Kinship structures and dynamics, with their gerontocratic and often patriarchal arrangement of power and privileges, contained the seeds of social inequality. In spite of their internal tensions and inequities, however, kinship structures provided the basis and language for solidarity and corporate citizenship. It took external developments, namely competition from other groups, as well as trade, to facilitate the development of more glaring forms of disempowerment and bondage like enslavement, pawnship and caste. Bondage and social exclusion based on pawnship and caste were concentrated in particular zones, but enslavement encompassed all the states and societies in the region.

External contacts, especially those that would eventually entail the trade of African peoples, like the trans-Saharan and Atlantic commercial networks, contributed greatly to the growth of strong states and military entities. These developments reinforced processes of social stratification, exclusion and subordination in the region. As these economic and political processes unfolded, especially over the last five hundred years, the different forms of bondage tended to reinforce one another. New language, cultural practices and identities had to be created to distinguish between those who were subjugated, alien and inferior, and those who were regarded as free, citizens (kin) and superior. By the turn of the twentieth century, the different forms of bondage and subjugation examined in this chapter had run their course and were largely eliminated during colonialism. Nonetheless, as these archaic forms disappeared, new forms of social exclusion and subjugation that colonialism facilitated emerged.

Recommended Reading

Arhin, Kwame (1983) 'Rank and Class among the Asante and the Fante', *Africa*, 53 (1), pp. 2–22.

Barry, Boubacar (1998) *Senegambia and the Atlantic Slave Trade* (Cambridge: Cambridge University Press).

Conrad, David. C. and Barbara E. Frank (eds) (1995) *Status and Identity in West Africa: Nyamakalaw of Mande* (Bloomington, IN: Indiana University Press).

Falola, Toyin and Paul Lovejoy (1995) *Pawnship in Africa: Debt Bondage in Historical Perspective* (Boulder, CO: Westview Press, 1995).

Lovejoy, E. Paul (2000) *Transformations in Slavery: A History of Slavery in Africa*, Second edn. (Cambridge: Cambridge University Press).

McIntosh, Roderick (1998) *The Peoples of the Middle Niger: The Island of Gold* (Malden, MA: Blackwell Publishers).

Meillassoux, Claude (1991) *The Anthropology of Slavery: The Womb of Iron and Gold* (London, Athlone Press; Chicago: University of Chicago Press).

Miers, Suzanne and Igor Kopytoff (eds) (1977) *Slavery in Africa: Historical and Anthropological Perspectives* (Madison, WI: University of Wisconsin Press).

Tamari, Tal (1991) 'The Development of Caste Systems in West Africa', *Journal of African History* 32 (2), pp. 221–50.

Searing, James (1988) 'Aristocrats, Slaves, and Peasants: Power and Dependency in the Wollof States, 1700-1850', *International Journal of African Historical Studies*, 21, pp. 475–503.

7

Religious Interactions
in Pre-Twentieth-Century West Africa

PASHINGTON OBENG

This chapter examines the nature, processes and construction of identities of religious entities and the development of communities that interacted with one another in pre-colonial West Africa. The discussion will address the multi-dimensional and dynamic aspects of religious practices and beliefs undergirding the diffusion of shrines. The chapter shows the relevance of religious interaction, migrations of deities and changes within religious structures and their relation to the everyday life of West Africans. Attention is paid to the critical role of African religious practitioners as actors who transformed religion. I also address how, as religions are experienced, expressed, and interpreted within the culture of their birth, and indeed outside those contexts, new meanings emerge, certain notions are dropped, identities are redefined and new alliances are forged. I show that, during religious encounter, religious experience and expression contain, shape and are shaped by culture, specific individuals or groups and historical processes.

The first part of the chapter addresses the translocal potential of indigenous African religions and ways in which they manifested variation and plurality as they crossed boundaries and shaped people's lives. The translocal potential of indigenous religions challenges the age-old view that indigenous religions are not mission-oriented. The second focus will be on how indigenous religions encountered Islam and the complex forms that these interactions took. The interactions of Christianity with indigenous religions and, in some cases, the encounters among all three religions will be the third concern of the essay. Finally, the chapter touches on the religious and cultural pluralism that emerged before and after the colonial period and continues to flourish in West

141

Africa. In attempting to show the nature and process of the interactions mentioned, the chapter also discusses the changing needs and methods of the practitioners and the religions engaged in the encounters. It thus contributes to African religious history and the current debate on identity reformulation and religious practice and belief. My analysis will draw heavily on Patrick Ryan's 'history of religions' approach, but I modify his analysis as the chapter develops.

Ryan divides the religious history of West Africa into ten separate but related periods.[1] He describes the first as marked by the intermarriage between pre-migrant and migrant religious ideas. The fusion, according to him, was between a universe populated by the direct ancestors of lineage groups and another transcendent world filled with a chieftaincy culture underpinned by a hierarchy of beings not necessarily the ancestors of the worshippers. The eighth to the eleventh centuries, he argues, witnessed the Ibadi Muslim merchants practicing a 'self-imposed mercantile quarantine' because they did not reach out to the West African communities. Ryan's third and fourth periods mark when Muslim and European Catholic societies, upon their arrival between the fifteenth and the nineteenth centuries, began to mix with the local people in a limited fashion. For instance, Christianity only reached beyond the castles and forts of the Europeans to mixed races or the mulatto population along the West African coast. By the time he gets to his tenth period, Ryan demonstrates how the twentieth century became the period for the re-Africanization of Islam and Christianity, although there are still some Muslims and Christians who associate indigenous practices with paganism or the lack of total devotion to Allah. Given the dynamic nature of religion, there will always be moments of convergence and divergence between some official positions of religious authorities and what happens on the ground.

Most scholarly writings on West African indigenous religions have generally focused on beliefs, practices, languages, and peoples. Those who pay attention to the history of indigenous religions tend to discuss interaction among Islam, Christianity and indigenous religions. They know full well that indigenous religions are not static and that politics, environment, economics and other aspects of West African peoples' lives were intertwined with their religions before the advent of Islam and Christianity. Such discussions often leave out the African agency factor, whereby individuals and communities have always played a key role in religious change.

---

[1] Patrick Ryan, 'Is it Possible to Construct a Unified History of Religion in West Africa?' (Accra, n.d.).

Mbiti's pioneering work on the religions and philosophies of Africa did awaken the world to the practices and ideas that undergird African religions. Yet his *African Religions and Philosophies* is an ahistorical analysis of African religions. Parrinder's equally helpful book, *Religions in Africa*, provides important information about indigenous African religions, Islam and Christianity. Parrinder, however, portrays Christianity and Islam as life-transforming and dynamic 'foreign' religions, while African religions seem frozen in time and place to passively receive or be shaped by the foreign religions. Fisher begins his analysis with a description of the sources for Akan religious phenomena and ends with a discussion of beliefs and practices among the Akan during their exposure to Islam and Christianity. He thereby inadvertently creates the impression that changes in indigenous religions occur only during their encounter with Islam or Christianity.

A focus on specific religions and social changes in West African societies can help illuminate how the interaction of shrines in communities affect power relations, people's identities and values in the societies, and how people deploy religion to reorient themselves and order their lives. This chapter thus focuses on changes within indigenous religions and the reforging of ideas and behavior between African religions, Islam and Christianity. This examination touches on how 'missionary' religions such as Christianity and Islam went through periods of quarantine before they broke out into the larger societies of West Africa and the changes which they underwent. Before, during and after the quarantine of the so-called 'missionary' religions, indigenous African religions were spreading. Prior to the nineteenth century, Christianity in West Africa was mostly confined to the coastal region — indeed to forts and castles and communities with resident European soldiers and traders. Islam which preceded Christianity in West Africa, went through a period of confinement at royal courts, where it was practised by visiting Muslims, a few rulers and some of their household members, before it spread through trade until the *jihads* of the late eighteenth and nineteenth centuries. While Christianity and Islam are often called 'missionary' religions, indigenous African religions have had their missionizing approaches. Literature that describes Christianity and Islam as 'missionary' religions — in contrast to indigenous African religions — gives the impression that the latter are somewhat perpetually quarantined. However, in pre-colonial West Africa as today, shrines and their devotees moved from place to place. Such movements resulted in the establishment of shrines and communities of indigenous religious practitioners in new and different parts of West Africa.

If 15–20 per cent of West Africa's population practise traditional religions as Boahen et al. contend,[2] and most of these religions have persisted through to the present day, it is critical to understand some of them, how they changed and how others interacted with one another. In addition, some adherents of Christianity and Islam may use and consult priests or priestesses of indigenous religions for protection, success, and so on. Belonging to multiple religions in West Africa has fostered the reconfiguring of religious ideas and practices. 'Devotees' are more than 'worshippers', they are political, social and economic agents, and, most of all, transmitters of cultural and religious ideas.

Identity, change and religion: translocal potential

Horton's point that indigenous African religions were responding to change long before encountering Islam and Christianity is useful for understanding pre-colonial religious interaction.[3] Change came from inside and outside the African religious sphere. Pre-colonial religions in West Africa have always been marked by diversity and variation; in addition, practitioners of those religions had interacted among themselves and with others outside their own societies through trade, intermarriage and other forms of social intercourse. Warfare, the fame of religious specialists and the power of their shrines, economics and politics also fostered the spread of indigenous religions across the borders of their origins.

Thus, as Africans confronted new realities, they sought ways of describing and elaborating their existing religious ideology and practice. In addition to the above observation, Opoku contends that religious and social change also created a gradual shift from the community ownership of deities to individual ownership of shrines, thereby privatizing some of the shrines, particularly in pre-colonial West Africa.[4]

Opoku points out that the tutelar deities of West Africa, especially of the Akan, preceded the medicine cults. The tutelar deities include Prah, Tano, and Bea. These antecedent deities belonged to the community, while the medicine shrines, that appeared later, were owned by individuals. While Opoku's general thesis about the privatization of cults is valid, the contemporary West African scene features both private and community-owned cults. Addressing the newly emerged shrines,

---

[2] A. A. Boahen et al., *Topics in West African History* (London: Longman, 1986).

[3] R. Horton, 'African Conversion', *Africa* 41 (2) (1971), pp. 85–108.

[4] A. Asare Opoku, *West African Traditional Religion* (Accra: FEP, 1978).

Field shows that such shrines appeared under economic, social and religious stresses that were unprecedented among the Akan.[5] He argues that the privately owned shrines sprang up between 1914 and 1919 in an atmosphere of tremendous insecurity due to the prevalence of influenza as well as economic pressures. People sought help from these medicine shrines for protection against witchcraft, bad luck and diseases.

Although indigenous Akan worshipped the Supreme Being, they did not have a priest or priestess who mediated between this being and its followers as practised in Christianity. The altars of the 'Sky God', shaped like a forked branch of *'Nyame dua'* (God's tree or *Astonia Congensis*) with a pot or basin containing a neolithic stone, convinced Rattray that the Ashanti knew and acknowledged a Supreme Being before the advent of Muslims and Christians.[6] In addition, the Ashanti have cultural elements that allude to the existence, influence and force of the Supreme Being. Yet, as he points out, the Asante have no priests or priestesses for the Sky God, and he asks how ideas about this being were transmitted from community to community and across generations. The answer is best given by the Akan proverb *'obi nkyere abofra Nyame'* (Nobody teaches the child knowledge about God); this affirms the tacitly shared experience and thus non-discursive transmission of aspects of religion among the Akan.

Missions within indigenous religions

The word mission comes from the Latin *'missio'* which means 'a sending'. When the word 'mission' is used, we often think of Christianity and Islam. For instance, the effort to extend or spread the Christian message and values through teaching, preaching and services to others, including non-Christians, with the goal of winning them, is generally referred to as a 'mission'. The person sent to proclaim the good tidings or news is the evangelist. The Greek verb *euggelizomai* means 'to announce the good news'. The Hebrew scriptures also describe a messenger (*mebasser*) who announces deliverance for the people and thus proclaims peace. The evangelist is thus one who travels proclaiming the good news.

In contrast, primal religions — as contended by Turner — are non-

[5] M. J. Field, *Search for Security: An Ethno-Psychiatric Study of Rural Ghana* (Evanston, IL: Northwestern University Press, 1960).
[6] R. S. Rattray, *Ashanti* (Oxford: Clarendon Press, 1923), p. 142.

missionary in nature and seldom spread across tribal boundaries.[7] He says they lack the eschatologies that go beyond traditional mythologies. He also believes that it is only the adoption of new religions that provides new mechanisms for practitioners to adjust to new situations. The spread of indigenous religions are never referred to as a missionary movement.

Although indigenous religions do not have elaborate infrastructures with institutions, preachers and the 'written word' for promoting and converting others, these religions have had their own modes for spreading. Indigenous religions spread not through written literature or written creeds, but by their 'evangelists' who proclaim news of cures, success, and the like. These religions have been used by people to face new situations, even though these indigenous religions did not have the Christian eschatologies that Turner describes. The spread of the good news about healing, newly gained spiritual power, blessing and success received from a shrine or a priest or priestess could be found in indigenous religions. Also, devotees acting as their own evangelists have spread indigenous religions along trade routes, at market centers, and in migratory patterns. The ease and flexibility surrounding the establishment of new shrines after consultation with religious specialists at the main or central shrine, played a major role in the spread not only of shrines but also of the power and influence of indigenous shrines in West Africa.

Like Field, Ryan argues that, due to the pressures exerted by rapid changes, West Africans were thrown into an era of 'insecurity — social and psychological — which stimulated the growth of interest in and, indeed, fear of witchcraft'.[8] The proliferation of medicine shrines — especially witch-catching shrines which became trans-ethnic — seems to have addressed these extra needs. Some of these shrines appear to have thrived directly as a result of their foreign-ness. People traveled long distances when necessary, to ask for, and be granted, the rights to establish replicas of shrines in their local communities. Among such shrines was Tigare, which originated in northern Ghana and spread to southern Ghana and even as far as Southwestern Nigeria, where it underwent transmutations and became known as Atinga. Though Ryan says the appeal of the exotic and the power attributed to a faith from an alien culture could account for the spread and popularity of such medicine shrines, it is also important to add that some of the priests

---

[7] H. W. Turner, *Religious Innovation in Africa: Collected Essays on Religious Movement* (Boston, MA: G. K. Hall & Co., 1979), p. 5.

[8] Ryan, 'Religion in West Africa', p. 105.

and custodians of the shrines did offer the support that their clients needed. At other times the spread of indigenous religion has been fostered by the priests' and priestesses' immense personal power to cure diseases, put an end to infant mortality, or ward off catastrophes that besieged towns and villages. The dynamic nature of religions is observed as the Nupe obtained deities from their neighbors: the Egwugwu from the Yoruba, the Sogha from the Gwari, and the Bori from the Hausa. Thus, as people's spiritual, economic and psychological needs changed, they acquired divinities that addressed those needs. These needs arose particularly during conflict between groups of people or when others waged war to expand their territories. War deities were deployed to wage war or at times their help was sought for protection and security. For instance, during the wars against the Fula of Wasulu in Upper Niger in 1851, Dyeri Sidibe of Ulundu selected warriors to wage war, relying on a vision from an indigenous spirit.

Besides the power of the deities, the spread and influence of some of the indigenous religions also depended on the military skills, personal strength and broad knowledge of the religious personality. For instance, Samori Toure, whose family was described as 'animist', had a strong personality and was also an itinerant trader. His trading activities exposed him to peoples and societies other than his own. In 1861, Samori would help his animist relations to resist Sise imperialism which threatened his people. Here we find another example of the fusion between cultic power and the personal force of a practitioner, highlighting African agency in spreading religion.

Religio-cultural creativity was further manifested in West African segmentary societies where religion fostered the integration of autonomous communities of villages. Dike, commenting on the integrative power of the Long Juju oracle among the Aro-Chukwu in Igboland, states that the oracle's advent among the Aros made them into a sacred people.[9] When the sacred Aros traveled among other Igbos and settled at various places, their relationship with Long Juju enabled them to establish critical links between the people and Aro-Chukwu. Aside from the Igbo, the Ijaw also acknowledged the judicial authority of the priests and custodians of the oracle. Indigenous religions have fostered the spread of religious power and personnel.

---

[9] K. O. Dike, *Trade and Politics in the Niger Delta, 1830–1885* (London: Oxford University Press, 1956).

African agency

The 'African' as a critical agent in the transmission of religious ideas and practices is what Sanneh and others have described as the 'African factor'.[10] When Berber Muslim merchants appeared around the upper Niger banks in the eighth century AD, these Ibadi Muslim merchants kept their faith to themselves thus practising what Ryan calls 'self-imposed merchantile quarantine'.[11] It was not until after the eleventh century that Islamic practices began to be adapted to the local customs. When Al-Bakri, the eleventh-century Spanish geographer, wrote on non-Muslim communities in ancient Ghana practising their religions, he described their practices as '*al-majusiyya*' (Magianism), and as simply in conflict with Allah or 'shirk' (polytheism). The appearance of the Europeans — the Portuguese Catholics of Elmina castle, and the Danes between the fifteenth and sixteenth centuries — was also marked by a period of segregation. During this time European religious people separated themselves from local people. When their Christianity began to influence the conversion of others, it reached the mulatto or mixed race Africans along the coast. These European traders were not missionaries. Their religion was incidental to their interest in gold, ivory, land and slaves and as Debrunner points out, Christianity was a bedfellow with the slave trade between the fifteenth and eighteenth centuries, and this fact overshadowed any genuine, if meager, effort at missionizing intending to elicit a positive response from local people.[12]

Post-colonial literature often gives the impression that Africans began to assert their agency after the 1960s when nations south of the Sahara gained their independence. However, Africanization did not start after the 1960s when nations were celebrating their independence. Religious and cultural interactions that stressed African agency preceded independence. In fact, the African as a responsible and creative agent has functioned during such religious interactions since before foreign religions arrived in West Africa.

Sanneh highlights the 'African factor' in mission in his book on West African Christianity. By the 'African factor', he refers to the significance of the response of African religions to foreign religions that have been brought to Africa such as Christianity and Islam. It is in the light of

---

[10] Lamine Sanneh, *West African Christianity: the Religious Impact* (Maryknoll, NY: Orbis, 1983), p. xii.

[11] Ryan, 'History of Religion in West Africa', p. 101.

[12] Hans Debrunner, *A History of Christianity in Ghana* (Accra: Waterville, 1967), p. 24.

African religious models and African agency, he argues, that the effective transmission of foreign religions can take place. He contends that when the African factor is given its due focus, 'It allows us to assess the respective impact of Christianity and Islam through the eyes of African religions and . . . release these two missionary faiths from the fixed motionless time frame in which they have been frozen. . . .'[13] He clarifies his argument with reference to the 'apparent failure' of missions between 1480 and 1785 and the successful period between 1785 and 1885. When Africans became equipped to engage in the mission, the foreign religions began to spread. The focus on African agency helps us to understand how Africans construct connections under the pressures of time and space; it also lays emphasis on addressing the cultural production of devotee religious knowledge and the people's ability to change ideas and practices.

As Sanneh discusses religious encounters among African religions, Christianity and Islam, his stress on the African factor seems to lead him to be a little heavy-handed in stating that the African response reveals African religious heritage which is brought to bear on the inter-religious encounter. Much as this African heritage is crucial, it is also important to mention that agency is shown when the African uses the models of a foreign religion to articulate aspects of his or her own religion. Furthermore, indigenous religions did and do sometimes use foreign religious models to renew themselves, or the foreign religion, to spread further. War medicines from shrines such as Krakye Dente were imported from the northern region of present-day Ghana to the Asante region to aid Asante warriors during the Asante wars of expansion. During the period of Asante expansion, Mande peoples and others who practised Islam at the trade centers in Western Sudan came under Asante control.[14]

Kwaku Dua was thus an ambivalent patron of Islam. Such strategic use of religion was not peculiar to the King. Asante political, cultural and military power was bolstered through the incorporation of the religions of some of the people they conquered. It was during Osei Tutu Kwame's reign (1804–23) in Asante that Muslims gained a stronghold in Kumasi, the Asante capital. Dupuis quotes Osei Kwame as saying 'the Koran . . . is strong, and I like it because it is the book of the great God; it does good for me, and therefore I love all the people that read it'.[15] Osei Kwame consulted Muslims for prayers and some

[13] Sanneh, *West African Christianity*, p. xvi.
[14] Ivor Wilks, 'The Northern Factor in Ashanti History' (Institute of African Studies Papers, University of Ghana, 1961), p. 19.
[15] J. Dupuis, *Journal of a Residence in Ashantee* 2nd edition (London: Cass, 1966), p. 161.

Muslims held responsible positions in the king's court. The widespread use of amulets and talismans was not restricted to the common people in Asante. The Asante war captains, the king himself, and other warriors all had battle garb on which were sewn bullet-proof amulets made by Muslims.[16] As Dupuis reports, the Asante accepted aspects of Islam believing that the Qur'an was a divine creation, and consequently that it contained ordinances and prohibitions, which were most congenial to the happiness of mankind in general.[17] The appeal of Islam was not necessarily the faith itself, but rather the efficacy of the religion, as it enabled the Asante to order their lives in relation to success, victory in battle, healing, and so on. Later, Asante Nkramo (Asante Muslims), who consisted of both Asante and non-Asante came, into being. The Asante king Kwaku Dua accepted certain aspects of Islam in Kumasi but did not convert. Conversion would have entailed his being circumcised, but this was impossible as an Asante king could not have any physical blemish — including circumcision. Circumcision would have spelled his overthrow.

Between 1879 and 1895, as Christian missionaries encountered Muslims in Nigerian cities such as Abeokuta and Lagos, they appeared to have admired 'a religion which taught sobriety, personal discipline and lay participation and which inspired self-giving and enforced a moral code'.[18] At the same time, while Christianity — especially Protestantism — saw local languages as essential to the spread of the religion, Islamists insisted on Arabic as the 'exclusive vehicle of revelation'.[19] The use of sacred language as a means of communication also has its appeal. Even those who do not understand Arabic can have respect and reverence for the language.

Renewal of religion: African religion, Christianity and Islam

Conventional wisdom, underscored by social evolutionary thought, tends to suppose that, in the light of social and religious change, practitioners of indigenous religions would discard their religions and embrace immigrant religions like Christianity and Islam. That if West Africans borrowed from the immigrant religions, they were bound to privilege the new religions so that indigenization would lead to African Islam and Christianity rather than Christianized or Islamized

---

[16] T. Bowdich, *Mission from Cape Coast Castle to Ashantee* 3rd edition (London: Cass, 1966), pp. 271–2.

[17] Dupuis, *Journal*, p. 248.

[18] Sanneh, *West African Christianity*, p. 220.

[19] *Ibid.*, p. 221.

indigenous religions. Santa Mariafo and Santonafo of Elmina are examples of indigenous religions that co-opted aspects of foreign religions to start new indigenous religions with a new priesthood structure.

After Christianity arrived in West Africa in the fifteenth century, accounts of travellers, such as Richard Jobson and a Portuguese Jesuit priest named Balthasar Barreira, recorded ways in which Africans had combined elements of indigenous African religions with Islam and Christianity. For instance, writing in the 1620s, Jobson reports that Muslims in Senegambia had used the cross to decorate their dresses and houses and had deployed the name of Jesus as a charm. Barreira is said to have found traditional rulers such as a Susu king of Sierra Leone embracing Islam and rejecting Christianity.[20] At other times religious tolerance has fostered a particular religion though the person in power might belong to a different or competing religious tradition.

Encounter between indigenous religions and Islam

Missionary religions do not always missionize. Sometimes they stall or become missionized by the so-called non-missionary African religions. Islam arrived in West Africa from North Africa between 1100 and 1600 and later could be found around the political capitals of West African states. When Islam first arrived in West Africa its practitioners were employed at some royal palaces as advisers, clerks, diplomats and medicine men. Though some West African rulers transmitted and embodied aspects of Islam, others did not embrace Islam because it threatened dimensions of their indigenous religions and polity. For example, Sonni Ali, in 1465 in the Songhay empire, purged some aspects of Islam and borrowed others to combine them with pre-Islamic practices for his political gains. People like Sonni Ali are sometimes called *Mukhallitwn* because they combine Islam with traditional faith. When Islam gained some roots among the ruling classes, the new Muslim chiefs and kings tried to marry the African religious underpinnings of their rule to Islam. This practice, according to Sanneh, produced an important environmental flexibility for the appropriation of Islam.[21] Such hybridized Islam was, however, disapproved of by the orthodox Muslims who sought to 'Arabize' the Africans. Sonni Ali and others like him demonstrated a politically astute and selective use of

[20] *Ibid.*, p. 214.
[21] *Ibid.*, p. 213.

Islam. On the other hand, the Askiya Muhammad Toure, who deposed Sonni Ali, embraced a zealous Islam and repudiated the hybridized Islam of his predecessor.[22]

The ninteenth century marked the beginning of substantial conversions to Christianity along the Atlantic coast in areas such as Freetown, Monrovia, Cape Coast (Gold Coast) and Abeokuta (Nigeria). During this period, according to Ryan, African converts were eager to discard aspects of their culture and religion in pursuit of European ways of life. For example, these Africans 'drank European tea, wore ill-fitted frock coats, and high hats were made to replace the palm wine and graceful cloth of traditional usage'.[23] This phase of 'Europeanized Christianization' lasted until Africans began to look for their own cultural links with Christianity. The seventh period, according to Ryan, was occasioned by the pressures of Islam and Christianity, the emergence of a money-based economy and improved communications throughout West Africa. This period was marked by a 'resurgence of traditional forms of faith'.[24]

African religious history witnessed the impact of Fulani *jihad* in the early nineteenth century, which was aimed at repudiating the mixing of religions (*Takhlit*) in West Africa. Such reform movements can be traced to the eleventh century Almoravid reforms in Western Sahara. Also the anti-mystical *Wahhabiyya* which began in the nineteenth century in Arabia rejected African traditional elements. Such stem purging of indigenous elements has resulted in clashes between the *Wahhabi* reformers and the *Tijaniyya* mystical confraternities in parts of northern Ghana. In his analysis, Ryan shows that the twentieth century has seen a re-Africanization of migrant religions although some of the de-Africanizing tendencies are still found in Islam and Christianity especially among those Africans who associate indigenous practices with 'paganism' and a lack of complete devotion to God/Allah.

Ryan's discussion gives the impression of a progression in the religious history of West Africa. For instance, in spite of the attempt by early Christian converts to Europeanize Christianity, and reform efforts by both Fulani *jihad* followers and the *Wahhabi*, 'mixing' has always happened on the ground. In spite of official positions against 'mixing', individuals and groups have continued to seek spiritual help from multiple sources to address their needs.

[22] *Ibid.*, p. 230.
[23] Ryan, 'History of Religion in West Africa', p. 104.
[24] *Ibid.*, p. 105.

The Kano Chronicle as cited, points to the influence of Nigerian local religion on Islam. The Chronicle states that Muslim rulers of Kano consulted the Tchunburburae cult at Gagua between 1063 and 1410. Before the rulers waged war, they consulted the oracle. When Islam entered the societies in the interior of Sierra Leone, the Muslim cleric, according to Sanneh, was incorporated into 'Poro hierarchy and given a role which suited his familiarity with the sacred Arabic script'.[25] The cleric, using his knowledge (*ilim awfaq*) of the science of magic squares, which is the basis of Islamic talismans, was able to give the Poro medicine power against malevolent spirits and enemies.[26] Other examples of mixing Islam with traditional faith exist especially at the courts of chiefs and kings in northern Ghana and in Asanteland. In Kito in northern Ghana, as Levtzion points out, is a shrine, Kagbir, where the shrine-priest Kagbir-Wura:

> prays twice a day (morning and evening) and fasts three days during Ramadan. He has a rosary, a Koran, and a bundle of Arabic manuscripts. He himself cannot read even an Arabic letter.[27]

We may also observe the case of the Qur'an's veneration at a shrine in Larabanga in Gonja of northern Ghana prior to the twentieth century. At the shrine, the adherents would sacrifice a cow or some other animal and after prayer would wipe the palms of their hands on their faces as Muslims do and the Qur'an would be folded and put away in a bag.

Thus, the sacred powers and skills of the cleric are tapped to foster a Sierra Leonean secret society's endeavors. In pre-colonial Middle Volta Basin in the Gold Coast (Ghana), according to Levtzion,[28] there were times when Muslim clerics gave up their practice as Muslims and served as diviners in local cults. At other times, the indigenous priests borrowed Islamic practices such as praying more than once a day, fasting during Ramadan, and carrying a rosary, a Qur'an and a few scraps of Arabic manuscripts even though many could not read Arabic. In addition to itinerant Muslim clerics and traders who frequented Asante in the eighteenth century, Muslim residents in and around Kumase (the capital of Asante) offered prayer amulets for protection and cure, and their leader performed a Friday *sadaqa* (almsgiving) at the Asante king's palace under the supervision of the *Nsumankwahene* (chief priest of the royal household). In the pluralistic religious atmosphere of Asante, the

---

[25] Sanneh, *West African Christianity,* p. 235.
[26] *Ibid.*
[27] Nehemia Levtzion, *Muslims and Chiefs in West Africa* (London: Oxford University Press, 1968), p. 66.
[28] *Ibid.*

royal family, starting with the Asante king Osei Tutu Kwame (1804-23) consulted Muslim clerics for prayers and amulets while also relying on religious specialists of the indigenous religions.

Owusu-Ansah asserts that Islam was put to many uses in Asante.[29] These uses included amulets for war medicine and cures for bed-wetting, small-pox, impotence, infertility, leprosy and ulcers, to name but a few. This demonstrates the African deployment of religious symbolism to generate spiritual power. In this case, foreign missionary religions were co-opted by indigenous religious practice.

The Aladura prophet and the Yoruba *babalawo* play very similar roles in their respective religions, in that they both receive dreams and visions and through them provide healing to their members or followers.[30] In Yoruba indigenous religion, the diviner receives insights for healing through Ifa divination and Ogun, while the Aladura prophet draws inspiration from the Holy Spirit. The Aladura church prohibits the use of herbal and Western medicines, but the *babalawo* may use oil, water and herbs to heal.

There are striking similarities between Islam and the Aladura church. The word *aladura* derives from the Arabic *Al-du'a*, meaning prayer. The five daily prayers are found in both Islam and the Aladura church. At the benediction in the church, the 'worshippers raise their arms with their hands open to catch the blessing from heaven',[31] as Muslims do at the end of the first chapter (*surat*) of the Qur'an. Aladura people remove their footwear at the entrance of their place of worship, as Muslims do. Thus we can see that indigenous African Christianity incorporates elements from Islamic practice.

There have been times when encounters between Islam and indigenous religions have led to the subversion of one religion. For instance, al-Bakri, the Spanish Muslim geographer writing in the eleventh century, describes an encounter between a visiting Muslim cleric and a local religious specialist in the Malinke Kingdom of Malal in the Western Sudan. Facing a national calamity of drought in Malal, the ruler sought help from the indigenous religious specialists, but the drought persisted. It was only when a visiting Muslim cleric prescribed prayers to be performed that rains fell to end the drought. This dramatic relief led the ruler to accept Islam and demolish the local palace shrines.

---

[29] David Owusu-Ansah, 'Prayer, Amulets, and Healing', in Nehemia Levtzion and Randall Pouwells (eds), *The History of Islam in Africa* (Athens, OH: Ohio University Press; Oxford: James Currey, 2000), pp. 477–88.

[30] Sanneh, *West African Christianity*.

[31] *Ibid.*, p. 225.

The ruler deployed his political power to end an indigenous religion and to embrace Islam, because of the need Islam met at that time.

In Dagomba, in northern Ghana, marriage is to be officiated by a *mallam* (Muslim religious specialist) if the prospective couple are Muslims. However, until recently, 'wanka', the indigenous practice of publicly bathing the bride on the evening before the marriage, was carried out. Similarly, some Christians still pour libations to call on their ancestors and deities or consult indigenous priests or priestesses in matters they believe Christianity does not adequately address.

Contact and context: emergence of indigenous religions

Debrunner writes:

> What remained of Catholicism at Elmina after 160–170 years of Portuguese rule? A pagan shrine — said to contain the statue of St Anthony, and to present certain Christian features and it is quite possible that some elements of Catholicism were thus absorbed into the pagan religion.[32]

Santa Mariafo and Santonafo

Frs Moreau and Murat reported in 1818 that they had found relics of the Virgin Mary and St Anthony of Padua in 'pagan homes in Elmina'. The two Catholic priests also observed that Elminians who possessed the relics of Mary called themselves 'Santa Mariafo'. As they performed certain rituals on Fridays, the Santa Mariafo repeated some phrases that contained the words 'Santa Maria'. The devotees wore long robes and carried candles as they processed through the major streets of Elmina.[33]

During the sixteenth and seventeenth centuries of Portuguese Catholic presence in West Africa, the church held big processions during which statues of saints were decorated and carried around. Among the statues were those of the Virgin Mary called in Portuguese 'Irmandade de Santa Maria'.[34] Wiltgen further suggests that during the Portuguese era (before the Portuguese were driven out by the Dutch in 1637), the African Christians in Elmina who carried the statues in the processions had to keep them until the next celebration. Thus, when the Dutch took over, the Elminians kept the relics of the saints and passed them on from generation to generation until the 1880s when

---

[32] Debrunner, *History of Christianity in Ghana*, p. 34.
[33] Ralph Wiltgen, *Gold Coast Mission History 1471–1880* (Techny, IL: Divine Word Publications, 1956), p. 142.
[34] *Ibid.*, p. 143.

the Society of African Missions (SMA) sent Frs Moreau and Murat to West Africa. By then the relics of the saints had become important ritual objects in the custody of Africans who had inherited ritual power from their forebears.

> When a member of Santa Maria died, the body was laid out, three burning candles were placed around it, and a small cross was placed on the person's breast. The statue of Santa Maria was set on a table nearby with a candle burning on either side of it.[35]

The funeral rites contained Christian elements, but they were used to perform and address an indigenous African belief system.

During the ceremony of the naming of a child, the devotees gave a crucifix and a lighted candle to the child involved. Naming ceremonies were practised among the Akan before the arrival of Christians. The inclusion of the crucifix and the candle in the ceremony was not intended to make the child a Christian; rather, it was to reinforce the child's Africanness. Similar deployment of immigrant religious objects to meet indigenous African religious needs was found in a village near Dakar by Fr Godefroy Loyer in 1701. He reported that he saw Africans who 'carried rosaries, recited some Portuguese prayers, and even baptized their own children'. Those Senegalese had no chapel, priest or catechists. The religion they practised was African though it used ritual objects and formulaic expressions and rites that happened to have come from Christianity.

Ntona Buw

The Ntona Buw in Elmina is an indigenous African shrine which contains relics of the statue of St Anthony of Padua, referred to by devotees as 'Nana Ntona' ('nana' being a term of respect for an elder in Akan). Santonafo or Antonifo, like the Santa Mariafo, must have shared in carrying the statue of St Anthony in processions. Hence when the Portuguese left in the seventeenth century, the Africans came to possess the statue. St Anthony was given a shrine and an indigenous priesthood emerged around it. As Wiltgen asserts, 'the once zealous confraternity slipped back into the pagan religious system of their countrymen who had never been baptized. But the shrine and the statue remained'.[36] With a new priesthood and a new shrine which was an amalgam of indigenous elements and the powerful St Anthony (a foreign spirit), the local deity Benja and his priests were eclipsed in power and importance.

---

[35] *Ibid.*
[36] *Ibid.*, p. 149.

The statue was washed annually before processions. The water used was believed to have special powers so it was sprinkled over parts of the town during the night to ward off bad spirits and to bring blessings. The priest and the devotees established an annual festival called Kotobum Kese, no longer on 13 June — the saint's feast. The celebration coincided with the planting season for peanuts because Nana Ntona is believed to be a rain-giver. When Elmina experienced drought, the people of Elmina made sacrifices to Nana Ntona and tradition had it that 'the priest hardly completed his prayers when the rain began coming down on him in torrents'.[37]

Devotion to Nana Ntona also took on political significance. The first sacred act the Elmina chiefs did after they had taken a ceremonial bath, before dawn at the time of their enthronement, was to pay a ceremonial visit to the shrine of Nana Ntona. Ntona's temple was also an asylum, so people who reached the 'priesthood's courtyard found a safe haven if they were fleeing danger or the consequences of an offense/crime'.[38] As we have discussed, the cult of St Anthony had roots in the earlier Portuguese era. However, from after 1637, until the arrival of the SMA in 1880, 'what once had been Catholic ceremonial was now completely absorbed into village fertility rites, initiation rites, and other ceremonial under the direction of the fetish priest'.[39] Santa Mariafo and Antonafo are telling examples of how Africans took hold of Christianity and reworked it to become an indigenous African religion with a new priesthood and practice that played a critical political role. Ntona Buw, for instance, overcame the significance of other indigenous cults and became a rain-giver for the Elminians. The institution that underpins Santa Mariafo and Antonafo had established its own policy, belief and practice. Africanness had been asserted not by integrating African elements into a foreign religion and labeling the result Christian or Muslim, but rather in the birth of an indigenous African religion. 'Fetish priests' had absorbed Catholic ceremonial into village fertility rites.[40]

Altered roles and identities

Mention should be made of identities and roles that have changed as a result of the interactions between religions in the same community. For

37 *Ibid.*, p. 150.
38 *Ibid.*
39 *Ibid.*, p. 152.
40 *Ibid.*, p. 150.

instance, the Hausa language of traders from Nigeria and other parts of northern Ghana has been worked into Qur'anic recitals and prayers in Islamic schools (Makarantas or Madrasas).[41] With state formation around some of the places that used to be acephalous societies, indigenous land priests (*tendaana kasa weliwura*) have lost some of their influence and prestige. For example, we can look to the 'diguit' who, among the Mandingo, were called 'master of the land'. In their society, the status of many members changed with the emergence of new political institutions and leadership. Chiefs and kings with their new political authority subordinated priests. Hence the latter played only a ritual role and are no longer viewed as the custodians of the land. With the emergence of chieftancy among the LoDagaa of northern Ghana, however, the Tallensi *na'am* (chief) and the *tendaana* share complementary roles in the politico-ritual domain. Thus under conditions of social change the status of indigenous religious specialists sometimes increased, or decreased, and at other times co-existed with other leaders in the community.

Muslims who spread their religion in upper Niger and other parts of West Africa were traders, manufacturers of charms and amulets, clerics and arbitrators. People sought advice from such Muslims because they believed them to possess fairness, integrity and knowledge of the occult. Both Haynes[42] and Ryan maintain that the mixing of Islam and African religions marked the early part of the African acceptance of new religions. This stage, according to them, was marked by the magical and ritual aspects of the professed religion. In different areas, Brenner[43] has addressed the dynamic relationship between African religions and Islam. He points out that the divination practice of '*khatt ar-ram*' (sand writing), which entails the diviner making marks in sand smoothed on a tray, was used by Muslim diviners in the court of Abomey (Dahomey) in the eighteenth century. Brenner further states that different forms of geomancy in non-Muslim communities in Mali are the result of *khatt ar-ram*. In Mali, a form of such geomancy is called *dion souttoun*. Aspects of Ifa divination in Nigeria, according to Brenner, reflect some influence of the classical Muslim practice of *khatt ar-ram*. Ritual practices found among some Muslim diviners did not enter non-Muslim practices, but West African religious specialists reworked those elements into their indigenous religions. Such religious borrowing points to the critical role of African agency in pre-colonial times.

[41] G. K. Nukunya, *Tradition and Change in Ghana* (Accra: Ghana Universities Press, 1992), p. 134.
[42] Jeff Haynes, *Religion and Politics in Africa* (London: Zed Books, 1996).
[43] Louis Brenner, 'Histories of Religion in Africa', *Journal of Religion in Africa* 30 (2) (2000), p. 157.

Pashington Obeng

Changes within indigenous religious concepts and religious entities

An important aspect of the dynamic nature of indigenous religions and their deities is manifested in how the practitioners draw on their environment, socio-cultural forces and notions of self to construct concepts of divinity and religious faith and practice. This section addresses the intertwining relations between African understanding of power, success and order, and the evolution of concepts of divinity.

Following the tradition of neo-Durkheimians like Mary Douglas in her *Natural Symbols: Explorations in Cosmology* (1973), Karin Barber argues that the Yorubas' ideas about their orisas' power is sustained and 'augmented by human attention'.[44] According to Barber, the Yoruba live in a society where an individual's power depends on the attention given to him or her by others in that society. When chiefly titles and ranks are the order by which people establish themselves, they can accentuate their power by recruiting those who can support and acknowledge that power. By extension, an orisa's power and influence are tied to the attention that many wealthy and influential devotees give to such orisa. Finally, Barber points out that there is a correlation between the power of the devotee and that of the deity. Thus, when the worshipper chooses a deity, that worshipper 'throws' her whole self into the service of the deity 'for she knows that enhancing its power is ultimately to her own benefit'. Although Barber's neo-Durkheimian approach is partly accurate, the disempowered in Yoruba society could turn to the orisa as sources of power, where such powerless devotees renew their strength, be it political or spiritual. Thus the Yoruba conception of power is implicated in their understanding of the power of their orisas.

Greene's discussion seems to follow Barber's approach, where she shows the necessary connection between human affairs and concepts of the Supreme Being. Greene contends that African conceptualizations about the Supreme Being are dynamic and thus shaped by the power relations and politics of communities in which such ideas function. She examines the problem of how conceptions of the Supreme Being can change over time in the same society, whereby that religious entity can be regarded as a lesser deity elevated to the level of a Supreme

[44] Karin Barber, 'How Man Makes God in West Africa: Yoruba Attitudes Towards the Orisa', *Journal of Religion in Africa* 51 (3) (1981), p. 274.

159

Being.[45] Greene illustrates this with the changing status and role of Mawu, a deity of Adja origin along the Slave Coast of West Africa, conceptualized either as a Supreme Being or as a lesser deity.

A society's religious knowledge is sometimes deployed by its leaders to legitimize their status. For instance, between 1740 and 1774, the Dahomean king Tegbesu is said to have drawn on his people's religious knowledge that Mawu created order in the world, and implicated such religious ideas in the Dahomey polity to legitimize his authority. In Dahomey, Nana Buluku, who was the Supreme Being, was replaced by Mawu, a deity borrowed from Whydah through economic interaction.[46] When Mawu was introduced into Dahomey, the attributes which were of a lesser deity became elevated to the status of a Supreme Being. Nana Buluku was superseded by Mawu and became the parent of all gods and controller of the universe.

Farther to the west among the Anlo-Ewe, Greene reports that Mawu was a powerful deity and the author of life, whose home was Notsie in Central Togo.[47] This Supreme Deity was cosmologically and geographically distant, hence no sacrifices were offered to it, as was the case with lesser divinities. Therefore, conceptualizations of the Supreme Being were intertwined with and mutually shaped by ideas and powers of lesser deities and the daily changing politics and economics of the communities. West Africans may conceptualize a divinity as a Supreme Being but there are differential emphases on the being's involvement in 'the work of origination'.[48] For instance, Ryan argues that the Akan Onyame (Onyankopong) is perceived as being more active in primordial creative acts than the Yoruba Olodumare (Olorun). Ryan's point underscores the fact that concepts of the Supreme Being also had varied attributes according to the society's values, history and polity.

Another manifestation of fluidity in the construction of religious ideas and spiritual beings is related to Mami Wata, the West African water divinity. Water divinities symbolize the merging of the spirit world and the material sphere. Such bridging of worlds has taken varying forms in shaping Mami Wata before the twentieth century. Water divinities' adaptability is expressed by Wicker as follows:

[45] Sandra Greene, 'Religion, History and the Supreme Gods of Africa: a Contribution to the Debate', *Journal of Religion in Africa* 26 (2) (1996), pp. 122–38.

[46] Robin Law, *The Slave Coast of West Africa 1550–1750* (Oxford: Clarendon Press, 1991), pp. 44–56.

[47] Greene, 'Religion, History and the Supreme Gods of Africa', p. 133.

[48] Patrick Ryan, '"Anse O God!" The Problems of "Gods in West Africa",' *Journal of Religion in Africa* 11 (3) (1980), p. 169.

They are characterized by shifting dispositions, genders and representations. This dispositional fluidity is probably why many Africans have an ambivalent attitude towards these divinities and spirits. They are, on one hand, considered beneficent providers of the bounty associated with water, especially fish, but more generally with riches of all kinds: knowledge of healing herbs, spiritual wisdom, creative inspiration, children, beauty in women, gold and gems, success in business. Conversely, they are also capricious spirits who, if offended, could cause disasters by drowning people who are attracted to water, capsizing their boats, rendering them childless or driving them mad.

The ambiguous nature of water divinities is reflected also in their gender identities and representations. Originally hermaphroditic, they are now more commonly portrayed as male-female pairs. They attract devotees of the same or of the opposite sex. They also assume a number of different nonhuman forms, including the rainbow, python, crocodiles, snakes and fish. The major symbolic value of water divinities and their representations in African cultures is to express the possibility of bridging worlds. Water divinities demonstrate by their very nature the intimate connection between the divine, the human, and the natural worlds.[49]

During the encounters between European merchants and Africans from the sixteenth century to the end of the nineteenth century, Africans fashioned hybridized forms of water mermaid/men called Mami Wata. This hybrid reflected the incorporation of West African water divinities into the half-human, half-fish European creatures.[50] No matter what form it took, the power of Mami Wata as a water divinity, was created, recreated and used to define, order and re-orient the lives of Africans both in Africa and among dispersed Africans.

Conclusion

This discussion has sought to shed light on ways in which religious interactions do not always produce hybridized forms that privilege immigrant religions. Indigenous African religions did, and continue to, undergo changes that are articulated in new religious practices, concepts and roles. In pre-colonial West Africa, the non-African religions were Islam and Christianity, which brought their personnel, values, institutions, faith and practice to 'missionize' Africans. As African indigenous religions spread, they borrowed from other resident religions and from those immigrant religions which, in turn, were themselves missionized at times. In other cases, indigenous African

---

[49] Kathleen O'Brien Wicker, 'Mami Wata in African Religion and Spirituality', in Jacob P. Olupona (ed.), *African Spirituality: Forms, Meanings, and Expressions* (New York: Crossroad, 2000), p.198.

[50] Gwen Benwell and Arthur Waugh, *Sea Enchantress: The Tale of the Mermaid and her Kin* (London: Hutchinson, 1961), pp. 51–85.

religious ways of life were borrowed by Islam and Christianity to 'missionize' Africans. Also during such religious, cultural and social encounters, new religions and religious institutions and offices emerged that did not exist prior to the interactions. The religious and social constructs and reconceptualizations of deities and their power that occur to address people's needs are part of the cultural and political reformulations that have been critical to the religious history of West Africa.

Recommended Reading

Brenner, Louis (2000) 'Histories of Religion in Africa', *Journal of Religion in Africa* 30 (2), pp. 143–67.

Blakely, Thomas D. et al. (eds) (1994) *Religion in Africa* (Portsmouth, NH: Heinemann).

Fisher, R. R. (1998) *West African Religious Traditions: Focus on the Akan of Ghana* (Maryknoll, NY: Orbis Books).

Greene, Sandra (1996) 'Religion, History, and the Supreme Gods of Africa: A Contribution to the Debate', *Journal of Religion in Africa* 26(2), pp. 122–38.

Haynes, Jeff (1996) *Religion and Politics in Africa* (London: Zed Books).

Horton, R. (1971) 'African Conversion', *Africa* 41 (2), pp. 85–108.

Levtzion, Nehemia and Randall Pouwells (eds) (2000) *The History of Islam in Africa* (Athens, OH: Ohio University Press; Oxford: James Currey).

Nukunya, G. K. (1992) *Tradition and Change in Ghana* (Accra: Ghana Universities Press).

Olupona, Jacob (ed.) (1991) *African Traditional Religions in Contemporary Society* (New York: Paragon House).

—— (ed.) (2000) *African Spirituality: Forms, Meanings, and Expressions* (New York: Crossroad).

Opoku, Asare A. (1978) *West African Traditional Religion* (Accra: FEP).

Peel, J. D. Y. (2000) *Religious Encounter and the Making of the Yoruba* (Bloomington, IN: Indiana University Press).

Ryan, Patrick (1980) '"Anse O God!' The Problems of "Gods in West Africa"', *Journal of Religion in Africa* 11(3), pp. 161–71.

Sanneh, Lamine (1983) *West African Christianity: the Religious Impact* (Maryknoll, NY: Orbis).

Turner, H. W. (1979) *Religious Innovation in Africa: Collected Essays on New Religious Movement* (Boston, MA: GK Hall & Co.).

Wiltgen, Ralph (1956) *Gold Coast Mission History 1471–1880* (Techny, IL: Divine Word Publications).

8

Poverty in Pre-Colonial & Colonial West Africa
Perception, Causes & Alleviation

OGBU U. KALU

Introduction

A number of concerns inform this reflection. The first concern is the apparent failure of West African states to respond adequately to the scourge of poverty that is ravaging the region harshly and unrelentingly. The increasing pauperization of communities constitutes the biggest challenge for the Economic Community of West African States (ECOWAS). Poverty also inhibits forms of cultural production and destroys the image of the region's populace. A historical approach may perhaps disclose the roots of the present dilemma in the structural faults of the past. Second, poverty alleviation schemes tend to emerge from the top of political hierarchies. There is a need to comprehend how communities understand the meaning of poverty and endeavor to combat its effects. This is a historical reconstruction that moves beyond the political arena to reconstruct the lives of common people. Third, and further informing this reflection, is a heightened awareness of the contribution of indigenous knowledge in response to modern social problems. This is an attempt to define poverty and wealth from an indigenous African perspective, and to examine how communities mitigated what they perceived as poverty. It uses language as an entry into indigenous thought and knowledge of these processes. It then examines how poverty was understood and combated through indigenous social and economic processes.

The emergence of the colonial project created a new type of poverty that was not conjunctural, but structural; the colonial political economy subjugated and eroded African social and economic structures, while racial prejudice held local knowledge in disdain.[1] The complexity of the colonial period was caused by the weaving of three cultures: the indigenous, the colonial Western culture and an emergent hybrid form that emerged from African appropriation and reinvention of the Western culture. This chapter explains the delayed colonial response — state, mission, and secular — to African poverty. The responses of these bodies would alter understandings of poverty in new ways. This method also enables the search for new insights into intractable contemporary problems from the debris of ancient theories of knowledge.

Some African leaders adopted this theory of ancient knowledge in their quest for new strategies of development in the early post-colonial period. For instance, the ideology of African socialism was an effort to harness the resources of indigenous knowledge for new solutions. As Julius Nyerere argued, in African indigenous culture 'nobody starved, either for food or of human dignity, because he lacked personal wealth; he could depend on the wealth possessed by the community of which he was a member. That was socialism'. Dame Lucy Mair made a similar statement in 1944 when urging that the colonial social welfare policy should center in towns instead of worrying about rural communities. 'There is no problem of delinquency in a village where the authority of chiefs or elders is respected and therefore effective, no unemployment or destitution where everyone draws his living from the land'.[2]

This portrait of indigenous culture may sound romantic and beg the question of whether traditional African societies lacked social and economic stratification. However, African indigenous vision, worldviews, and cultural practices have potential to help provide viable solutions to the current state of poverty that many West Africans endure. What manner of social ethics and resource allocation prevented or alleviated the scourge of abject levels of poverty in West Africa's past?

Nyerere did more: he rooted Africa's modern faces of poverty in the colonial experience and alleged that alleviation strategies, dubbed as development projects, had failed; that there was a need for a radical

---

[1] Structural poverty is a permanent or long-term condition, which exists due to personal or social circumstances. Conjunctural poverty refers to temporary poverty resulting from a specific political or environmental crisis such as war or famine. John Iliffe maintains that structural poverty has changed little in Africa, even with the introduction of colonialism, whereas the nature of conjunctural poverty altered greatly during the twentieth century and in fact merged with structural poverty. See John Iliffe, *The African Poor: A History* (Cambridge: Cambridge University Press, 1987).

[2] Julius K. Nyerere, 'Ujamaa: the basis of African Socialism', in *Freedom and Unity, Uhuru na umoja: a selection from writings and speeches, 1952–65* (London, Nairobi, Dar es Salaam: Oxford University Press, 1966), p. 164; Lucy P. Mair, *Welfare in the British Colonies* (London: Royal Institute of International Affairs, 1944), pp. 109–10.

paradigm shift. Scholars have followed him to draw a connection between colonialism and poverty. It is admitted that the colonial phase was a short timeframe in the lives of many communities, extending through less than a lifetime, but its transformative impact was tremendous as it reshaped the socio-economic, political, religious and moral foundations of communities. For example, as Falola and Ahazuem would argue, using the underdevelopment model, the colonial project exploited and transformed Nigerian peasants into producers of raw materials for the benefit of Lebanese traders and European exporters. This commercialization of agriculture partially explains the sudden increase in poverty. Onimode specified how the production of cash crops incorporated the rural peasants into the imperial economy and diminished their food security.[3]

Within this perspective, a revisit to the world of ordinary West Africans living during colonial times might provide clues about the changing faces of poverty, specifically the perception, causes and alleviation strategies that were attempted in the past. The question could be raised as to whether these strategies hold any insights for today's impoverished communities. They may fare better in assisting Africans, however, given that the definitions of poverty and alleviation strategies implemented today derive from Western communities that operate from an Enlightenment worldview. Could it be that the wrong medicine is being dispensed to people who diagnose their maladies differently? To put the matter in another way: do World Bank technocrats and the average West African understand poverty in the same way? When Britain and France partitioned West Africa, was there a shared perception of poverty and its alleviation in their so-called development projects? In brief, the dilemma of poverty in West Africa arises from external prescriptions, marginalized indigenous knowledge and failed state policies. As Keith Hart points out, analysts of West African political economy and agriculture often gloss over the massive impediments to growth that originate from local and social conditions.[4]

The rationale for privileging indigenous knowledge stems from the consideration that, during the colonial era, the West African region was predominantly rural and agricultural, with strong traditional socio-economic, political and religious moorings. However, colonial urbanization and its emergent culture, which Fela Ransome-Kuti

---

[3] Toyin Falola (ed.), *Britain and Nigeria: Exploitation or Development?* (London: Zed Press, 1987), pp. 80–90; B. Onimode, *Imperialism and Underdevelopment in Nigeria: The Dialectics of Mass Poverty* (London: Zed Press, 1982).

[4] Keith Hart, *The Political Economy of West African Agriculture* (Cambridge: Cambridge University Press, 1982).

dubbed as 'shakara culture' (neither traditional nor Western) brought to the attention of the new rulers the disparaging neglect of the rural areas. This captured the imagination of West African novelists such as Chinua Achebe, Wole Soyinka, Kofi Awonoor, Mongo Beti, Sembene Ousmane and others.

To reconstruct the perception of poverty and its alleviation, case studies of certain rural communities will be examined. It is important to note that, though certain aspects of worldviews are shared among West Africans, vast ecological and therefore cultural differentiations do exist, which range from living in tropical forests to savanna to mangroves. The core of the argument of this chapter is that poverty is as much a cultural fact as it is economic, and its meaning is embedded in language and culture. Culture itself emerges from the interaction between people and their environment, particularly in the face of certain ecological challenges. Culture is not heuristic but is produced as communities seek out a sustainable existence from the ecosystem they inhabit. A meaningful discussion of poverty must be specific with regard to cultural context. The faces of poverty varied from the savanna mosaic zone of West Africa to the forested south of the Atlantic littoral. An example from the Igbo of southeastern Nigeria will be used to deal with the language of poverty and the social mores of wealth, but other regions will also be explored.

The language of poverty: perceptions and causes

Language is more than the outer skin of cultures; it reveals their heartbeat. Even when Europeans ruled, African people expressed their understanding of the increasing levels of poverty in their indigenous vernaculars which disclosed the meaning and typology of poor conditions. Explanations of causes and strategies for alleviation took root in the meaning and typology. For instance, the Hausa have incorporated into their language the *matsiyat* (destitutes), *kutare* (lepers), *guragu* (cripples), *makafi* (blind), *kusanti* (deformed), *mahankata* (mentally ill), and *talakawa* (poor people). Each word indicates varying indigenous perceptions of social conditions, providing a composite picture. From the worldview of a particular culture, it may mean that a beggar acting from an ideological mandate may actually be an ascetic, rather than a poor, man. Thus, studies of poverty lack consensus about its meaning because of varied cultural perceptions. Whose reality is to be used? What level of deprivation could be perceived as subsistence insecurity? Other factors further complicate this problem. First, there is the *spatial factor* because of the differences between urban and rural contexts. Though urbanism preceded the colonial period, the new urban centers that emerged during and after colonialism created a new face of poverty. Secondly, the *time factor* emphasizes that the 'hunger gap', which occurs in African societies between the planting season and harvest time, is not perceived as poverty among indigenous people. For instance, a survey team working among the Massa and Mussey — two savanna populations of northern Cameroon and Chad that are spread along the Logone River south of N'jamena — found that the people perceive the food shortage that occurs in this period as a 'normal' period of hunger, or *mayra*. It neither elicits panic nor limits consumption or the level of hospitality required by custom. Such a *conjunctural* or *relative* type of poverty differs from *structural* types that bite more deeply into the roots of a community's life, threatening food security and health-care systems.[5] Moreover, most studies tend to approach poverty as an economic fact rather than a moral, ethical matter. In using static numerical indices, they miss the historical perspective that recognizes societies as living, evolving structures whose internal contradictions continuously produce new forms and perceptions of poverty and wealth.

The argument here is that a viable analysis should explore indigenous language and knowledge in order to interrogate poverty from strong cultural and historical perspectives. Jan Vansina and other scholars have urged the value of deploying comparative linguistics as a means of recovering the past because of the 'special property of words as joiners of form and meaning'.[6] Vocabulary concerning a certain subject matter will enable a reconstruction of the social systems that communities employed in negotiating continuities amidst the invasion of change agents. These systems constitute valuable cultural capital for contemporary struggles. The social structures through which communities met change agents were more resilient than colonial propagandists would acknowledge. Typology and periodization are, therefore, essential in understanding poverty.

---

[5] Igor de Garine, 'Seasonal food shortage, famine and socio-economic change among the Massa and Mussey of Northern Cameroon', in Hans G. Bohle (ed.), *Famine and Food Security in Africa and Asia: Indigenous Response and External Intervention to Avoid Hunger*, vol. 15 (Bayreuth: Naturwissenschaftliche Gesellschaft Bayreuth, 1991), pp. 83–99.

[6] Jan Vansina, *Paths in the Rainforests: Toward a History of Political Tradition in Equatorial Africa* (Madison, WI: University of Wisconsin Press; London: James Currey, 1990), p. 11; J. Fairhead and M. Leach, *Misreading the African Landscape: Society and Ecology in a Forest-Savanna Mosaic* (Cambridge: Cambridge University Press, 1996); D. L. Schoenbrun, *A Green Place, A Good Place: Agrarian Change, Gender, and Social Identity in the Great Lakes Region to the Fifteenth Century* (Portsmouth, NH: Heinemann; Oxford: James Currey, 1998).

Case study: poverty in Igbo language and culture

As an example, in the language of the Igbo in southern Nigeria, persistent lack of material things is denoted as *ubiam*. However, when taking cultural perspectives into account, this word may in fact mean that a person does not produce enough to exchange for other things that he may need. The person may have some things but needs other resources to fulfil social obligations. The deficit model in Igbo culture operates by emphasizing lack and need. *Ubiam* refers to conjunctural poverty. A more sustained structural, or generic, lack is denoted as *ogbenye*. A very acute form of poverty is the inability to feed oneself. This is described as a condition where one's mouth is covered with ashes, *ogbenye onu ntu*. Why ashes? Perhaps the person does not have enough firewood and must continue to blow into the hearth to keep the little fire aflame. For a man, being designated as *ogbenye onu ntu* may mean that he cannot marry and has to make the cooking fire for himself. It may also refer to the connection between food and the ashes of the hearth, or an expression that the person's teeth have bitten the dust, defeated by harsh circumstances. In sum, *ogbenye* is abject poverty, a structural lack or need.

Ogbenye, however, does not always refer to lack of material things but sometimes includes lack of kinship support, relations, family network and social security. A proverb says that any one who lacks a kinship group would be more likely to lose a legal case: *Onye enwegh ummunna, ikpe mara ya*. This is not for the lack of justice in the community, but an assertion that poverty engenders vulnerability: that a poor person is voiceless. Another proverb, reflected in personal names, asserts that to have a large extended family is to have both wealth and strength just as 'children are wealth'. This is perhaps the source of the anecdote about a missionary, who, when describing to a group of villagers the tortures that the Jews meted out to Jesus, was asked by an old man whether Jesus did not have a kin group. The old man then concluded that if they did not rise up to avenge him, he must have been a bad man! The village folk thus designated what they perceived to be a materially wealthy person as poor, given his lack of kinship ties. Indeed, before the colonial cash nexus predominated, poverty and wealth were conceptualized within the social values of the communities. Indigenous knowledge constructed the family and community as the key determinants of poverty or its absence.

The understanding that wealth and poverty are connected to family and community value systems raises questions about the moral dimensions of individual responsibility and the obligations of the

168

extended family. Implicit is the notion that the socialization process inculcates the knowledge and skills required for sustainable living in a particular ecosystem. Poverty, therefore, goes beyond the lack of material things to include the lack of knowledge and skill that enhance participation in the socio-economic and political life of the community. Poverty is a combination of the lack of material things, knowledge, skill, dignity, sense of well-being, political voice, and a social support system or family. Poverty is the lack of power to be truly human; the lack of the 'moral foundations of abundant life'.[7] It can arise from personal failure, political or environmental factors, or the failure of others to exercise adequate responsibility towards the poor.

Beyond the perception of poverty as relational, the meaning was deduced from the accepted communal value described as *nka na nzere*, long life and dignity. A person who lived with good health and fulfilled social obligations would be perceived as rich, *ogaranya*. Such a dignified person would show *ogaranya* by taking traditional titles to indicate the hierarchy of local prominence. Thus, a scantily clad man with a rope tied around his ankle, a stool in one hand, and an *ofo* stick in the other, may appear to an outsider as a poor man but in fact is an *ozo* titled man, a fully achieved person holding a symbol of his authority. He sits among the judges, endowed with moral transparency. In indigenous societies, institutions, such as the family, age grades and community, confer certain obligations on the individual. In a society oriented towards achievement, primacy is allocated to the performance of these responsibilities. This is dignity, and the pursuit of a dignified living is the path to abundance. Wealth and character are linked.

Failure is perceived as poverty because it diminishes the person; it robs the person of political voice in the market square, among the age grade, and in the gender relations within the society. Concerning the latter, women may taunt the person as *ofeke*, a useless human being, or *okokporo*, a man who is unable to marry a wife. Such a person would be regarded as being less than a man, a mere human being with a scrotum. The person's freedom and basic human rights may be violated by his inability to marry, unless his kin group responds to the challenge and, as a proverb puts it, 'provides the person with a wife and a mat'; in other words, pays the bride price and provides him with shelter. A person is not regarded as poor as long as the kinship system, with its network of extended family remains functional. There are, in common parlance, people standing behind the person.

[7] Laurenti Magesa, *African Traditional Religion: The Moral Foundations of Abundant Life* (Maryknoll, NY: Orbis, 1997).

Within such a value system, there was a great tendency to taunt and label people who failed to achieve social obligations. For instance, if a person could not afford to join secret societies, he would be labeled as *ikpo,* a weakling, and forced to hide indoors with women and children during the ritual curfew. Constraints of space would hinder the exploration of the negative aspects of traditional life, such as oppressive and dehumanizing patterns of power relations, institutionalized injustice, social violence, the politics of exclusion, and cultural mores that engendered fear and vulnerability. For instance, festivals were periods of high consumption that reduced the level of stress. But they also exposed sex, wealth and class differentiations. During festivals, some masquerades set out to humiliate and terrorize the uninitiated. Life in traditional communities was not a romantic revelry. Much to the contrary, certain social control models intimidated the poor, infirm, disabled and the stranger. Yet a tradition of humane living was embedded within a restrictive social control model that employed satirical songs, dances, gossip and peer-group joking relationships, in order to restrain the wealthy from preying on the less fortunate. The accepted ethics of power dictated that festivities must be exercised in moderation.

Poverty and the West African landscape

Other causes of poverty can be connected to subsistence production, modes of food procurement, distribution networks, allocation of wealth, patterns of environmental degradation, demographic pressure, quality of infrastructure, models of socialization or access to knowledge, patterns of coping with psycho-social stress and health-care delivery. The first six of these factors link land, ecology and food security. As James Fairhead and Melissa Leach argue, the tendency in the literature has been to 'misread' how Africans responded to environmental challenges, emphasizing soil degradation, forest loss and vulnerable food security, thereby ignoring the regenerative techniques in traditional agricultural practices. They showed that in the savanna mosaic of West Africa, people staved off hunger by adopting many innovative production practices. Using Kissidougou, Guinea, as an example, they argued that

> . . . shifts in the balance of farming practices with different vegetational effects, have reflected how changes in migration, farm-household structure, marketing conditions and gender relations have come together at different times and in different places. Once such conjunctural history is appreciated, unilineal arguments about people's effects on the environment — including arguments concerning social

breakdown and demographic change—appear theoretically inadequate and misleading. [8]

Fairhead and Leach demonstrate their claims with numerous examples: in Côte d'Ivoire, farmers have developed reforestation techniques; in Ghana, Krobo-speaking farmers developed regenerative technologies that reverse desertification; shifting cultivation, forest fallows, trees and forest crops helped to maintain Togo's forest-savanna mosaic; while Susu farmers of northwestern Sierra Leone have tried to maintain forest thicket fallows and employ intensive grazing and organic matter to enhance their food procurement.

Other factors that alleviate poverty among many communities in West Africa include land tenure or holding patterns and rotational cultivation. Land is held by extended families, an entire community, or by individuals. At the planting season, and after the elders designate what land is to be cultivated, landholders allocate portions of their farms to family members and outsiders, the latter being required to pay fees. The accrued income from the harvest is then shared among family members. A rotational farming or shifting cultivation system ensures that some people's land would be declared fallow for a number of years, while other familial or communal land would be farmed. Bush burning may have harmed soil nutrients but rotation gave respite to arable land and enhanced productivity. Admittedly, there were some African communities that did little to conserve their natural resources by not replanting forests and expecting the gods to replenish the earth.[9]

Another misreading of the landscape suggests that West Africa was saved from a breakdown of food security by the introduction of maize and cassava from overseas. It has been argued that cassava along with maize was introduced from the Americas during the Atlantic slave trade. Cassava became the staple diet of many West Africans, an important buffer during famine and hunger gaps. Among the Ewe of Ghana, for example, the name of cassava means, 'there is life'. However, yam, the major agricultural product of the region, has grown wild in West Africa for millennia in both toxic and non-toxic varieties. The yam belt runs from Côte d'Ivoire in the west to Cameroon in the east. Studies abound with regard to the origin of these crops and their import for food security throughout the region.[10] These studies contest the following assumptions: that poverty was endemic to the African

[8] Fairhead and Leach, *Misreading the African Landscape*, pp. 288–9.
[9] Ogbu U. Kalu, 'The Gods Are To Blame: Religion, Worldview and Light Ecological Footprints in Africa', *Africana Marbugensia* (University of Marburg), 32 (1/2) (1999), pp. 3–26.
[10] See P. J. Ucko and G. W. Dimbley (eds), *The Domestication and Exploitation of Plants and Animals* (London: Duckworth, 1969), pp. 419–21.

context because of the threatened ecological balance in tropical temperatures; that shifting agriculture demanded an immense amount of land that could not be sustained in the face of population explosion; that tropical diseases affected animal production and protein intake; that subsistence production limited the required surplus for responding to natural disasters and increased food demand; and that many communities had thin, infertile soil.[11]

Rebuttals abound because these negative assertions do not describe specific contexts and historical periods. One example comes from Senoufo in southern Mali. A study shows how climatic changes (variability of rainfall), soil structure and official agrarian policies challenged food security. However, the communities fought back through shifting cultivation that privileged maize, exploited the diversity of local food crops, deployed a broad spectrum of labor organization based on extended family production units (*senyon*), individual farming (*jongenni*), and division of labor between males and females. They also turned to mixed cropping, agro-forestry and other supplementary income sources such as hunting and raising poultry.[12] The resilience of this community is instructive.

Subsistence agriculture served until other external change agents degraded the environment, encroached on arable land and changed the mode of production. There was no lack of technological inventions, which developed over time: large hoes for cultivating heavy soils, new forms of traps for hunting, nets for fishing, and creative devices for the preservation of crops. The agricultural cycle followed the contours of the natural seasons. Inaccessibility to land and labor did indeed cause poverty but this seemed to have occurred when natural disasters (drought and flood), war and infirmity reduced an individual's capacity to farm. Inter-group tensions sometimes resulted in wars, which in turn disrupted trade and exchange systems. Wars could result in conjunctural poverty and often caused children and wives to become orphans and widows. Attitudes towards orphans and widows were embedded in social norms, which shaped societal responses to the material needs of widows and orphans. Meanwhile, age grades and a number of social control mechanisms were employed to maintain the infrastructure of the community.

---

[11] Robert W. July, *A History of the African People* (New York: Charles Scribner, 1970), p. 570.

[12] Thomas Krings, 'Indigenous Agricultural Development and Strategies for Coping with Famine: The Case of Senoufo, Southern Mali', in Bohle (ed.), *Famine and Food Security in Africa and Asia*, pp. 69–81.

Ogbu U. Kalu

Poverty and social norms in indigenous West African communities

On this point, John Iliffe's canvas about orphans needs to be repainted.[13] Some West African communities tended to fear orphaned children whose parents died of illnesses or inexplicable diseases. Among the communities of southern Nigeria, this fear arose from the belief that some children came from the spirit world to haunt parents. It was believed that the orphans made a pact either to die early or to kill any parents who would obstruct their design. The Yoruba called them *abiku*, and the Igbo referred to such children as *ogbanje*. People dreaded orphans who lost both parents. Similarly, twins were considered unnatural and, in the patriarchal ideology, the mothers were the ones ostracized with the children. Thus, certain social norms created poverty.

At the root of poverty in indigenous communities was a combination of individual failure and power relations. Until the colonial project changed the economic structure, patriarchy engendered the feminization of poverty. This is the intriguing argument in D. U. Iyam's *Broken Hoe*, which reconstructs the social history and cultural reconfiguration in Biase in southeastern Nigeria.[14] An illustration is the treatment of widows. Widowhood practices have generated much literature as a part of resurgent gender studies. Responses to widows differed in many culture areas. They were either looked after by their original families or children, or remarried within the husband's family in a levirate ritual. A widow without children was buried in her natal home. The threat to a widow was the tendency of the husband's relations to treat her as if she had killed her husband by witchcraft, and to seize the property of the deceased man. When indigenous family ties weakened, the fate of the widow became more harrowing. In polygenous contexts, many widows were left to fend for themselves unless they were protected by their children.

Other social norms caused poverty as well, including domestic slavery that arose from war, outright sale of slaves, or pawning. A family may pawn a member as collateral for a debt. Slave status conferred a stigma that continued through the generations, and it evoked discrimination and denial of the means of production, social status, human rights and political freedom. Another type of servitude with a religious undertone

[13] John Iliffe, *The African Poor*, pp. 88–94.
[14] D. U. Iyam, *Broken Hoe: Cultural Reconfiguration in Biase, Southern Nigeria* (Chicago: Chicago University Press, 1995), pp. 2–7.

was the caste system consisting of people who were sacrificed to deities. Male caste members served in the precincts of the shrine and female members functioned as temple prostitutes. People from this caste did not marry and they ceased to belong to any families. There are many more examples that show how poverty could be caused by ecological, economic, social, and religious norms.

In a worldview that was suffused with religion and where socio-economic and political processes were sacralized, religious causes for poverty were paramount. Indeed, it was believed that the failure of individuals to produce and reproduce could come from curses, ancestral spirits, witchcraft and sorcery. An unstable woman would be declared as being troubled by a marine spirit. Diviners would try to liberate the hapless one; often they would declare that the woman was married to a spirit husband residing in the water and that she would need to be divorced before she could function normally in the human world. They would demand an expensive catalogue of sacrificial items that deepened the poverty of the votary. Barrenness was a serious matter, because it contested a core value, which was to preserve one's name: 'may my name not be lost'. Other religious sources of poverty include the destiny of a person who is controlled by a demon. Sometimes, the co-operation between the individual and this spirit force, which causes achievement or failure, would be embodied in a figurine to which the individual offered sacrifices. A proverb says that a poor person's personal god eats only kolanut, while a rich man's god eats chicken. The quality of one's moral life was important because those who offended their ancestors might find their life paths blocked. Hateful neighbors might use sorcery to cause ill health or even death. Causality was always explained by an appeal to spiritual sources. This is why the levels of witchcraft accusations revealed the degree of social disharmony.

When the level of such deaths increased, the chiefs would invite a strong medicine man from a neighboring village to dispense detection potions that would ferret out sorcerers. At other times, litigating individuals made pilgrimage to powerful oracular deities for arbitration. For instance, at the turn of the nineteenth century, the Aro slave traders in the Cross River basin established a fake arbitration divinity, *Ibin Ukpabi*, that the British colonial officers referred to as *Long Juju*. The Aro traders sold the votaries into slavery by pretending that the deity had 'eaten' the culprits. The colonial officers' intensive efforts to destroy the groves of the Long Juju between 1912 and 1925 failed.[15]

---

[15] Ogbu U. Kalu, 'Missionaries, Colonial Government and Secret Societies in South Eastern Igboland', *Journal of the Historical Society of Nigeria* 9 (1) (1977), pp. 75–90.

Certain inexplicable diseases such as smallpox and leprosy evoked ostracism from the frightened communities who acted in self-preservation and from an ideology that placed primacy on group survival over that of the individual. Leprosy was dreaded as an infectious disease caused by the spirits and poisoning. Extended family structures proved incapable of responding to the challenge that leprosy brought to communities. Gradually, leprosy communities sprouted in the forests and the number of such clusters in Igboland left the impression of a dreadful level of poverty in the hinterland.[16] New diseases came into West Africa following the influenza epidemic in the interwar years to exacerbate this source of poverty.

In his poverty register, which is derived from missionary records, Iliffe shows that infirmity was a major cause of poverty. This may lead to a discussion on health and health-care delivery in colonial West Africa. Suffice it to say that traditional methods remained dominant in the colonial era, especially in rural areas. The limitations of traditional methods made health issues major concerns which were manifested in taboos, as well as in cultic and herbal practices. Health was a major concern in traditional religions, and therapy was diagnosed through divination and incantation. The register of therapeutic practices included herbalism, massage, hydrotherapy, pasting, blood letting or cupping, heat treatment and faith healing. Health was perceived both as the absence of disease and as the peace existing between the human, spirit and natural worlds. Dissonance within this three-dimensional perception of reality might trigger ill-health, both physical and psychological. Indeed, certain features of indigenous life raise moral questions about people's sensitivity to the suffering of others. The ridicule and harsh responses to people who were mad, deformed, or suffering from elephantiasis or incurable sores (possibly as a result of diabetes) indicate a poor level of sensitivity. These people were the sources of proverbs that indicated the society's abhorrence of weakness.

Early contact with Europeans intensified the formation of towns and exposed certain cultures to a sustained assault on indigenous mores, and created the types of poverty that nineteenth-century missionaries described. For instance, take the incidence of begging. It was more common in the northern sahelian zone where it was sustained by Islamic religious values, but it also carried a stigma in much of West

---

[16] For a study of Presbyterian leprosarial work, see Ogbu U. Kalu, *A Century and Half of Presbyterian Witness in Nigeria, 1846–1996* (Enugu: Presbyterian Church Publication, 1996), pp. 193–219. See also, Stephen Addae, *History of Western Medicine in Ghana, 1880–1960* (Durham: Academic Press, 1996), pp. 8–25.

Africa. Olaudah Equiano declared in the eighteenth century that the Igbo had no beggars, not even ascetic, religious types.[17]

The incidence of slavery intensified as the trans-Atlantic slave trade increased slave raiding and kidnapping in the interior. Abolition of the slave trade created a surplus of slaves in the interior, and the incidence of cultic blood sacrifices increased in the regions that could not utilize this large number of slaves in plantation farming. Indeed, a tradition of absorbing slaves into families began. In many cases, slave villages that had been founded grew rich, and successful farmers were beginning to challenge the master villages by the mid-1920s.[18]

In indigenous communities, poverty was less a matter of material things and more a matter of relationships, dignity, power and moral stability. Poverty alleviation, therefore, involved ritualized stabilization of relationships between the human and the divine. The maintenance of moral order ensured that human activities succeeded and that evil was warded off. Alleviation was not merely achieved by an intensification of human activities, but by first restraining the capacity of negative moral forces to ruin human projects. When moral order was abused, poverty entered the domains of individuals, families and communities, especially when the head of a family indulged in a lifestyle of laziness, drunkenness and sexual immorality.[19]

Community and communal ethos provided a solidarity network proffering rewards and responsibilities. Food security and safety were the responsibilities of the entire community. The elders made the rules for economic activities following communal decision-making processes. People were involved in determining the strategies for ensuring their food security. They understood their ecosystem so well that their proverbs and myths were suffused with images from the world of animals and nature. Two East African political leaders, Nyerere and Kaunda, referred to this communal ethos as the moral foundation of African socialism; Kaunda in particular found resonance in Christian social ethics and, therefore, christened his own political design as Christian humanism. Chinua Achebe's novel *Things Fall Apart* is built around the struggle to adjust indigenous ethics to a new worldview

[17] John Iliffe, 'Poverty in Nineteenth-Century Yorubaland', *Journal of African History* 25 (1984), pp. 43–57. Olaudah Equiano, *The Interesting Narative of the Life of Olaudah Equiano* (Norwich, 1789; repr. Abridged and edited by Paul Edwards, *Equiano's Travels*, London: Heinemann, 1967).

[18] Carolyn Brown, 'Testing the Boundaries of Marginality: Twentieth-Century Slavery and Emancipation Struggle in Nkanu, Northern Igboland, 1920–1929', *Journal of African History* 37 (1) (1997), pp. 51–80. See also Ogbu U. Kalu, *Embattled Gods: Christianization of Igboland, 1841–1991* (Lagos/London: Minaj Publishers, 1996), chapter 5.

[19] See Jean H. Kopytoff, *A Preface to Modern Nigeria* (Madison, WI: University of Wisconsin Press, 1964).

introduced by the colonial project, a worldview that embraced individualism. In that unequal contest, the ancestral barrier that had protected the community gradually fell apart. Other scholars have canvassed a resistance narrative. The jury is still out.

In the nuclear family, the gender factor is paramount, as women's ingenuity could sustain families, especially during the hunger gap. Women gathered firewood, assisted by their daughters; searched for berries and food seasoning from the forest; grew vegetables in farms and gardens; and cultivated root crops such as cassava and coco yams. Here again, the socialization model enabled young people to know their ecology, its resources and challenges, and gain a higher level of sustainability. Those in forest regions taught their young to farm, set traps and hunt. Riverine people ensured rich harvesting techniques of marine resources. Indigenous knowledge is rich with minutiae of surviving strategies in each ecosystem. Apprenticeship served as an instrument for training young people to engage in such technologies.

Alleviation strategies built on consultants' cursory studies, which ignore the rich reservoir of indigenous knowledge of the ecosystem, will inevitably fail. A gendered division of labor existed in communities. Men harvested palm trees, tapped wine and cultivated yams. Some men also engaged in long-distance trade, while women dominated the eight-day markets. Women took responsibility for feeding the entire family. In some villages, if a man collapsed in public because of hunger, his wives would be severely fined and accused of a plan to kill him. However, an economic revolution was in process as women became engaged in the cash-crop economy, giving them more economic power with vast social consequences. Some women became richer than men. The impulse of the womenfolk to produce and reproduce to sustain their families led to the dominant market women of today. Polygyny, once supported by the argument that it provided labor for farms, was attacked; matters worsened when the children went off to school and disdained farm labor. Many anthropological studies have shifted from strident ideological feminism to reconstruct the domestic and market roots of feminine power found in contemporary Africa.[20] Indeed, Lugard, architect of indirect rule in British Africa pointed with respect to the rising power of women when the system that he built was stung by their organized rebellion in 1929. Writing the preface to Sylvia Leith Ross's *African Women*, Lugard rejected the portrait of the invisible woman and contended that the African woman is 'ambitious,

---

[20] Jane L. Parpart (ed.), *Women and Development in Africa* (New York: University of America Press, 1980); Ifi Amadiume, *Reinventing Africa: Matriarchy, Religion and Culture* (London: Zed Press, 1997).

courageous, self-reliant, hardworking and independent . . . she claims full equality with the opposite sex and would seem indeed to be the dominant partner'.[21]

In summary, community, culture and family engendered significant moral principles and served as structural agencies that staved off poverty, except the kinds of poverty caused by natural and spiritual forces. This may suggest that neighborhood associations, village community development agencies and other types of civil societies, whether based on ethnicity or beyond ethnic boundaries, could serve as poverty alleviation agencies because they possess organic roots and bonds that ensure viability. From this perspective, ethnicity, which has been vilified as tribalism and as a dysfunctional force in the modern public space, may have its uses in designing poverty alleviation strategies.[22] The artificial character of non-governmental organizations and impersonal government agencies cause development failure.

The effects of colonial rule: embattled values and new vistas

Colonialism was a system consisting of administrative machinery, a judiciary and an economic order, all sanctified by a monotheistic religion imbued with 'civilized' values. The colonial project sought to entrench a new moral economy in other cultures in order to remodel them into reflections of its own image. It was built on a racial ideology that perceived the Western Enlightenment worldview as truly capable of enlightening 'dark' cultures. It sought to reconfigure both the mindset of its victims and the features of their everyday lives. Much of its character has been subjected to criticism which bears little repetition. Suffice it to say that development failures in contemporary West Africa could be traced to many of the unresolved aspects of colonial hegemony and the clash of worldviews; the failure of poverty alleviation strategies emanates more from privileging the neocolonial models than from a congenital African pathology.

But it must again be stressed that the colonial period was brief in many parts of West Africa, and that hegemony was consolidated amidst African resistance until the First World War. Colonialism never possessed the manpower necessary to create or sustain truly imperial rule. The colonial achievements witnessed during the interwar years

---

[21] 'Foreword' in Sylvia Leith Ross, *African Women: A Study of the Ibo of Nigeria* (London: Routledge, 1939).

[22] The argument has been pursued at greater length in Ogbu U. Kalu, 'Religion, Ethnicity and Development in Africa', in N. Onwu (ed.), *Reforming the Reformed Tradition: African Presbyterianism in the 21st Century* (Enugu: Presbyterian Church Publications, 2001), pp. 54–84.

were overshadowed by the Great Depression and the build-up to the Second World War. The aftermath of that war fuelled political nationalism, as the indigenous African elite voiced opposition to colonial rule and sparked off discussions leading to eventual decolonization. Decolonization was not a passive revolution; that is, the colonial powers did not orchestrate decolonization in anticipation of neocolonialism. African interests and agendas shaped both decolonization and the nature of neocolonialism. This brief periodization of colonialism and decolonization argues that the force and style of the colonial presence oscillated, due to the forces of global geopolitics. Thus, colonial perceptions and responses to poverty varied during the periods between 1900 and 1914, 1914 and 1945, and thereafter.

The greatest 'achievement' of colonialism was its creation of a new socio-economic context that, in turn, created a new face of poverty. Colonialism transformed geography by establishing urban centers. Rural-urban migration and population shifts produced an emergent public and culture that was neither indigenous nor fully Western. Wole Soyinka's *The Interpreters* and Cyprian Ekwensi's *Jagua Nana* give us glimpses into this raucous context. The market economy followed suit, as the growth of urban markets and nascent industrialization lured migrant laborers. Merchant houses and government offices needed clerks. In this period, the definition of urban life went beyond the number of inhabitants to include semi-industrial capitalism, job differentiation and an improved infrastructure.

The colonial powers emphasized the building of roads and railways, as well as the use of waterways. Each project created new towns. The presence of colonial government structures enhanced the status of towns whose space allocation defined new social classes and wealth differentiation. Many towns remained semi-urban. Yet urban slums sprouted because little attention was paid to the crowded neighbor-hoods where the indigenous people lived. Meanwhile, the new economy caused new socio-economic problems such as unemployment, and a new class of labouring poor emerged who earned meager wages. Disruptive consequences followed as the politics of urban penury intensified. In Nigeria, for example, taxes were introduced in 1926 to the consternation of many. Dependence on wages to pay taxes and to sustain one's family replaced reliance on land. Particularly in urban settings, the youth demographic swelled and created problems of delinquency. The Human Development Indices, which evaluate problems concerning water, food, shelter, employment, lack of voice, and loss of dignity, arose from the social and cultural changes induced by the urban situation and new modes of production. Official economic policy focused on agricultural cash crops. In some places, scientific agriculture, a plantation economy, experimental farms and new food crops were introduced. The towns were the centers of exchange, and this export-driven economy fed on rural production and thereby transformed it. Chima Korieh and Olatunji Ojo have researched some aspects of the cash-crop economy and its dire impact on the macroeconomic pattern and on gender relations in colonial Nigeria.[23]

Two major concerns of this chapter are, first, the impact of the colonial economic pull that put pressure on rural subsistence societies and, second, the new social values generated by urban life that threatened pre-colonial social control models without yielding a sustainable alternative. People tried to recreate their village ethics in towns. Village organizations, town unions, community development associations and thrift clubs, all enabled people to thrive in the colonial economy. There are instances where a few people from the same village would form a friendship club based on trust, and would contribute monthly to pool resources to support one of their members financially in a business endeavor. People invented many ways to survive in the new colonial economy.

Despite these strategies, new alluring aspects of city life did create habits that countered village norms: new consumption habits for Western products and disdain for rural ethics crept in. The gathering of people from many cultures and subcultures created a new cultural context − an open society. Education, which was often missionary-driven, became the greatest instrument for attacking indigenous values, and installing a social control system and a colonial counterculture. In every town, people appeared to have attained new freedoms and anonymity. Urban life provided opportunities for the accumulation of wealth without the obligations of helping the poor.

From its inception, colonial ideology was built on replacing the slave trade with legitimate trade. The focus was on the production of cash crops such as cocoa, groundnuts, cotton, palm oil and palm kernel, which served as raw materials for European factories. Every District Officer included a table demonstrating cash-crop production in his reports to the Provincial Commissioner who, in turn, included a longer table in reports to the Lieutenant Governor. The production of cash crops dominated the concern of colonial officers. Local producers sold

---

[23] See Chima J. Korieh, 'State Policy, Agricultural Transformation and Decline in Eastern Nigeria, 1960–1970' and Olatunji Ojo, 'More than Farmers' Wives: Yoruba Women and Cash Crop Production, c. 1920–1957' in Adebayo Oyebade (ed.), *The Transformation of Nigeria* (Lawrenceville, NJ: Africa World Press, 2002), pp. 223–60 and 383–404 respectively.

to middlemen, who made their way through villages or carried their products to markets. In exchange, these middlemen brought European goods such as cloth, helmets, hats, mirrors, guns, swords, machetes, handkerchiefs, ivory bangles, walking sticks and shirts. These articles became the means of wealth and social differentiation among rural peasants. To display their new wealth, the successful women of one particular village performed a dance with mirrors that were framed in carved wood and tied with colorful handkerchiefs. They would flash the mirror in the sun so that the poor people could watch the reflection of the sun with admiration. Social differentiation intensified in the rural sector as consumption habits changed and palates for foreign goods sharpened.

The focus on cash crops diminished the concern for subsistence agriculture, and rural-urban migration drained the labor supply of village communities. Increasingly, some villages lacked able-bodied young people to farm. Some youth insisted on being hired to work for older relations and kindred. Markets also became more important, not only as spaces of exchange but for social occasions as well. Furthermore, the status of women changed in the new economy, as many of them became traders — a transformation which contested the authority of male leaders whose income was diminishing. Men held authority, while women had the power. Educated young people and female traders contested the authority of village elders — some overtly, others covertly. These social and cultural changes, generational opposition, new values and the insertion of a new worldview, all created new forms of poverty and attacked the alleviation strategies, values and agencies that worked in pre-colonial societies.

The new context that the British colonial regime created in particular is important for understanding its responses to poverty. Before 1914, colonial officers showed little concern for poverty. They left the matter to indigenous communities, missionaries and local philanthropists. They believed that indigenous structures and values had the capacity to respond to poverty. When the population of towns continued to grow and the incidence of urban poverty became more critical, the colonial response focused on towns to the neglect of the rural areas. The colonial regime applied conceptions of poverty based on conditions in Britain, and resorted to the solutions of correction institutions. As John Iliffe concluded,

> In British colonies, government made little provision for the poor before the Second World War. Officials believed that African families and communities looked after their needy members and that any supplementary care could best be given by missionaries. Government provided general services: increasing control of famine;

free but limited public health services; legislation against abuses; rudimentary urban sanitation and control of working conditions. District Officers generally had small discretionary funds to relieve distress.[24]

Conditions after the First World War drew attention to the issues of poverty, and the Great Depression exacerbated matters. Even then, poverty was misconceived as it only pertained to the disabled: those who were sick, dying, deaf, blind, leprous, vagrants or physically incapacitated. The missionary strategy was based on the use of charitable institutions and schools as a means of evangelization. Thus, missionary groups competed among themselves to establish industrial institutions for the acquisition of skills: hospitals, dispensaries, primary schools, homes for the destitute, leprosaria and orphanages. They paid much attention to the rescue of twins, the training of girls and care of the sick. In a few cases, missions engaged in creating wealth, such as their role in cocoa production in Western Nigeria and the Basel Trading Company in Ghana and Cameroon. The greatest 'achievement' of missions remained in the field of education. The colonial government aided missionary schools because they produced clerks and health-care workers. Mission education remained at the primary level for a long time in many parts of Nigeria. Only in the 1940s did secondary schools develop due to the initiatives of African entrepreneurs.

At this time, both rival mission bodies and the government joined the affray. Perhaps social Catholicism and the social gospel among Protestants inspired the intervention of missions, but it is certain that rivalry and evangelical strategy determined the pace and direction of alleviation interventions. Some missions achieved more in certain areas than in others. For instance, the Presbyterians and Methodists left indelible imprints on the fight against leprosy. The Salvation Army focused on urban welfare intervention. Roman Catholic leadership in the medical and educational apostolates remains incontrovertible. Increasingly, the government intervened to control the quality, curricula and location of schools. Grants-in-aid, based on reports of education inspectors, became an instrument of pressure.

Secular institutional charity followed the poor laws instituted in Britain. Initially, the government established welfare officers and institutions to handle cases of juvenile delinquency, the disabled (blind, crippled, insane) and beggars. These services remained rudimentary until after the Second World War. The government encouraged indigenous philanthropists to assist. In the mid-1930s, secular charity institutions such as the Red Cross (founded in 1863) gained access to

---

[24] Iliffe, *The African Poor*, p. 200.

the colonies in Kenya, Ghana and Nigeria. Others would follow as late as the 1950s. By this time, the concept of social welfare was challenged because of its narrow purview in urban areas, while the majority of the populace lived in the rural hinterland. It was also felt that intervention should focus on community development. In the late 1950s, eastern Nigeria's mobilization of rural labor for government projects was achieved with a propaganda machine that sent mobile units into villages to show a film entitled 'Planning for Prosperity'. The film showed happy villagers working on new roads, people constructing a rural dispensary, and contented coal miners waving their pickaxes. Meanwhile, predatory sanitary inspectors roamed through village markets collecting bribes from hapless traders.

There was difficulty in integrating welfare practices with indigenous poverty alleviation strategies; official policy and practices remained inchoate. State, religious and secular agencies often moved in different directions. The great irony was that the government recognized the strength of indigenous knowledge and practices, but failed to tap the resources.

Quite disheartening was the failure to link poverty reduction to environmental protection. Industrial development was barely built on wholesome ecological ethics. But the development theory that dominated colonial ideology privileged the exploitation of natural resources for foreign markets and degraded the environment. Aggregate indices computed the wealth of the colonies by their export capacity and consumer potential. The neglect of ecological health was related to racial ideology. The dominant theory in African sociopolitical analysis, dubbed as 'Afro-pessimism', leaves the impression that there is no strategy for African problems that could adequately confront the hardship of poverty: that the lack of leadership, as well as other debilitating factors, has doomed the continent. A shift to a more hopeful model, namely, an African renaissance, enhances a social analysis that sees potential in indigenous knowledge. This model is predicated on the belief that a part of the African problem is rooted in the exploitative ideology and practices of colonialism.[25]

Conclusion

In conclusion, the past has uses for the present. This reflection on the colonial period of West African history shows that post-colonial regimes

[25] See Ogbu U. Kalu, *Power, Poverty and Prayer: The Challenges of Poverty and Pluralism in African Christianity, 1960–1996* (Frankfurt am Main: Peter Lang, 2000), chapters 2 and 3.

in Africa inherited the colonial lack of understanding and concern for the poor and the environment. Modernization theories of the 1960s focused on using Western indices in mapping developmental strategies. The object was to 'catch up' with the West or to repackage the continent in the Western image. Black skins wore white masks. These theories collapsed even before they were implemented. The proto-Marxist 'under-development' theories that followed in the 1970s proved better at criticism than prescription. African nations that turned Marxist watched their economies collapse. In the Cold War, both pro-Western and pro-Eastern nations fell into debt traps. Ideological vanguards turned into dictators, and slogans which catered for the masses rang hollow. Pessimists dominated the 1980s. The second liberation of Africa from dictators in the 1990s was constructed with the promise of democracy following the collapse of Communism. However, this renaissance in the new millennium might be stillborn unless there is renewed respect and appreciation of African indigenous knowledge.

The lessons learned from poverty alleviation strategies during the colonial period are many. African countries must acknowledge the plight of poverty. Sustainable projects must be woven into the contours of communities' ecological, developmental and cultural systems. To tap the salient aspects of indigenous knowledge, there must be an in-depth understanding of the ecological resources of our communities; that is, how the people cope and what factors inhibit or alter these coping mechanisms. This understanding will reclaim the value of culture and ethnicity and mobilize all the resources of the communities, including the power of women and youth. It may require the integrating of central cultural values into alleviation strategies. It will recover the moral dimension of poverty and restore those communal ethics and social control models that created the tradition of humane living. It must be reaffirmed that life is sacred and that poverty is the single force that is eroding the dignity of Africans. Poverty is the source which deprives the African continent of its human resources.

Recommended Reading

Amadiume, Ifi (1997) *Reinventing Africa: Matriarchy, Religion and Culture* (London: Zed Press).

Bohle, Hans G. (ed.) (1991) *Famine and Food Security in Africa and Asia: Indigenous Response and External Intervention to Avoid Hunger*, vol. 15 (Bayreuth: Naturwissenschaftliche Gesellschaft Bayreuth).

Fairhead, James and Melissa Leach (1996) *Misreading the African*

Landscape: Society and Ecology in a Forest-Savanna Mosaic (Cambridge: Cambridge University Press).

Hart, Keith (1982) *The Political Economy of West African Agriculture* (Cambridge: Cambridge University Press).

Iliffe, John (1987) *The African Poor: A History* (Cambridge: Cambridge University Press).

Kalu, Ogbu U. (1999) 'The Gods Are To Blame: Religion, Worldview and Light Ecological Footprints in Africa', *Africana Marbugensia* (University of Marburg), 32 (1/2), pp. 3–26.

—— (1996) *Embattled Gods: Christianization of Igboland, 1841–1991* (Lagos/London: Minaj Publishers).

—— (1977) 'Missionaries, Colonial Government and Secret Societies in South Eastern Igboland,' *Journal of the Historical Society of Nigeria,* 9 (1), pp. 75–90.

—— (2000) *Power, Poverty and Prayer: The Challenges of Poverty and Pluralism in African Christianity, 1960-1996* (Frankfurt am Main: Peter Lang).

Magesa, Laurenti (1997) *African Traditional Religion: The Moral Foundations of Abundant Life* (Maryknoll, NY: Orbis).

9

Disease in West African History[1]

EMMANUEL KWAKU AKYEAMPONG

Introduction

Disease, together with the environment, set some of the important parameters within which West African societies and communities have operated, reflecting the challenges of both settlement and ecology, as well as documenting the history of contact between peoples. The African environment, and especially the tropical rainforests, supports a mass of bacteria and parasites, where even single-celled organisms can flourish. Indeed, for William H. McNeill, the migration of the first Africans from the tropical climes of their homeland — the cradle of humans — to the temperate climes of Europe, marked the beginning of an important developmental divide:

> In leaving tropical environments behind, our ancestors also escaped many of the parasites and disease organisms to which their predecessors and tropical contemporaries were accustomed. Health and vigor improved accordingly, a multiplication of human numbers assumed a hitherto unparalleled scale.[2]

For McNeill, the disease epidemiology of the tropics represents a burden on development:

> That, more than anything else, is why Africa remained backward in the *development of civilization* [emphasis added] when compared to temperate lands (or tropical zones like those of the Americas), where prevailing ecosystems were less elaborated and correspondingly less inimical to simplification by human action.[3]

---

[1] The author is grateful to James Webb Jr, Michael McCormick, Myles Osborne, and Harmony O'Rourke for their comments on an earlier draft of this chapter.
[2] William H. McNeill, *Plagues and Peoples* (New York: Anchor Doubleday, 1997 [1976]), p. 47.
[3] *Ibid.*, p. 67.

186

Defining 'civilization' from the Western perspective has always been a messy business, and the inherent problems in the above statement are apparent. This statement also creates the erroneous impression that the only factor Africans have had to battle with in the quest for their development is the environment, eliding the pivotal role that people — including outsiders — have played in the political economy of Africa. Jared Diamond's *Guns, Germs, and Steel* uses science in a historical context to illuminate the processes of human development from an even starting line, not just to rationalize the contemporary state of affairs by reading back into history.[4] But McNeill was right about the rich biodiversity of the tropics and the presence of disease vectors that have afflicted humans and their livestock.

This chapter reviews the disease environment of West Africa, examining some of the challenges Africans have faced epidemiologically, and the physiological and cultural adaptations and innovations that have enabled them to subsist and prosper in their settled environments. Diseases in Africa include those rooted in the physical environment and others introduced through external contact. Disease or bodily disorders arise from human encounters with parasitic organisms; parasites include bacteria and viruses that are unable to replicate without a host cell (plants and animals). Some parasites require a non-human intermediate host, and they step off other animals, fleas, lice and rodents in their propagation. Diseases such as malaria spread by the anopheles mosquito, trypanosomiasis (sleeping sickness) by the tse tse fly, onchocerciasis (river blindness) by the black simulium fly, and schistosomiasis (bilharzia) by the snail are tropical diseases indigenous to West Africa. Other diseases that afflict humans pass directly from host to host with no intermediary carrier and no delay, and many of these have been introduced to West Africa through cultural contact. Examples of these diseases, such as the common cold, measles, and chicken pox, entered West Africa through Atlantic trade.

This chapter covers the period from medieval times to the present, although its scope prevents detailed coverage of every disease or epidemic. A number of important questions are raised, including the epidemiological impact of the Atlantic trade and colonialism. In present-day Africa, most of the diseases that were present in 1900 have resurfaced, with the notable exception of smallpox. Major environmental changes, such as global warming and changes in land use, have transformed higher and cooler areas in Africa that were previously

---

[4] Jared Diamond, *Guns, Germs, and Steel: The Fates of Human Societies* (New York: W. W. Norton, 1999).

malaria-free into malaria zones. In 2000, malaria, and not AIDS, remained the number-one killer in Africa, accounting for between 20 and 30 per cent mortality in school-age children and for the whole population.[5] New diseases such as HIV/AIDS and Ebola have complicated disease patterns.

This chapter endeavours to shed light on the dismal state of health in contemporary Africa. The author utilizes medieval Arabic sources for medieval West Africa and contemporary European documents for the sixteenth to the nineteenth centuries. His archival research provides an important basis for the discussion of the colonial and post-colonial periods. There is a vast volume of secondary literature on disease in African history, a small proportion of which has been carefully selected and appears in a bibliography at the end of the chapter.

Environment and disease in West Africa

The physical environment of West Africa is a good starting point for examining diseases endemic to the region, and how West African peoples have responded to these diseases. The issue of African therapies and whether these adequately addressed the burden in African disease challenges is an important question that needs to be raised in spite of the absence of substantial evidence to resolve this query.[6]

James Webb in Chapter 2 of this volume has provided a useful review of the physical geography of West Africa, examining rainfall patterns, vegetational zones and the network of major rivers. He discusses how the flora and fauna of West Africa harbored a universe of microparasites that shaped disease epidemiology. Vegetation belts expanded and contracted in response to fluctuations in rainfall, determining the presence of vectors such as the tse tse fly and the incidence of trypanosomiasis. Webb's chapter also reviews early settlement history in West Africa, the impact of climate changes on settlement patterns, and the cultural and linguistic groups that emerged. The prehistory of West Africa is ably examined by Susan McIntosh in Chapter 1 of this volume. Most of the large polities that emerged in West Africa in the early medieval period — Takrur, Ghana, Mali, and Songhai — were located in the sahel belt or the northern savanna. As George Brooks

---

[5] Maureen Malowany, 'Unfinished Agendas: Writing the History of Medicine of Sub-Saharan Africa', *African Affairs* 99 (2000), pp. 325–8.

[6] This is an issue raised in Joseph Inikori, *The Chaining of a Continent* (Mona: University of the West Indies, 1992). See also, Steven Feierman, 'Struggles for Control: The Social Roots of Health and Healing in Modern Africa', *African Studies Review* 28 (2–3) (1985), pp. 105–110.

has highlighted, these polities all emerged during more favourable climatic periods.[7]

J. H. Greenberg classified most of the languages of West Africa as falling under the Niger-Congo group of languages, with the exception of Hausa, an Afroasiatic language. Linguists have accepted Greenberg's classification of African languages as a useful tool. But one may further divide the Niger-Congo group in West Africa into the West Atlantic (for example, Jolof, Sape), the Mande (for example, Soninke, Mandinka, Fula), the Western Kwa (for example, Akan, Ewe, Ga), and the Eastern Kwa (for example, Yoruba, Igbo). Our historical evidence for the medieval period is particularly strong for the Mande area, which was drawn into the trading and diplomatic networks of the wider Muslim world. We also have good coverage of the coastal communities with European maritime commerce, especially from the sixteenth century.

In addition to commenting on trade conditions, politics, religion and the social norms of the West African places they read and wrote about or visited, Arab chroniclers also included information on the health conditions of the towns and the prevalent diseases or illnesses. Al-Bakri, who died in 1094 CE, in his major work *The Book of Routes and Realms*, provided useful information on health in Ghana. He described Awdaghost, a populous and prosperous town in northern Ghana, as a country 'where the inhabitants have yellow complexions because they suffer from fever and splenitis. There is hardly one who does not complain of one or another'.[8] Here, al-Bakri seems to be describing the symptoms and an effect of malaria: the fevers that characterize the illness and the inflammation of the spleen that results from frequent bouts with malaria. Africa, home to the most virulent form of malaria (*plasmodium falciparum*) carried by the mosquito *Anopheles gambiae*, appears to be the birthplace of malaria. The *Aedes aegypti*, another species of mosquito, is also the vector for yellow fever, a disease that has plagued West Africans and visitors to West Africa for centuries. Al-Bakri added, further:

> The countryside of Ghana is unhealthy and not populous, and it is almost impossible to avoid falling ill there during the time their crops are ripening. There is mortality among strangers at time of the harvest.[9]

Perhaps what al-Bakri is describing here is the abundance of flies during harvests and when crops are ripening, which could then serve as vectors

---

[7] George E. Brooks, 'A Provisional Historical Schema for West Africa based on Seven Climate Periods', *Cahiers d'études Africaines* 26 (1–2) (1986), pp. 43–62.

[8] J. F. P. Hopkins and N. Levtzion (trans. and eds) *Corpus of Early Arabic Sources for West African History* (Cambridge: Cambridge University Press, 1981), p. 68.

[9] *Ibid.*, p. 81.

for diseases, especially of the intestinal variety. The incidence of malaria would also have been higher following the end of the rainy season, when crops would also have been ripening.

Ibn Battuta, who actually visited the empire of Mali from 28 July 1352 to 27 February 1353, described a place along a channel connected to the River Niger in Mali — when he traveled from Timbuktu to Kawkaw — as having 'many mosquitoes and nobody passes there except by night'. This place probably proliferated in pools and puddles, which are fertile breeding places for mosquitoes. (In addition, the fringes of channels, lagoons and slow-moving bodies of water can be prolific breeding places for mosquitoes.) Malians obviously labored under the misapprehension that mosquitoes did not feed at night. Ibn Khaldun in his universal history incorporated information on Mali recorded in 1393–4. He mentioned another enemy of health in Mali, sleeping sickness, the culprit of the death of the thirteenth *mansa* or king of Mali, Mari Jata ibn Mansa Magha (1360–73/4).

> He was stricken by sleeping sickness (*'illat al-nawm*), a disease which often afflicts the inhabitants of that region, particularly the aristocracy. The victim suffers from attacks of sleepiness at all times until he hardly wakes except for short intervals. The disease becomes chronic and the attacks are continuous until he dies. This Jata was afflicted by this disease for two years and died in 775/1373-4.[10]

Sleeping sickness may have been a disease of the aristocracy in Mali because the latter placed a premium on equestrian skills as part of the trappings of power, and tse tse flies are attracted to horses — and their riders. The thirteenth to the fifteenth centuries CE, which witnessed the emergence of the Mali Empire, was a period of progressive desiccation and a southward retreat of the tse tse fly belt. The expansionist activities of Malian horsemen who raided along the southward-moving borders of the savanna-woodland zone may have exposed many to tse tse flies.[11]

West Africans responded to their disease environment by striving to attain ecological balances that kept local diseases at a lower level of endemicity. Folk environmental knowledge promoted the control of vegetation and game, which kept trypanosomiasis and other epidemics and epizootics at bay.[12] Warfare — which intensified with the rise of

---

[10] *Ibid.*, p. 336.

[11] Brooks, 'Provisional Historical Schema', pp. 52–3.

[12] The literature on Eastern, Central and Southern Africa is much stronger in this respect, though mostly for the nineteenth and twentieth centuries. See, for example, John Ford, *The Role of Trypanosomiasis in African Ecology: A Study of the Tsetse Fly Problem* (Oxford: Clarendon Press, 1971); Leroy Vail, 'Ecology and History: The Example of Eastern Zambia', *Journal of Southern African Studies* 3 (2) (1977), pp. 129–55; and James L. Giblin, *The Politics of*

the Atlantic slave trade — destroyed these balances and endemic diseases then became epidemic in various parts of Africa. Genetic or biological modification was another response to the disease environment. The penchant of the *Anopheles gambiae* for cleared spaces in the forest ensured high malaria morbidity and mortality for forest communities in West Africa. As a coping device against the malaria parasite, sickle cell emerged in the gene pool of Kwa forest agriculturalists as early as 700 CE. The Akan of present-day Ghana have sickle cell heterozygotes as high as 30 per cent, reflecting a long period of settlement and genetic adjustment in the forest region.[13]

Atlantic trade and epidemiology in West Africa

The onset of Atlantic trade from the fifteenth century complicated disease patterns in West Africa. European viral diseases such as measles, the common cold, smallpox and rubella, as well as bacterial diseases like tuberculosis and syphilis, spread to the region.[14] The insecurity of the slave trade encouraged West Africans to cluster in denser settlements for protection; ironically, this crowded environment could have increased the infection rates of these diseases, though population requirements differ for different diseases. Klein highlights how the Akan responded to increased mortality rates with a cultural emphasis on female fertility and the celebration of fertile mothers with several living children. The Akan also imported large numbers of slaves to balance the demographic consequences of a hostile disease environment. Ships traversing the Atlantic carried peoples, crops, goods, ideas and diseases. Epidemiological zones merged as previously isolated peoples were brought into contact. Crosby has ably documented the consequences for the New World, and the horrendous impact of smallpox and measles on the American Indian population.[15] Malaria and yellow fever crossed on slave ships from West Africa to the New World, and yellow fever

---

Environmental Control in Northeastern Tanzania, 1840–1940 (Philadelphia, PA: University of Pennsylvania, 1992). For an important West African study of the management of the environment, though not centering on disease but with important implications, see James Fairhead and Melissa Leach, *Misreading the African Landscape: Society and Ecology in a Forest-Savanna Mosaic* (Cambridge: Cambridge University Press, 1996).

[13] A. Norman Klein, 'Towards a New Understanding of Akan Origins', *Africa* 66 (2) (1996), pp. 248–73.

[14] Europeans of the 1490s regarded syphilis as an American disease that returned to Europe with Christopher Columbus and his crew. Alfred W. Crosby, *The Columbian Exchange: Biological and Cultural Consequences of 1492* (Westport, CT: Greenwood Press, 1972), pp. 122–3.

[15] Crosby, *Columbian Exchange.*

made its first documented appearance in Barbados in 1647.[16] These West African diseases would exact a heavy toll in European lives in the New World. When an influenza epidemic hit in 1558–9, it was felt on both sides of the Atlantic in the Old and New Worlds.[17] It is also worth remembering, on the other hand, that the introduction of American crops such as maize and manioc (cassava) to Africa revolutionized agriculture and improved nutrition and immunity to diseases.

Syphilis and typhus appear to have made their debut in recorded history during the Italian wars of 1494–1559. European therapies were useless against these diseases. Europe did not adopt smallpox inoculation until the late eighteenth century. The professionalization of medicine in Europe really took effect from 1850, but prior to this date doctors were expensive and their treatments often ineffectual. In addition to endemic local diseases, West Africans thus had to deal with new viral and bacterial diseases introduced from Europe and for which the Europeans had no effective medical remedies. Pieter de Marees, a Dutchman, captured this combined effect in his description of the main diseases afflicting the Gold Coast around 1602.

> The diseases and plagues from which they suffer are: pox, the clap, gonorrhea, worms [Guinea worm] headache and hot fevers. . . . Even though they catch some of these diseases, which are not without peril [to them], they do not pay much heed to their injuries or illnesses and go around as if they are not suffering from any infirmities.[18]

For the treatment of syphilis and worms the Africans close to European forts and castles deferred to the European barbers (the surgeons of the day) in these settlements:

> They [the barbers] often use Salsaparille, which is brought to them by the Dutch ships, against the pox and the clap. They boil the ointment in fresh water and drink it as a draught against the pox and similar diseases, and also against the worms which they get in their legs. . . .[19]

Another Dutchman, Willem Bosman, writing on the Gold Coast in 1702 from the experience of fourteen years' residence, spoke disparagingly of these European barbers as 'unskilled physicians' using 'corrupted medicines', who endanger the lives of many people.[20]

[16] Sheldon Watts, *Disease, Power and Imperialism* (New Haven, CT: Yale University Press, 1997), pp. 213–14.

[17] McNeill, *Plagues and Peoples*, p. 218.

[18] Pieter de Marees, *Description and Historical Account of the Gold Kingdom of Guinea* (1602), trans. and ed. by Albert van Dantzig and Adam Jones (Oxford: Oxford University Press, 1987), p. 173.

[19] *Ibid.*

[20] William Bosman, *A New and Accurate Description of the Coast of Guinea: Divided into the Gold, the Slave, and the Ivory Coasts*, 4th edition (London: Frank Cass, 1967), p. 106.

Unlike de Marees, Bosman had a healthy respect for African therapies, emphasizing the curative effect of some herbs. He distinguished between illnesses for which local remedies sufficed, and others such as venereal diseases against which African medicines were helpless. Africans on the Gold Coast were unfamiliar with surgery aside from the superficial cuts made on the skin for the rubbing in of medicinal herbs. Serious wounds and internal bleeding were definitely beyond the scope of African therapies in the Gold Coast:

> The natives are very much to be pitied, that being shot, cut or otherwise wounded in their wars, they neither know nor have any other way of cure other than green plants, which they boil in water and foment that part with the decoction; which proves effectual in some cases, the vegetables being endowed with a wonderful sanative vertue [sic]. But others either not knowing the simples, or being ignorant how to apply them aright, apply their fomentations in vain. . . . Those seized by the Venereal Distemper, are also incurable, except they happening to be near our Fort fall into our Barber's hands; who for a good large summ [sic] of money cure them.[21]

Bosman listed native remedies in use as including lime juice, malaget (also called the grains of paradise), cardamom, the roots, branches and gums of trees, and 'about thirty several sorts of green herbs, which are impregnated with an extraordinary sanative virtue'.[22]

In a 1974 bibliographical essay on disease and medicine in African history, K. David Patterson opined that: 'Any consideration of disease and medicine in Africa must of course consider local theories and cures, even though present health conditions on the continent suggest that indigenous medical systems are relatively ineffectual'.[23] Joseph Inikori also raises the issue of whether African therapies in the pre-colonial era were competent in dealing with indigenous diseases or illnesses.[24] We have very little record of how these therapies functioned in the pre-colonial era, aside from the usually uninformed comments of European observers. There are some notable exceptions, however, and European travelers with medical training have left valuable accounts of West African diseases and therapies. Mungo Park, the Scottish doctor, botanist and explorer, traveled though the region of present-day Gambia, Senegal and Mali between 1795 and 1797. He lists common diseases among the Africans as fevers, fluxes, dysentery, yaws, leprosy, elephantiasis, Guinea worm and goiters, the first two being the most frequently fatal. Park had high regard for local therapy where fevers

---

[21] *Ibid.*, p. 110.
[22] *Ibid.*, p. 224.
[23] K. David Patterson, 'Disease and Medicine in African History: A Bibliographical Essay', *History in Africa* 1 (1974), p. 142.
[24] Inikori, *The Chaining of a Continent.*

and the management of dislocations and fractures (bone-setting) were concerned.[25]

Henry Tedlie, a surgeon and member of a British diplomatic mission to Asante in 1817, wrote a paper on *materia medica* and diseases in Asante.[26] Tedlie gives a list of herbal remedies used by the Asante as purgatives, to cause abortion, as treatment for a sprained foot or ankle, for stomach pain, acidity in the stomach and heartburn among pregnant women, dysentery and diarrhoea, boils and swellings, earache, coughs, eye pains, yaws and other ailments including venereal disease. Considering that Tedlie enumerated the diseases most common in Asante as lues, yaws, itch, ulcers, scald-heads, venereal disease and gripping pains in the stomach, Asante herbal remedies may have proved proficient for these common ailments, though this cannot be argued with great certainty. Tedlie confirmed Bosman's above observation that the Asante were unacquainted with any method of stopping haemorrhage.[27]

T. E. Kyei's autobiography, *Our Days Dwindle*, reveals that growing up in rural pre-colonial or early colonial West Africa entailed the acquisition of knowledge crucial for the reproduction of the community, including herbal knowledge.[28] There was a shared body of herbal knowledge in rural, agrarian communities such as Agogo in early colonial Asante. Kyei (1908–99), a non-specialist, enumerates several well-known herbal remedies for the cure or treatment of stomach upsets, constipation, fever, cuts and bruises, boils, coughs, chest pains, headaches, conjunctivitis, convulsions, yaws and other complaints.[29] This list of common ailments is very similar to that compiled by Tedlie in Asante in 1817, suggesting an established pattern of maladies and, perhaps, a coherent response to these through indigenous therapy. In spite of the European missionary bias against African healers in the pre-colonial era, it was one such skilled herbalist who nursed Andreas Riis of the Basel Mission through the worst convulsions of what was evidently malaria in the 1830s. Riis's two colleagues, Peter Jäger and Christian Friedrich Heinze, the latter a medical doctor from Saxony, had earlier succumbed.[30]

---

[25] Kate Ferguson Marsters (ed.), *Travels in the Interior Districts of Africa by Mungo Park* (Durham, NL: Duke University Press, 2000), pp. 248–50.

[26] This appeared as a chapter in T. E. Bowdich, *Mission from Cape Coast Castle to Ashantee* (London: Frank Cass, 1966 [1824]), ch. XI.

[27] *Ibid.*, pp. 371–7.

[28] T. E. Kyei, *Our Days Dwindle: Memoirs of my Childhood Days in Asante* (Portsmouth, NH: Heinemann, 2001).

[29] *Ibid.*, ch. 6.

[30] Peter A. Schweizer, *Survivors of the Gold Coast: The Basel Missionaries in Colonial Ghana* (Accra: Smartline, 2000), p. 20.

European colonial rule changed the praxis of therapy, with African healers being declared illegitimate under the new political dispensation. Indeed, even Western-trained African medical men would be pushed into subordinate positions from the beginning of the twentieth century, and few experienced illustrious medical careers such as James Africanus Horton (1835–83).[31] As Feierman and Janzen accurately observed, the diagnosis of illness is closely connected to power and authority, and 'whoever controls the diagnosis of illness . . . shapes cultural ideas on misfortune and evil. The power to name an illness is the power to say which elements in life lead to suffering'.[32] The desire to claim hegemonic space for Western biomedicine during the colonial era would lend biomedicine an imperialist edge in the colonial setting.

Colonial rule, 'colonial diseases' and Western biomedicine

The Cape Verde Islands represent the first European colony in West Africa, claimed by the Portuguese in 1455 and with a small Portuguese community by the sixteenth century. French presence was particularly strong along the coast of Senegal by the end of the sixteenth-century, especially at Saint Louis. The nineteenth-century move towards the formal acquisition of colonies in West Africa began with the assumption of British control over Sierra Leone in 1808 and the establishment of Bathurst at the mouth of the river Gambia in 1817. The mid-nineteenth century witnessed a quickening of imperialist ambitions, with French activity intensifying in Senegal, and the British declaration of Lagos and the Gold Coast as colonies in 1861 and 1874. The entry of new European powers in the rush for colonies, notably Germany and Belgium (under King Leopold II), precipitated the Berlin Conference of 1884–5, and the establishment of ground rules for the peaceful colonization of Africa. Effective claim to any African territory was to be supported by treaties with local chiefs and European occupation on the ground. Earlier treaties signed with African kings and chiefs for the purposes of trade were now used as evidence of spheres of European influence.

The period between the 1890s and the 1920s has been described as an ecological disaster in Africa, as colonial conquest, pacification and

---

[31] Christopher Fyfe, *Africanus Horton 1835-1883: West African Scientist and Patriot* (New York: Oxford University Press, 1972); Adell Patton, *Physicians, Colonial Racism and Diaspora in West Africa* (Gainesville, FL: University of Florida Press, 1996).

[32] Steven Feierman and John M. Janzen (eds), *The Social Basis of Health and Healing in Africa* (Berkeley, CA: University of California Press, 1992), p. 18.

the re-settlement of new colonial subjects altered the equilibrium between African communities and their natural environments. That colonization followed close on the heels of cattle diseases such as lung sickness, rinderpest and recurrent drought — particularly in East and Southern Africa — meant that Africans were simultaneously faced with epidemiological, environmental and political challenges.[33] In the West African colony of Senegal, colonial expansion in the nineteenth century coincided with unusually low rainfall, and colonial conquests together with locust plagues led to widespread famines in the sahel region between 1901 and 1903. Drought and poor harvests characterized the period between 1910 and 1915, and the colony between 1880 and 1915 also suffered smallpox, cholera and bubonic plague epidemics.[34] The divergence between knowledge and power was an important paradox of this period: Africans who had enough knowledge about their environment and knew how to manage it to keep endemic diseases at a low level were politically disempowered, and Europeans who now had political power lacked knowledge of the African environment. Indeed, some of the disease epidemics of the period of conquest were actually linked to the process of colonization, as John Ford demonstrated in his seminal study of trypanosomiasis.[35]

Developments in biomedicine or Western science had emboldened the European colonizers; the post-1880 period witnessed a 'germ revolution', made possible by the Industrial Revolution. The microscope, developed by a new technology of optics, and the intellectual curiosity spawned by the Enlightenment, pushed aside the old belief that reality was what the eye could see. Tropical medicine came to constitute the frontier of medical science in the second half of the nineteenth century, as the European desire to colonize the tropics created the impetus for medical discoveries. The discovery by Louis Pasteur of the bacilli of anthrax and tuberculosis between 1877 and 1879, and Robert Koch's discovery of the bacteria that caused cholera in 1883 gave birth to the so-called 'germ theory' of disease. In the mid-1890s Dmitri Ivanovski in Russia and Martinus Beijerinck in the Netherlands demonstrated the existence of viruses. Indeed, the colonization of Africa might well have been impossible without the industrial and medical revolution of the nineteenth century.

[33] Malowany, 'Unfinished Agendas', p. 326; Terence Ranger, 'Plagues of Beasts and Men: Prophetic Responses to Epidemic in Eastern and Southern Africa', in Terence Ranger and Paul Slack (eds), *Epidemics and Ideas: Essays on the Historical Perception of Pestilence* (Cambridge: Cambridge University Press, 1992), pp. 231–68.

[34] Myron Echenberg, *Black Death, White Medicine: Bubonic Plague and the Politics of Public Health in Colonial Senegal, 1914–1945* (Portsmouth, NH: Heinemann; Oxford: James Currey, 2002).

[35] Ford, *Trypanosomiasis in African Ecology.*

Yet it was two old diseases which posed the greatest challenge to the European colonization of Africa: malaria and trypanosomiasis. In the early decades of the twentieth century, human trypanosomiasis erupted in a series of epidemics in Africa with great cost in human life. However, it was only during a study in The Gambia in 1901 that J. E. Dutton established that the disease could affect humans. Dutton named the parasite seen in the blood of a patient *Trypanosoma gambiense*, and in 1903 the vector was identified as the tse tse fly. Very little was available in terms of effective medical treatment, and atoxyl, the only known drug for this disease in the early twentieth century, caused blindness in about 30 per cent of those injected.[36] Malaria was perhaps the most formidable foe, and had earned Sierra Leone — and the rest of West Africa — the title of 'the White Man's Grave' from the early nineteenth century. Though the cinchona bark was known to seventeenth-century Europeans to be a possible antidote for malaria, it had a mixed reception. Quinine was used irregularly in the nineteenth century, until Dr T. R. H. Thompson demonstrated its effectiveness as a prophylactic during the 1841 Niger expedition. It was not until Dr Baikie kept the entire crew of the Niger Expedition in 1854 alive through daily doses of quinine that it became popular as a prophylactic.

The disease cycle of malaria was determined by the 1890s through the combined research of several scientists. In 1880, Alphonse Laveran had discovered the plasmodia in the blood of a patient. Laveran came to suspect the mosquito as the vector for malaria. In 1898 Ronald Ross worked out the entire cycle of the disease, tracing how the plasmodia moved back and forth between people and mosquitoes. Ross became one of the first Britons to win the Nobel Prize. However, knowing the disease cycle, or the potential effectiveness of quinine, did not alleviate the devastation of malaria wreaked on Europeans and Africans in Africa. The separation of Europeans from African carriers of malaria — that is to say, segregation — was adopted as the official policy of British West African colonial governments at the beginning of the twentieth century. Segregation occurred on the recommendation of J. W. Stephens and S. R. Christophers, members of a Royal Society of London expedition to West Africa to study malaria in 1900. Stephens and Christophers declared as unrealistic Ross's position that the mosquito vector could be eradicated, suggesting instead the separation

[36] Other important works on trypanosomiasis include Vail, 'Ecology and History', and Maryinez Lyons, *The Colonial Disease: A Social History of Sleeping Sickness in Northern Zaire, 1800-1940* (Cambridge: Cambridge University Press, 1992).

of Europeans from Africans.[37] Cantonments and hill stations were established in West African towns as European residential areas. The Medical and Sanitary Report for the Gold Coast in 1903 confidently stated:

> That segregation is of the greatest efficacy in preventing the spread of malaria is now generally admitted; it has been carried out in building residences for European officials in nearly every station in the Colony, and the remarkable fall in the death rate speaks for itself.[38]

But a perusal of medical reports for French and British colonies in West Africa even in the mid-1920s still listed malaria as the number-one cause of morbidity and mortality.[39] As Rupert Boyce had commented in 1909, concerning European presence in colonial Africa, it was a question of 'mosquito or man'.[40]

New infectious diseases also entered Africa through the colonial context, and they underscore how African colonies had become part of wider European empires, including a global economic and maritime network. Non-African diseases would enter African ports, and quickly spread along the roads and railway lines that colonial governments had constructed to facilitate colonial administration and the extraction of natural resources. A good example is cholera, native to India. A cholera epidemic broke out in 1817 in Calcutta. The presence of British troops and ships ensured that the disease was spread beyond the original area of outbreak. British imperialism took over, and by 1821 cholera had made its way to Muscat and from there to the east coast of Africa.[41] Cholera would strike Senegal in 1868–9, and among its victims was the governor of Senegal, Pinet-Laprade. In 1893, cholera struck Senegal again, causing great devastation among the urban poor of St Louis.[42]

Two other new infectious diseases caused much consternation in colonial West Africa because of the high rates of mortality and the

---

[37] Philip Curtin, 'Medical Knowledge and Urban Planning in Colonial Tropical Africa', in Feierman and Janzen, *Social Basis of Health and Healing*, pp. 235–55; and John Cell, 'Anglo-Indian Medical Theory and the Origins of Segregation in West Africa', *American Historical Review* 91(2) (1986), pp. 307–35.

[38] Public Records and Archives Administration Department (PRAAD), Accra, ADM 5/1/80. Gold Coast, *Departmental Reports*, 1903. Medical and Sanitary Report.

[39] Public Records Office (PRO), London, CO 554/71/9/ Memorandum of the Activities of the Medical Departments in West African Colonies (1926). For French West Africa, see Dr Abatucci, 'Extract from a Report on the Sanitary Organization in the French Colonies' (c.1925), in CO 554/69/1, 'Study Tour for Colonial Medical Officers in West Africa (1925–26)'.

[40] Roy Macleod and M. Lewis, 'Introduction', p. 7, in Macleod and Lewis (eds) *Disease, Medicine and Empire: Perspectives on Western Medicine and the Experiences of European Invasion* (New York: Routledge, 1988).

[41] McNeill, *Plagues and Peoples*, p. 268.

[42] Echenberg, *Black Death, White Medicine*, p. 24.

inability of biomedicine to deal with these health threats: bubonic plague and influenza. The etiology of both diseases underscored how ports, valued within the political economy of colonialism, had become instrumental to the introduction of new viral diseases. Plague was new to West Africa, which seemed to have escaped two earlier pandemics ascribed to the pathogen, the first in 542 CE ('Justinian's plague'), and the second in the mid-fourteenth century (the 'Black Death').[43] West Africa was included in the third plague pandemic, which was first detected in Hong Kong in 1894. At this time West Africa had become an integral part of empire and the global economy. Grand Bassam in the Ivory Coast was one of the first places to experience plague in 1899. Dakar and the interior of Senegal suffered recurrent attacks of bubonic plague between 1914 and 1945, when the combination of DDT pesticide and new chemotherapy (sulpha drugs and later penicillin) curtailed its endemic status in the colony.[44]

The Gold Coast went through two plague epidemics in 1908 and 1924. The 1908 outbreak started in Accra and spread quickly to other towns along the coast line, causing 288 deaths in 336 officially reported cases.[45] The second Gold Coast plague epidemic started at another port town, Sekondi.[46] In both Senegal and the Gold Coast, bubonic plague entered through ports with infected rats. *Y. pestis* is a disease of rodents and only spreads from rodents to humans through flea bites in exceptional cases. These infected rodents must have spread the pathogen to local rats, and the enlarged pool of infected rodents traveled along the coast and into the interior via railways and roads. Traders, migrants, pastoralists and those in other mobile professions contributed to the dissemination of the disease by carrying along rodents in their possessions and goods. Thus in Senegal, the railway capital, Thiès, was constantly threatened by plague between 1914 and 1945. In the Gold Coast epidemic of 1924, Kroos from Liberia, who worked as stevedores at the port in Sekondi, and Hausa and Yoruba traders in the *Zongos*

[43] John Iliffe, *Africans: The History of a Continent* (Cambridge: Cambridge University Press, 1995), p. 113, notes that 'the black rat often associated with plague existed in the Zambezi and Limpopo Valleys early in the second millennium AD, and plague was one of the acute diseases which Ganda called *kawumpuli* . . .' Recent work suggests that *Yersinia pestis* might have been born in Africa, and that the Justinian plague stemmed from Africa. See, for example, Peter Sarris, 'The Justinian Plague: Origins and Effects', *Continuity and Change* 17 (2002), pp. 169–82.

[44] Echenberg, *Black Death, White Medicine*. Subsequent references to plague in Senegal are from this excellent source.

[45] PRAAD, Accra, ADM 5/1/85. Gold Coast, *Departmental Reports, 1908*. Report of the Medical and Sanitary Department.

[46] PRAAD, Accra, ADM 5/1/100. Gold Coast, *Departmental Reports, 1923–24*. Report of the Medical Department, April 1923–March 1924.

(stranger settlements) in Sekondi were disproportionately affected.

The Spanish influenza pandemic in 1918–19 also exacted a heavy toll in Africa as an estimated 2 per cent of the African population died. About 33 million people died worldwide from this pandemic. It was dramatic in its sudden appearance and quick retreat. Less publicized is the fact that the aftershocks of the epidemic continued through 1920 with less remarkable outbreaks of a mild type of flu. The flu epidemic of 1918 was not the first in West Africa; that of 1889–93, for example, reached the Gold Coast in 1891. However, the widespread manifestation of the pandemic of 1918 was unique. The current interpretation of this pandemic is that American soldiers from Kansas took the microbe to Europe in the First World War. Transferred from military camp to military camp the microbe mutated and accompanied servicemen returning from the arena of war. About 450,000 soldiers from French Africa had fought during the war in Europe. When flu struck simultaneously in New England (United States), Sierra Leone, and Brest (France) in August 1918, the disease was unrecognizable in its new form. The futility of therapy (both African and Western) created a cognitive crisis in areas of Africa and gave birth to anti-medicine movements. In Nigeria the epidemic underpinned the rise of the Aladura Church.

Again, the disease had made its entry through ports. In the Gold Coast, Cape Coast was the point of entry on 31 August when an American vessel, the *S. S. Shonga*, made a brief call on its way from Sierra Leone. The ship also stopped at Accra on 3 September and infected the town. Another port town, Sekondi, received infected members of a ship's crew who were brought ashore for treatment on 5 September.[47] The disease then made its way inland along roads and railways. Commenting on how the colonial infrastructure ironically serviced new infectious diseases, Ohadike observed of the 1918 flu pandemic in Nigeria that, 'In sum, in 1918 and 1919 the entire population of Nigeria was called upon to pay the price of being integrated into the world capitalist system'.[48] In Nigeria the disease was supposedly introduced from Sierra Leone or the Gold Coast, and then penetrated the interior via boats on the river network, roads and the railway. The government estimated that about 4 per cent of the

---

[47] PRAAD, Accra, ADM 5/1/95. Gold Coast, *Departmental Reports, 1918*. Medical and Sanitary Report; and D. K. Patterson, 'The Influenza Epidemic of 1918-19 in the Gold Coast', *Journal of African History* 24 (4) (1983), pp. 485–502.

[48] D. C. Ohadike, 'The Influenza Pandemic of 1918-19 and the Spread of Cassava Cultivation on the Lower Niger Delta: A Study in Historical Linkages', *Journal of African History* 22 (3) (1981), p. 386.

Gold Coast's population (1911 Census) succumbed to the disease, approximately 60,000 deaths. Patterson views this figure as a gross underestimate and adds on a further 30,000.[49]

The flu pandemic overlapped with seasonal patterns of illness with devastating effect. In West African countries, respiratory diseases peak during the cool dry season, when the dry harmattan wind blows south from the Sahara. Intestinal diseases increase in the rainy seasons, the period also of widespread malaria. As the Gold Coast medical report for 1918 remarked:

> Unhappily the appearance of the pandemic in this neighborhood synchronized with a spell of unusually cold weather with high winds, and to this unfortunate coincidence may be attributed the grave character of the outbreak and the high ratio of pulmonary complications.[50]

This made the death toll particularly high in the dry savanna of the Northern Territories of the Gold Coast, where flu's presence was particularly felt during the harmattan season between October and February. There was also a generational dimension to the flu pandemic, which hit young adults hardest.[51] Young adults in their twenties and thirties constituted the bulk of servicemen and wage workers and were thus at the center of the colonial political economy. As migrants and a mobile category, this group perhaps also suffered from nutritional deficiencies that lessened their immunity to disease. In a colonial context in which Western biomedicine reigned supreme in the realm of therapy, it was ironic that colonial representatives lacked an antidote or coping mechanism for a flu pandemic that was viewed by all Africans as a European disease. That many of the medical discoveries between 1880 and 1920 dealt with the tropics indicates the central importance of empire in Europe.

The extermination of yaws is one of the success stories of colonial medicine in Africa. Remarkable advances in pharmaceuticals would come in the 1930s and 1940s, particularly with the invention of antibiotics. The 1940s and 1950s witnessed decolonization in West Africa, and the training of African medical practitioners was part of the process of preparing Africans to take over the government and management of their countries. By the 1960s most West African countries had attained their independence, with Guinea Bissau and Cape Verde the last in 1975.

---

[49] Patterson, 'Influenza Epidemic'.
[50] PRAAD, Accra, ADM 5/1/95. Medical and Sanitary Report (1918).
[51] Patterson, 'Influenza Epidemic', p. 499; Howard Philips, 'Bloemfontein and the Consequences of the Spanish Flu Epidemic of 1918', *Journal of Southern African Studies* 13(2) (1987), p. 222.

Independence, the challenge of development and the reality of medical pluralism

Both French and British West African colonies had medical branches that comprised curative medicine, sanitary work and medical research. The structure in French West Africa was more hierarchical than in the British territories; positions such as those of the Medical Inspector of the Colonial Health Service and the Inspector-General of Public Health and Medical Services were federal positions and these two appointees (resident in the federal capital, Dakar) were at the helm of public health in French West Africa. Just before the First World War, a Bacteriological Laboratory of French West Africa was opened in Dakar. Each separate colony in French West Africa had its Chief of the Medical Service and its own Public Health and Sanitation Board. Both colonial systems had initiated training of African medical personnel, though African medical doctors were assigned a subordinate status by the British West African Medical Association. More African dispensers and nurses were trained than doctors, as the British medical profession had reservations about establishing a fully-fledged medical school in colonial West Africa. With independence, various African countries would set up medical, pharmaceutical and nursing schools, and move to intensify the training of medical personnel. As heirs of colonial rule and with the high expectations of African populations resting on their shoulders, the new African governments were expected to deliver rapid socio-economic development — including excellent health-care. West African countries have since discovered that solid health care systems are the products of strong economies, and that health and disease are firmly rooted in political economy.[52]

Older diseases such as malaria, trypanosomiasis, schistosomiasis (bilharzia), and onchocerciasis (river blindness) remained potent challenges at the time of independence. In addition, other diseases such as tuberculosis, described by health officials as a relatively minor threat in the early colonial years and often restricted to coastal towns, had begun to grow in prominence during the colonial era, with the rise of underground mining and increased overcrowding in towns. In 1969 Lassa fever, spread by rats of the *Mastomys* genus, was first observed in Nigeria. Its high level of contagiousness and case fatality has compelled Nigerian hospitals — even today — to close down as soon

[52] See, in general, Toyin Falola and Dennis Ityavyar (eds), *The Political Economy of Health in Africa* (Athens, OH: Ohio University Press, 1992).

as a single case of Lassa fever is detected.[53]

From the early 1980s HIV-AIDS caught the world's attention. Its confinement to the so-called 'AIDS Belt' in Central Africa — Uganda, Kenya, the Democratic Republic of the Congo and Zambia — may have given West Africans a false sense of immunity. But the disease's presence in Senegal in the late 1980s was a grim reminder that no one was immune. In the 1990s the disease spread southwards into Southern Africa, to Botswana, Zimbabwe and South Africa, and westwards to Nigeria, Togo, Burkina Faso, Ghana, Côte d'Ivoire and Liberia. The 1990s also witnessed a decline in HIV-AIDS prevalence levels in parts of East Africa, notably Uganda, and in Senegal. Statistics such as those for Botswana, where 38 per cent of the adult population are currently HIV-positive, have energized West African countries in their AIDS control measures to ensure that they do not reach a prevalence rate of 5 per cent, seen by experts as the take-off point for hyper-infection.

The mandate of accelerating socio-economic development in independent Africa could itself bring health complications, as the construction of hydro-electric dams has demonstrated in various parts of the continent. With the construction of the Volta Dam in Ghana in the 1960s, schistosomiasis, present before the dam in the lower Volta, has increased as the dam has slowed down significantly the flow of the River Volta and enabled the snail host (*Bulinus rohlfsi*) to thrive. However, the dam has eliminated onchocerciasis from the lower Volta, as the blackfly vector, *Simulium damnosum*, thrives only in fast-flowing rivers and streams.

The decline in world prices for African primary exports from the 1960s placed African governments in a weakened financial position, unable to deliver on the promise of rapid economic growth and good health care. Criticism elicited political repression, and in the mid-1960s a wave of military coups overthrew the first democratically elected governments in Togo, Ghana, and then Nigeria. Military adventurism and ethnic tensions have resulted in the current state of political fragility with civil wars having been fought in Nigeria, Liberia, Sierra Leone and Côte d'Ivoire, the last three of them, largely post-1990 phenomena, drawing in countries from the entire West African region either as collaborators or as peace keepers. Economic decline and political instability have consequently weakened the health-care infrastructure.

The few successes in the fight against disease in the post-colonial era have often been achieved with the assistance of the international community. This fact underscores the internationalization of disease and medicine in the contemporary world, as well as the weak state of

---

[53] Diamond, *Guns, Germs and Steel*, p. 208.

health care in African countries, where health does not attract a significant portion of the national budget. Some of these successes also reveal that weak African countries lack even the ability to insist on their health-care priorities in their relationship with the international community. When the World Health Organization (WHO) launched a global malaria eradication campaign in 1955, it excluded Africa, the birth place of malaria and the continent most in need of its eradication. It considered that Africa was not ready for the exercise, citing the poor health-care infrastructure. Yet when the WHO declared a smallpox eradication program barely a decade later — significantly at the prompting of the Soviet Union and the United States during their Cold War tussle — West and Central Africa were used as testing grounds for the program, even though rates of smallpox infection in Africa were falling. The much-needed measles eradication was attached to smallpox to encourage the co-operation of African countries.[54]

Unfortunately, the civil wars and political instability of the past two decades in West Africa have promoted the resurgence of diseases once eradicated; for example, sleeping sickness — eradicated in 1965 — returned in 2000. Research programs implemented with the assistance of external organizations have been disrupted or aborted. The Lassa fever project in Sierra Leone, established in 1976 by the Centers for Disease Control (CDC) in the United States, had to be abandoned with the outbreak of civil war in March 1991. Yet tests by CDC scientists had established that nationwide about 9 per cent of the Sierra Leone population tested positive for Lassa fever antibodies. The mutual suspicion of the United States and the Soviet Union, that the other might be developing Lassa fever for biological warfare, compelled both countries to end their Lassa fever studies in West Africa.[55] Lassa fever is also endemic in Guinea and Liberia. Some of the most advanced medical research in West Africa at present is being conducted by the Medical Research Council in The Gambia, an institute run by the Wellcome Institute and the London School for Hygiene and Tropical Medicine.

Today, HIV-AIDS is promoting the convergence of disease patterns, as AIDS compromises the immune system and enables other opportunistic diseases to invade the bodies of patients. The result has

---

[54] Malowany, 'Unfinished Agendas'; William Foege et al., 'Smallpox Eradication in West and Central Africa', *Bulletin of the World Health Organization* 52 (2) (1998), pp. 233–5; D. A. Henderson, 'Smallpox Eradication — A Cold War Victory', *World Health Forum* 19 (2) (1998), pp. 113–19.

[55] Laurie Garrett, *The Coming Plague: Newly Emerging Diseases in a World Out of Balance* (New York: Farrar, Straus & Giroux, 1994), ch. 7.

been an increase in diseases such as tuberculosis. Recent political upheavals have been a major contributor to ill health in the West African sub-region. The movement of peoples fleeing conflicts, war that is characterized by sexual violence, deep-rooted poverty and the weak position of women in African societies have opened the flood-gates to HIV-AIDS. In 1988 Sierra Leone had one of the lowest HIV-AIDS levels in Africa, with only five patients diagnosed with AIDS and a further six identified as non-symptomatic HIV carriers.[56] By 1992, the country registered a prevalence rate of 2.7 per cent for HIV-AIDS, and was worried by evidence that tuberculosis was on the rise, as well as the prevalence of sexually transmitted diseases (STDs).[57] It has been scientifically established that STDs increase vulnerability to HIV-AIDS, and that the incidence of tuberculosis rises in HIV-AIDS patients. Today, health care in Sierra Leone is largely dependent on international non-governmental organizations. Preliminary studies in early 2002 on HIV-AIDS reveal a very different picture from 1992, and a decade of civil war has certainly reconfigured the manifestation of the disease.

After an initial climb in life expectancies during the late colonial and early independence periods, AIDS threatens to lower life expectancy drastically in African countries. In 2002, 25 million people in Africa had HIV-AIDS. Thirteen million AIDS orphans lived in Africa. But AIDS-ravaged Africa is being subjected once more to discriminatory treatment. In 2001, only 20,000 people died of AIDS in the West, compared with Africa's 2.2 million. Yet GlaxoSmithKline, the largest British pharmaceutical company, sought legal injunctions to prevent South Africa and other developing countries from accessing or producing generic antiretroviral drugs based on its patents. These drugs have been proven to lengthen the life expectancy of AIDS patients and to make living with AIDS possible for extended periods. It took the public court of international opinion to compel the British pharmaceutical giant to withdraw its legal suit. At an annual cost of $10,000 per patient, no African country could afford antiretroviral drugs. Yet Indian pharmaceutical companies are able to produce generic antiretroviral drugs based on Western patents for less than $1 a day. On 28 April 2003, GlaxoSmithKline announced that it had almost halved the price of its Combivir treatment in poor countries to 90 US cents per day. This comes to about $330 a year per patient, but the per capita income for Ghana in 2002 was only $390.

[56] Republic of Sierra Leone with WHO, *AIDS Prevention and Control Programme: Medium Term Plan 1989–1993* (Freetown and Geneva, 1988).
[57] National AIDS Prevention and Control Programme, *Sierra Leone Annual Report, 1992* (Freetown, c. 1993).

Medical pluralism is the reality on the ground, not just because medicine in West Africa has always drawn on multiple therapies, but also because of pragmatic considerations. Health care maintained its urban bias in the post-colonial era, and aside from the issue of cost, great distances to health-care centers encouraged rural dwellers to seek local therapies. Thus, Freetown in 1979 had 7 per cent of the population of Sierra Leone, but retained 70 per cent of all doctors and 40 per cent of all hospital beds. Even in 2002, a little under 70 per cent of Sierra Leone's population lived in rural areas. Indeed, sometimes local therapies turn out to be more expensive than health care provided at the health centers, and it is the distance from the centers that compels rural denizens to patronize local therapies.[58] At the Fevers Unit in Korle Bu Teaching Hospital in Accra, a cash-strapped administration, in a desperate endeavor to at least ameliorate the suffering of AIDS patients in the absence of antiretroviral drugs, arranged for a herbalist in the Eastern Region of Ghana to supply a herbal tonic that allegedly improved the appetite of AIDS patients. Several AIDS patients showed up religiously on Wednesdays in 2002 with their plastic containers to receive the tonic. Today, health remains a challenge and an indictment for contemporary West African governments. One significant result is that both patients and medical providers explore relief through medical pluralism.

Conclusion

This chapter demonstrates the importance of disease as a lens for West Africa's history. The changing patterns of disease enable us to examine people's relationships to the physical environment, to explore the nature of towns and their surroundings, and to interrogate West Africa's incorporation into the wider world. That colonial rule marked an important transition in West Africa's history of disease is clear from the ecological devastation that marked colonial pacification, as well as the elimination of epidemiological boundaries through maritime revolution, especially with the introduction of the steam ship in the 1850s. As colonial rule stabilized, European officials benefited from research into tropical medicine, and health services were gradually extended to Africans with the realization that the health of Africans and Europeans were connected. A healthy African labor force was

---

[58] Joshua Lacsina, '"Lassa Fever No Good-O": Community Theatre and the Prevention of Lassa Fever in Sierra Leone' (Seminar Paper, Harvard University, January 2003).

also crucial to the colonial economy. Today, Western pharmaceutical companies are less interested in developing drugs for tropical diseases. Though driven by the search for profits, the internationalization of disease has meant that drugs developed by pharmaceutical companies with Western patients in mind — such as antiretrovirals for HIV-AIDS — can be of benefit to African patients as well. The issue then becomes affordability, as West Africans with low incomes are unable to purchase these Western-manufactured drugs. Most African countries feature among the list of the world's poorest nations. The brain drain has deprived African countries of most of their qualified medical staff. Financial and human resources are thus lacking to facilitate top-level medical research in West African countries. Disease and health in West Africa's history cannot be removed from the context of political economy.

Recommended Reading

Abdalla, Ismail H. (1997) *Islam, Medicine and Practitioners in Northern Nigeria* (Lewiston, NY: Edwin Mellen).

Addae, Stephen (1996) *History of Western Medicine in Ghana 1880-1960* (Durham, NC: Durham Academic Press).

Conklin, Alice L. (1997) *A Mission to Civilize: The Republican Idea of Empire in France and West Africa, 1895–1930* (Stanford, CA: Stanford University Press).

Echenberg, Myron (2002) *Black Death, White Medicine: Bubonic Plague and the Politics of Public Health in Colonial Senegal, 1914–1945* (Portsmouth, NH: Heinemann; Oxford: James Currey).

Feierman, Steven and John M. Janzen (eds) (1992) *The Social Basis of Health and Healing in Africa* (Berkeley, CA: University of California Press).

Ford, John (1971) *The Role of Trypanosomiases in African Ecology: A Study of the Tsetse Fly Problem* (Oxford: Clarendon Press).

McMillan, Della (1995) *Sahel Visions: Planned Settlement and River Blindness Control in Burkina Faso* (Tucson, AR: University of Arizona Press).

Patton, Adell (1996) *Physicians, Colonial Racism and Diaspora in West Africa* (Gainesville, FL: University of Florida).

Silla, Eric (1998) *'People Are Not The Same': Leprosy and Identity in Twentieth-Century Mali* (Portsmouth, NH: Heinemann; Oxford: James Currey).

10

Urbanization in Colonial
& Post-Colonial West Africa

ANDREAS ECKERT

This chapter attempts to provide an overview of the field of African urban studies and to present some of the central issues in the urbanization of West Africa. After outlining the important urban developments from the pre-colonial period to recent times, the chapter looks specifically at colonial efforts to order urban space and African strategies to find a place within that new urban order. Moreover, it focuses on urban land, landowners and conflict as tools with which to explore broader issues of urban society and economy.

Urbanization in West Africa: developments and issues

Of all the major regions in the world today, Africa is still one of the least urbanized.[1] During the twentieth century, however, rapid urbanization 'has been the most significant and pervasive socio-economic trend across the African continent'.[2] It is widely held that the colonial experience had the greatest effect in urban formation and function south of the Sahara.[3] Although dramatic urban growth is a relatively recent phenomenon, which dates back only to the post-Second World War period, West Africa's urban history covers a far longer period of time. Archaeological evidence and a variety of other sources,

[1] Richard Stren and Mohamed Halfani, 'The Cities of Sub-Saharan Africa', in Ronan Padison (ed.), *Handbook of Urban Studies* (London: Sage, 2001), p. 466.
[2] David Anderson and Richard Rathbone, 'Urban Africa. Histories in the Making', in Anderson and Rathbone (eds), *Africa's Urban Past* (Oxford: James Currey, 2000), p. 1.
[3] See, among many others, Catherine Coquery-Vidrovitch, 'Villes Coloniales et Histoire des Africains', *Vingtième Siècle* 20 (1988), pp. 49–73.

such as travel accounts, suggest complex pre-colonial urban settings.[4] Many West African 'trading towns' developed rapidly from the fifteenth century onwards in response to the economic stimuli of overseas trade. It is important to note that these towns, such as Ouidah, Bonny and Calabar, were not mere reflections of the contemporary European urban order, but were always characterized by the African inhabitants' own conceptions of urban space.[5]

The transition from slave trade to 'legitimate' commerce in the nineteenth century brought to West Africa both a greater European influence on urban designs and settlement patterns and the rise of some commercial centers such as Dakar, Douala, Freetown and Lagos, at the expense of hitherto important centers such as Ouidah.[6] The population of Lagos, for instance, grew from about 5,000 inhabitants in 1800 to 25,000 people in 1850. At this time, however, Ibadan, the largest Yoruba town, had more than twice as many inhabitants.[7] During the second half of the nineteenth century, the scale of West African cities was certainly not comparable to European or North American metropolises. In the 1890s, Paris had 2.5 million inhabitants, an industrial city like Manchester had about 550,000, and New York had already exceeded 1 million inhabitants in 1860.

While many pre-colonial West African commercial centers gained further in importance after the establishment of colonial rule, other cities that became important during the colonial and post-colonial periods, such as Abidjan or Yaoundé, had colonial foundations.[8] Another important urbanizing effect of colonialism in West Africa was the rise in the level of migratory activity from rural areas to urban centers, although most colonial migration remained rural-rural. The decade immediately following the Second World War witnessed a major acceleration of African migration from the countryside to cities. The annual population growth rate in places like Abidjan was more than

---

[4] Graham Connah, *African Civilizations. An Archaeological Perspective.* Second Edn (Cambridge: Cambridge University Press, 2001); Catherine Coquery-Vidrovitch, *Histoire des villes d'Afrique noire: Des origines à la colonisation* (Paris: Albin Michel, 1993).

[5] Anderson and Rathbone, 'Urban Africa', p. 4. For an excellent case study see Robin Law, *Ouidah. The Social History of a West African Slaving 'Port', 1727–1892* (Athens, OH: Ohio University Press; Oxford: James Currey, 2005).

[6] Anderson and Rathbone, 'Urban Africa', p. 5. For the transition see generally Robin Law (ed.), *From Slave Trade to 'Legitimate' Commerce: The Commercial Transition in Nineteenth-century West Africa* (Cambridge: Cambridge University Press, 1995).

[7] See A.L. Mabogunje, *Urbanization in Nigeria* (London: Pall Mall Press, 1968), chapters 3 and 4. An excellent study of Ibadan is Ruth Watson, *Civil Disorder is the Disease of Ibadan: Chieftaincy & Civic Culture in a Yoruba City* (Athens, OH: Ohio University Press; Oxford: James Currey, 2003).

[8] For Abidjan (and other Ivorian cities) see the voluminous study by Pierre Kipré, *Villes de Côte d'Ivoire 1893–1940*, 2 vols (Abidjan, Dakar and Lomé: Nouvelles Éditions Africaines, 1985).

10 per cent: Côte d'Ivoire's biggest city had mushroomed from a population of 58,000 in 1948 to 198,000 in 1960.[9] Lagos's population had swollen from 267,000 in 1952 to 665,000 in 1963.[10] The key to the pace of urbanization can be seen in colonial economic policies.[11] Africans were encouraged to leave the countryside because marketing controls limited the immediate returns to cultivators. The general post-Second World War expansion of education and health services occurred mainly in cities. And while the development programs of the period such as the French FIDES (Fund for Economic and Social Development) largely failed to transform the rural areas (or even brought about disastrous results), they provided the urban centers with a new set of functions and institutions in managing and servicing these efforts. In West Africa, large numbers of migrants flocked into the cities looking for urban employment which paid far higher returns than agrarian enterprise. However, only a small proportion of these migrants found work in the formal sector. The majority struggled along with casual jobs, petty trade or service occupations; an increasing number turned to criminal activities.[12]

During the late colonial and early post-colonial periods, everywhere in West Africa the physical growth of cities and towns far outstripped the capacity of urban resources and services. In many places housing provision proved to be the most precarious issue.[13] After independence, many West African countries attempted to respond to rapid urban growth by executing 'master plans', and by large-scale, government-sponsored construction of residential dwellings, which was often accompanied by the systematic eradication of 'slums'. These independent governments also regularly continued efforts instituted during the late colonial period.[14] However, the gap between the supply of, and demand for, good housing dramatically widened. The housing problem worsened after independence as the flow of rural migrants to the cities continuously swelled. The most important impulse for this

[9] Stren and Halfani, 'Cities', p. 467.

[10] Margaret Peil, *Lagos. The City is the People* (London: Belhaven Press, 1991), p. 19.

[11] For the rest of this paragraph see Ralph A. Austen, *African Economic History: Internal Development and External Dependency* (London: James Currey, 1987), pp. 230f.

[12] Laurent Fouchard and Isaac Olawale Albert (eds), *Sécurité, crime et ségrégation dans les villes d'Afrique de l'Ouest du XIXe siècle à nos jours* (Paris: Karthala, 2003).

[13] Philip Amis and Peter Lloyd (eds), *Housing Africa's Urban Poor* (Manchester: Manchester University Press, 1990).

[14] Stren and Halfani, 'Cities', pp. 469–71; for late colonial residential development efforts in West Africa see Jacqueline Poisnot et al. (eds), *Les villes d'Afrique noire. Politiques et opérations d'urbanisme et d'habitat entre 1650 et 1960* (Paris: Ministère de la coopération et du développement, 1989).

development can be seen in the 'urban bias' of the new West African states, which until the 1980s privileged the urban sector and especially the capital cities at the expense of rural areas. Urban growth was also fuelled by the high rate of natural population growth. Improved health conditions brought about not only a decline in mortality but also an increase in fertility.[15] In many rural areas, these changes led to growing population pressures, which in turn led to growing migration into the cities. Although the number of urban jobs in the formal sector (administration, parastatals, processing industries, banking, tourism, etc.) grew considerably in the first decades after independence, the urban labor market could never keep up with the explosion of urban population.

'From being places of accumulated wealth and prosperity, by the 1970s Africa's leading cities were increasingly coming to be seen as centers of poverty and social deprivation.'[16] Similar to the rest of the African continent during the 1980s and 1990s, West Africa faced an 'urban crisis' which was mainly characterized by three components: the formal job market shrank considerably while the 'informal sector' grew enormously; basic services deteriorated; and there was a severe decline in the quality of urban environments, for instance restricted access to various institutions, increasing criminality, or massive pollution. The poor were particularly affected.[17] Moreover, all big cities in West Africa, be it Abidjan, Accra, Dakar or Lagos, have become marginal at the global level. They have to cope with demographic pressure, economic stagnation and social deterioration, and lack the infrastructural and institutional requirements to attract private investments, which in turn could support the participation in global transactions.[18] Another recent feature of West African cities is the growing importance of urban agriculture.[19] One effect of this development is that the economic and cultural differences between city and rural areas have become blurred.

These blurred differences between the urban and the rural lead to the question of definition. 'Everyone knows what a city is except the

---

[15] Josef Gugler, 'Urbanization in Africa South of the Sahara: New Identities in Conflict', in J. Gugler (ed.), *The Urban Transformation of the Developing World* (Oxford, New York: Oxford University Press, 1996), p. 221.

[16] Anderson and Rathbone, 'Urban Africa', p. 8.

[17] Stren and Halfani, 'Cities', pp. 474f.

[18] David Simon, 'Urbanization, Globalization and Economic Crisis in Africa', in Carol Rakodi (ed.), *The Urban Challenge in Africa: Growth and Management of its Large Cities* (New York and Tokyo: United Nations University Press, 1997), pp. 74–108.

[19] Christine Schilter, *L'agriculture urbaine à Lomé: approches agronomique et socio-économique* (Paris and Geneva: Karthala and IUED, 1991).

experts.[20] Horace Miner's observation nicely refers to the eternal problem of definition, what is a city? Is there a specific African or even West African city? How does one define urbanization? The general literature on urbanization is full of complaints about the lack of satisfying definitions. While there seems to be a consensus that 'city' cannot be generally defined, at least among historians, hardly anyone embarks upon further suggestions. In a recent handbook article, two demographers suggested that definitions of the city may need to differ by levels of development and city function, and introduced the notion of the 'Functional Community Area'.[21] It seems doubtful whether this concept, based upon the example of the United States, can help to clarify the problems of definition in the African context. Even a closer look at Max Weber's famous typology of cities will not solve the problem, as the German sociologist did not include Africa in his study.[22] However, John Peel reminded us more than twenty years ago that it was Weber who showed that 'it is general historical issues which give towns their particular importance and the explanation of urban phenomena always depends on their location within a wider context.' Thus, Peel concludes, 'West African towns must always be viewed in relation to both the rural hinterland and the national and international systems of power in which they are set.'[23]

For a long time, historians of West Africa did not bother about problems of definition and how to conceptualize urbanization. Facing the rapid post-Second World War urbanization, sociologists, demographers, social anthropologists, economists and geographers were the first to discover African cities as a field of research. They usually tended to set aside the historical dimensions of urban Africa and treated urbanization as a modern phenomenon.[24] Furthermore, those historians who started to focus on urban areas during the 1970s were not concerned with urbanism itself, but with social, political or economic history that took place within cities.[25] Only recently has a

[20] Horace Miner, 'The City and Modernisation: An Introduction', in H. Miner (ed.), *The City in Modern Africa* (London: Pall Mall Press, 1967), p. 3.

[21] William H. Frey and Zachary Zimmer, 'Defining the City', in Padison, *Handbook*, pp. 14–33.

[22] Max Weber, *Wirtschaft und Gesellschaft. Die Wirtschaft und die gesellschaftlichen Ordnungen und Mächte. Nachlaß, Teilband 5: Die Stadt*, ed. by Wilfried Nippel (Tübingen: Mohr, 1999, orig. 1921); see Hinnerk Bruhns and Wilfried Nippel (eds), *Max Weber und die Stadt im Kulturvergleich* (Göttingen: Vandenhoeck & Ruprecht, 2000).

[23] John D.Y. Peel, 'Urbanization and Urban History in West Africa', *Journal of African History* 21 (1980), p. 277.

[24] This is still true for a number of more recent studies. See, for instance, Guy Mainet, *Douala. Croissance et Servitudes* (Paris: L'Harmattan, 1985).

[25] See the excellent overview by Catherine Coquery-Vidrovitch, 'The Process of Urbanization in

deeper interest in urban history emerged, which also includes work on pre-colonial West Africa. The remaining parts of this chapter attempt to build on the work noted above, while mainly focusing on urban land, real estate and the transformation of urban space.

Ordering urban space

Since Pierre Bourdieu's seminal studies on the theory of practice based on fieldwork in Kabylia (Algeria), we know that relations of power and social stratification are reflected in space, that we can discern in the order of space something like a lived map of daily life.[26] Space is an important and contested area of colonial and post-colonial daily life. Power structures are inscribed in space, and space reflects social organization and defines the people in it. Space is a central object of rule. In this context, an important aspect is the keeping of distance: rule is based upon distance. This is especially true in the colonial context, since in the colonies a small European minority faced a large indigenous majority. The thin foundations of colonial control made urban planning and architecture an important symbol of colonial hegemony. Colonial planning did not promote integration: it did not even pretend to be willing to integrate. On the contrary, it emphasized difference and hierarchy.

The most striking aspect of colonial urban planning in West Africa was the partition of urban space into two zones, a thinly populated 'European city', provided with all modern comforts, and the 'indigenous city', usually overpopulated and inadequately provisioned. This dualism was expressed in legislation that allowed only a restricted number of African individuals access to specific urban areas. It was also conveyed in architectural regulations or in the distribution of urban services. It would be misleading, however, to view West African colonial cities exclusively as 'dual cities', because colonial societies cannot be understood by the simple dichotomy 'European versus Indigenous'.[27]

The bifurcated nature of colonial urban space in West Africa was originally conceived to 'protect' Europeans from 'disease' thought to be

Africa (From the Origins to the Beginning of Independence)', *African Studies Review* 34 (1991), pp. 1–98.
[26] Pierre Bourdieu, *Outline of a Theory of Practice* (Cambridge: Cambridge University Press, 1977; French orig. 1972).
[27] Frederick Cooper, 'Conflict and Connection: Rethinking Colonial African History', *American Historical Review* 99 (1994), pp. 1516–45.

carried exclusively by Africans — the 'sanitation syndrome'.[28] Usually town planning promoted the separation of 'races'; in many West African cities one of the most important elements of this policy was the establishment of a 'free zone' or 'cordon sanitaire', as it was called in Francophone Africa. This policy was based on tropical hygienic arguments in connection with malaria prophylaxis.[29] The years between 1880 and the First World War were a key period for city planning in Africa, and also a period of rapid advance in tropical medicine. Until the late nineteenth century the thought was widespread, that malaria fever, which made parts of West Africa a 'white man's grave', was caused by 'toxic airs'. Then it was discovered that Anopheles mosquitoes were the principal carriers of malaria and that Africans, especially African children, were important carriers of the plasmodium of malaria.[30] The proposals of European medical specialists to fight malaria through segregation were usually conditioned by the pervasive racial thinking of the time. As Albert Wirz has noted:

> The historical tragedy is that at the very moment when a scientific revolution permitted for the first time a rational attack and prevention against malaria, in the social arena a racist ideology of dominance replaced the previous Enlightenment ideology. In the end only the mosquitoes profited from it.[31]

The most elaborate project in West Africa to fight malaria took place at the turn of the century in Freetown, Sierra Leone, reputedly the place most prone to malarial disease in the British Empire.[32] A government plan proposed the building of a new segregated suburb,

---

[28] This term has been coined by Maynard W. Swanson, 'The Sanitation Syndrome: Bubonic Plague and Urban Native Policy in the Cape Colony, 1900–1909', *Journal of African History* 18 (1977), pp. 387–410.

[29] See especially Philip D. Curtin, 'Medical Knowledge and Urban Planning in Tropical Africa', *American Historical Review* 90 (1985), pp. 594-613; also John W. Cell, 'Anglo-Indian Medical Theory and the Origins of Segregation in West Africa', *American Historical Review* 91 (1986), pp. 307–35; Daniel R. Headrick, *The Tentacles of Progress. Technology Transfer in the Age of Imperialism, 1850–1940* (Oxford: Oxford University Press, 1988), esp. chapter 5: 'Cities, Sanitation, and Segregation', pp. 145-70. Besides malaria, other diseases also justified segregation measures, for example the plague in Dakar. See Elikia M'Bokolo, 'Peste et Société Urbaine à Dakar: L'Epidémie de 1914', *Cahiers d'Etudes Africaines* 22 (1982), pp. 13-46; Myron Echenberg, *Black Death, White Medicine. Bubonic Plague and the Politics of Public Health in Colonial Senegal, 1914-1945* (Portsmouth, NH: Heinemann; Oxford: James Currey, 2002).

[30] See Emmanuel Akyeampong's chapter on the history of disease in West Africa, this volume.

[31] Albert Wirz, 'Malaria-Prophylaxe und kolonialer Städtebau. Fortschritt als Rückschritt?', *Gesnerus* 3 (1980), p. 222.

[32] For the rest of this paragraph see Leo Spitzer, 'The Mosquito and Segregation in Sierra Leone', *Canadian Journal of African Studies* 2 (1968), pp. 49–61; Curtin, 'Medical Knowledge', pp. 600f; Odile Goerg, *Pouvoir colonial, municipalités et espaces urbains. Conakry — Freetown des années 1880 à 1914, Vol. II: Urbanisme et Hygiénisme* (Paris: L'Harmattan, 1997).

which was called Hill Station, following an Indian model. The site chosen was about 750 feet above sea level and four miles from central Freetown, surrounded by a strip of land in which no African house-building or occupation of land was to be permitted. A mountain railway for both passenger and freight traffic opened in 1904. As mosquitoes were believed to bite only at night, African servants were allowed to work at Hill Station during the day but had to leave at night. However, Freetown's African elite of Western-educated journalists, doctors and lawyers strongly opposed this project because they realized that racial segregation was not only motivated by medical reasons, but by social and racist reasons as well. In fact, a number of British colonial officers wanted to enjoy 'the absence at night of the noises and smells of a native town', but not to such a degree that they had no African house servants. Moreover, the 'scientific' arguments for separating Europeans and Africans soon proved to be tenuous. In 1913, the British administration had to note: 'The health of officials who reside in Freetown . . . appears to be no worse than that of their fellow officials on the hill'.[33]

While in most West African cities segregation efforts took place in the early twentieth century, the extent of related measures varied according to not only the racist and chauvinist attitudes of local administrators but also the counter-activities and protests of local African elites. In Lagos, for instance, the local British Governor, William MacGregor, was a medical doctor himself and entertained serious doubts about the Colonial Office's idea of demolishing parts of the city to create 'free zones'. He initiated a large quinine-prophylaxis effort which was directed at both government officials and the African population. In 1907, however, the colonial administration made an effort to implement sanitary segregation by expropriating a central area of Lagos to create an exclusive European settlement. The Africans living there, mainly successful merchants and professional people, immediately mobilized against this plan. In the end, a European residential area came into existence, but the government was unable to get all Africans to leave.[34] Similar developments took place in Bathurst (Gambia) and Accra.

Probably the most radical attempt to establish an *apartheid* city in

---

[33] The two quotes are taken from Stephen Frenkel and John Western, 'Pretext or Prophylaxis? Racial Segregation and Malarial Mosquitoes in a British Tropical Colony: Sierra Leone', *Annales of the Association of American Geographers* 78 (1988), p. 227.

[34] Curtin, 'Medical Knowledge', pp. 602f.; Thomas S. Gale, 'Segregation in British West Africa', *Cahiers d'Etudes Africaines* 20 (1980), pp. 495–508.

West Africa was made by the Germans in Douala, Cameroon.[35] In 1910, the German administration drew up an elaborate plan for the segregation of Douala into European and African districts. The Europeans were to occupy the land along the Wouri River, where the original settlements of the leading Duala clans were located. Duala inhabitants of this riverine zone were to move inland to new settlements (called 'New Bell') and to receive compensation at a very low rate fixed by the government. The two social areas were to be separated by a one kilometer wide 'free zone' containing no residences. The chronology of the conflicts which followed this initiative is well covered in other historical studies. In summary, after the announcement of the expropriation plan in 1911, the Duala protested strongly, under the leadership of the Bell clan chief, Rudolf Duala Manga Bell. They first petitioned the local administration, and later the German Parliament. The Duala engaged a German lawyer, and the Reichstag debated the expropriation at considerable length during the first half of 1914, before finally accepting the local Cameroonian government's position. Meanwhile, the authorities in Douala completed the annexing of the major Bell area, partly by the use of force. Duala Manga and some of his followers were arrested on charges of high treason. On 8 August 1914, following the outbreak of the First World War, Duala Manga Bell was executed by hanging. The primary motivation for the expropriation plan did not begin with the economic needs of European enterprises but rather the government's vision of an orderly and sanitary gateway to its West Central African domain. The Duala appeared to threaten this vision both in general terms, because of their presence as an African group with claims to a position beyond that of colonial subjects, and more specifically by supposedly harboring disease. The Duala elite were very conscious of their privileged access to European educational institutions and argued, among other things, that a movement away from the Europeans in general, and missionary schools in particular, would mean 'cultural ruin'.

The expropriation conflict continued throughout the first decade of French rule in Cameroon. The new mandatory power did not fulfil the Duala hope of regaining the annexed land. The French argued that the German expropriation was legal and that, according to the Treaty of Versailles, that land was their property. The French, nevertheless,

---

[35] For the case of Douala see Ralph A. Austen and Jonathan Derrick, *Middlemen of the Cameroons: The Duala and their Hinterland, c.1600-c.1960* (New York: Cambridge University Press, 1999), esp. pp. 128–37; Andreas Eckert, *Grundbesitz, Landkonflikte und kolonialer Wandel. Douala 1880-1960* (Stuttgart: Steiner, 1999), esp. pp. 112–29. Note that 'Douala' refers to the city, 'Duala' to the ethnic group.

concluded that the Germans had mistreated and insulted the Duala through their exaggerated and perhaps insincere belief in the need for total segregation of the city's African and European populations. They limited segregation to a few areas of the city and paid some compensation for the land lost.[36]

In Douala, as in most other Francophone African cities, the French carried out an urban policy which stressed cultural difference and took architectural style as a criterion for ordering urban space. The 'European city' was to be open for Europeans and those Africans willing and capable of living in 'European style'. In Dakar, Abidjan and Conakry, the French administration created spacious 'European cities' often equipped with elegant boulevards and government buildings. These buildings symbolized the most important institutions of colonial power and displayed its permanence: European individuals would come and go, but these buildings clearly showed that colonial rule as such was meant to be permanent.[37] Another important structural element of colonial cities in West Africa emerged from efforts to further organize the 'European city'. European women had to structure their leisure time, and children had to be kept occupied in parks and green areas as in Europe, if possible. The 'domestication' of urban vegetation as well as the creation of large green spaces and public gardens were a part of this project.[38] In the end, only very few Africans 'achieved' the status required to live in the 'European city', while the majority settled in suburbs and *bidonvilles*.

While a number of historians stress that French and British colonizers had fundamentally different approaches to urbanism and segregation in their respective colonies, it should be emphasized that one usually finds the same discourse of racial separation. All colonial powers used the hygiene paradigm to enforce a clear division between so-called races and ethnic groups, and to make these categories visible in everyday life.[39] By segregating 'races', the European colonizers introduced a new

---

[36] Jonathan Derrick, 'Douala under the French Mandate, 1916 to 1936' (unpublished PhD Thesis, London University, 1979).

[37] Raymond F. Betts, 'Imperial Designs: French Colonial Architecture and Urban Planning in Sub-Saharan Africa', in G. Wesley Johnson (ed.), *Double Impact. France and Africa in the Age of Imperialism* (Westport, CT: Greenwood, 1985), pp. 191–207; Gwendolyn Wright, *The Politics of Design in French Colonial Urbanism* (Chicago and London: University of Chicago Press, 1991).

[38] Odile Goerg, 'Entre nature et culture: La végétation dans les villes coloniales (Conakry, Freetown)', *Revue Française d'Histoire d'Outre-Mer* 83 (1996), pp. 43–60.

[39] Odile Goerg, 'From Hill Station (Freetown) to Downtown Conakry (First Ward): Comparing French and British Approaches to Segregation in Colonial Cities at the Beginning of the Twentieth Century', *Canadian Journal of African Studies* 32 (1998), pp. 1–31.

element into the African urban order. However, in pre-colonial West African societies space had social dimensions. In numerous pre-colonial West African cities there had been the creation of districts based upon ethnic, religious or professional criteria. West African rulers often allocated separate settlements to traders and other travellers. Sometimes this traders' district constituted a specific part of a city, and it was often distinctly separated from the city center.[40] In the eleventh century, the Arab geographer Al-Bakri described Kumbi-Saleh, the capital of the Ghana Empire, as a twin city, where the immigrant Muslim traders settled spatially separated from the site of the ruler.[41] However, the categorization of human variety according to 'races' is a European invention and alien to African cultures. Moreover, in most pre-colonial African towns and cities the formation of districts was relatively spontaneous, not centrally decreed. And it was strangers, not indigenous people, who were referred to distinctive areas on the periphery. Finally, the structuring of African cities according to ethnic or other criteria did not exclude the possibility that there was a city center accessible to all. Unlike the racially segregated colonial city, this kind of structure allowed for common social life.

By creating segregated 'African' districts, the colonial officials had to realize that they had also created spaces difficult to control. Especially after 1945, it proved to be impossible to 'channel properly' migration to the cities. Although the colonial state's land regime accorded no new rights of ownership in most cities deemed either 'traditional' or 'new', in the increasingly crowded urban areas an active 'illegal' trade in plots, buildings, and rooms soon became a feature of urban life. Activities such as prostitution and the distilling of liquor, which the administration deemed 'illegal' or even 'criminal', were widespread. Moreover, this 'illegal space' became a center of trade union activities and political opposition.[42]

However, West African cities never became the cultural melting pots that a number of colonial officials so greatly feared; rather, the opposite occurred. Increasing competition for jobs, space and power hardened rivalries. In numerous places these struggles were increasingly configured in ethnic terms. Long-established residents and members of majority communities defended access to jobs and living space against

---

[40] Philip D. Curtin, *Cross-cultural Trade in World History* (Cambridge: Cambridge University Press, 1984), pp. 38–59.

[41] Richard W. Hull, *African Cities and Towns before the European Conquest* (New York: W.W. Norton, 1976), pp. 80f.

[42] For the case of New Bell, Douala, see Richard Joseph, *Radical Nationalism in Cameroun: Social Origins of the UPC Rebellion* (Oxford: Clarendon Press, 1977), pp. 160ff.

immigrants. Minorities banded closer together to increase their influence.[43] Still today, access to urban land is a particularly contested area, which not only sets ethnically defined groups against one another, but also creates divisions along age and gender lines. In Douala, for example, younger sons and women are regularly excluded from access to landed property with the argument that they have no traditional rights to it.

Urban land, landowners and conflicts

The literature on issues such as control over land, land conflicts and land law has almost exclusively dealt with rural areas. And although the importance of landed property and conflicts over land is frequently mentioned in the fast growing literature on Africa's urban past, only a very few scholars have used land issues as a tool to explore broader questions of urban development during the colonial and post-colonial periods.[44] The importance of access to land in urban West Africa has varied considerably. Lagos ranks high among those cities where a market for rental property had already developed during the second half of the nineteenth century and where the value of land as an economic resource constantly increased. Anthony Hopkins has argued with good reason that Britain's annexation of Lagos in 1861 was primarily motivated by the need to have property rights.[45] Population growth and commercial development following the annexation combined to increase the demand for land to build residences and storehouses. Immigrants from the interior obtained use-rights to land from chiefly and other local families. A number of immigrants settled where they chose. Usually no one made attempts to expel them: the local population seldom made efforts to formally protect their rights in land, which had been in abundance since time immemorial. In the face of numerous land conflicts and fraudulent transactions, in 1863 British Governor Freedman already felt obliged to establish a land register in order to allocate land titles. From this date on, land occupants received

[43] Anderson and Rathbone, 'Urban Africa', pp. 7f.
[44] For a recent exception that confirms the rule see Laurent Fourchard, *De la ville coloniale à la cour africaine: espaces, pouvoirs et sociétés à Ouagadougou et à Bobo-Dioulasso (Haute Volta), fin 19ème siècle–1960* (Paris: L'Harmattan, 2002); and 'Propriétaires et Commerçants Africains à Ouagadougou et à Bobo-Dioulasso (Haute Volta), fin 19ème Siècle–1960', *Journal of African History* 44 (2003), pp. 433–61. See also Eckert, *Grundbesitz*.
[45] Anthony G. Hopkins, 'Property Rights and Empire Building: Britain's Annexation of Lagos, 1861', *Journal of Economic History* 40 (1980), pp. 777–98. The following paragraphs draw heavily drew from this article.

Crown grants. Between 1863 and 1899, the government issued about 3,500 Crown grants. Hopkins' analysis of the grantees' names suggests that about 100 grants were issued to Europeans, about 1,100 to Christian Africans, and the rest, roughly 2,300, to indigenous Lagosians.[46]

Although heavily contested, from the outset Crown grants were treated as if they conferred absolute rights of individual ownership. The occupier became a freeholder with the right to alienate his land; he also acquired the opportunity to procure lands which he did not occupy personally. Filing a mortgage on one's landed property in order to obtain credit or loans was a widespread practice already in the 1860s.[47] Moreover, the transformation of Lagos into an important colonial trading and administrative center created a busy real-estate market. Although African merchants ceased to compete with European firms after the turn of the century, they and their families clung tenaciously to landed property wherever possible. In becoming landowners who rented out their property, they retained their gentility and used the income from this source to finance the education of their children. In this way they helped to generate new forms of property based on the service industries, notably the professions such as journalism and legal business and government employment. In 1908, the Commissioner of Land stated: 'There is no doubt that the value of land in Lagos has increased very rapidly. It is the ambition of every man to own land in Lagos and money saved is at once invested in land'.[48]

In the course of the twentieth century real estate further gained in importance. Everywhere in Lagos, urban land proved to be an investment which paid off in political, economic and social respects. As Sandra Barnes noted: 'Nothing attracted as much respect as owning a house: it was a necessary requirement of any claim of eminence or affluence in a community'.[49] Access to this resource was linked to many conflicts and brought about numerous judicial and political conflicts. Struggles over urban land, on the one hand, led to deep rivalries, but,

[46] *Ibid.*, p. 791. On Lagos society at the turn of the century see Kristin Mann, *Marrying Well: Marriage, Status and Social Change among the Educated Elite in Early Colonial Lagos* (Cambridge: Cambridge University Press, 1985); Patrick Cole, *Modern and Traditional Elites in the Politics of Lagos, 1884–1938* (Cambridge: Cambridge University Press, 1975).

[47] Kristin Mann, 'The Rise of Taiwo Olowo: Law, Accumulation, and Mobility in Early Colonial Lagos', in Kristin Mann and Richard Roberts (eds), *Law in Colonial Africa* (Portsmouth: Heinemann; Oxford: James Currey, 1991), p. 87.

[48] Hopkins, 'Property Rights', pp. 793, 790 (quote).

[49] Sandra T. Barnes, *Patrons and Power: Creating a Political Community in Metropolitan Lagos* (Manchester: Manchester University Press, 1986), p. 47. See also by the same author: 'Migration and Land Acquisition: The New Landowners of Lagos', *African Urban Studies* 4 (1979), pp. 59–70.

on the other hand, new loyalties were created and promoted. Those who succeeded in accumulating landed property constituted a heterogeneous group, but they shared an important characteristic feature: their property earned them a privileged position in the urban social hierarchy. There are to date no detailed studies of Lagos landowners, but apparently the Yoruba own a majority of the real estate in many areas. In old city districts, those families who bought land during the nineteenth century are still among the notable landlords.[50] Today, the process of acquiring land puts much more emphasis on social networks than on estate agents. Prospective buyers must locate a family that may be willing to sell a plot and come to an agreement with the elders. These arrangements are often contested by other family members. Few sales were registered before the 1950s; and although transfers were increasingly certified after that period, there is still much land whose ownership is ambiguous.[51]

Turning to colonial Douala, the most important landlords organized their access to urban land by claiming their 'traditional' rights, as well as relying on modern land law and the real-estate market.[52] In the 1940s and 1950s, real estate not only symbolized economic success, but also reflected a person's power both in 'traditional' and 'modern' society. Those who had been able to achieve access to land had shown that they could either raise traditional rights in land or master modern capitalistic ways of land acquisition. Ideally, a person had access to both possibilities. However, the rise of real estate did not produce a new class transgressing older hierarchies in Duala society. Towards the end of the colonial period, it was the chiefs and notables who were in a position to make the most of the new economic resource. But the system eventually opened up. During the late colonial period not only the old elite, but any Duala who skilfully used European land decrees and the options produced by the urban real-estate market, had access to property and could use it to sharpen his social and political image. However, women were still excluded from obtaining real estate, because they had neither 'traditional' nor 'modern' options.[53]

The growing conflicts over land within the Duala community and family units after the Second World War reflected basic conflicts in

[50] Peil, *Lagos*, pp. 142f.

[51] *Ibid.*, p. 142.

[52] This and the following paragraphs are based on Eckert, *Grundbesitz*.

[53] For women's access to urban real estate in other colonial West African cities, see Claire C. Robertson, *Sharing the Same Bowl. A Socio-economic History of Women and Class in Accra, Ghana* (Bloomington and Indianapolis, IN: Indiana University Press, 1984); Kristin Mann, 'Women, Landed Property, and the Accumulation of Wealth in Early Colonial Lagos', *Signs* 16 (1991), pp. 682–706.

society. During the post-war boom, the more important land plots became as an economic resource, the more intense were the struggles over access to this resource. 'Customary law' played an important role in these struggles: those who succeeded in fixing 'traditional' modes of land acquisition according to their own interests usually emerged victorious in these struggles. Furthermore, land conflicts clearly show the growing loss of authority on the part of chiefs and elders, who, on the one hand, tried to make a mark for themselves as representatives of their commoners in land issues, while on the other hand, considerably benefiting from their privileged access to land — a privilege based on colonial ideas about the importance of chiefs in land matters and in the colonial legal system generally.

Another important relationship in the conflict was the presence of elder and younger sons within a household. Using 'tradition' as an argument, the elder laid claim to inherited real estate. These claims usually brought the younger brothers into the arena, as they feared exclusion from the economic use of urban family land. Conflicts between the sexes also increasingly took the form of struggles over land. Men successfully interpreted the Duala customary land law in the sense that women were to have no access to this resource. Moreover, the accusation of slave origin was used by Duala individuals to prevent others from claiming 'customary' rights in urban land plots.

The adaptation of European land law may have been part of the Duala elite identity, and was therefore used as a vehicle for their 'modernization' efforts: the demand for land titles could be interpreted as an effort to meet the standards set by Europeans, to demonstrate aspirations towards equality. People requested land titles for the same reasons they constructed European-style houses, bought European furniture, or wore three-piece suits. Cities have always been places where Africans simultaneously adapted to and transformed urban lifestyles. Leisure and recreational activities, such as football, fashion and dance, built up social networks, humanized daily life, and forged new identities in the colonial context.[54] These activities became even more important after independence. In Pikine, a densely populated district of Dakar, young people in sport clubs 'shape the cityscape, modulate the public sphere, and negotiate their own position in society'.[55] In the context of deteriorating social and economic conditions

---

[54] Phyllis Martin, *Leisure and Society in Colonial Brazzaville* (Cambridge: Cambridge University Press, 1995); Paul Tiyambe Zeleza and Cassandra Rachel Veney (eds), *Leisure in Urban Africa* (Trenton, NJ: Africa World Press, 2003).

[55] Susann Baller, 'Creating the Postcolonial City: Urban Youth Clubs in Senegal', in Toyin Falola and Steve Salm (eds), *African Urban Cultures* (Durham, NC: Academic Press, forthcoming).

in African suburbs, young people use these clubs to find entry into economic independence and adulthood.

Conclusion

As previously mentioned, African cities are in a position of global marginality. However, in the last decade local community organizations in many West African cities have created a new political culture, recognizing the plurality of actors in urban society. In the course of the twentieth century, cities have become places that millions of Africans call 'home'. However, they have also sought to reinvent these urban spaces. New efforts to transform African cities' physical landscapes, as well as their social and political structures, must better reflect these cities' unique cultural and historical conditions. This is all the more important given that, in 2025, it is highly probable that more than 50 per cent of Africa's population will be living in large metropolitan areas, a number of which will probably become the mega-cities of West Africa.

Recommended Reading

Anderson, David and Richard Rathbone (eds) (2000) *Africa's Urban Past* (Oxford: James Currey).

Barnes, Sandra T. (1986) *Patrons and Power: Creating a Political Community in Metropolitan Lagos* (Manchester: Manchester University Press).

Connah, Graham (2001) *African Civilizations. An Archaeological Perspective*, second edn (Cambridge: Cambridge University Press).

Coquery-Vidrovitch, Catherine (1993) *Histoire des villes d'Afrique noire. Des origines à la colonisation* (Paris: Albin Michel).

Eckert, Andreas (1999) *Grundbesitz, Landkonflikte und kolonialer Wandel. Douala 1880-1960* (Stuttgart: Steiner).

Goerg, Odile (1997) *Pouvoir colonial, municipalités et espaces urbains. Conakry – Freetown des années 1880 à 1914*, 2 vols (Paris: L'Harmattan).

Mabogunje, A. L. (1968) *Urbanization in Nigeria* (London: Pall Mall Press).

Martin, Phyllis M. (1995) *Leisure and Society in Colonial Brazzaville* (Cambridge: Cambridge University Press).

Rakodi, Carol (ed.) (1997) *The Urban Challenge in Africa. Growth and Management of its Large Cities* (New York and Tokyo: United Nations University Press).

PART III

Understanding
Contemporary West Africa through Religion
& Political Economy

11

Commodities, Mercedes-Benz & Structural Adjustment
An Episode in West African Economic History[1]

CELESTIN MONGA

Introduction

'In much of Africa, it is easier to find a bottle of beer than a glass of clean water.' — Ali Mazrui.

By all accounts, Africa's economic performance since 1960 (the year of independence) has been dismal. Much has been said and written about the 'disappointments of independence', the fact that the advent of *Uhuru* (freedom) may have been 'worse than colonialism', to use the words of the poet Okot p'Bitek. Yet, many other post-colonial societies in Asia and Latin America have managed to escape the burden of history and establish themselves as self-sufficient, economic powerhouses. While it is difficult to generalize about West Africa, a quick anatomy of its economies suggests that their structural patterns and the engines/drivers of economic growth over the past decades have often been similar. Performance has been dismal. Agricultural growth, which determines the livelihood of 60 to 80 per cent of African people, has been unable to keep up with needs. Because of ineffective strategies and population growth, food production per capita has declined since independence and many countries depend on imports — which creates serious foreign-exchange needs and balance-of-payments problems. Production is typically oriented to the limited processing of commodities and other low value-added activities. Even countries that have experienced

---

[1] The findings, interpretations, and conclusions expressed in this chapter are entirely those of the author. They do not necessarily represent the views of the World Bank, its Executive Directors, or the countries they represent.

industrial growth have done so by relying on a small sector of the economy (mostly oil), scarce and volatile foreign capital and skills, and import-intensive technologies. Faced with the shortage of financing, poor infrastructure and ineffective government policies, the services sector has mushroomed into a large informal sector which provides subsistence employment but not the productivity and income levels that can reduce poverty.

Exploring the reasons for this state of affairs has been a battle of narratives. This chapter discusses Africa's economic development through one particular narrative, the structural adjustment programs (SAPs) designed by the Bretton Woods institutions (World Bank and International Monetary Fund) as a framework for growth and poverty reduction. The package of economic and social policies known as SAPs emerged in the early 1980s and quickly became a central feature in the discourse on African economic development. A famous quote attributed to Adebayo Adedeji, former Executive Secretary of the UN Economic Commission for Africa (ECA), is that SAPs did more harm to the continent than all the decades of colonialism put together! There are obviously many other narratives to the story.

The remainder of this chapter is organized as follows. First, there is a brief survey of the main theoretical frameworks offered by economic historians as the key explanations for the continent's poor performance, plus the consensus view among mainstream economists on the determinants of growth and welfare for small open economies. Second, there is an explanation of how SAPs fit into the dominant (neo-classical) economic paradigm. Thirdly, how these programs have been assessed in Africa, and the shortcomings of the theoretical underpinnings of the prevailing model, are discussed as well as the alternative frameworks for economic development put forward by African leaders. The chapter concludes by suggesting the criteria for an adequate economic development strategy, together with a road map for moving beyond the current 'commodities and Mercedes-Benz economies'.

African economies in a historical perspective

In analyzing the genesis and effects of SAPs in sub-Saharan Africa, it is useful to put them in historical perspective and at least sketch the wider economic and socio-political contexts in which they emerged. While these programs, as they came to be known in the economic literature, only occurred in the 1980s and determined most of economic policy in many Third World countries, their particular importance in

Africa stems from the very nature of the long history of the continent's economies. A brief survey of the dynamics of African pre-colonial and colonial economies is therefore in order if one is to understand how post-colonial economies so quickly became trapped into the need for structural adjustment.

Competing theoretical frameworks

The difficulty of providing powerful organizing concepts and frameworks that would explain Africa's economic past is illustrated by the large volume of work with purely descriptive accounts of agriculture, crafts, trade and industry across the continent during pre-colonial times.[2] Fortunately, the lack of theoretical statements and the rather limited usefulness of broad-encompassing, long-run historical studies have been compensated since the 1970s by the many insights from more geographically focused research. Thus, the study of the history of West African economies, at least for the period ranging from the beginnings of food-source domestication to the post-colonial regimes of the contemporary era, has been marked by what Austen called 'ideologically charged debates.'[3] Long before the advent of structural adjustment programs, various competing frameworks were offered by historians and social scientists to explain the continent's sluggish economic performance.

Austen identified two major camps: one committed to a market or neo-classical perspective and using rational choice theory as the main tool of analysis, and the other sub-divided into substantivist, Marxist, and dependency theory. Obviously, in their approach to African economic history, these two camps rely on sharply different models of the behavior of economic actors and their motives. Market theorists consider the actor to be an individual or a firm whose only objective is to use production factors to maximize benefits or returns under specific constraints imposed by circumstances, while minimizing risks. Structuralists tend to focus on collective entities such as a harmonizing social order determining the rules of economic behavior (for substantivists), or a hierarchical system in which dominant and

---

[2] See, for instance, Wickins, which attempts a general survey of African economic history from the fifth millennium BC to around AD 1900 with no clear rationale for what seems to be a randomly selected period of time: P.L. Wickins, *An Economic History of Africa from the Earliest Times to Partition* (Cape Town: Oxford University Press, 1981). In the same vein, Z. A. and J. M. Konczacki mostly offered a narrative account of African integration into the world economy but did not engage with some key issues explaining these patterns of engagement: The *Economic History of Tropical Africa*, vol. 1, *The Pre-Colonial Period*, vol. 2, *The Colonial Period* (London: Frank Cass, 1977).

[3] Ralph Austen, *African Economic History* (London: James Currey and Portsmouth, NH: Heinemann, 1987).

subordinate social groups or world regions struggle over economic control (Marxists and dependency theorists).

Such schematic classification obviously does not capture all the nuances of the intellectual discussion on African economic history. Nevertheless it helps sort out the main themes underlying the competing theoretical frameworks at work, and their relative strengths and weaknesses. With his radiography of West Africa's patterns of involvement in world trade, Hopkins stands as one of the main proponents of the market-oriented school.[4] He explains that a market system initially failed in that part of the world not because economic agents did not want it but because domestic resources were not sufficient to spur the growth of effective demand. It was constrained, on the one hand, by the low density of population, and, on the other hand, by the high cost of transportation. Thus, the first phase of international trade failed to act as an engine of growth in West Africa because the slave trade, besides being criminal and immoral, created only a very small export sector, one that had 'few beneficial links with the rest of the economy'. However, at the beginning of the nineteenth century, there was a major turning point in the development of these economies: trade became more legitimate and more intense, as warrior entrepreneurs who had dominated the scene up to that time faced a large number of small producers and traders. This shift in the structure of export-producing firms was sustained throughout several decades by some internal dynamics in African societies (the emergence of a highly industrious class of local entrepreneurs), and the increasingly important role of France as a colonial power in West Africa.

By the end of the nineteenth century, this new economy suffered a major setback. There was a general economic crisis which can be explained by economic and political factors: a prolonged fall in the price of palm oil and groundnuts after 1860 and desperate attempts by the oligarchs of the slave-trade networks to maintain their grasp on the economy. Furthermore, some poor business practices on the part of the trading firms eventually encouraged colonialism: in response to declining profit margins, monopolies became popular and business relations more politicized. Colonial powers felt compelled to become more involved in the ruling of these territories.

Rodney attempts to explain the gap between the rich and poor nations that has been growing for centuries, and offers a completely different economic history of Africa.[5] His book is considered a major contribution

---

[4] A. G. Hopkins, *An Economic History of West Africa* (London: Longman, 1973).

[5] Walter Rodney, *How Europe Underdeveloped Africa* (London: Bogle-L'Ouverture Publications, 1972).

to dependency theory. His scope is larger than economic growth, as it addresses issues of development — defined as growth in economic production, equity in the distribution of social product and autonomy of people in colonial territories in the control over social processes. Interestingly, he rejects the notion that underdevelopment could be the natural, initial stage of any society, and sees it as the distorted result of European hegemony which has been imposed on the world since the fifteen century. As Legassick noted, Rodney asserts that 'metropolitan capitalist development and peripheral underdevelopment are two sides of the same coin'.[6]

Relying on Marx's ambiguous development theory, Rodney affirms African capability and business sense but stresses its limitations in the context of externally imposed constraints. The core of the issue is the fact that capitalism can promote growth almost everywhere, but development (equity and autonomy) nowhere — neither in the metropolis nor in the periphery. The logic of capitalist accumulation is to mobilize forces of production to the point where the concentration of ownership lies in ever fewer hands, which then produces a high level of inequalities of wealth and power. But the process is not inconsistent with the fact that higher real wages and higher living standards can occur for the working class. Indeed, higher living standards for the masses can be compatible with a higher technical rate of their exploitation.

Such a framework obviously raises questions about the meaning of development, especially in the African context. Rodney argues that, prior to European penetration, African societies were at various stages of development, from communalism to a 'transitional' stage 'below class-ridden feudalism'.[7] Thereafter, European-generated activities created underdevelopment. Specifically, the external domination of merchant capital through the slave trade, unequal exchange and the destruction of domestic economies (especially handicraft production and trade) promoted development in Europe and mostly misery and inequality in Africa.

The economics of colonialism and commodities

One of the preliminary issues to be addressed is that of 'periodization', the optimal or relevant sequencing of time and periods of analysis. While the conventional wisdom among Western historians is to

---

[6] Martin Legassick, 'Perspectives on "African Underdevelopment"', *Journal of African History* XVIII (3) (1976), pp. 435–40, p. 436 (quote).

[7] Rodney, *How Europe Underdeveloped Africa*, p. 80.

distinguish between traditional time categories like Antiquity, the Middle-Ages, the Enlightenment, etc., some African historians question what they consider to be an ideologically designed sequencing of events. Instead, Amara Cissé, for instance, suggests that a completely different and longer timeframe (starting from the Neolithic) be used for assessing performance over time.[8] Another important issue is the accuracy of the information on pre-colonial economies. A third issue is the debate over the actual impact of colonialism on African societies. Hicks' distinction between 'colonies of settlement' and 'trading post colonies' is an interesting conceptual categorization. But it is not very useful in assessing what impact colonialism had on African economies, especially since he also observes that many colonies started for settlement gradually became trading posts, that is 'plantation colonies'.[9]

These three issues are relevant to the analysis of SAPs. However, the 'periodization' debate and the quality of the information on African pre-colonial economies are still ongoing conceptual discussions among historians. They are therefore beyond the scope of this chapter. The issue of the impact of colonialism is a more legitimate one: because SAPs have been conceived outside of the continent and have been implemented under the pressure of the Bretton Woods institutions in which Western countries are major shareholders, it is impossible to discuss them in isolation from the broader debates in African economic history. Indeed, many African intellectuals have clearly linked SAPs to imperialism and colonialism.[10] It is, therefore, useful to start with a brief overview of the discourse on the impact of colonialism on the structure and performance of African economic performance today.

The age of colonialism began soon after the discoveries of the sea route around Africa's southern coast (1488) and of America (1492). According to Cooper, after the Industrial Revolution, the elaboration of military technology and the self-confidence of the bourgeois culture gave European elites a sense that their ways of organizing life stood not only for might but also for progress. 'Africa became a salient object of reformist imperialism because it could be portrayed as a slavery-ridden continent, held in check by tyrants, isolated from the beneficial

---

[8] Daniel Amara Cissé, *Histoire économique de l'Afrique noire*, 4 vols. (Abidjan and Paris: Presses Universitaires et Scolaires d'Afrique and L'Harmattan, 1988).

[9] John Hicks, *A Theory of Economic History* (Oxford: Clarendon Press, 1969), pp. 51–3.

[10] The words *imperialism* and *colonialism* are used here as defined by Frederick Cooper: 'The exercise of power by a state beyond its borders' for the former, and 'the erection by a state of an apparatus of administrative control over peoples who are defined as distinct' for the latter; 'Colonialism and Imperialism: An Overview', in John Middleton (ed.), *Encyclopedia of Africa South of the Sahara*, 4 vols. (New York: Charles Scribner's Sons, 1997), pp. 316–21.

effects of commerce'.[11] The slave trade took a heavy toll on African economies by depriving them of manpower and resources, and European imperialists did penetrate inland and tried to remake African societies in a European image starting in the nineteenth century. Furthermore, the effects of Europe's economic power — demonstrated through trade in gold, ivory and other commodities — were widely although unevenly felt throughout the continent, influencing the political and economic structures of coastal and inland communities. According to Cooper, this initial justification of colonialism assumed the superiority of the free market system, along with the rationalist heritage of the Enlightenment, and a particular organization of state-society relationships.

While the debate over the economic impact and balance sheet of colonialism in Africa is far from settled, there is little discussion about the magnitude of the structural changes that took place in the continent during the time of European domination.[12] The colonial powers initially considered their role in 'structuring' African economies with pride. In the 1930s, several large exhibitions were organized in Europe to display what was then considered the accomplishments of colonization: the familiar argument that, thanks to European rule, foreign trade (especially commodity trade) had acted as the main engine of growth, drawing the dark continent into the international economy; the launch of major public works; and the ability of colonial states to bring together diverse populations and cultures into harmonious, peaceful nations. Free market historians have endorsed that view, focusing on attempts at industrialization that were not even made by economic agents prior to colonialism, and on the surplus that was not generated.

According to Hopkins, colonialism marked 'a new and broadly speaking, expansionist phase in the evolution of the modern market economy'. Such statements and the assertion that 'Britain [for instance] . . . had a moral obligation to support her traders in international markets',[13] if need be by conquering territories like Nigeria, explain why he has been dismissed in some circles as a colonial apologist.

On the other hand, structuralist and Marxist economic historians of Africa tend to consider the colonial moment as the 'crucial' determinant of underdevelopment.[14] The fact that economic dependence on the West and on commodity markets outlived colonialism in Africa has given

---

[11] Cooper, 'Colonialism and Imperialism', p. 316.
[12] Peter Duignan and Lewis H. Gann (eds), *Colonialism in Africa, 1870–1960*, vol. 4, *The Economics of Colonialism* (Stanford, CA: Hoover Institution Press, 1988).
[13] Hopkins, *An Economic History*, p. 157.
[14] Rodney, *How Europe Underdeveloped Africa*, p. 308.

life to anti-capitalist theories. Following Lenin[15] and taking up variants of his approach, many economic historians consider colonialism as a purely extractive process designed to produce profits for colonial capitalists, prevent capital accumulation in African economies, and perpetuate their dependence on commodities and imports. Brett[16] presents evidence of colonial authorities acting decisively to block attempts at industrialization, and to redistribute the surplus in ways that favored the metropolis. Hobson[17], though a liberal economist, linked colonialism and capitalism, arguing that underconsumption in Europe was the main driver of imperialism. By keeping workers' wages very low and consistently investing profits in more production, Western capitalists quickly faced insufficient domestic markets to absorb their surplus. Each national group then pressured their government to find new, protected, colonial markets overseas. While Robinson and Gallagher[18] argue that Britain's role in the partition of Africa after 1880 was largely determined by political and strategic considerations, Hynes[19] demonstrates the importance of economic motives in determining British action. Using records of the Chamber of Commerce and Colonial Office papers, he shows the heavy pressure brought to bear on various British governments by merchants and manufacturers to persuade them to extend British influence in various parts of Africa and South-east Asia. As a result of the decline in traditional outlets for British goods and the rise of protectionism in world markets, the interest in African markets grew sharply between 1880 and 1895, shaping the pattern of British involvement in West Africa.

French authorities were even more direct in putting forward an economic rationale for their involvement in African colonies. They decided to build railroads and motor roads, introduced their currency, imposed a monetary union among territories under French rule in 1939, and made labor more mobile through the end of slavery and peace-keeping. Suret-Canale[20] shows that the authoritarian and oppressive administrative system put in place by the French government served to

[15] Vladimir Ilitch Lenin, *Imperialism: The Highest Stage of Capitalism* (New York: International Publishers, 1939).

[16] E. A. Brett, *Colonialism and Underdevelopment in East Africa: The Politics of Economic Change, 1919–1939* (London, Heinemann: 1981 [1973]).

[17] John Atkinson Hobson, *Imperialism: A Study* (London: Unwin Hyman, 1988 [1902]).

[18] Ronald Robinson and John Gallagher, *Africa and the Victorians: The Climax of Imperialism in the Dark Continent* (New York: St. Martins Press, 1961).

[19] Williams G. Hynes, *The Economics of Empire: Britain, Africa, and the New Imperialism, 1870–95* (London: Longman, 1979).

[20] Jean Suret-Canale, *French Colonialism in Tropical Africa, 1900–1945* (London: C. Hurst and Co., 1971).

force Africans into the colonial economy, compelling local producers to supply primary products for the profit of a French commercial oligarchy. Marseille[21] makes the same point, stressing, however, the divergence of views between politicians and businessmen in France towards the end of the colonial period.

Well before the nineteenth century, Africa had established strong trading networks based on the marketing of locally produced agricultural and industrial goods. As noted by Akinola, 'Africa was Europe's trading partner, not its economic appendage'.[22] Colonialism changed that dynamics. An important step was to wrest the control of trade from middlemen, like the Swahili states of the East African coast, and powerful magnates, like Ja Ja, king of the Niger Delta state of Opobo. Indeed, several of the wars resisting European penetration in the Lower Niger, in East Africa, and in the Congo Basin were precipitated by European measures to take control of trade. The subsequent colonial boundaries and the smothering of pre-colonial industries through the flooding of African markets with European consumer goods contributed to the export-import orientation of the colonial economy — still a dominant feature of African economies today.

In fact, economic growth and progress in West African living standards throughout the nineteenth century and most of the colonial period were primarily driven by innovative business strategies developed by African migrant workers, cocoa farmers, groundnut-buyers, and road hauliers. Cooper writes that some of the economic success of colonial regimes came about more through African than European agency. 'The vast expansion of cocoa production in the Gold Coast at the turn of the [twentieth] century, in Nigeria from the 1920s on, and in Côte d'Ivoire beginning in the 1940s took place in the absence of colonial initiatives to develop this crop'.[23] Yvette Monga[24] presents evidence of the way Duala entrepreneurs used their social networks creatively in the early twentieth century to beat their German competitors.

The benefits of the so-called open economy which some authors (including Hopkins) claim was brought to bear by colonialism,

---

[21] Jacques Marseille, *Empire colonial et capitalisme français: histoire d'un divorce* (Paris: Albin Michel, 1984).

[22] G. A. Akinola, 'Colonialism and Imperialism: The African Experience', in John Middleton (ed.), *Encyclopedia of Africa South of the Sahara*, 4 vols. (New York: Charles Scribner's Sons, 1997), pp. 321–8, p. 324 (quote).

[23] Cooper, 'Colonialism and Imperialism', p. 319.

[24] Yvette Monga, *'Les entrepreneurs Duala, ca 1890–1930'* (PhD dissertation, University of Aix-Marseille, 1996).

underestimate the extent to which most West African territories were connected to their metropolis rather than to the world economy during the whole colonial period. Therefore, in spite of their internal dynamism, African societies did not fully benefit from international trade. In any case, colonial open economies were put under severe strain after 1930 with the world depression, the consequences of the First World War, and the restrictive policies adopted by the colonial administration to please powerful business interests in the West. In her analysis of the balance sheets and investment patterns of two major colonial French companies (*Société commerciale de l'Ouest africain*, SCOA and *Compagnie française d'Afrique occidentale*, CFAO), Coquery-Vidrovitch shows that these firms benefited enormously from their business in colonies at least until 1952 − the year when commodity prices reached their peak but were reluctant to modernize their structure and organization thereafter.[25]

In fine, the colonial record on inducing Africans to produce cash crops may well be considered mixed and the geography of economic colonialism across the continent uneven. However, the patterns of African involvement in world trade during the late nineteenth and the twentieth centuries, and the profound impact of the 'colonization of the mind', have made the colonial order an important variable of African economic performance today. In the early twenty-first century, five decades after independence, the basic organization, structure and performance of African economies have not changed much. They still rely mostly on primary commodities for foreign exchange and for a large share of their government revenues.

It is estimated that about 25 per cent of world merchandise trade consists of primary commodities. More than 50 developing countries − many of them in Africa − depend on three or fewer commodities for more than half their merchandise export earnings. Reliance on commodities for increasing national income is not a bad development strategy in itself − countries like Australia or even the United States have successfully done so over the course of their history. But to stick to that pattern of growth for several centuries in the face of evidence of little structural transformation, high price volatility and the major external shocks associated with it, raises questions about the appropriateness of the economic development strategy followed by most African countries.

Both short-term and long-term commodity price fluctuations are

---

[25] Catherine Coquery-Vidrovitch, *L'Afrique noire de 1800 à nos jours* (Paris: Presses Universitaires de France, 1974).

important determinants of development in the world economy. Using 140 years of commodity price data, Cashin and McDermot[26] observe that there has been a long-run downward trend in prices, but that such trends are small and variable, especially in comparison with the large variability of the prices of various commodities. They also find that markets for primary products have exhibited changing patterns of instability, which have become much larger over the past 30 years. Analyzing commodity price cycles, one can conclude that price slumps tend to last much longer than price booms, with the severity of positive or negative changes in prices being unrelated to their duration. This makes policy prescription for African countries that rely on a few commodity prices particularly difficult. Even more worrisome is the observation that shocks to commodity prices are usually long-lasting, with half-lives typically in excess of five years — which complicates the search for the appropriate policy and institutional response to smooth the effects of such shocks.

Empirical studies have identified the supply of commodities on the world market (which is strongly affected by climatic variability and subsidies), the real exchange rate of the US dollar, and world industrial production as the key determinants of price fluctuations for non-oil commodity prices. In macroeconomic terms, the impact of constantly changing prices in African countries is better captured through their effects on the terms of trade — a measure of the purchasing power of a country's exports. In fact, terms-of-trade shocks have had a big impact on fluctuations in national output and the real exchange rate, especially for CFA countries. Even temporary terms-of-trade shocks have a large impact on private saving and the current account balance. Also, there is a clear link between the evolution of the real price of commodity exports and the real exchange rate — a key indicator of external competitiveness for the small open economies of sub-Saharan Africa.

Clearly, because African economies are still largely dependent on a limited number of commodities, they are even more vulnerable to shocks in the early twenty-first century than they were at the end of the 1950s. Moreover, prior to colonization, the main problems of production were low human capital (in spite of relatively abundant labor) and absence of infrastructure and technology. By the time of independence, all these problems were unresolved, if not made worse. Today, after at least two decades of SAPs, it is hard to make the case that they have been addressed satisfactorily. One of the main ideas heavily promoted with

---

[26] Paul Cashin and C. John McDermott, 'The Long-Run Behavior of Commodity Prices: Small Trends and Big Variability', *IMF Staff Papers*, 49 (2) (2002), pp. 175–99.

SAPs was the need for the diversification of national economies. It has not taken place.

The unexplored benefits of economic backwardness

Regardless of the actual importance of colonialism in Africa's economic performance, the success stories during the twentieth century of many previously colonized countries indicate that there may be some truth in the so-called model of late-comer economic development. Suggested by Gerschenkron[27] who studied the experiences of countries like Russia, Germany, France, Italy, Austria and Bulgaria, that model's central hypothesis is the positive role of economic backwardness in inducing systematic substitution for supposed prerequisites for industrial growth. Rejecting the English Industrial Revolution as the normal pattern of economic development and the accumulation of capital as a prerequisite, Gerschenkron observed that disadvantageous initial conditions could indeed be overcome. His hypotheses are as follows.[28] First, relative backwardness motivates institutional innovation and promotes locally appropriate substitution for the absent conditions of growth. Second, the more backward the economy, the more interventionist is the successful channeling of capital into nascent industries. Third, the greater the degree of backwardness, the more likely are: coercive measures to reduce domestic consumption; an emphasis on producers' goods rather than consumers' goods; reliance on borrowed, advanced technology rather than indigenous techniques. Fourth, the more backward the country, the less likely is the agricultural sector to provide a growing market for industry through rising productivity.

If indeed these lessons from comparative economic history indicate that state intervention did compensate for the inadequate supplies of capital, skilled labor, entrepreneurship and technological capacity found in developing countries, then the key question for African economies is why post-colonial states and policymakers did not manage to achieve the kind of economic success that Indonesia, South Korea, Malaysia, Costa Rica or Chile have been able to achieve in recent decades. Insofar as SAPs have played a role in African economic development, related questions are: why has institutional innovation been so elusive? Why

---

[27] Alexander Gerschenkron, *Economic Backwardness in Historical Perspective* (Cambridge, MA: Harvard University Press, 1962).

[28] I borrow this summary of Gerschenkron's model from Albert Fishlow, 'Gerschenkron, Alexander', in John Eatwell et al. (eds), *The New Palgrave: A Dictionary of Economics* (New York: Stockton Press, 1987), pp. 518–19.

has the state been so ineffective in promoting entrepreneurship or channeling resources into nascent industries? Why has agriculture — commodities specifically — remained the only (volatile) engine for economic growth? And why have Mercedes-Benz and other consumer goods been consistently the most popular features in these economies? Why have former African colonies remained trapped in economic backwardness?

There are at least two possible broad answers to these questions — which are not mutually exclusive. One is that, contrary to European, Asian and Latin American countries, African countries have not managed to free themselves from colonialism, and that even in the early twenty-first century, post-colonies still operate as territories under domination. Another is that independent African countries have not learned the lessons of history and economic theory. This second hypothesis would be consistent with the findings of the large literature on cross-country analysis of growth. According to Barro[29], the leading researcher in this field, growth differences between countries depend first on each country's existing level of output. If a country's current output is below its so-called steady-state potential, there is a catching-up process, which occurs mainly through technology transfer. He even estimates that each year's growth should eliminate some 2.5 per cent of the gap between actual and steady state output. However, this does not necessarily imply that poor countries will always grow faster than rich ones, or that inequalities will necessarily fall over time, for other factors too (propensity to save or have children, access to technology, government policies, etc.) affect growth. In the African context, the question is why this catching-up process has not taken place.

How economists explain growth and welfare

Growth versus development

The vigorous debates and the subsequent progress in knowledge gathered by economic historians working on Africa are not always consistent with the fundamental framework through which macroeconomists explain economic growth across countries and over time. To a large extent, the various schools of thought at work in African studies have been observed in academic debates all over the world. In particular, the controversies between neo-classical theory on the one

---

[29] Robert J. Barro, *Determinants of Economic Growth: A Cross-Country Empirical Study* (Cambridge, MA: MIT Press, 1999).

hand, and Keynesian and Marxist theories on the other, which have dominated much of macroeconomics throughout the twentieth century, are somewhat reminiscent of those chronicled by African economic historians.

In recent years, there seems to be an emerging consensus within the so-called mainstream economic profession on the mechanics of growth and welfare, the role of governments and the effectiveness of the main economic instruments at their disposal. An important caveat here is that one should draw a clear distinction between economic *growth* and economic *development*, two fundamentally different notions which are too often used confusedly by social scientists. While economists seem to agree on the main ingredients for growth, there is still a lot of debate about what should be the definition, objectives, prerequisites, policies, instruments and monitoring indicators for development, a more philosophical and elusive notion.[30] This partly explains why SAPs, which aim to foster both development and growth, have been so controversial. Clearly, African societies and governments are still struggling to define precisely whether public policies should be tailored to achieve one or the other, or both.

Macroeconomic theory and lessons of history

Focusing only on growth, the prevailing consensus is quite straightforward. In the short run, movements in economic activity (including economic growth) are dominated by movements in aggregate demand. Also known as aggregate expenditure, aggregate demand is the sum total of nominal expenditures on goods and services in the economy, that is, consumption, investment, government expenditures together with exports, less imports. In the long term, any economy tends to return to what is called a steady-state growth path, which is determined by supply factors: labor, capital and technology.[31]

Growth accounting exercises provide a breakdown of observed

---

[30] Economic growth refers to the combination of factors of production to increase a country's national income, while economic development involves a deeper analysis of the variables that influence changes in the relative contribution of each factor of production. For a discussion, see Célestin Monga and Robert M. Solow, *Réflexions sur l'équation secrète du progrès économique* (Cambridge, MA: MIT Press, 1995). For definitions of economic development, see: Markos Mamalakis, 'Economic Development, Theories of', in Barbara A. Tenenbaum (ed.), *Encyclopedia of Latin American History and Culture*, vol. 2 (New York: Charles Scribner's Sons, 1996), pp. 439–44; and Goran Hyden, 'Development: Trends and Issues', in John Middleton (ed.), *Encyclopedia of Africa South of the Sahara*, 4 vols. (New York: Charles Scribner's Sons, 1997), pp. 424–9.

[31] Olivier Blanchard, 'Is There a Core of Usable Macroeconomics?' *American Economic Review*, 87 (2), Papers and Proceedings of the 104th Annual Meeting (May, 1997), pp. 244–6.

economic growth into components associated with changes in factor inputs (capital, labor) and the so-called Solow residual (total factor productivity) that reflects technological progress and other elements.[32] Depending on the availability and reliability of data, economists usually undertake the accounting exercise as a preliminary step for the analysis of fundamental determinants of economic growth. This is particularly useful when the most important determinants for factor growth rates are substantially independent from those that matter for technological change. Because of data limitation, many studies of African economies focus more on the final step of the analysis of determinants of growth, which involves the relations of factor growth rates, factor shares, and technological change to elements such as government policies and institutions, initial levels of physical and human capital, natural resources, household preferences, etc.

The steady upward trend in growth recorded in industrialized countries during the twentieth century is driven mainly by factors on the supply side like an increase in the capital stock per worker and the replacement of obsolete equipment, improvements in human capital, better access to and use of technology by firms, etc. Short-term fluctuations within the broader upward trend suggest the existence of business cycles, which are primarily driven by demand-side forces — basically changes in the ability or willingness of domestic and foreign economic agents to buy domestic goods and services. Understanding such two-way chains of causation is the main goal of economic policy.

If the strategic goal of policymakers is to end a recession, a temporary slowdown of economic growth, and bring the economy closer to its potential output, public policies are usually directed to increasing private and public spending on goods and services for public and private consumption, business investment and durable goods. When policymakers adopt a longer-term vision of trying to steepen the growth trend, then policy should focus on improving human capital, promoting capital investment, and encouraging research and development to improve productivity. However, demand-side and supply-side measures are not completely independent of each other. Business investment, for instance, could stimulate both short-term and long-term growth. When a firm builds a new factory, it adds to the country's potential output. But building a recreational room of the same value does not. Likewise, some supply-side business decisions like producing faster computers could induce consumers to spend more on new goods, which stimulates demand.

---

[32] See R. Barro, *Notes on Growth Accounting*, WP 6654 (Cambridge, MA: NBER, July 1998).

The big debate in macroeconomics during the past century has been over the type of policies that would allow for a better understanding of interactions between the business cycle and the growth trend, and allow policymakers to disentangle demand-side and supply-side factors. The dominant view so far has been that of neo-classical economists, which emphasizes the self-balancing properties of the free market economy, and plays down the occurrence of gaps between a country's potential output and its actual output. SAPs have emerged mostly from that policy framework. Yet, lessons from economic history show that the development of the supply-side forces necessary for growth (physical capital, human capital) and technological progress is always at least partially determined by political decisions and government actions about public investment in infrastructure, education, health — and by the demand for expanding markets. Indeed, the now standard recipe for improving the standards of living in almost any poor, open economy includes an important role for the state.

The standard recipe for improved living standards

In order properly to assess the design of SAPs, the objectives they were supposed to achieve, their effectiveness and the relevance of the debate over their features, it is necessary to discuss what would constitute a proper macroeconomic strategy for African countries. Given their current structure, their fragmented nature and their dependence on external trade for foreign exchange, the ability of African countries to improve their standard of living will ultimately depend on two key notions: higher productivity growth (output per worker) and better terms of trade (the price of exports relative to the price of imports, or, put another way, the quantity of imported goods a country receives per unit of export).

Why is productivity important? In principle, any given country that would not trade with others could raise its consumption per capita in only three ways: (i) by putting aside as investment for the future only a smaller fraction of current output, and by devoting more of its productive capacity to manufacturing goods for current consumption; (ii) by putting a larger fraction of its population to work; and (iii) by increasing its productivity so that each worker produces more. Clearly, option (i) would not be sustainable, as lower levels of investments will eventually cut into the country's ability to produce and to consume. Option (ii) could work for a while in countries where a substantial fraction of the population is unemployed, or if the social dynamics of the country bring new groups into the work force; this would clearly be the case in most African countries where a very large segment of the work force are unemployed or under-employed. But option (iii), namely, raising productivity, would really be the only important way to achieve sustained long-term growth in living standards. Empirical studies show that, in most countries, the evolution of real consumption per capita is usually very closely correlated with that of productivity.

Because African economies are 'open' and rely heavily on trade, an important part of their output is sold abroad as exports so that they can earn foreign exchange and pay for their imports, which they consume. Therefore, these countries can also increase their per capita consumption in two ways: (i) by importing more without selling more abroad — which implies that they have to find the money to pay for the extra imports (by borrowing or sale of their assets); or (ii) by managing to obtain better prices for their exports so that they do not need to pay the extra cost of their additional imports. Option (i) is possible only for countries with sufficient reserves and excellent creditworthiness to pay the extra cost, but, in any case, it cannot be sustained for a long period of time — as borrowing needs to be repaid at some point. Option (ii) is the more realistic but it implies that African countries are able to persuade foreigners to pay more for their exports. This can only be done through higher productivity, that is, producing better goods and services. This shows the importance of terms of trade.

How SAPs fit into the dominant economic paradigm

The first two decades of independence (1960s and 1970s) did not fundamentally change the course of African economic history. On the contrary, a combination of factors led to a new macroeconomics of nationalism that reinforced the dependence path initiated by colonialism. In the view of their promoters, SAPs were designed in the early 1980s to free African economies from that path, and to address the two important issues identified above; the evolution of terms of trade and productivity. If chosen correctly, the policy measures advocated by SAPs should have fostered each country's terms of trade and prospects for change. They should also have stimulated the reallocation of resources from the low-productivity sectors to better performing sectors in order to increase the economy-wide productivity and standard of living. They should have facilitated the review of the market mechanism for factors of growth, and the analysis of whether governments maintain labor in low-productivity areas by distorting prices and policies (including commercial and exchange-rate policies).

They should have reviewed the role of the public sector itself as a possible low-productivity user, and also the second channel through which labor productivity is usually increased, namely, capital accumulation and technical progress.

The macroeconomics of nationalism and Mercedes-Benz

The above summary of views on African economic history, and of the debate surrounding its importance in underpinning contemporary issues, offers some clues as to why almost all African countries faced the need for a 'structural' or 'macroeconomic' adjustment, starting in the 1980s onwards. Such a need arose mainly from the conditions under which growth occurred during the first two decades of independence and from the failure of African post-colonial states in their ambitious role of managing the economy.

Starting in the early 1960s, most of the newly independent sub-Saharan countries benefited from a rapid rise in the value of their exports. This led to an increase in their foreign exchange revenues and government revenues. This surge in income stimulated ambitious public policies aimed at increasing both investment and consumption. While often justified by the poor state of the infrastructure and the huge social needs of the population (especially in the areas of education and health) who had suffered centuries of slavery and colonization, a lot of these investments were over-sized and ill-designed. Fueled by the nationalistic dream of the new political leaders, large projects and programs dominated government plans — often conceived on the model of the Soviet Gosplan, regardless of the ideological background of the ruling elites. These projects and programs also generated large current expenditures, as they required a large number of civil servants with salary levels often equivalent to ten times the average income per capita, or high levels of operation and maintenance spending. Furthermore, for ideological, political and sometimes economic reasons, and also for reasons of pure greed, many countries opted for the nationalization of a large fraction of the production apparatus. They were encouraged along this direction by the ease with which they could obtain foreign loans, owing to abundant international liquidity.

In the 1970s, many private American, European and Japanese banks had at their disposal important deposits from members of the Organization of Petroleum Exporting Countries (OPEC) cartel — the so-called petrodollars. Acting on the assumption that even poor developing countries cannot go bankrupt, these banks started lending money to African countries with little rigorous analysis of its justification.

Countries like Mobutu Sese Seko's Zaïre, Jomo Kenyatta's Kenya or even Félix Houphouët-Boigny's Côte d'Ivoire were provided with large loans which, under normal circumstances, would have been considered unwise. They were considered financially viable, as the prices of commodities (coffee, cocoa, copper, diamonds) through which they obtained foreign exchange were relatively high.

These loans were used to finance huge investment projects with little or no economic rationale, imports of luxury goods (symbolized by Mercedes-Benz), and personal bank accounts in European banks. Yet, by the early 1980s, the situation had changed considerably. OPEC had become less effective as a cartel, which drove down oil prices and substantially reduced the petrodollars held as deposits in Western banks. Also, the United States had elected as President Ronald Reagan, whose fiscal policy consisted mainly of large tax cuts and a big build-up in military spending. The combination of these two factors (the limited availability of petrodollars on the international lending market and the need for funds to finance the large US fiscal deficit) drove interest rates upwards. To make matters worse, the world economy faced a major recession in the early 1980s and commodity prices on which African countries relied for foreign exchange fell to historic lows. Confronted with the rapid increase of interest rates on their variable-rate loan repayments, these countries were on the verge of default on their external debt. Since the loans they obtained in the 1970s were used to pay for politically motivated projects or expensive luxury goods — not productive investments — only one option was left to them: to turn to multilateral financial institutions like the World Bank and the IMF for help.

In macroeconomic terms, the evolution of sub-Saharan Africa in the 1960s and 1970s can be described as follows: after independence, most African countries quickly experienced a persistent imbalance between aggregate domestic demand and aggregate supply, and this was reflected in a worsening of their external payments and an increase in inflation. In certain cases, the main explanation was the importance of external factors such as a rise in foreign interest rates or an exogenous deterioration in the terms of trade. But in most cases, the so-called demand-supply imbalance could be traced to the inappropriate government policies that expanded domestic demand (consumption, investment) too rapidly relative to the productive capacity of the national economy.

For over a decade, foreign financing was available and allowed these countries to sustain the large expansion of demand, albeit at the cost of a widening deficit in the current account of the balance of payments, a worsening of external competitiveness, and heavier foreign debt. This was eventually accompanied by declining growth rates, the aggravation of poverty, and the loss of creditworthiness. Indeed, as foreign investors and creditors who had been too lax in their willingness to put money in sub-Saharan Africa suddenly became irrationally reluctant to do so, these countries had no other choice but to undergo a macroeconomic or structural adjustment.

Genesis, rationale and objectives of structural adjustment

SAPs were designed by the Bretton Woods institutions as a remedy for the macroeconomic problems facing Third World countries. They aimed at eliminating the imbalances of their economies and putting them back on the path to long-term sustainable growth. SAPs thus combined two overlapping objectives: stabilization and adjustment. Stabilization as the reduction of national expenditure to bring it in line with national output or income, and structural adjustment as policies to increase national income/output through a more efficient use of resources. Stabilizing the economy implies adopting policies that lower the rate of inflation, reduce the current account deficit, restore external competitiveness, and limit the fiscal deficit. When this is achieved, there is the need for structural adjustment, that is, implementing policies to increase the productive capacity of the national economy and to improve the efficiency with which the country's resources are utilized. Macroeconomic success is usually considered to be achieved when the economy has reached domestic balance (loosely defined as full employment without a large distortion in economic policies) and external balance (a sustainable position of the current account balance). Economic theory and empirical evidence suggest that successful programs to get to that point are the ones that combine effectively stabilization and structural adjustment policies and measures. But the optimal sequencing of the various policy options and use of instruments is still a matter of vigorous debate.

In plain English, the theoretical framework underlying SAPs simply provides that, when a country is experiencing the kind of serious balance-of-payment problems and a shortage of external financing that most of sub-Saharan Africa was confronted with in the early 1980s, it must eventually confront the issue. The only known technical way to do this is to redress the aggregate imbalances. The way this is done may be subject to discussion. But the consensus among mainstream economists is that it requires a contraction of domestic spending, which is most easily done by a tightening of monetary and fiscal policies. When the imbalances are too large, a real depreciation of the currency may also be required. In general, there is no quick fix or easier way to secure external financing and avoid some form of stabilization, when the country is in the midst of a financial crisis. However, it is also true that, in specific country cases, various specific policy instruments could be used in different ways to achieve that goal, taking into account all the constraints, circumstances and opportunities. Depending on the country, its size, performance and the structure of its economy, there may also be different ways to move from stabilization to growth, and to combine demand-restraining and supply measures. But the bottom line is that, in an interdependent world, small open economies with low levels of domestic savings like those of Africa desperately need to develop trade and attract foreign savings to be able to pay for their imports and investments, use their resources more efficiently, create jobs, raise their income and reduce poverty. Therefore, the general direction of stabilization and structural reforms is likely to be the same across countries.

SAPs and the Washington consensus

Proponents of SAPs relied on three simple ideas: the belief in the virtues of the market economy, the importance of macroeconomic discipline, and the need for all economies to open up to trade and foreign direct investment. These basic ideas also constitute the foundations of what Williamson called 'the Washington Consensus'.[33] Even though this particular term was coined only to describe the set of ideas that 'most people in Washington believed Latin America (not all countries) ought to be undertaking as of 1989 (not all the times)', many critics quickly lumped together SAPs and the so-called Washington Consensus. The fact that Williamson went on to become one of the most influential Regional Chief Economists at the World Bank reinforced that view.

While there was indeed a consensus in the policymaking circles of Washington in those days about the big objectives and the general directions in which Latin American countries — and most of sub-Saharan Africa — ought to reform their economies, the specific policy instruments and the way to use them, and the sequencing of actions, were never clear-cut. Here are the ten reforms that Williamson initially presented as the Washington Consensus:

---

[33] John Williamson, 'What Washington Means by Policy Reform', in J. Williamson (ed.), *Latin American Adjustment: How Much Has Happened?* (Washington D.C.: Institute of International Economics, 1990).

1. *Fiscal Discipline.*
2. *Reordering Public Expenditure Priorities.* This suggested switching expenditure in a pro-poor way, from things like indiscriminate subsidies to basic health and education.
3. *Tax reform.* Constructing a tax system that would combine a broad tax base with moderate marginal tax rates.
4. *Liberalizing Interest Rates.*
5. *A Competitive Exchange Rate.*
6. *Trade Liberalization.*
7. *Liberalization of Inward Foreign Direct Investment.*
8. *Privatization.*
9. *Deregulation.*
10. *Property Rights.*

In spite of the consistent analytical framework underpinning SAPs and the very strong theoretical foundations of the mathematical models used to explain them, there was still room for discussion of some of the targeted objectives, uncertainty about how best to achieve them, and flexibility on how and when to use some key policy instruments like monetary and fiscal policies. Unfortunately, confusion and incompetence on the part of some Washington bureaucrats, compounded with the intellectual laziness of African political leaders and the often tense and brutal political environment prevailing in African countries, led to poor implementation of what was often a radical, free market reform agenda. It is therefore not surprising that, even today, assessing the outcomes of these programs is still considered a 'political' exercise, either simply to justify them, or bluntly to reject their policy agenda.

Assessing SAPs: the trouble with the narratives

From an economic perspective, the relevance and effectiveness of SAPs and, more generally, any economic development strategy designed for sub-Saharan Africa should be addressed with a focus on the two following questions: Why has productivity growth in Africa been slower than in other parts of the world over the past decades? And is there anything that can be done either to improve the terms of trade or at least to limit their deterioration?

There are many methodological difficulties in the assessment of SAPs. First, a basic question with no straightforward answer is the period of analysis. The time lags between changes in public policies in any country cannot be determined precisely, especially when comparison is made with other countries. Secondly, even if in theory new econometric techniques may be useful for this purpose, in practice it is often impossible to disentangle the effects of SAPs from other influences observed in African economies. A related issue is the choice of adequate performance indicators. Even if one considers the improvement in the balance of payments (BoP) as a measure of success or failure, the question is what particular quantitative indicator to choose within the BoP. The overall balance is commonly used by some evaluators, yet it is heavily influenced by other factors outside the SAPs. Another option often used is the current account balance. But, again, countries facing foreign-exchange difficulties manage to find ways of limiting their current account deficit (including through severe import cuts) to whatever level they can finance. Therefore, it may be misleading to conclude from a mere reduction of that indicator that the BoP has improved, as cuts in imports may have negative impact on economic performance, and on the capacity to export.

Third, as noted by Killick,[34] it is difficult to distinguish between the impact of policies promoted by the World Bank and the IMF and the effects of the finance that comes with them. Fourth, there is the issue of the severity of conditionality and the degree of implementation of SAPs, which vary considerably among countries (sometimes even depending on the personalities negotiating adjustment programs both on the government side and on the side of the Bretton Woods institutions). Fifth, it is difficult to elaborate a counterfactual scenario that can be used as a yardstick to assess the impact of SAPs in Africa. Widely employed in economics as a tool to measure the effects of government policies, counterfactuals would have to be constructed for each African economy. But in policy environments where unpredictable severe weather conditions, brutal political changes, civil wars or persistent social violence can derail almost any programme, it is impossible to come up with reasonable counterfactual scenarios. Against this background, one can inscribe most of the literature assessing SAPs in Africa either in the narrative of justification, or in the narrative of dissent.

Narrative of justification: the World Bank-IMF perspective

The measurement of progress in structural adjustment policies is acknowledged to be a philosophical mystery even by the most vocal supporters of SAPs. The timing of the program (beginning and end),

---

[34] Tony Killick, *IMF Programs in Developing Countries: Design and Impact* (London: Routledge, 1995).

the amount of loans underpinning it, the policies whose impact is to be assessed, are all subject to uncertainty and change, making the difficulties of identifying and making sense of its effects all the more challenging.

The 1989 World Bank report entitled *Sub-Saharan Africa: From Crisis to Sustainable Growth* attempted to address some of the development issues that were omitted by SAPs (institutional weaknesses and insufficient technical and administrative capacity, the role of external factors in African economic crises, the legacy of colonial history, etc.). The report also identified investments in infrastructure and in human capital (education and development) as pre-requisites for long-term success. However, five years later, another World Bank report, entitled *Adjustment in Africa*, adopted the narrow focus of short-term financial crises and concluded that adjustment policies were working. The 1994 report insisted that African countries that reduced their deficits through real exchange-rate depreciation, liberalization of their trade and foreign-exchange allocation system, liberalization of marketing of inputs and outputs in the agricultural sector, and reduction of agricultural taxation, achieved a turnaround in their macroeconomic performance. The report also acknowledged that 'adjustment alone is inadequate for long-term sustainable development', but did not elaborate much on the findings of the 1989 report. Since then, the World Bank has released several other performance evaluations with more or less the same key finding: countries that implement SAPs consistently eventually experience improvements in their economic performance. Over recent years, the Bank has emphasized in its evaluation the fact that foreign aid and SAPs are most effective in countries with 'good' policy and institutional environments.

Cross-country analyses carried out by the IMF on the experience of their programs also conclude that they are, by and large successful — however success is defined. In a report, Hadjimichael et al. note that 'on the whole, African countries that have effectively implemented comprehensive adjustment and reform programs have shown better results'.[35] The IMF also notes that policy recommendations tend to vary considerably in terms of the emphasis put on each of their major components, and that the size of adjustment they require (as measured by the proposed reduction in the fiscal deficit, the current account deficit and the rate of inflation) is typically a monotonic function of the size of the pre-existing imbalances. Therefore, according to IMF experts, it cannot be said that these programs only contain the same

---

[35] M.T. Hadjimichael et al., *Adjustment for Growth: The African Experience,* Occasional Paper 143 (Washington DC: IMF, 1996), p. 1.

type of policy recommendations, or that they advocate the same size of adjustment. One piece of evidence is usually presented in support of this claim: the fact that in several of the debt-crisis countries of the 1980s, massive and unsustainable fiscal deficits were major problems and lay at the core of balance-of-payments difficulties and high inflation. Correspondingly, objectives for fiscal consolidation in IMF programs had to be very ambitious. 'This was much less so for the programs with Mexico and Argentina in the tequila crisis[36] and for those with Indonesia and Korea in the 1997 Asian crisis, but was again a more critical issue in recent arrangements with Russia and Brazil'.[37] It is interesting that only large, non-African countries like Mexico, Argentina, Indonesia or Korea are quoted as counter-examples of the similarity in the design of IMF programs. Clearly, most IMF programs in sub-Saharan Africa over the past two decades have offered the same features.

Narratives of dissent: some African perspectives

African criticism of SAPs usually falls into three broad areas: the ideological foundations, politics and legitimacy of these externally designed frameworks — which is not surprising, given the competing historical perspectives from different schools of thought about African economic history; the overall design, purpose and perceived toughness of the conditionality attached to SAPs, the sequencing of the various reforms and the implementation mechanism; and the relevance, effectiveness (contents) and impact of these programs. Let us briefly review these criticisms in turn before exploring alternative ideas put forward over the past two decades by African intellectuals.

SAPs as illegitimate and ineffective frameworks
With or without explicit reference to dependency theory, some African intellectuals have rejected SAPs on the basis that they are entirely imposed from outside. In the introductory chapter to their book *African Voices on Structural Adjustment*, Mkandawire and Soludo, for instance, note that there has been hardly any development program in much of Africa without the tacit or explicit involvement/endorsement of the donors. In several important aspects, many of the policies/programs

---

[36] The so-called 'Tequila crisis' refers to the financial crisis that started in Mexico in December 1994 and created confusion, a wave of investor stampedes and fear in other emerging markets (Argentina, Brazil, Chile, the Philippines and Poland).

[37] Michael Mussa and Miguel Savastano, *The IMF Approach to Economic Stabilization*, Working Paper WP/99/104 (Washington DC: IMF, 1999), pp. 24–5.

which have turned out to be 'bad' were at their insistence. With Africans adjudged 'incapable of thinking for themselves and implementing policies', a deluge of over 100,000 foreign technical experts costing over $4 billion annually to maintain have literally taken over the process of policy/project design and sometimes implementation. In what has ensued, 'Africa has turned into a pawn on the chessboard of experimentation for all manner of ill-digested development theories and pet hypotheses'.[38] Considering that they are too often damaging to economic growth, harmful to the poor, inflexible in their design and contents, unresponsive to the particular needs and circumstances of African countries, and based on the rigid application of discredited neo-classical economic models, Mkandawire and Soludo conclude that SAPs have consistently failed to reach their stated development objectives, and that they have been 'grossly defective'.[39]

Economics does not take place in a vacuum. African political scientists have emphasized the deleterious context in which public policies are designed and implemented in sub-Saharan Africa. Olukoshi, one of the most articulate critics of SAPs, has highlighted the need to tackle 'governance' issues as a prerequisite for economic development. Observing that 'governance, like obscenity, is difficult to define in a legal phrase', IMF expert Premchand also notes that 'the lack of it seems to be more easily felt than governance itself'.[40] In its search for an operational framework to address governance issues, the World Bank has suggested the following principles: rationality and predictability in governmental decisions; transparency in governmental procedures; fight against corruption; greater accountability (financial and political) by public officials; adoption of a system of checks and balances; judicial autonomy and the rule of law; and protection of property rights and enforcement of contracts.[41] But many African intellectuals have not been convinced by this 'technocratic' approach to the matter. According to Olukoshi, the World Bank's governance program is, in fact,

> reduced to a managerial/technocratic affair tailored to the goals of an adjustment program that, in the view of many, has, at the very least, contributed to the reproduction/intensification of authoritarianism in Africa. The question of democratic governance in Africa is, therefore, one which is still unresolved.[42]

[38] Thandika Mkandawire and Charles Soludo (eds), *African Voices on Structural Adjustment* (Dakar: Codesria, 2003), p. 3.

[39] *Ibid.*, p. 2.

[40] A. Premchand, *Public Expenditure Management* (Washington DC: IMF: 1993), p. 16.

[41] World Bank, *Governance: The World Bank's Experience* (Washington DC: World Bank, 1994).

[42] Adebayo O. Olukoshi, 'The Elusive Prince of Denmark: Structural Adjustment and the Crisis of Governance in Africa', in Mkandawire and Soludo, *African Voices on Structural Adjustment*, pp. 229–73, p. 254 (quote).

Is it possible to reform African economies without changing the political context? Some other African intellectuals have criticized the rather narrow focus of the SAP features and the lack of realism of their sponsors who believe naively that the main problem facing African economies is to free them from the dominance of the state and open them up to markets.[43]

Criticism of the overall design of SAPs and sequencing of reforms
Those who criticize the macroeconomics of SAPs usually stress the sometimes obvious disjunction between their stated objectives (higher growth, lower inflation, poverty alleviation, an adequate supply of key public goods — especially in social sectors) and their core elements.[44] Moreover, they do not accept the premise that these medium- and long-term objectives cannot be achieved without some costs in the short run. Yet economic reforms and adjustment are always costly, especially since most African leaders only agree to put their economic house in order when their countries are on the brink of financial crisis.

Some other African critics have pointed out that the design and implementation of SAPs have ignored the appropriate sequencing of the reforms. Indeed, for free market reforms to work, for privatization to yield results and for competition to take place in any previously centralized economy, the key first step in the reform program should be the design of new rules and regulations. Yet, as Lipumba[45] rightly noted, the reform program underpinning SAPs in many African countries in the 1980s entailed the liberalization of imports, for instance, before removal of the policy restrictions that discouraged exports and before adequate adjustment of the exchange rate. As a result, small closed economies that had relied for decades on protectionism and import-substitution strategies eventually opened up to relatively cheap consumer goods (French champagne and red wine, German luxury cars, Swiss cheese) from mostly Western countries. They continued to rely heavily on a limited number of commodities with volatile prices for foreign exchange and an important fraction of government revenues. The deterioration of the trade balance created by higher imports and

---

[43] See, for example, Mahmood Mamdani, 'Democratization and Marketization', in Kidane Mengisteab and B. Ikubolajeh Logan (eds), *Beyond Economic Liberalization: Structural Adjustment and the Alternatives* (London: Zed Books, 1995), pp. 18–19.

[44] Charles Chukwuma Soludo, 'In Search of Alternative Analytical and Methodological Frameworks for an African Economic Development Model', in Mkandawire and Soludo, *African Voices on Structural Adjustment*, pp. 17–71.

[45] Nguyuru H. I. Lipumba, *Africa Beyond Adjustment*, Policy Essay no. 15 (Washington DC: Overseas Development Corporation, 1994).

stagnant exports compounded the balance-of-payment difficulties that the SAPs were supposed to address.

Similarly, commercial banks were privatized in other countries without prior strengthening of the supervisory capacity of the central banks. State enterprises, including in key sectors of the economy like water supply or electricity, were sold to private businessmen — mostly foreign — before the creation of an independent regulatory agency functioning properly. As a consequence, public monopolies were replaced in several countries by private monopolies run by new oligarchs with strong political ties, to the detriment of consumers who never benefited from the drop in prices expected from privatization and competition. Interest rates were substantially increased as part of strategies to reduce inflation. But since this was often done prior to the privatization of public enterprises — the main borrowers from the banking system — and before the adoption of policy measures to reduce the fiscal deficit, the banking system accumulated bad debts and became even more vulnerable. In fact, African countries that rushed to implement SAP reforms focused on short-term concerns (high inflation and high external deficits) neglected to start with a comprehensive long-term development strategy with optimal sequencing of the reforms.

Criticism of the relevance of SAPs
Lipumba notes that SAP reforms 'have focused on policy-induced distortions that discourage efficiency in the use of resources and have ignored the physical bottleneck that requires investment expenditure'. He also points out that the World Bank 'ignores the role of the state in planning public investment expenditure by anticipating sectors and areas that are likely to be socially and privately profitable'.[46] Mamdani rejects the short-term focus on demand management of SAPs:

> There must be a difference between the perspective of an accountant and that of a development economist: the former can even balance the budget in the midst of the Ethiopian famine by reducing demand — perhaps at the cost of another million lives![47]

Olukoshi[48] and many others have stressed the social cost of poorly designed SAPs.

[46] *Ibid.*, p. 2.

[47] Mamdani, 'Democratization and Marketization', p. 19.

[48] Adebayo O. Olukoshi, 'Extending the Frontiers of Structural Adjustment Research in Africa: Some Notes on the Objectives of Phase II of the NAI Research Program', in P. Gibbon and A. O. Olukoshi, *Structural Adjustment and Socio-Economic Change in Sub-Saharan Africa: Some Conceptual, Methodological, and Research Issues*, Research Report no. 102, (Uppsala: Nordiska Afrikainstitutet, 1998), pp. 49-99.

Over recent years, the World Bank has acknowledged the failure of initial adjustment programs (essentially derived from the so-called Washington Consensus) to tackle social issues, and has focused more attention on the importance of education and health in its programs. Nevertheless, some African critics assert that adjustment policies did not go far enough in stimulating the restructuring of African economies, and that the implementation was weak.

Theoretical shortcomings of SAP models

The theoretical shortcomings of the macroeconomic models underpinning SAPs explain most of the criticism of their design. Both the IMF's and the World Bank's theoretical models for stabilization and adjustment policies[49] can be challenged at several levels: their objectives, their conceptual framework and the type of econometric techniques they rely upon. First, the objective of the two models is rather limited. The IMF core model was designed in the 1950s simply to ensure that countries encountering deficits in their balance of payments that could not be financed by their reserves, and seeking credit from the IMF, would correct their payments position within a few years. The model thus attempted to study the effects on both the balance of payments and income formation of what were seen as the two most important exogenous variables affecting many economies in the early postwar period: changes in exports and the creation of bank credit.[50] For designing its programs all over the world, the IMF has continued to use this simple model, with a very limited number of variables, subject here and there to minor elaboration on an ad hoc basis. The World Bank model was initially designed in 1971 under the name Minimum Standard Model (MSM) primarily to estimate the financing gap facing developing countries and to calculate precise aid requirements. In 1973, it was slightly updated and renamed Revised Minimum Standard Model (RMSM) but kept the same focus.

Second, the limited conceptual framework of the two models is

---

[49] The IMF's stabilization model was developed in the 1950s and has not evolved substantially. See Jacques J. Polak, *The IMF Monetary Model at Forty*, Working Paper WP/97/49 (Washington DC: IMF, 1997). The Bank's RMSM-X was initially designed as a six-week tool and is still used in 2004. See William Easterly, *The Elusive Quest for Growth: Economists' Adventures and Misadventures in the Tropics* (Cambridge, MA: MIT Press, 2001).

[50] See IMF, *The Monetary Approach to the Balance of Payments* (Washington DC: IMF, 1977). The simplicity of the IMF model was understandable, given the absence of national income and GNP data for many countries in the 1950s, and the need to focus on the main variable under the control of the government, domestic credit creation, an important means to correct balance-of-payments problems.

obviously linked to their rather focused objectives. They both have a coherent macroeconomic accounting framework that is very useful for financial programming and macro modeling exercises. In particular, they focus on the financial sector of the economy and often include fairly detailed current and capital account activities of economic agents (government, private sector, financial sector, and the rest of the world). The World Bank RMSM-X (as it is called these days) allows for various 'closure' options, which is useful when used not only to estimate the availability of financing, but also to compute the required financing in a particular policy scenario. It also produces standard indicator tables; this facilitates sensitivity analyses and comparison between a baseline scenario and alternatives.

However, the simplicity of these two models comes at the price of excluding many variables that the economic literature considers relevant for growth, and relying on some key assumptions chosen in a very arbitrary manner. For instance, the IMF model assumes that stabilization is a direct consequence of restrictions on money demand and supply, but makes no explicit reference to the savings-investment dynamics, or even to growth; yet this should be the ultimate objective of any economic policy. In other words, while the model defines fairly well the relationship between money, the balance of payments and domestic prices, it devotes almost no attention to the effect of policies on the real sectors of the economy (agriculture, industry, services). Most economists would agree that a restrictive monetary policy will reduce inflation and the deficit of the balance of payments; but it would also lead to an undesirable loss in output in the short term. Yet the size of this loss and the specific period over which it occurs — which are of crucial importance to policymakers concerned with many other economic and social objectives — are largely unknown and neglected in the design of IMF programs in African countries.

The RMSM-X is basically a computerization of a model developed independently by Rod Harrod and Evsey Domar in the 1930s, which suggests that the economy's rate of growth depends on the level of saving and the productivity of investment — the capital-output ratio. The model initially focused on the analysis of business cycles. However, it was later adapted to explain economic growth. It states that economic growth depends on the amount of labor and capital. Developing countries often have an abundant supply of labor but they also lack physical capital. Yet, in principle, more physical capital generates economic growth. Net investment leads to more capital accumulation, which generates higher output and income. And higher income allows higher levels of saving. The key to economic growth is therefore to expand the level of investment in terms of both fixed capital and human capital. Policies should encourage saving or generate technological advances which enable firms to produce more output with less capital, i.e. lower their capital-output ratio.[51]

Building upon the Harrod-Domar philosophy, the RMSM-X makes two crucial assumptions which are not supported by empirical evidence. First, it assumes that higher aid volumes lead to higher investment levels — which is obviously incorrect, as shown by the large literature on the economics of incentives, the functioning of bureaucracies and the politics of adjustment. In practice, it is difficult to stimulate the level of domestic savings, particularly in developing countries where incomes are low. Furthermore, borrowing from overseas to fill the gap created by insufficient savings eventually causes debt-repayment problems when the money is not used to finance productive investments. Secondly, the model states that higher investment levels translate into higher growth rates. Following the Harrod-Domar model which suggested that one simply had to multiply the targeted growth rate by the incremental capital-output ratio (ICOR) to obtain the required level of investment, the RMSM-X provides a theoretical justification for foreign aid when savings rates are lower than investment rates. Yet, Solow[52] demonstrated convincingly that, because of diminishing returns, there is no one-to-one relationship between investment and growth: as investment increases, the productivity of the capital will diminish and the capital to output ratio rise. And if such a linear relationship does not exist, the so-called ICOR can be misleading.

Reflecting these shortcomings, the real sector module in the standard RMSM-X is not very sophisticated. There are few behavioral equations, which are specified in a rather crude way — namely, using ratio or constant elasticity methods. More importantly, gross domestic product, as well as prices, are exogenously specified, which is a major impediment for an instrument aiming at macroeconomic policy simulation. Finally, the econometric analysis on which the estimation of parameter values for key functions is based is often limited by poor data quality. Furthermore, African economies are too often subject to negative shocks (drop in commodity prices or depreciation of the US

---

[51] The capital-output ratio shows the amount of units of capital that are needed to produce a certain level of output. For example, if $100 worth of capital equipment produces $10 of annual output, the capital-output ratio is 10 to 1. A 5 to 1 capital-output ratio indicates that only $50 of capital is required to produce each $10 of output annually. The lower the capital-output ratio, the better the efficiency level of the economy.

[52] Robert M. Solow, *Growth Theory: An Exposition* (New York: Oxford University Press, 1987 [originally published in 1970]).

dollar). This implies that parameter values for important behavioral functions are unstable. Given the similarity of structure of these economies, the right econometric technique for mitigating data inconsistencies, and obtaining robust estimates and viable projections would come from 'pooling' time-series for each African economy with that from neighboring countries.

Shortcomings of African alternatives to SAP

The Lagos action plan
After the wave of independence and before the advent of SAPs, African leaders and intellectuals had put forward various economic policy frameworks as part of their development strategies. Perhaps the most famous of these ideas emerged in 1979-80 when heads of state adopted the so-called Monrovia declaration, and later the Lagos Plan of Action and the Final Act of Lagos.[53] It was a rather grandiose attempt by African political leaders in post-colonial times to enunciate a development strategy of their own, which would be underpinned by regional integration. Inspired by the pan-Africanist philosophy of Kwame Nkrumah and others, the main idea behind the Plan was that African countries were too small to be economically viable, and that there would be economies of scale as well as enormous political benefits in pursuing common economic goals and launching transnational investment projects.

The Plan was endorsed as the 'official' economic development strategy for the Organization of African Unity (OAU) and validated by a United Nations resolution. Yet it quickly faded away, for several reasons. First, the economics underpinning the ambitious objectives and largely vague statements of faith behind the Plan was almost non-existent. Second, there was no real commitment to flesh it out clearly and implement it systematically, as almost all the African heads of state who were behind it were perceived in their own countries as politically illegitimate, if not dictators, and therefore could not mobilize the financing and political

[53] Following a series of discussions and meeting by experts and ministerial-level meetings, the OAU leaders adopted in July 1979 the 'Monrovia Declaration of Commitment of the Heads of State of the OAU on the guidelines and measures for national and collective self-reliance in economic and social development for the establishment of a new international economic order'. The pomposity of the title itself should have made them more cautious. The heads of state and government charged the OAU Secretary General and the Executive Secretary of the UN Economic Commission for Africa to come up with a sound plan for putting in place their objectives. This is what led the Second Extraordinary Session of the Heads of States and Governments held in Lagos in July 1980 to pass the Lagos Plan of Action and the Final Act of Lagos for the economic development of Africa. The Plan was recently reprinted and is available online at www.uneca.org/itca/ariportal/docs/lagos_plan.PDF.

support for it. Third, the idea of hastily grouping poorly managed small economies into larger geographic entities with little administrative and financial capacity and working under unclear political arrangements was doomed to fail. Fourth, from the perspective of the African people (identified in official speeches as primary beneficiaries of the Plan, yet not involved in the discussion prior to the decision), all this was simply another manifestation of political posturing by the ruling elites who seldom carry out a clear cost-benefit analysis before embarking on action.

The African alternative framework to Structural Adjustment Programs
Reacting to the dominance of SAPs, a group of African professionals led by Adebayo Adedeji, the Executive Secretary of the Economic Commission of Africa (ECA), decided to take a more proactive approach and to offer their own economic policy prescription for the continent. This new proposal still underscored the need for massive capital investment in African economies so as to kick-start economic growth, and the need to pay attention to vulnerable groups and to include social safety nets in economic policies. But that same year, political issues dominated the development agenda in Africa: the Berlin Wall fell, Nelson Mandela was released from prison in February 1990 and a 'sovereign national conference' was held in Benin, triggering massive popular protests throughout the continent. The ECA prepared for and held the famous Arusha conference on Popular Participation for Democracy in Africa and subsequently produced the African Charter for Popular Participation for Development (1990). The AAF-SAP was never the subject of serious debate.

More recently, the New Partnership for Africa's Development (NEPAD) has been adopted by African heads of states as a 'vision' and a 'framework for Africa's renewal'. The 37th Summit of the OAU in July 2001 formally adopted it as the new, official strategic framework document. It has four stated primary objectives: to eradicate poverty; to place African countries, both individually and collectively, on a path of sustainable growth and development; to halt the marginalization of Africa in the globalization process and enhance its full and beneficial integration into the global economy; and to accelerate the empowerment of women. Yet, beyond these good intentions and some rather ambitious infrastructure projects with no clear link with national development strategies, the NEPAD is off to a dubious start. Appearing as just another wish-list in its official statement, it has no rigorous analytical background and presents no clear strategy that takes into account both the challenges facing African economies today and the opportunities offered to them by globalization.

Beyond the Commodities – Mercedes-Benz Economy

Partly for historical and structural reasons, partly for managerial and ideological reasons, most African countries have been trapped into the commodity-and-Mercedes-Benz economies, and the SAPs have been unable to break what has become a vicious circle of high consumption, low capital accumulation, low productivity, low value-added activities and external dependency. For any economic development model to suit the needs of African countries today, it must address two central questions:

- On the purely macroeconomic and financial front: What will it take (in terms of financial resource requirements) to push – in a 'voluntarist' manner – these economies to a higher growth path of, say, 8–10 per cent a year, in real terms for a minimum period of five to ten years while maintaining a certain 'desired' level of consumption?
- What is the path from macroeconomic performance to poverty reduction? How does a given pattern of GDP growth translate into poverty reduction in the context of Chad, Burkina Faso, Angola or Zimbabwe? For example, how do we infer that a pattern of sectoral growth, which yields an aggregate income growth of 8–10 per cent will lead to the kind of massive poverty reduction (of 50 per cent by 2015) the international community is contemplating?[54]

Answering the first question can be relatively straightforward, even with SAP types of models, provided that they are calibrated to address more than the short-term balance-of-payments issues, and completed with the longer-term perspective (a sharper focus on building human capital and public infrastructure) suggested by Lipumba and others. Addressing the second issue is a far more difficult exercise that requires fairly elaborate empirical methodology and policy simulation instruments. Conceptually, the challenge is to establish an empirical link between economic growth patterns and poverty. This would make

---

[54] The United Nations adopted in 2000 the Millennium Development Goals (MDG) which are a series of measurable goals and targets for combating poverty, hunger, disease, illiteracy, environmental degradation and discrimination against women. The first and perhaps most important of these MDG (now endorsed by 191 countries) is to reduce poverty in the world by half by 2015. See http://www.un.org/millenniumgoals/.

Célestin Monga

it possible to state a global policy objective in terms of poverty reduction, and then simulate through various policy options the growth patterns and levels that may lead to the desired outcome — with the financial resource requirements. Once such a consistent strategy is elaborated on paper for each country, a further challenge is to implement it.

Given the lack of expertise in many African public institutions, another issue to be addressed in the design of the strategy would be the need for capacity-building. The key issue here is not so much to come up with another tool for 'linking' macro policies to poverty and human development, but that the thinking and linkages captured in any strategy or model should also permeate the thinking of African policymakers at all levels in their country. After all, policy design and its effective implementation is primarily their responsibility, regardless of how much intellectual and technical assistance can be gathered from outsiders.

Such an approach would allow for a rethinking of African economic development strategies, and outline a path for the type of structural changes needed. It would imply a rather ad hoc series of tasks tailored to particular country circumstances. They are likely to include:

- A statistical analysis linking growth patterns to poverty, for a given poverty profile. Information on household income shares in various sectors are often available from existing surveys. These shares are to be obtained by combining data on functional income distribution (income from activity sectors such as agriculture, industry, services, and aggregates factors such as labor, capital and land), with data on institutional income distribution (from factors to various agents, households included). Assuming that distribution patterns are stable, it is then possible to trace growth patterns in activity sectors to income growth for households and make some inferences on changes in the incidence and severity of poverty.[55]
- A second step will be a macro-modeling exercise to operationalize a methodology for growth and poverty reduction policy analysis. For this to be a simulation tool through which macro policies can be considered, and their aggregate macroeconomic and financial

[55] This is a simplification, but a useful one. Let us assume, for example, that poor households receive 75 per cent of their income from agriculture (wages, profit, rent combined), 15 per cent from industries and services, and 10 per cent from direct government transfers. The income growth rate for poor households will be a weighted average of exogenously specified GDP growth rates in these sectors, the weights being the above income shares. Therefore, knowing changes in mean poverty income relative to the exogenous poverty line, and with the simplifying assumption on distribution patterns, one can make rough inferences on the evolution in the poverty rate.

261

effects captured, economic growth (measured by improvements in GDP) and inflation must both be endogenous — unlike the IMF and World Bank existing models. Furthermore, such a framework should include a sound knowledge of intersectoral relations in the economy. This 'mapping' exercise is important for tracing policy effects from activity sectors (prices, production and income) to institutions (income and demand), especially the households. It is also important to ensure consistency between output, income and spending at the aggregate level (the entire economy), and to allow for inferences in income distribution and poverty incidence to be drowned by the growth effects of macroeconomic policies.

Neither the IMF-World Bank economic models, nor the rather general policy statements released by African leaders in reaction to the SAP, were designed to address these fundamental issues. They all attempted either to make the best out of the current basic structure of African economies (commodity exporting economies), or to 'modernize' them in a way that would allow some social groups to obtain foreign exchange for luxury consumption (Mercedes-Benz and the like).

Establishing the macro-poverty linkages

For any economic development strategy to be viable in the African context, an additional conceptual feature should be added to the framework: the linkage between macroeconomic policies and poverty reduction. First, economic development strategies should rely on macro-simulation tools. Not only should macroeconomic policies be implemented, but their aggregate macroeconomic and financial effects (economic growth, inflation, fiscal and external balances, etc.) must also be fully understood and integrated into the strategy. This requirement disqualifies the World Bank and IMF models, as GDP growth and inflation should be *endogenous variables*, that is, generated in the model itself depending on policy options, not externally and arbitrarily set outside the model. Second, the strategy must be rich enough in its analysis of intersectoral relations. Third, the strategy and models used should capture the dynamics of government expenditure policies — especially on infrastructure, education, health — on households' current well-being and future income-generation capacity, which determine present and future prospects for poverty reduction.

This would imply carrying out on a systematic basis public expenditure reviews and poverty profile analyses in African countries, and ensuring that the results of these exercises are included in the macro-modeling framework. For example, it is crucial to get a quantitative measure (incidence analysis) of: how each CFA franc or naira of public spending allocated to education affects the primary school enrolment rate; how the higher enrolment rate translates into higher productivity of human capital in the country; and how this may affect sectoral growth patterns. With this type of information, public expenditure policies could be related to household income and inferences could be drawn for welfare and poverty strategies. Also, more directly, knowing the incidence of government spending in such sectors as education, health and infrastructure is useful for assessing changes in social indicators in addition to the poverty rate.

The difficulty in the above approach stems from the complicated dynamics involved. Public spending programs and capital spending generally take time to be fully executed, and even more time to yield results. Furthermore, relating a stated policy goal to specific spending patterns is not a straightforward exercise (linking, for example, an amount of x CFA francs spent on primary education to y percentage points improvement in the enrolment rate). Nevertheless, nowadays when country programs are focused on poverty reduction objectives, this must be done to provide a strong justification for decisions on economic strategy. A crucial requirement for this approach to yield results is to stop relying on foreign experts for policy advice, and to build or strengthen local expertise for economic analysis in all African countries.

Recommended Reading

Austen, Ralph (1987) *African Economic History* (London: James Currey; Portsmouth, NH: Heinemann).

Devarajan, Shantayanan, David Dollar, and Torgny Holmgren (eds) (2001) *Aid and Reform in Africa: Lessons from Ten Case Studies* (Washington DC: World Bank).

Duignan, Peter and Lewis H. Gann (eds) (1988) *Colonialism in Africa, 1870–1960*, vol. 4, *The Economics of Colonialism* (Stanford, CA: Hoover Institution Press).

Easterly, William (2001) *The Elusive Quest for Growth: Economists' Adventures and Misadventures in the Tropics* (Cambridge, MA: MIT Press).

Hopkins, A. G. (1973) *An Economic History of West Africa* (London: Longman).

Killick, Tony (1995) *IMF Programs in Developing Countries: Design and Impact* (London: Routledge).

Lipumba, Nguyuru H. I. (1994) *Africa Beyond Adjustment*, Policy Essay no. 15 (Washington, DC: Overseas Development Corporation).

Mkandawire, Thandika and Charles Soludo (eds) (2003) *African Voices on Structural Adjustment* (Dakar: Codesria).

Monga, Célestin (1997) 'A Currency Reform Index for Western and Central Africa', *World Economy* 20 (1), pp. 103–25.

—— (1997) *L'argent des autres: Banques et petites entreprises en Afrique – le cas du Cameroun* (Paris: LGDJ).

Sandbrook, Richard (1985) *The Politics of Africa's Economic Stagnation* (Cambridge: Cambridge University Press).

World Bank (1994) *Adjustment in Africa: Reforms, Results, and the Road Ahead* (New York: Oxford University Press).

12

Ethnicity, Conflict & the State in Contemporary West Africa

CYRIL K. DADDIEH

Introduction

West Africa came of age politically in 1960. Of the seventeen countries that gained their independence and were admitted to the United Nations in that watershed year, sixteen were African, around half of them from the West African sub-region. The struggle for black African liberation had been spearheaded by Kwame Nkrumah roughly a decade earlier and had culminated in Ghana's attainment of independence in 1957. This was followed a year later by the repudiation of France's Fifth Republic Constitution by Sékou Touré's Guinea, with strong backing from Nkrumah, his ideological soul-mate. Thus, by 1960, the nationalist leaders of ten of the sixteen African countries had succeeded in wresting political control from their European rulers. For the most part, West African leaders achieved this successful recovery of Africa's lost independence by mobilizing masses of people into peaceful but formidable nationalist coalitions that cut cross ethnic, religious, regional and class cleavages. In short, the new political kingdom or state was an entity superimposed on a pluralistic society.

As we shall see, the articulation of the post-colonial state with social pluralism was later to become a vexing political issue. But in the heady euphoria of the 1960s, issues of ethnic pluralism and ways to achieve genuinely balanced ethnic representation and protection of minority rights were subordinated; the nationalist state project of nation-building, the attempt to forge national unity among disparate socio-cultural groupings at different levels of economic and political development, was considered imperative. At one level, the moment appeared auspicious. The nationalist leaders had already demonstrated their political prowess and efficacy by orchestrating the formal departure of the colonialists. Many of them were also regarded as very charismatic. This combination of charisma and efficacious leadership generated widespread popular support and legitimacy for the new leaders. However, legitimacy was highly contextualized in the sense that the mobilized masses developed an instrumentalist conception of political independence. They viewed it as a prelude to material progress and social welfare. In short, legitimacy was based on a fundamental African social compact in which the new political elites promised, at least implicitly, to produce less poverty and less inequality, in exchange for popular support. An expectant and results-oriented polity was willing to give support and legitimacy for as long as the new leaders produced material benefits for all. Any prolonged frustration of popular expectations could result in the disintegration of the social glue that bound different communities to each other as well as to the state itself. This, in a nutshell, is one of the sources of social conflict and the dissolution of state-society relations in post-colonial West Africa.

Post-war political activism and colonial state reactions

As suggested in the introduction, West Africa came of age in the independence decade of the 1960s when broad nationalist coalitions waging anticolonial struggles triumphed over European colonial rule. Unlike the cases of settler colonialism in North, East and Southern Africa as well as the Portuguese colonies of Guinea Bissau and Cape Verde, the process of decolonization in West Africa was remarkably uncomplicated and less messy because it was relatively devoid of major violence. For the most part, it was characterized by piecemeal reformism and gradualism rather than radicalism or revolutionary transformation. In the Gold Coast (Ghana), nationalist groups such as the United Gold Coast Convention (UGCC) under J. B. Danquah and later the Convention People's Party (CPP) under Kwame Nkrumah; in Nigeria, the National Council of Nigeria and Cameroon (NCNC) under Nnamdi Azikiwe; in Sierra Leone, the Sierra Leone People's Party (SLPP) under Sir Milton Margai (later known as the United National Front, UNF); and in the Gambia, the People's Progressive Party (PPP) and the United Party (UP), to name just a few, all resorted to such 'civilized' or reformist tactics as letter writing campaigns, deputations to metropolitan capitals, peaceful pressures in the form of protest marches and rallies, boycotts of European merchants and goods, strike actions, crop 'hold-ups', and other forms of civil disobedience or 'positive action'.[1]

The response of the colonial states in West Africa was equally remarkable for its gradualism and seeming complacency, as epitomized by the gradual lifting of the ban on political organizing, the rise of mass political parties, voter registration campaigns and, finally, the staging of multiple competitive elections to fill positions in local, municipal and national legislatures. This was true not only of British West African colonies where decolonization may have been planned.[2] In the case of Francophone Africa also, France took the first tentative steps towards granting political concessions in February 1944 at the Brazzaville conference. In contrast to British plans, the Brazzaville Declaration made it abundantly clear that 'The colonizing work of France makes it impossible to accept any idea of autonomy for the colonies, or any possibility of development outside the French empire. *Even at a distant date, there will be no self-government in the colonies'* (emphasis added).[3]

Nevertheless, Brazzaville and the subsequent Fourth Republican Constitution, ratified in a national referendum in October 1946, provided the necessary legal and political framework to allow African nationalists like Gabriel d'Arboussier and Léopold Sédar Senghor of Senegal, Ahmed Sékou Touré of Guinea, Félix Houphouët-Boigny of Côte d'Ivoire, Mamadou Konaté and Modibo Keita of French Soudan (Mali), to organize and participate in elections to the French National Assembly in Paris and to improve African representation in that body. Yet the status of the colonies remained virtually unchanged; they retained their colonial status within the framework of the French Union (*Union Française*). However, in a subsequent development, the passage of the enabling legislation (*loi cadre*) in 1956 paved the way for further constitutional progress to be achieved, including the creation of territorial assemblies, greater national autonomy especially post-1958, and eventually formal political independence in 1960, thus bringing the historically anachronistic Franco-African Community to an abrupt end.

Again, the decolonization process in West Africa was comparatively tame and proceeded more smoothly once the colonial powers became

---

[1] Decolonization was largely an urban affair and led by urban elites. The 'cocoa hold-ups' of the 1930s in the Gold Coast represented one of the few instances in which rural resistance to the economics of colonial rule intersected with urban political protests.

[2] See John Flint, 'Planned Decolonization and its Failure in British Africa', *African Affairs* 82 (328) (July 1983), pp. 389-411.

[3] See Basil Davidson, *Modern Africa: A Social and Political History*. Second Edn (London and New York: Longman, 1989), p. 126.

convinced of the historical inevitability of the 'wind of change' blowing across the continent. Or it may well be that the colonial powers had realized that the emerging leaders were likely to become far more efficacious indirect rulers than the *obas* and *mwamis* (traditional chiefs) of the colonial period. Nevertheless, even in West Africa, colonial administrators found the allure of what Basil Davidson calls the 'colonialist fight-back' too tempting to resist, especially given that the *Bula Matari* complex was considered an indispensable component of the colonial enterprise.[4]

Thus, even in the model colony of Ghana, the colonial state not only sought to discredit the CPP leaders by branding them as communists and traitors and throwing them into jail, but also its security personnel fired on peaceful demonstrators, killing and wounding several. In Francophone West Africa, the strongest of the emerging territorial parties, the Democratic Party of Côte d'Ivoire (Parti démocratique de Côte d'Ivoire, PDCI) led by Félix Houphouët-Boigny, was subjected to vicious repression. Following the recall to Paris of the more sympathetic Governor Latrille, Governor Laurent Péchoux was dispatched to Abidjan apparently with a mandate to crush the PDCI. Although Péchoux failed in his primary mission, he did succeed in causing the deaths of several dozen party members; hundreds more were incarcerated in the infamous Bassam prison. Houphouët-Boigny himself narrowly escaped arrest in January 1950. On the one hand, such tactics may have backfired because they provoked a backlash in Abidjan that resulted in the famous march on Bassam by women demanding the release of their men.[5] On the other hand, they did succeed in altering the political posture of the PDCI leadership, especially that of Houphouët-Boigny, from radicalism to accommodation to constructive engagement with the French authorities, a posture he maintained for nearly 35 years of uninterrupted rule.[6]

This pattern of relatively peaceful protest and reactionary colonialist fight-back was repeated throughout West Africa. Nevertheless, nationalist persistence paid off and many leaders who had become 'prison graduates' went straight from the jail house to government

[4] The *Bula Matari* (he who breaks all rocks) complex refers to the authoritarian model of state-society relations which was so integral to colonial rule, and to the ability of the colonizing powers to crush all resistance to colonial rule. The title itself was bestowed on the famous explorer, Henry Stanley, after he succeeded in forcing a caravan of African porters to dismantle and head-carry several steamships up the Congo River.

[5] The gender dimension of decolonization remains a relatively unexplored subject.

[6] For more on this, see Cyril K. Daddieh, *Côte d'Ivoire in Crisis: The Sins of the Fathers or Houphouët-Boigny's Revenge* (Accra: The Institute of Economic Affairs Occasional Papers No. 38, 2003).

house after securing majority votes in winner-takes-all (first-past-the-post or majoritarian) preindependence elections. The departing colonial governments bequeathed to the emerging states freshly minted liberal democratic constitutions that at least on paper guaranteed civil and political rights and the related freedoms of the press, expression, assembly and association, as well as the right to vote and hold political office. The inherited model featured the Westminster parliamentary system for Anglophone Africa and, for Francophone states, strong presidential systems. Everywhere central government powers were considerably enhanced at the expense of community self-government. Even the emerging legislatures and judiciaries proved too weak to act as a check on executive power, especially under the more presidential model of Francophone Africa.

Ethnicity and the emerging post-colonial state

Significantly, with the exception of Nigeria whose initial three-state federal structure at least tacitly recognized its ethnic diversity or cultural pluralism, all the other West African states achieved independence within highly centralized or unitarist political structures. Admittedly, despite the preference for centralized governance, at least a modicum of decentralization was built into the new constitutions, primarily through local government provisions. However, the relevance of local government as a locus of political learning and contestation was highly circumscribed, in most cases deliberately so, by lack of autonomy and independent resources. Furthermore, almost everywhere a deliberate attempt was made to deny the very existence of this pluralism or to prevent it from confounding the nationalist project. Pluralism was erroneously, in some cases cynically, equated with tribalism. Tribalism was considered atavistic, a throw-back to a more primitive past. It was also much feared as a primary source of primordial loyalty, with the power to cause potentially destructive social conflict, if not state collapse and national disintegration. Thus, tribalism was vilified and, as a result, treated by virtually all West African leaders like a plague to be avoided. Guinea's Sékou Touré (President 1958–84) may have pursued the most systematic and sustained policy to wipe it out. He is reported to have told his compatriots that 'no one will remember the tribal, ethnic or religious rivalries which, in the recent past, caused so much damage to our country and its population'.[7]

And yet, ethnicity remains resilient as both paradigm and praxis.

[7] See Crawford Young, *Politics of Cultural Pluralism* (Madison, WI: University of Wisconsin

Indeed, while most nationalist leaders preached against the dangers of tribalism, they were not averse to mobilizing along ethnic lines. They routinely co-opted ethnic intermediaries into cabinets or civil service positions as largesse for getting their ethnic clients to demonstrate their loyalty to the national leaders. In the case of Côte d'Ivoire, a pragmatic, even programmatic, acceptance of ethnic corporatism and skilful ethnic calibration of government and administrative posts contributed significantly to the Ivoirian political miracle of ethnic co-existence, relative peace and regime longevity under Houphouët-Boigny. This helps to explain the proliferation of 'hometown associations' and their manipulation by ethnic leaders or sponsors in Côte d'Ivoire as well as elsewhere across West Africa. This stands in stark contrast to the rather clumsy attempt in the 1995 elections by former President Henri Konan Bédié and his successors to restrict access to the Ivoirian state within the context of an ongoing crisis of accumulation and dwindling state resources. Here as elsewhere, the state sought to link political and economic rights to the concept of *indigeneity* (in this case *ivoirité*). *Ivoirité* was intended to be used to drive a wedge between migrants (strangers) and indigenous (native) Ivoirians, and to exclude the former from civic (voting, elected office) and economic (jobs and land especially) rights.[8] Instead, this latest West African revival of the classic *divide et imperum* (divide and rule) ideology has provoked an unresolved ethnic-based struggle for control of the state. Similar developments have taken place, with much more tragic consequences, in Liberia, Sierra Leone and Nigeria.

The West African state in the 1960s: from liberal democracy to the rise of authoritarianism

The states that were inherited by West African leaders at independence were not only post-colonial; they were also notoriously weak and fragile. They were poorly endowed with woefully inadequate administrative capacity for policy formulation and implementation, due in large part to the scarcity of trained and skilled manpower. They were also faced with pluralistic societies, with arguably unrealistic or exaggerated expectations that long-neglected material needs would finally be

Press, 1976), p. 6; also Marina Ottaway, 'Ethnic Politics in Africa: Change and Continuity', in Richard Joseph (ed.), *State, Conflict, and Democracy in Africa* (Boulder, CO: Lynne Rienner Publishers, 1999).

[8] For an earlier attempt to theorize on the subject, along with some highly suggestive essays, see William A. Shack and Elliott P. Skinner (eds), *Strangers in African Societies* (Berkeley, CA: University of California Press, 1979).

addressed. The solution to this paradox of great expectations and limited state capacity entailed at least three responses: accelerated manpower development, greater attention to security, and pleas for maximum political and social tranquility or national unity. It is in this context that everywhere new universities were created and existing ones vastly expanded to meet national administrative manpower needs. The creation of national universities was complemented by scholarships for study abroad, financed by both national governments and the former colonial powers. This was especially true of Francophone Africa where study abroad and employment in the civil service provided some of the finest opportunities for the best and the brightest, as well as individuals with the right political connections, to achieve rapid upward social mobility. Such opportunities or avenues also built up support and loyalty for the new leaders. This dual usage of the bureaucracy partly explains the rapid expansion of the bureaucratic state shortly after independence.

Manpower training was combined with the transformation of colonial constabularies into greatly expanded national armies, supplemented by 'presidential guards', and the indigenization of their officer corps, in order to provide greater security for the state and the new rulers. Over time, the state became overdeveloped, used increasingly as a source of patronage and an instrument of control and even terror. In short, overdeveloped, post-colonial West African states produced fewer results such as sustained social welfare and even less security for their citizens. Paradoxically, these same states created a security dilemma for their own rulers who felt even more insecure. To counteract pluralism and its attendant centrifugal forces, some leaders and Western scholars even argued that a degree of authoritarianism was acceptable. The pursuit of the dream of nation-building or national unity demanded, to borrow Chinua Achebe's poignant invocation, 'that all argument should cease and the whole people speak with one voice and that any more dissent and argument outside the door of the shelter would subvert and bring down the whole house'.[9] A little later, it was the development imperative that provided the pretext for autocratic rule. It was as if, as the late Claude Ake quipped, a banner had been unfurled across Africa, proclaiming 'Silence. We are developing'.[10]

By employing a combination of charisma, newly minted national symbols, exhortations, political pressure and, at times, outright repression, African leaders hoped to secure acquiescence in ongoing efforts to shrink the political arena. Initially, moves toward the

---

[9] Chinua Achebe, *A Man of the People* (London: Heinemann, 1967), p. 37.
[10] Claude Ake, *Democracy and Development in Africa* (Washington DC: Brookings Institution, 1996), pp. 1–17.

narrowing of the scope of political participation and competition or the re-channeling of participation into state-controlled institutions were fairly subtle. It usually began, as Ghana under Nkrumah illustrates, innocuously enough with the promulgation of legislation prohibiting the formation of political parties along narrow ethnic, religious or regional lines. This was followed by a retreat from constricting Constitutional provisions, including those mandating decentralized government, coupled with the gradual expansion of presidential powers, the elimination of constitutional checks on the executive branch of government, and culminating, finally, in the imposition of one-party rule. This pattern was repeated elsewhere in West Africa.

With single-party rule firmly entrenched, strenuous efforts were made to incorporate all autonomous civil society organizations into state structures in order to bring them under tighter political control. In Côte d'Ivoire, for instance, all civil servants were compelled to become, willy nilly, card-carrying members of the ruling PDCI. Various laboring and professional classes — ranging from farmers, fishermen, bakers and transporters, to doctors, lawyers, secondary school teachers and university professors — were all cajoled or pressured into joining the state-sponsored federation of Ivoirian workers, the *Union Générale des Travailleurs de Côte d'Ivoire* (UGTCI).

Military intervention in West Africa

From the mid-1960s, West African militaries began to enter the political fray. They began to intervene in their countries' political processes, thereby completing the ongoing political enclosure begun earlier by their civilian counterparts. Indeed, military coups became so contagious and so commonplace that they appeared as a *de facto* institutionalized model for the transfer of power. Thus, with the exception of Côte d'Ivoire (until 1999), Guinea (until 1984), Gambia (until 1994), and Senegal, the men in khaki from virtually all the West African countries left their barracks, usurped political power, disbanded national parliaments, banned political parties and began to rule by force or decree. Invariably, they made strike action by workers and professional bodies illegal, shut down independent newspapers, and promulgated draconian libel laws designed to muzzle the press or to compel journalists to practise self-censorship. Many dissident politicians were tried in extra-judicial or kangaroo courts and sentenced to death or to extended periods of incarceration with hard labor. Even ordinary citizens were not immune to arbitrary arrest and prosecution. Much of this might even have been palatable if only the military rulers had succeeded in turning the West African states into developmental ones. Instead, most of them produced first-class venality. A West African case in point is Major General Ibrahim Babanginda who has earned opprobrium as the most massively corrupt ruler in Nigerian political history.

Military interventions were emblematic of the basic breakdown of constitutional order and governmental instability in the post-colonial period. Moreover, as the line-up of countries that have experienced coups reveals, colonial heritage, regime type and national income were unreliable predictors of coups. Francophone and Anglophone countries, one-party regimes (Ghana and Mali) and multi-party states (Dahomey in 1963 and Gambia in 1981, failed coup; 1994), an oil-rich, rentier state (Nigeria) and desperately poor countries (Niger and Burkina Faso) have all succumbed to military rule, sometimes many times (for instance, Nigeria, Ghana, Burkina Faso, Mali). The first generation of military coups was partly a function of perceived threats to the corporate interests of the military and the ambitions of individual officers. They also reflected the weakness of civilian political institutions. However, international actors contributed to either successful military takeovers or, in a few cases, their rollback. By virtue of its strategic presence in Senegal, Côte d'Ivoire, Gabon, Cameroon, etc., and the centrality of Africa to its major power status and ambitions, France was more likely to intervene in Francophone West Africa and to get away with it.

At the same time, praetorianism (a state leader supported by a powerful personal guard) deprived the African masses of their right to meaningful political participation and undermined their capacity to hold the new rulers accountable through the electoral and other decision-making processes, and democratic institutions. In short, military intervention was a setback to political institutionalization. However, as the popular West African saying goes, 'No Condition is Permanent'. Since the beginning of the 1990s, West African states have come full circle and joined their counterparts elsewhere in Africa in accepting, sometimes grudgingly, multi-party competition and citizen participation in the selection of their rulers. These elections now proceed within a framework of nationally approved democratic constitutions.

Simultaneously, West African states have also witnessed a real flowering of associational life, including an unruly and, at times, irreverent free press. National governments no longer have monopoly control over information. Private FM radio stations now rule the airwaves. In short, parts of West Africa, including Ghana, Senegal, Benin, Mali and Nigeria, are currently experiencing a 'second independence'. The unevenness of the democratic resurgence in West

Africa can be inferred from the nightmarish civil wars in Liberia, Sierra Leone, Guinea and even Côte d'Ivoire. We return to these issues below.

Economic crisis and loss of legitimacy

Whether the regime in question is characterized as being single-party, one-man-dominated or a military junta, West African states became highly authoritarian and gendered (male-dominated partly by virtue of limited female access to education and involvement in the military profession). Authoritarianism took the peculiar form of neopatrimonialism. The hallmarks of this variety of authoritarianism were the personalization of authority, institutionalized relations of loyalty and dependence, and the construction of patron-client networks. Although the limits to such patron-client relationships were real and not hard to discern, they were apparently ignored. As a model of governance, it was expensive to administer because it relied heavily on the state's capacity to distribute economic and symbolic goods, combined with careful calibration of bureaucratic and political appointments along ethnic and regional lines in order to maintain loyal support. To be sure, the longer-term viability of a strategy of distributive politics hinges on a robust economy and the generation of increasingly expanding economic resources. Such economic success was the key enabler, permitting the state to broaden its distribution of economic and job opportunities as well as facilitating the co-optation of key political actors such as heads of corporatist groups (ethnic intermediaries) and real or imagined dissidents with offers they could not easily refuse. Kwame Nkrumah's Ghana came up against this limit early in the post-independence era and Houphouët-Boigny's Côte d'Ivoire belatedly experienced it. Indeed, it continues to be challenged by the limits to economic growth and redistributive politics.

Another key feature of neopatrimonialism was the systematic concentration of political power in the hands of one individual who stubbornly refused to delegate authority, let alone share power. This led inexorably to the cultivation of a 'cult of personality' which was unmistakably celebrated in monuments and statues, and in images of the president emblazoned on national currencies and special anniversary cloth and tee-shirts, coupled with the appropriation of various honorific titles (praise names).[11] These initiatives were

---

[11] The following is a sample of these honorific titles: Julius Nyerere became 'Mwalimu' (the beloved and respected teacher); Jomo Kenyatta became 'Mzee' (wise elder, counselor, arbiter); Kwame Nkrumah became 'Oyeadiyie' (one who puts things right); 'Kantamanto' (he who is

supplemented by self-serving representations of leaders as 'fathers of the nation' who knew what was best for their extended national households, and who were indispensable to the continued survival of the nation and must therefore live and rule forever (the 'life excellencies' or 'presidents-for-life' syndrome). Another significant component of neopatrimonialism was the projection of aristocratic effects in both lifestyles and physical appearance, to wit, bellies protruding from 'too much eating'.[12] The resultant 'politics of the belly' only fuels kleptocratic rule. The line between the latter and the felonious and criminalized state may be considerably blurred, as the notorious examples of Foday Sankoh of Sierra Leone and Charles Taylor of Liberia reveal.

In order to maintain their grip on power and the associated lifestyles, West African leaders centralized all state power. They shifted from multi-party to one-party regimes and then to highly personalized one-man rule on the pretext that (a) the shift was more in line with African tradition; (b) it would permit the people to speak with one voice and thereby facilitate efficient governance; (c) it would concentrate the national collective mind on the tasks of nation-building and development. In addition it would allow the West African states to avoid dissipating their national energies in pursuit of narrow, ethnic claims or spare them the financial cost of putting out inter-ethnic fires sparked by multi-party competition, as happened in several countries during the run-up to independence.

Not surprisingly, in the process, the West African state became both grossly overdeveloped and highly predatory. A sprawling network of bureaucratic institutions was created to manage not only production and marketing, but people's lives as well. In particular, West African peasants were exploited through the ubiquitous colonial-era Marketing Boards that used their monopoly buying powers to purchase export

---

never guilty); 'Kasapreko' (a man of his word); 'Osagyefo' (redeemer, the messiah); Houphouët-Boigny was 'Nana' (traditional chief); Le Vieux (wise old man); Kamuzu Banda was 'Ngwazi' (the champion, the messiah); Emperor Haile Selaissie was 'the elect of God, son of David, Son of Solomon, King of Kings, Lion of Judah'; Joseph Désiré Mobutu became 'Mobutu Sese Seko Koko Ngbendu wa za Banga (the all-powerful warrior who because of his endurance and inflexible will to win, will go from conquest to conquest leaving fire in his wake)'; Samuel Doe fancied himself as 'the redeemer' and Rawlings became popularly known as 'JJ – Junior Jesus'. It must be said that honorific titles seem to be going out of favor. Contemporary African leaders would rather be known as technocrats. Thus, Thabo Mbeki has conjured up the image of 'African Renaissance'; Abdoulaye Wade has initiated the 'Omega Plan' and Mbeki, Wade, and Obasanjo have together spearheaded the NEPAD (New Partnership for African Development) initiative.

[12] The 'before and after' images of Master Sergeant Doe of Liberia and Jerry John Rawlings of Ghana provide the best visual reminders of such a transformation: from skeletal junior officers to obese presidents.

cash crops at well below world market prices. Such exploitation notwithstanding, the material base of the state continued to be undermined by unfavorable world market conditions for primary export commodities. The problem was exacerbated by peasant attempts to avoid capture of their products by the governments. The worsening terms of trade against the countryside and the ongoing urban bias in state policies prompted the normally apolitical peasants to exercise their exit or withdrawal options by smuggling crops across national boundaries, reverting to subsistence production, substituting crops that were not under state buying control, selling crops 'illegally' on the black market or simply voting with their feet and migrating elsewhere.

It is hardly surprising that most of the states in West Africa began to experience fiscal crises in the late 1970s that continued into the lost decade of the 1980s. By the late 1980s, West Africa had experienced more than a decade of a combination of bad policies, bad governance, bad luck (devastating drought and bush fires in the 1970s) and a double whammy of external shocks — unfavorable world market prices for primary commodities and devastating oil price hikes at both ends of the decade. The resultant crisis of accumulation and political instability pushed African states into international receivership, making the continent ripe for external co-optation of its policy-making by the international financial institutions, most notably the International Monetary Fund (IMF) and the World Bank. Thus, virtually all West African countries were compelled to embrace neoliberal economic orthodoxy, popularly known as structural adjustment programs (SAPs), in return for balance of payments and other policy supports.

Broadly, SAPs involved two sets of conditionalities: trade liberalization and privatization of both investments and production. These twin conditions were aimed at promoting exports while simultaneously constraining imports, especially of nonproductive consumer goods. They targeted government finances, aiming to bring them into balance or eliminate chronic budget deficits by subjecting national currencies, considered grossly overvalued almost everywhere, to massive and repeated devaluations. These measures were coupled with exchange-rate liberalization, the tightening of money supply, and the dismantling of government price controls and import/export regulations. Another target of SAPs was the overdeveloped state. Liberalization, privatization, deregulation and downsizing entered the lexicon. The bureaucracy, a major source of employment and patronage, was trimmed down and civil servants retrenched (a euphemism for being laid off).

The drive to unburden the treasury and curtail government

expenditures even further led to government subsidies for basic needs such as education and health care being drastically reduced or eliminated altogether. Instead, 'cost recovery measures' or 'user fees' for public services were instituted. SAPs were aimed at not only downsizing the state but also reducing its interventionist role through the privatization of state-owned enterprises and other government assets. In sum, SAPs were designed to discipline a predatory and unruly state, shrink its size and diminish its appetite for economic intervention. It was hoped that these measures would unleash market forces that would create incentives for private entrepreneurship, stimulate competition, ensure a more rational allocation of scarce resources, channel investments into more productive rather than consumptive activities and make African economies more attractive for capitalist penetration and foreign direct investments.

After more than two decades of SAPs, the results have not been very edifying. Witness the fact that Ghana, the IMF's model adjusting country since 1983, and Côte d'Ivoire, the former 'economic miracle', have both been declared HIPC — that is to say, 'heavily indebted poor countries'. Indeed, critics have questioned the wisdom and efficacy of structural adjustment. SAPs imposed short-term hardships in anticipation of future economic and social recovery or development. Instead, wherever they have been implemented, from Senegal to Nigeria, they have increased the burdens and misery of long-suffering vulnerable groups such as children, women and the laboring poor. Rather than restructuring West African economies away from their traditional roles in the old international division of labor, and towards new and higher forms of production and incorporation, they have merely reinforced that role and low power status while producing, as Zimbabweans have quipped, results in 'Suffering for African People'. It is arguable that given the lackluster performance of nearly all African economies beginning in the 1970s and the absolute declines in incomes and standards of living in the lost decade of the 1980s, African states had little choice but to turn to these international financial institutions.

Social conflict and state disintegration/collapse

Significantly, as the crisis of accumulation gathered momentum and state resources dwindled, West African regimes exhibited a number of contradictory responses. First, access to the state became increasingly restricted to the fortunate few elites from the right ethnic groups (Americo-Liberians, Mandingo, Krahn, Gio or Mano in Liberia; Creole in Sierra Leone; Baoulé in Côte d'Ivoire; Kabye in Togo; Hausa-Fulani or Kaduna Mafia in Nigeria; Wollof in Senegal, and so on) or those with the right political connections. Not surprisingly, this government response only provoked greater resentment among disaffected groups and stimulated fierce competition for control of the state in order to redefine who got political access or to determine who received what, when and how. This, in turn, led to state repression to fend off real and imagined threats. Thus, the new struggle for power became literally a life and death affair. In such an atmosphere, it was not surprising that loyalty fragmented and legitimacy became a scarce commodity. As Ake contended, the trauma of repeated subjection to arbitrary and coercive rule had turned West African societies into a 'hostile force to be feared, evaded, cheated and defeated as circumstances permit. They turn their loyalty from the more ecumenical level of the state and localize it in community groups, kinship groups, ethnic associations, or even religious organizations'. He went on to assert that, *'What is happening in Africa now is in effect the strengthening of the process of the localization of loyalties. We might say that as a result of political repression, we are witnessing, not nation building, not development, but in fact, the dissolution of society'* (emphasis added).[13]

Second, faced with societies that had turned decidedly hostile, several regimes in West Africa appeared to disengage from them. They had all but lost their ability to exert effective political and administrative control or to perform the most basic functions of statehood and simply withdrew inwards. Many West African societies reciprocated in kind. For a time, states were sustained by their juridical status even though they demonstrated little or no empirical statehood, as Jackson and Rosberg Jr had argued.[14] Such states remained authoritarian, especially in core areas, without being authoritative. They were unable to command voluntary compliance and lacked the power to compel societies to obey their edicts.

Furthermore, both civilian and military office-holders pursued a third response which exacerbated the already worsening situation. They began to subvert the state from within, making the crisis of legitimacy even worse. The state became not only highly predatory but increasingly inverted. State institutions became increasingly dysfunctional and state

---

[13] See Claude Ake, 'The Case for Democracy', in *African Governance in the 1990s: Objectives, Resources, and Constraints* (Atlanta, GA: The Carter Center of Emory University. Working Papers from the Second Annual Seminar of the African Governance Program, 23-25 March), p. 2.

[14] Robert H. Jackson and Carl G. Rosberg, Jr, 'Why Africa's Weak States Persist: The Empirical and Juridical in Statehood', *World Politics* 35 (October 1989), pp. 1–24.

functionaries ended up turning inwards on themselves rather than outwards facing society. In such a situation, as Joshua Forrest has argued, state units become transformed into factionalized pockets of power, each enjoying access to one or more illegal markets. This, in turn, further accentuates the institutional and political fragmentation of state power.[15] The military, which is often the only state institution capable of preventing the actual break-up of the nation and the total disintegration of the state, is increasingly unable to do so because its integrity and coherence have suffered a serious decline from years of praetorian adventurism. Moreover, the armed forces themselves have become divided into component sections that parallel the fractured structure of the state itself.

A key outcome of extreme state inversion appears to be organized and pervasive violence in which surviving elements of the state become immersed in or devoted to warfare. Sectors of society ally with rebels or become super-saturated with social banditry. When such a crisis of governance degenerates into fully-fledged civil war, the state often breaks down along patterns reflecting its ultra-privatized character. The result is that military and political factions become linked to informal economic networks. In such an atmosphere, different politico-military units seek control over informal markets such as stockpiles of food, arms trade (the cases of Somalia, Ethiopia and Sudan), or diamond mining and precious gems trading (the cases of Liberia, Sierra Leone, Zaire and Angola). Social banditry becomes a generalized social phenomenon, fueled in part by the proliferation of small arms. Thus, by coincidence or not, there is an intriguing conjunction of SAPs and small arms proliferation.

While virtually all West African states were faced with serious challenges to their rule and several were 'verging on dissolution',[16] in Liberia and Sierra Leone the specter of anarchy was unmistakable. War raged in Liberia from 1989 to 1996 and in Sierra Leone from 1991 to 2002. These two West African states represented one of two patterns of challenge to the state and Africa. They became notorious for the most grotesque form of mobilized social banditry, which was characterized by plunder and pillage and barbarism on the road from the countryside to the national capitals of Monrovia and Freetown respectively.[17] In both cases, disaffected members of the governing class

---

[15] See Joshua B. Forrest, 'State Inversion and Nonstate Politics', in Leonard A. Villalon and Phillip A. Huxtable (eds), *The African State at a Critical Juncture: Between Disintegration and Reconfiguration* (Boulder, CO and London: Lynne Rienner Publishers, 1998), chapter 3.
[16] See Aristide R. Zolberg, 'The Specter of Anarchy: African States Verging on Dissolution', *Dissent* 39 (October 1992), pp. 1–24.
[17] *Ibid.*

formed armed movements, seeking to wrest control of the state from their former colleagues. Most of these rebel movements were ethnically based. They also had a propensity to fracture into different organizations as evidenced by the experiences of Liberia's ULIMO-J and ULIMO-K.

What was particularly novel and different about Liberia and Sierra Leone was that the struggle for state power did not take the traditional form of army officers staging a military coup. Rather, rebel leaders put together ragtag, but highly motivated, armies and launched insurrections from the countryside, often with the collusion of neighboring states. This raises the specter of a wider regional conflict. Unlike coups d'état, such bids took much longer to prosecute. The resulting civil wars were often protracted, and were fought with unprecedented brutality. All kinds of atrocities were perpetrated against innocent civilian populations. It seemed nothing was off limits: amputations, rape, forced murder of some family members by others and various other fratricidal tactics, as well as scorched earth policies, such as the burning of entire villages. In short, every kind of devilry was unleashed. Villages and refugee camps were raided and civilians abducted and inducted into rebel armies.

The widespread use of child soldiers became another striking feature of this new challenge to the state. Child-soldiers were recruited, drugged, and psychologically inoculated against the fear of death and dying and forced to go into harrowing battles. Indigenous fighters were often supplemented with mercenaries or soldiers of fortune who commanded a hefty price and were therefore only available to those rebel movements which controlled resources bringing in a steady stream of revenue. Indeed, these wars were fueled by the allure of the control of precious metals. Since these assets were often insufficient to secure outright victories, these uncivil wars produced inconclusive, mutually damaging stalemates. As such, they provided an opportunity for oftentimes difficult peace negotiations and the subsequent injection of ECOWAS and UN peacekeepers as well as post-conflict reconfigurations of the state. The potential for spillover was one reason for the involvement of regional and international actors. Overall, the consequences of state collapse and civil wars were horrendous. Life became rather Hobbesian: nasty, brutish, solitary and short.

Fortunately, the second pattern of challenge to the state which unfolded in the latter part of the 1980s and the first half of the 1990s was less dastardly and less anarchic. It took the form of increasingly massive and sustained protest demonstrations that reflected urban discontent over capricious governance as well as unrelenting economic hardships (high prices, high unemployment even for university graduates, depressed wages, shortages of essential commodities and so on), despite repeated adjustments. It metamorphosed into demands for political liberalization reforms, including the abolition of military or one-party rule, the legalization of opposition parties, the staging of competitive elections and the transfer of power to democratically elected governments. This chorus of demands was tantamount to calls for a 'second independence'.

Across the sub-region, university and even secondary school students played a vital role in the democratic transitions.[18] Campus politics and student activism enabled political parties, professional bodies, business associations, other civil society organizations and even military factions to prise open sufficient political spaces for autonomous action. This sustained pressure compelled even the most recalcitrant regimes to give in to multi-party competitive politics, albeit often grudgingly. By 1994, not a single *de jure* one-party state remained. Benin's so-called 'velvet revolution' provided a template for the transition in Francophone Africa. In Benin, students at the national university demanded the disbursement of long delayed scholarships and the restoration of public sector employment for university graduates. They were later joined by civil servants, school teachers and a military which refused to use its muscle to quell a growing opposition to military strongman and self-proclaimed Marxist, Mathieu Kérékou.

These demands evolved into a National Conference that claimed sovereignty and stripped Kérékou of all but symbolic power. The National Conference then controlled the transition process by abolishing the one-party military state rule, reinstating multi-party competition, establishing a constitutional assembly consisting of a wide variety of civil society organizations, and writing a new constitution which was massively ratified in a referendum in December 1990. All this served as a prelude to competitive multi-party legislative elections in February 1991 which were supervised by international observers and certified as 'free and fair'. Indeed, a repentant and apparently reformed Kérékou lost his bid for democratic confirmation in the presidential elections of March 1991 to Nicephore Soglo, and accepted defeat, only to be returned to power by the voters five years later.

The combination of the National Conference model and the alternation in office has made Benin something of an icon in democratic transition and consolidation. Another Francophone West African

---

[18] For more on this student role in the democratization process, see Cyril K. Daddieh, 'Universities and Political Protest in Africa: The Case of Côte d'Ivoire', *ISSUE: A Journal of Opinion* XXIV/I (Winter/Spring, 1996), pp. 57–60.

country that has passed the test of democratization, even though it eschewed the National Conference route, is Senegal. The defeat of the long-ruling incumbent Socialist Party of Senegal and its presidential candidate Abdou Diof by Abdoulaye Wade presages a transformation of Senegal's 'semi-democracy' to consolidated democracy. By contrast, Togo has not been so fortunate. Its National Conference initiatives have been repeatedly guided and subverted by its strongman, Gnassingbé Eyadema, although part of the fault may also lie with an intransigent opposition. Eyadema's death in February 2005 brought no reprieve for the Togolese as the army conspired to elevate his son Faure to the Presidency.

Meanwhile, the guided democratic transitions of Nigeria and Ghana are maturing into consolidated democracies. In the case of Ghana, Flt. Lt. Jerry Rawlings (Head of State 1981–92 under military government, President 1992–2000) controlled and effectively guided the transition process. Not surprisingly, he also managed to win the transitional parliamentary and presidential elections. The opposition boycotted the presidential vote, claiming that the people's verdict had been stolen by Rawlings and the New Democratic Party (NDC). In the subsequent balloting four years later, Rawlings again won, thus serving two consecutive terms as president. Since the constitution barred him from serving more than two terms, his handpicked successor and former Vice-President, Professor Atta Mills, became the party's flag-bearer in the 2000 elections. However, he and the NDC could not hang on to the reins of power; they were defeated by John A. Kufuor and the New Patriotic Party (NPP). Kufuor and his NPP were again victorious in the elections of December 2004, but the strong showing by the opposition NDC leaves little doubt that Ghanaian democracy is verging on maturation.

By contrast, neighboring Côte d'Ivoire, which also experienced guided democracy without alternation under the leadership of its founding father and an ardent foe of multi-party competition, Félix Houphouët-Boigny, is currently in the throes of political instability. Houphouët-Boigny's successors inherited a prolonged economic downturn, diminished state resources, increased overall population and rapid urbanization, the presence of millions of migrant workers (strangers), some of whom had lived in the country for several generations, growing competition for access to public schools, and increasingly scarce public sector jobs, urban joblessness, youth restlessness, vagrancy and violence, bank robberies, and other forms of social banditry. Diminished access to land was also producing periodic inter-ethnic violence in the countryside. It was within this context that the transitional elections took place in 1990. The turning point came because the much vaunted Ivoirian economic miracle (which had lasted from independence through to the 1980s) and related welfare benefits that had mediated opposition to the monopoly power of the 320 families that controlled the system had by then become considerably tarnished. The challenges to the regime had begun to multiply from a variety of social groups. More importantly, the continuing crisis of accumulation had begun to erode the hitherto seemingly unassailable cohesion of the elite.

While the ruling party won the flawed transitional elections in 1990, the state did not fully recover from the political blows it had suffered. Both the political system and society in general were far from pacified. Three years later, Côte d'Ivoire narrowly averted a succession crisis when President Houphouët-Boigny died on 7 December 1993, and the reins of government were handed over to his heir apparent, Henri Konan Bédié, the incumbent president of the National Assembly. President Bédié's legitimacy was challenged almost immediately by incumbent Prime Minister Alassane Dramane Ouattara and some of the other opposition leaders. The new president's position was made even more tenuous because he lacked the charisma and political acumen of his more revered predecessor to which the society had grown accustomed. Nevertheless, the country's political elites agreed to bury the hatchet while they prepared to bid *Le Vieux* a fond farewell. Moreover, the country weathered the storm of devaluation of the CFA franc in January 1994 better than most of the other members of the franc monetary zone. However, social and political unrest continued unabated until the political death-knell was tolled by the military on Christmas Eve 1999, thus producing the country's first successful coup against President Bédié.

The entrenched power of the ruling Parti Démocratique de la Côte d'Ivoire (PDCI) was swept aside with astonishing ease and replaced by a joint civilian-military junta under the leadership of General Robert Gueï. Although General Gueï professed his lack of interest in power, proclaiming that he merely wanted to 'sweep the house clean' and that 'once we know that the house is clean and politicians can dance without slipping, we will withdraw after holding transparent elections', he changed his tune a few months later and contested the October 2000 elections as a no-party 'candidate of the people'. When the people rejected him, he tried in vain to nullify the verdict by falsifying the official results. This move occasioned three days of spectacular displays of people power that forced him to flee the capital and brought the subsequent swearing-in of Laurent Gbagbo as president on 26 October 2000. Since Gbagbo's ascendancy, Côte d'Ivoire has been mired in political violence, including attempted coups, abductions and gruesome killings by shadowy death squads. The manipulation and politicization of ethnicity by the country's political contenders, and the pursuit of exclusionary ethnic politics by incumbent presidents since 1993, in particular the ongoing attempts to redefine Ivoirian identity and link it to civic and economic rights, have culminated in the virtual partition of the country into two, with the government clinging to the south, the rebels holding on to the north and a corner of the 'wild West', and the French military and ECOWAS (now UN) forces providing a buffer and monitoring a shaky truce.

Conclusion

If the 1960s was a decade of independence, optimism, even euphoria in West Africa, the 1970s was a decade of frustrations. The optimistic expectations of independence had been dashed. Material progress was limited. Political enclosure, authoritarianism and patron-client networks deprived ordinary West Africans of genuine involvement in the political process. The state and society were at loggerheads because of the inability of the authoritarian rulers to transform the post-colonial state into a developmental one. They forfeited legitimacy, especially during the lost decade of the 1980s when incomes, even for middle-class professionals, plummeted and food and other shortages became widespread. The economic crisis of the 1980s led to external co-optation of West African decision-making via neo-liberal structural adjustment measures. The hardships imposed by SAPs on all groups, especially the more vulnerable ones, provoked a societal backlash. Sustained protest demonstrations against SAPs spilled over into demands for political liberalization. Civil society organizations emerged and gradually gained confidence in their capacity to challenge authoritarian governments that were presiding over the suffering of African peoples. The resultant democratization has produced uneven results, with some countries verging on maturation or democratic consolidation (Ghana, Senegal, Benin), while others remain fragile or at risk of policies being reversed (Côte d'Ivoire, Togo, Guinea, Guinea-Bissau, Sierra Leone, Liberia, Burkina Faso). Perhaps such unevenness is to be expected. It is certainly consistent with Antonio Gramsci's memorable observation that: 'The old is dying, and the new cannot be born; in this interregnum a great variety of morbid symptoms appear'.[19]

[19] Antonio Gramsci, *Selections from the Prison Notebooks of Antonio Gramsci*, ed. and trans. by Quinton Hoare and Geoffrey Nowell Smith (New York: International Publishers, 1971), p. 276.

Recommended Reading

Adebayo, Adekeye (2002) *Building Peace in West Africa: Liberia, Sierra Leone and Guinea-Bissau* (Boulder, CO: Lynne Rienner Publishers).

Bayart, Jean-François (1993) *The State in Africa: The Politics of the Belly* (Harlow and New York: Longman).

Bayart, Jean-François, Stephen Ellis and Béatrice Hibou (1999) *The Criminalization of the State in Africa* (Oxford: James Currey; Bloomington: Indiana University Press).

Berdal, Mats and David M. Malone (eds) (2000) *Greed and Grievance: Economic Agendas in Civil Wars* (Boulder, CO and London: Lynne Rienner Publishers).

Davidson, Basil (1992) *The Black Man's Burden: Africa and the Curse of the Nation State* (New York: Random House; Oxford: James Currey).

Donald Crummey (ed.) (1986) *Banditry, Rebellion and Social Protest in Africa* (London: James Currey).

Ellis, Stephen (1999) *The Mask of Anarchy: The Destruction of Liberia and the Religious Dimension of an African Civil War* (New York: New York University Press).

Falola, Toyin (1999) *The History of Nigeria* (Westport, CT: Greenwood Press).

Fatton, Robert Jr (1992) *Predatory Rule: State and Civil Society in Africa* (Boulder, CO: Lynne Rienner Publishers).

Hirsch, John L. (2001) *Sierra Leone: Diamonds and the Struggle for Democracy* (Boulder, CO: Lynne Rienner Publishers).

Reno, William (1998) *Warlord Politics and African States* (Boulder, CO: Lynne Rienner Publishers).

Richards, Paul (1996) *Fighting for the Rainforest: War, Youth and Resources in Sierra Leone* (London: James Currey; Portsmouth, NH: Heinemann).

Rothchild, Donald and Naomi Chazan (eds) (1998) *The Precarious Balance: State and Society in Africa* (Boulder, CO and London: Westview Press).

Sørbø, Gunnar M. and Peter Vale (eds) (1997) *Out of Conflict: From War to Peace in Africa* (Uppsala: Nordiska Afrikainstitutet).

Young, Crawford (1977) *The Politics of Cultural Pluralism* (Madison, WI: University of Wisconsin Press).

Zartman, I. William (ed.) (1995) *Collapsed States: The Disintegration and Restoration of Legitimate Authority* (Boulder, CO: Lynne Rienner Publishers).

13

Pentecostalism, Islam & Culture
New Religious Movements in West Africa

BRIAN LARKIN & BIRGIT MEYER

Introduction

The most striking aspect of religious revitalization in West Africa over the last two decades has been the rise of evangelical Pentecostalism along the coastal and southern parts of the region, and of reformist Islam in the hinterlands. At first glance, these represent two almost diametrically opposed religious movements. Pentecostalism is marked by a return to mysticism and to practices of possession over the intellectualist worship of mainline Christian churches, while Islamism attacks Sufi mysticism and calls for a return to a legalistic, rationalist Islam. Pentecostals preach prosperity and parade the accumulation of wealth as a sign of God's blessing, as Islamist leaders criticize the materialism of Sufi elites. Pentecostalism links African Christians to a worldwide congregation of born-again believers and a set of doctrines and bodily practices, derived from southern American televangelists. Reformist Islam is part of the thoroughgoing reform of West African Islam through the increased penetration of Islamic beliefs and procedures from the wider Muslim world, most especially Saudi Arabia. Both are, of course, fiercely outspoken religions; enmity between them runs deep, and the consequence has been that disagreements and mutual suspicion have often degenerated into violent conflict.

At second glance, however, both movements share a great deal of common ground and, while disagreeing strongly on doctrine, overlap strikingly in the procedures by which they have come to prominence, the practices on which they depend, and the social processes they set in motion. Indeed, in the wake of the reconfiguration of African states and the progressive disembedding of the African economies from the formal world market, both Pentecostalism and Islamism can be seen as two new kinds of social imaginaries which thrive on religion's ability to render meaningful the unstable and often depressing flux of life in Africa. They do this through a conversion process that marks a deep transformation and reconstitution of the person by redefining established forms of religious practice such as prayer, and by transforming intimate relations of dress and deportment, commensality and social interaction. In this way, Pentecostalism and Islamism offer new ways for people to imagine both collective life and their position as individuals in contemporary Africa.

Therefore, instead of taking for granted the oppositions between reformist Islam and Pentecostalism, this chapter explores their commonalities, seeing both as examples of structural shifts in the way religion articulates relations between society, the individual and modernity. Both religions copy from one another, thus crossing boundaries and blurring sharp distinctions, while at the same time stereotyping and objectifying the other in order to generate the energy for 'crusades' or 'jihads'. In this way both are doppelgangers, enemies whose actions mirror those of the other, and whose fates are intertwined.

This occurs in three main ways. First, the Pentecostalist and Islamist desire to remake religious practice in West Africa is enacted through a sustained attack on 'culture' in a way that is nothing short of revolutionary. By 'culture' we mean here local religious and cultural traditions that now take in Catholicism as well as *orixas*, Sufism as well as *bori* spirit possession. Once thought constitutive of social and religious identities and still hailed in state politics of identity, these practices are now revealed through the new revivalisms to be the cause of mishap and apostasy, backsliding and syncretism. To carry out this attack, Pentecostalism and Islamism depend on seizing a pre-constituted, objectified conception of culture, and then subjecting it to a new form of objectification − in a process not unlike that of colonial rule itself. Secondly, both Pentecostalism and Islamism self-consciously offer new ways of becoming modern both through religious practice (modern orientated versus 'backward' looking) and in terms of the access to economic networks, material goods and lifestyles associated with modernity. Pentecostalists pursue this through links with Europe and especially the United States, while Muslim networks head in a different direction, to religious and economic centers in Saudi Arabia, Lebanon and Dubai.

Thirdly, and related to the above, both Pentecostalism and reformist Islam represent new eras in the globalization of religion − inherent in

287

the operation of both Christianity and Islam in West Africa — and the intensified interaction of West Africa religiously and economically with other centers. For both born-again Christians and reformist Muslims, the transformations inherent in this shift are played out at the level of doctrine, but also in the ways in which religious practices control and delimit the micro-processes of everyday life: the way one dresses, prays, or addresses elders and superiors. These bring theological issues down into the daily routines of everyday life, and it is these routines — and how one is to live in the world — that are often the most intense battlegrounds where the influence of these new religious movements are revealed and fought over.

While we concentrate on the mirroring of Pentecostalism in Islam and vice versa, most scholars have focused on conflicts *within* Christianity and Islam, between mainline Protestants and born-again Christians on the one hand, or Sufi orders and Salafi-inspired reformers on the other.[1] This stems from the still common habit in certain fields of African studies (especially history and anthropology) of dividing countries into different regions and treating them as inward-looking wholes. Studies of Islam in West Africa tend not to concern themselves with Christianity (or vice versa), studies of southern Ghana often proceed as if the north did not exist, or those of northern Nigeria as if Yoruba and Igbo belonged to a different world. The exception to this, of course, is the scholarship on religious conflict itself which, while informative, takes as its starting point the opposition between Islam and Christianity.[2] While not wishing to downplay the dynamics internal to Christianity or Islam, we choose rather to focus on their interrelations.

While Pentecostalism and Islamism are perhaps the most dynamic religious forces in Africa at present, mainline Christian churches and Sufi brotherhoods have proved themselves more than competent in the task of updating and transforming basic aspects of their organization and ritual so as to adapt to the perceived challenge from these new outsiders. Aspects of Pentecostal and Salafi critique are accepted and internalized while others are rejected, testifying to an impressive ability to withstand sustained assault and carry on. Moreover, there is a solid

---

[1] Salafis, also known as Wahhabis (though this term is often used by others to describe them), subscribe to a literalist interpretation of Islam based on a return to the core texts of Islamic belief: the Qur'an and Hadith. Salafism is also variously known as reformist Islam, Islamism and fundamentalist Islam.

[2] Toyin Falola, *Violence in Nigeria: The Crisis of Religious Politics and Secular Ideologies* (Rochester, NY: University of Rochester Press, 2001); Jibrin Ibrahim, 'The Politics of Religion in Nigeria: The Parameters of the 1987 Crisis in Kaduna State', *Review of African Political Economy* 45/46 (1989) pp. 65–82.

intellectual reason for keeping in mind the interrelations between 'older' forms of Christianity and Islam and their revivalist cousins: this is the fact that many of the dynamics that might at first sight be identified as new in contemporary Pentecostalism and reformist Islam — revolutionary transformations of everyday personhood and bodily practices, access to modernity, objectification of conceptions of traditional culture and displacement of it at the same time — have actually been long-standing in the articulation between religion, colonialism and society. What we see at play in the rise of new religious movements, then, is an *extension* as well as a transformation of processes established during the colonial period.

In this chapter, we make assertions about new religious movements that we believe have resonance for the region as a whole; yet our specific analyses will be on the areas of our own expertise: Pentecostalism in southern Ghana and Islamism in northern Nigeria. This is therefore a partial rather than a comprehensive study. We think that there is merit in understanding the national contexts of transnational religious movements; religious movements are articulated in particular national arenas — for instance, the tensions between Islam and Christianity in Nigeria are not what they are in Ghana — but once those religious movements are formed as a result of a specific set of national circumstances, they can create a template to be exported elsewhere. This is especially the case for Nigeria whose dynamic Pentecostal churches have tremendous influence in the Anglophone region of West Africa, and whose Islamist movements are highly influential in Niger and elsewhere.

Pentecostalism

As elsewhere in Africa, the religious regimes of Ghanaian so-called mission or mainline churches were contested throughout the twentieth century. Prayer groups emerged which placed much more emphasis on the Holy Spirit and prayer healing than Protestant and Catholic church authorities, and these eventually developed into Independent African Movements. Also, from the 1920s onwards, American and European Pentecostal Churches began to proselytize in Gold Coast/ Ghana with much success.[3] Since the mid-1980s, a period of political

---

[3] Scholars of Pentecostalism trace the beginnings of this movement, which is indebted to pietist forms of religious experience and the nineteenth-century awakening movement, to the Azuza street revival in a poor predominantly black congregation in Los Angeles in 1906. Pentcostalism is characterized by its strong emphasis on the Holy Spirit, whose presence is sought to be

upheaval following the 1981 military coup staged by J. J. Rawlings,[4] as well as severe economic hardships, have resulted in the creation of a new type of Pentecostal-charismatic mega-church which has become popular in southern Ghana. Sporting suggestive names like International Central Gospel Church, Action Faith Ministries, Winner's Chapel, Global Outreach Church, and International Bible Worship Centre, these churches pose as access points for the global networks of born-again believers. Linking the prospect of prosperity with deliverance from evil forces such as witchcraft, ancestral spirits and other demons, these churches have had tremendous appeal for people, and in particular young men and women, who desperately seek to make progress in life (and often think, perhaps realistically, that the only way to succeed is by way of a miracle).

The popularity of Pentecostal-charismatic churches has led many African Independent Churches and older Pentecostal churches to adapt their practices so as also to appeal to a mass audience, and even many mainline churches have institutionalized prayer groups with a strong charismatic orientation so as to prevent members from attending the Pentecostal-charismatic churches.[5] Non-denominational organizations such as the Full Gospel Men's Fellowship, which addresses Christian businessmen and meets in up-market venues such as hotels and conference centers, and the Scripture Union, which is active among university students, have played a crucial role in spreading charismatic Christianity far beyond the confines of Pentecostal-charismatic churches.

The new type of Pentecostal-charismatic church is usually founded by a flamboyant African leader, has a transnational outlook and often branches in other African countries and overseas, and is devoted to the so-called Prosperity Gospel.[6] As well as having links with white

---

evoked so as to allow for deep experiences of divinity and prayer healing. Pentecostalism has tremendous global appeal, and encompasses a wide array of movements and members of different class and culture. See Allan H. Anderson and Walter Hollenweger (eds), *Pentecostals after a Century: Global Perspectives on a Movement in Transition* (Sheffield: Sheffield Academic Press, 1999); David Martin, *Pentecostalism: The World Their Parish* (Oxford and Maldan, MA: Blackwell, 2002); Karla Poewe (ed.), *Charismatic Christianity as Global Culture* (Columbia, SC: University of Carolina Press, 1994).

[4] Flight-Lieut. J. J. Rawlings seized power twice through a military coup (in 1979 and 1981). When Ghana returned to a democratic constitution in 1992, Rawlings' party, the NDC, won the 1992 and 1996 elections. In 2000 the opposition took over.

[5] According to the last census (Ghana Statistical Service, 2000), 24.1 per cent of the Ghanaian population describes itself as Pentecostal-Charismatic. In Greater Accra, the figure even amounts to 37.7 per cent; almost half of the Christians in Greater Accra are Pentecostal-charismatic.

[6] According to the theology of the Prosperity Gospel, God bestows spiritual and material

and black American Pentecostal churches, they also have close contacts with Nigerian Pentecostal-charismatic organizations. Not only do Nigerian churches open branches in Ghana and Nigerian preachers and their books circulate in Ghanaian charismatic circles, but Ghanaian preachers are also inspired by the new styles of worship coming from Nigeria, and in some cases have even traveled to learn these styles in Nigeria. In this respect, Ghanaian and Nigerian Pentecostal-charismatic churches are a truly transnational phenomenon operating on a global scale.

As the strong charismatic, and for that matter Protestant, emphasis on personal contact with God invites fission,[7] there are plenty of Pentecostal-charismatic churches operating more or less independently of one another, yet having much in common. In many respects, these churches claim to make up for the perceived shortcomings of the mainline churches, which tend to emphasize discipline above the Holy Spirit, Bible reading above prayer healing, and a more or less rational outlook above a strong conviction that occult forces exist and do harm.

Disappointment about Christianity's incapacity to achieve health and wealth through prayer have instigated many believers to turn to alternative options: secretly 'sliding back into heathendom', attending native prophets or becoming members of Independent churches. In contrast to the mainline churches, Pentecostal-charismatic churches offer elaborate ritual devices in order to cope with Satan and his demons. In a sense, they offer a version of African Christianity that does not make it necessary to (secretly) seek for help outside the confines of the church. During so-called deliverance prayers, people with physical and spiritual troubles are called forward and prayed for by the laying-on of hands. This gives rise to spectacular sessions in which evil spirits are cast out.[8] These sessions form a source of inspiration not only for pastors writing books about the power of prayer, but also for Ghanaian and Nigerian video-film producers, who claim to make films that offer visualizations of the realm of the 'powers of darkness' that

blessings on those he loves, whereas the devil is responsible for the Spirit of Poverty, which has so many Africans in its grip. As a good Christian is held to be well-to-do, charismatics seek to call upon the Holy Spirit to liberate believers from occult bonds and open them up to becoming prosperous. Cf. David Maxwell, 'Delivered from the Spirit of Poverty?: Pentecostalism, Prosperity and Modernity in Zimbabwe', *Journal of Religion in Africa* XXVIII (3) (1998), pp. 350–73.

[7] Martin, *Pentecostalism: The World Their Parish*, p. 176.

[8] See K. Asamoah-Gyadu, '"Missionaries without Robes": Lay Charismatic Fellowships and the Evangelization of Ghana', *Pneuma* 19 (2) (1997), pp. 167–87; Birgit Meyer, *Translating the Devil. Religion and Modernity among the Ewe in Ghana* (Edinburgh: Edinburgh University Press, 1999), pp. 155ff.

Fig 13.1 Poster for the film
'Deliverance from the Powers
of Darkness', Sam Bea
Productions
(Photo by Birgit Meyer)

holds such a central place in Pentecostal-charismatic speech practices
(see Figure 13.1).[9] The circulation of such books and films, as well as
the movement of traveling preachers across national boundaries, has
led to the emergence of a transnational born-again audience.

Diabolizing culture

As suggested in the Introduction, strong opposition to local cultural
and religious traditions is a key feature of contemporary Pentecostal-
charismatic churches. This opposition clearly links Pentecostalism with
nineteenth-century missionary reifications of culture as 'heathendom'.
Key to this reification was the recurrence of a temporalizing ideology
which cast local cultural and religious practices as 'matters of the past'
into which one could only 'slide back', although, of course, these

---

[9] Birgit Meyer, 'Praise The Lord. Popular Cinema and Pentecostalite Style in Ghana's New
Public Sphere', *American Ethnologist* 31 (1) (2004), pp. 92–110. Azonzah Franklin Ukah,
'Advertizing God: Nigerian Christian Video Films and the Power of Consumer Culture',
Journal of Religion in Africa 22 (2), pp. 203–31. Obododimma Oha, 'The Rhetoric of Nigerian
Videos: The War Paradigm of *The Great Mistake*' in. J. Haynes (ed.), *Nigerian Video Films*
(Athens, OH: Ohio, University Center for International Studies, 2000), pp. 192–8.

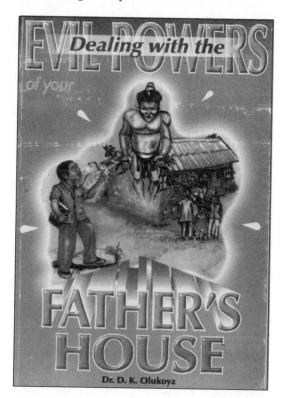

Fig 13.2 Cover image of
*Dealing with the Evil Powers of
your Father's House,* by Dr D.
K. Olukoya
*(Published by Battle Cry Ministries,
Lagos)*

practices actually co-existed with Christianity in time and place. This construction of local culture as a matter of the past bound up with the devil, and of missionary Protestantism as a harbinger of modernity and progress, proved to be very powerful. It was perpetuated in the mainline churches which grew out of the missionary enterprise in the early twentieth century and is still operative today. This association of African culture with the past and even with the devil gave way to continuous debates about 'how to be African and Christian at the same time' which have never been resolved.[10]

Since the 1980s, both Protestant and Catholic mainline churches have gradually sought to develop a more positive attitude towards African culture and have striven to accommodate certain local elements, for instance the pouring of libations, into Christian worship.[11] As, in this

[10] Christian G. Baëta CG (ed.), *Christianity in Tropical Africa: Studies Presented and Discussed at the Seventh International African Seminar, University of Ghana, April 1965* (London: Oxford University Press, 1968); E. Fasholé-Luke, R. Gray, A. Hastings and G. Tasie (eds), *Christianity in Independent Africa* (London: Rex Collings, 1978).

[11] Especially theologians of the mainline churches seek to develop a more adequate and 'authentic' synthesis (Meyer, *Translating the Devil,* pp. 122ff; Peter Sarpong, *Libation* (Accra: Anansesem,

view, true faith can only develop in conjunction with, rather than in opposition to, local culture, there is a strong link between Christianity and ethnic identity. The Pentecostal-charismatic churches, by contrast, adopt a significantly different view, which maintains that culture and religion are virtually impossible to disentangle and hence potentially demonic. It is maintained that traditional cultural practices such as the pouring of libations bring participants in touch with the realm of occult, invisible forces, especially ancestor spirits. There is a strong obsession with occult powers originating from 'the past' that are held to prevent believers from progressing in life. Being born-again is perceived as a radical rupture not only from one's personal sinful past, but also from the wider family and village of origin.

In Ghana, the question of ancestral curses that hold sway over individual believers' lives or 'evil powers from your father's house' — as a popular booklet by the Nigerian pastor Dr D. K. Olukoya puts it[12] (see Figure 13.2) — is much emphasized in Pentecostal-charismatic circles. Many sermons thrive on a moral geography which associates the village with occult forces and talks about the witches in the extended family, who are jealous of a person's progress in the city and seek to bring him or her down by spiritual attacks. This negative attitude towards the village feeds into more general misgivings about the realm of tradition or culture. Hence Pentecostal-charismatic churches strongly oppose attempts on the part of theologians in mainline churches to rehabilitate tradition from being represented as 'heathendom', as well as state policies seeking to re-evaluate tradition in terms of national heritage. The culture lessons institutionalized in public schools are as much scorned as the National Commission on Culture's attempts to recast local chieftaincy festivals and other ethnic celebrations as part and parcel of national culture and heritage.[13]

In recent years there have been numerous conflicts between traditional authorities and Pentecostal-charismatic churches about the performance of traditional rituals and the obligation to observe

1996), yet the underlying problem of these attempts consists in the fact that they are based on a reified notion of culture, which represents Christianity and African culture as closed and bounded wholes. This view unconsciously adopts a typically Western notion of culture in terms of a bounded system and neglects the initially open and extravert manner which characterized African ways of negotiating foreign influences, at least up to the colonial period. Thus, in a sense the critical insistence on 'authentic African culture' is part and parcel of the reification of culture in the colonial period.

[12] D. K. Olukoya, *Dealing with the Evil Powers of your Father's House.* (Np: The Battle Cry Ministries, 2002).

[13] Cati Coe, 'Not Just Drumming and Dancing. The Production of National Culture in Ghana's Schools' (Ph.D. Dissertation: University of Pennsylvania, 2000).

traditional taboos. The Pentecostals even took these issues to the newly established Commission of Human Rights, so as to assert that freedom of religion entailed that there was no need to obey and respect the rules of traditional religions. For Pentecostals the emphasis on culture is misguided and potentially dangerous in that it hampers progress. Conversely, progress requires that one is able to domesticate the past, even though this past is discursively constructed in the arena of deliverance prayers, and is thus always co-present.

Hailing Christian modernity

Yet it would be mistaken to limit an analysis of the appeal of Pentecostal-charismatic churches to their obsession with miracles and victory over demonic forces, and their critical attitude towards culture. At the same time, they present themselves as successful embodiments of − and gatekeepers guarding − modernity. These churches have done much to create an image of successful mastery of the modern world: building mega-size temples with a seating capacity for thousands of believers (see Figure 13.3); making use of the latest audio-visual technology to use closed video-circuits for mass scale sermons; producing programs

Fig 13.3 Christ Temple, Headquarters of the International Central Gospel Church in Accra
(Photo by Marleen de Witte)

on TV and radio; organizing spectacular crusades throughout the country in order to convert so-called nominal Christians, Muslims and supporters of traditional religions; creating avenues for high quality Gospel music; and instigating trend-setting, yet 'decent' modes of dress. Of course, the modernity advocated by these churches highlights the necessity for moral behavior and Christian ethics in a world in turmoil. Essentially, the modern world is represented as thriving on temptation, as the devil is supposed to operate not only through blood ties linking people to the extended family in particular and local culture in general, but also as being at the heart of modernity, the sphere of consumption.

While these churches represent prosperity as a God-given blessing, they admonish believers not to lose themselves in selfish, consumptive behavior, and to make good use of their money (the fact that believers are expected to pay tithes may also induce a more administrative attitude towards money). Born-again Christians are forbidden to drink alcohol, have sex outside of marriage, and — especially in the case of married men — are expected to control their libido and remain faithful to their wives. The nuclear family being the ideal form of life (much preferred to the extended family), churches offer elaborate lessons on marriage which young couples have to attend prior to their wedding and special hours for marriage counseling. Also, against the background of the perceived threat of moral decay, which has recently become a matter of much debate in Ghana in the aftermath of the AIDS epidemic and the rise of a new fashion (very short skirts and tight tops) called *Apuskeleke*, many churches explicitly insist on certain dress codes.[14] The ideal is a moral self, not misled by the glitzy world of consumer capitalism nor misguided by the outmoded world of tradition, but instead filled with the Holy Spirit.

This does not, however, entail the necessity of adopting a stance similar to the ascetic denial of consumption that Max Weber found to be typical of early Protestantism. As the example of the exquisitely dressed pastors, wearing expensive garments and driving posh cars shows, prosperity and being born-again are held to be two sides of the same coin. This idea is upheld although numerous scandals show time and again that power and wealth may lead even the staunchest believer to go astray,[15] whereas believers may become disillusioned because the promised wealth fails to arrive (a question which is hardly addressed in current research on the Pentecostal-charismatic churches). In order

---

[14] Brigid Sackey, '*Apuskeleke*. A Youth Fashion Craze, Immorality or Female Harassment?' *Etnofoor* 16 (2) (2003), pp. 57–69.

[15] For a study of this issue in Nigeria cf. D. J. Smith, '"The Arrow of God". Pentecostalism, Inequality, and the Supernatural in South-Eastern Nigeria', *Africa* 71 (4) (2001), pp. 587–613.

to help believers advance, many churches offer them small loans which should enable them to engage in trade and become financially independent — an aim not only desirable to the person in question, but also to the church, as members are expected to donate 10 per cent of their income to the church.

In a sense, as argued earlier, these churches claim to be able to guide people in handling modernity and surpassing the limits of locality. The experienced impossibility of distancing oneself from the past — that worries people in their dreams and seems to be the reason behind all mishaps — testifies to the difficulties arising from the striving to become a modern person, more or less independent from the extended family. The Pentecostal-charismatic churches do not simply lead people into modernity, they also offer a space to think about its failures, the clash between modernity's aspirations and its malcontents.[16] In this sense, these churches are not only a discourse within modernity which is historically linked with the nineteenth-century missionary project, but also a discourse about the specific problems and aspirations generated by modernity in the context of globalization.

Pentecostalism as a global religion

While Pentecostal-charismatic churches appear to link up with precisely that missionary heritage — the representation of traditional culture as heathendom — from which contemporary mainline churches are struggling to free themselves, it is important to realize that they also offer something distinctly new. Whereas mission societies, which stood at the cradle of contemporary mainline churches, sought to create Christian subjects rooted in their native language, present-day Pentecostal-charismatic churches have a much more global perspective and challenge both ethnic and national definitions of identity. Globalization, as Appadurai suggests, entails that the work of imagination, vital for notions of selfhood and being, is less and less dominated by the forces of the nation-state.[17] Indeed, as Marshall-Fratani argues, 'it is not so much the individualism of Pentecostal conversion which leads to the creation of modern subjects, but the ways in which its projection on a global scale of images, discourses and ideas about renewal, change and salvation opens up possibilities for local actors to incorporate these into their daily lives'.[18] In other words,

[16] See Jean and John Comaroff (eds), *Modernity and its Malcontents* (Chicago: University of Chicago Press, 1993).

[17] Arjun Appadurai, *Modernity at Large. Cultural Dimensions of Globalization* (Minneapolis and London: University of Minnesota Press, 1996).

[18] Ruth Marshall-Fratani, 'Mediating the Global and the Local in Nigerian Pentecostalism', in A.

contemporary Pentecostal-charismatic churches incite imaginations of community that surpass the space of the ethnic group or the nation, in that they are delocalized and represent believers as 'brothers and sisters in Christ'. This stance materializes in widely available (cassette and video) sermons, music and literature which circulate in global Pentecostal networks and entice the constitution of a new public of born-again believers with a strong global outlook. It also plays an important role in the diaspora, where many Ghanaians do not have a residence permit, yet are entitled to get married in the church, thereby surpassing national identity politics.[19]

However, the fact that the Pentecostal project of the imagination of community is much broader in scale than the state's national project, does not mean that Pentecostal-charismatic churches do not address matters of national concern. They certainly do — it seems increasingly so — thereby deliberately assuming a voice in the public sphere and challenging the state as the privileged space for the imagination of modern identity. For example, prior to the elections in 2000, Pentecostal-charismatic churches organized mega-prayer meetings, in which they prayed for peace and the choice of a leader who had God's consent. Many Pentecostals believed that state affairs had been damaged by corrupt leaders seeking refuge in occult practices, and argued that Ghana needed to become a Christian nation. Far from taking for granted a modern secular order as the missions did in the nineteenth century, many current Pentecostal-charismatic churches dream, more or less openly, about a Christian nation. Given the close links with Nigerian Pentecostal leaders, who seem to mirror Islamic reform movements' appropriation of a number of federal states in Northern Nigeria, this move is not surprising. It testifies to the emergence of new ways of thinking about the relationship between religion and the state that surpass modernist ideas about the place and role of religion in society and deliberately assume its public role.

Islamism

While a student in Kano, the young Abubakar Gumi, fresh from the province of Sokoto and soon to be the most important religious reformer in Nigeria, approached a group of older men to ask for directions. They

Corten and R. Marshall-Fratani, *Between Babel and Pentecost* (Bloomington, IN: University of Indiana Press, 2001), p. 80.

[19] Rijk Van Dijk, 'The Soul is the Stranger: Ghanaian Pentecostalism and the Diasporic Contestation of "Flow" and "Individuality", *Culture and Religion* 3 (1) (2002), pp. 49–66.

remained silent, so he asked again and one replied, 'Man from Sokoto, why should you come so close to us with your shoes on? Didn't you hear what God says to Moses . . . that he must remove them as a sign of respect?' The speaker was referring here to the common practice in northern Nigeria of showing respect to seniors by removing one's shoes when in their presence. The young Gumi was angry at being put down and was outraged by these remarks, especially so because the men acted as if they were religiously learned when to Gumi, their comments were 'due to ignorance' and therefore 'totally unjustified'.[20] Gumi argued that the men had mistaken the religious message of the parable: the reason Moses had to remove his shoes was because he was in the Holy Valley and not because of the presence of God. 'Is this the Holy Valley?' the young Gumi retorted to his seniors as he walked away.

Gumi includes this story in his autobiography as an early example of one of the central themes of his life: that existing Hausa practices of status and hierarchy were wrong. While they were justified as being 'Islamic', they were in fact based on poor interpretation and ignorance of religious knowledge. In his life, Gumi's mode of operation was to take certain social and religious practices that had been acceptable for centuries in Islam and redefine them as 'cultural'. In a similar way to Pentecostalism, reformist Islam asserts its modernity through rearticulating older religious practices as 'culture' and relegating this culture to the non-Islamic past. And what is interesting and typical in this example is that this theological conflict is conducted at the level of the everyday, the intimate and the apparently non-religious: taking off one's shoes, everyday manners and the relations of respect a junior owes to his senior.

The rise of Islamism in Nigeria is manifest in a variety of movements with both mass and elite followings, but what unites many of them is an assertion of a new type of Islamic identity. This is one that is intimately engaged with the West and with modernity at the same time as being fiercely critical of it; one that seeks to intensify connections — theological, economic, social and linguistic — between Nigeria and the wider Islamic world (whether Egypt, Saudi Arabia or Iran); it is also one that is increasingly ready to assert its authority in the political realm, notably in the call for Islamic law and an Islamic state; and is also one that is openly critical of existing royal and religious hierarchies in Hausa society. Islamists are split between those oriented towards Saudi Arabia — such as Abubakar Gumi's *Izala*[21] movement and Sheikh

---

[20] Abubakar Gumi with Ismaila Tsiga, *Where I Stand* (Ibadan: Spectrum Books, 1992), p. 34.
[21] *Izala* stands for *Jama'at Izalatu al-Bid'a wa Iqamat al-Sunna*, Society for the Removal of Innovation

Aminudeen Abubakar's *Da'wa* group — and those inspired by the Islamic revolution in Iran, such as Ibrahim El Zakzaky's Muslim Brothers. Differences between them are important. The Muslim Brothers' call for Nigeria to be ruled by Islamic law is part of their strident opposition to the Nigerian state and to traditional royal elites.[22] Izala, while critical of royal elites, has been identified more with its theological attack on Sufism (an issue on which the Muslim Brothers have been relatively quiet) and has strong ties to the political and military organs of the Nigerian state. Da'wa, while calling for Islamic renewal and clearly pro-Saudi, has been careful to do so without launching polemics against either Sufis or the *sarauta* (aristocracy). Nevertheless all three have become successful by articulating a new way of being Muslim to the new sector of Hausa society that emerged in the post-colonial period.

The new Muslim subject that is offered by Islamism is one that is largely Western-trained, but seeks modernity through the Islamic as well as the Western world. On an ideal level, it is a profoundly cosmopolitan subject, speaking English as well as Arabic, which uses the authority, knowledge and networks of the transnational Islamic world as a base from which to fund and criticize existing injustices in Hausa society associated, depending on one's affiliation, with Sufis, the Sultan and Emirs, and the Nigerian state. This cosmopolitanism is significant because it is also the trope through which the parochialism of traditional religious leaders is stereotyped and lampooned. Monolingual in Hausa (or at best also speaking Kanuri or Fulfulde), 'local' Sheikhs are accused of lacking the connections and the knowledge derived from either the Western or Islamic worlds in which Islamists are culturally fluent. Islamists, because of their proselytizing movements, have also been intimately involved in articulating religious ideas in new media as part of their wider attempt to reform and revise Islamic education. Abubakar Gumi, fluent in English, Arabic, Fulfulde and Hausa, was the first Sheikh to preach on the radio and television, as well as writing a regular religious and political column in the main (state-owned) Hausa language newspaper. Ibrahim El Zakzaky, fluent in English, Farsi and Hausa, banned from all state media because of his inflammatory attacks on the secular state, turned instead to cassette tapes as a means of distributing his message, while his followers set up

and the Maintenance of the Sunna. The movement, perhaps the largest mass Islamic movement in the last quarter of the twentieth century, was founded by followers of Gumi in 1978 and he remained its spiritual head until his death in 1992.

[22] With the introduction of Islamic law in several northern Nigerian states in 2001, it is easy to forget how the call for Shari'a was, for most of the 1980s, profoundly anti-status quo, and part of an explicit attack on the oppressiveness of existing royal authority in Nigeria.

the pro-Zakzaky paper *Al-Mizan*. This represents the migration of religious discourse into new fora of communication that were wholly outside traditional procedures for the production of religious authority.

It is the diversity of Islamism that has enabled it to gather together followers attracted to a range of different aspects of its message. Gumi's early support came from that fraction of Hausa society — Western educated, working in the new organs of colonial and post-colonial rule, the bureaucracy and military — which was deeply Muslim yet was regarded with suspicion by traditional religious elites because of its association with Western lifestyles. Gumi, the first English-speaking religious leader, offered a way of being Muslim that denied the association of Western education with *kafir* (non-Muslim) lifestyles, turning the accusation around to question the religious legitimacy of traditional *malams* (religious teachers).

At the same time, the egalitarianism inherent in Gumi's attack on royal authority, and El Zakzaky's full-scale assault on the *sarauta* system and the secular state, drew into these movements a mass of young, uneducated followers disaffected by the increasing inequalities of wealth and the general insecurity of society. Zakzaky, in particular, and despite his Shi'ite leanings (which are wholly unorthodox in West Africa), articulated the anger of these youths. His charisma and uncompromising attitude resulted in his being thrown out of Ahmadu Bello University while a member of the Muslim Students' Society; he and his followers have been accused of being behind several violent confrotations with the state (notably in Katsina in 1991); and he was imprisoned several times which gave him widespread respect among the younger Hausa. Finally, because of the increasing religious connections with the Middle East, certain Islamist movements attracted wealthy business people whose religious affiliation with Salafi views from Saudi Arabia enabled them to combine religious with economic networking. The intensified connection of Nigeria with the Arabian Gulf should be seen as part of the economic as well as religious restructuring of Hausa society; northerners look to the profitability of new economic centers like Dubai and Jeddah. Izala and Aminudeen's Da'wa were famous for their prominent membership of wealthy businessmen.

Islamism, Abubakar Gumi, Izala and the attack on Sufism

One of the key features of the rise of Islamism is the emergence of a religious class trained in a Western educational style and often working in the Western-oriented sectors of society such as the military and the post-colonial bureaucracy. For many years this class of *'yan boko*

Fig 13.4 Islamic stickers.
The Tijaniyya leader, Sheikh
Ibrahim Niass of Kaolack
Senegal (*below*)

(Western-educated Muslims) were regarded with suspicion by many Hausa Muslims, and up to the 1970s it was not uncommon to find parents refusing to send their children to Western schools. Islamism, in contrast, shares a social base with Pentecostalism that is young, Western-trained and relatively well educated.[23] As a consequence the secular institution of the university has been a crucible of religious militancy in Nigeria. Pentecostalism has deep roots in the rise of 'Campus Christianity' just as the radicalism of Islamism was forged in groups like the Muslim Students' Society, which has been at the forefront of espousing radical Islamist ideas. University campuses are theaters where Islamist and Pentecostal militancy is and has been defined. They were some of the first sites for 'crusades' and 'jihads', and where these competing groups fight against each other, they also learn from one another and share social space.[24]

[23] As mentioned above, Islamism later came to rely on a mass as well as an educated membership.

[24] It is no accident that several riots in northern Nigeria were sparked off by incidents at institutions of higher education, emerging from conflict between Muslims and Christians most notably in the case of the riots in Kafanchan in 1987 said to be fired by the response of the Muslim Students' Society to an evangelical crusade. See Ousmane Kane, *Muslim Modernity in Postcolonial Nigeria* (Leiden: Brill, 2003); Rev. Matthew Hassan Kukah, *Religion, Politics and Power in Northern Nigeria* (Ibadan: Spectrum Books, 1993).

Fig 13.5 Billboard for the Asrami Islamic Video and Cassettes Shop,
Kaduna

Fig 13.6 Billboard for the shop, Qur'an on Cassettes, Kaduna

As the Grand Khadi of the Northern Region of Nigeria at independence, and the main religious adviser to the Sardauna of Sokoto (the leader of the Northern Region), Gumi was unique as a religious leader in being situated at the heart of the emerging political machinery of independent Nigeria. Not only did he remain well connected with the political and military elite throughout his life, but he was also championed by this group, and their support was vital to the rise of Izala in the 1970s.

Izala, founded by Ismaila Idris in 1978, rose to prominence with a series of attacks against Sufism, the religious orders that up to that point had effectively dominated Islam in Nigeria. Borrowing heavily from the teachings of Abubakar Gumi, and articulated in mosque sermons, newspapers, radio programs, mass meetings and audio cassettes, Izala attacked core Sufi practices such as the worship of saints, practices of possession (both seen as a form of *shirk* or a denial of the oneness of God), the magical uses of Islamic knowledge for healing or prosperity, and the recitation of secret prayers passed down only to initiates. To Izala, these were evidence of syncretic innovations that marked the intrusion of pre-Islamic Hausa culture into Islam, or deviation from orthodoxy via the innovations of maverick religious figures. Before Izala, religious polemics were regular occurrences in Nigeria with conflict breaking out both within orders (such as the Tijaniyya) and between orders as evidenced by the long-standing enmity between Tijaniyya and Qadiriyya. Izala, however, accused Sufis not just of being poor Muslims but of not being Muslim at all. This was not only a total redefinition of who could be called a Muslim, but it also initiated a full-scale attack on the way Islam had been practised by generations of Hausa Muslims. Unsurprisingly, this was intensely polarizing and provoked a backlash from Sufis, resulting in sustained and often violent conflict.

Izala proposed the creation of a more rationalist and intellectualist Muslim, who came to knowledge of Islam through his or her (and Izala was innovative in promoting women's education) own reading of the core texts of Islam — the Qur'an and Hadith — and not through the intercession of a sheikh. Undergirding this pedagogical shift was a rejection of the scholarly and charismatic authority of Sufi sheikhs, along with a redefinition of status as something that is acquired and proved through argument rather than inherited. This created a strikingly different style of religious presentation. Abubakar Gumi, for instance, was famous for allowing questions from anyone 'no matter how small' — as his followers would say — indicating that the worth of a statement lies in the quality of evidence marshaled rather than the social position of the questioner. This openness was manifest in the youth of Izala organizers who would lead *wa'azi* (religious teachings or admonitions to follow the right path) and take the lead in organizing religious and political gatherings, where previously their inexperience and lowly status would have made this impossible.

Unlike Gumi, whose personal manner was polite and restrained even when his statements were inflammatory, the teachings of younger Izala members tended to be aggressive. Many younger, Western-educated followers were openly contemptuous of 'local mallams' whom they saw as poorly educated Muslims, backward, and unclear of the separation between Islam and culture in religious practice. Izala delineated new ways of studying Islam, new modes of reciting the Qur'an, and new mosques for followers to worship in. Moreover, Izala's theological controversies were translated into a series of everyday prohibitions that moved the conflict from an intellectual terrain to an everyday, bodily one. Izala followers refused to attend Sufi mosques or even to be led in prayer by Sufi members. They rejected traditional forms of status and the markers of bodily respect that went with it: refusing to remove their shoes, or to crouch down and salute in respect when in the presence of seniors. Some with Sufi names (such as Tijani) changed them to more orthodox ones. Kane cites rumors spread among Sufis that Izala supporters went so far as to give their mothers boxes of milk (in compensation for having nursed them) and their fathers rams (in compensation for the animal sacrificed at their birth.)[25] These actions and stories about them exemplify the sense that Izala's reforming zeal represented a challenge to existing forms of family hierarchy since Izala, like Pentecostalism, offered a network of support and a realm of individual freedom outside the traditional hierarchies of family (and Sufi) religion.

Christianity, Saudi Arabia and the rise of political Islam

The rise of Islamist movements is not restricted to intra-Muslim conflict, but it cannot be understood except in relation to the rise in prominence of Christianity in the north. Gumi, for instance, is well known in Nigeria for asserting a religious voice in the general political arena through the mobilization of Muslims to vote *as Muslims* in an explicitly religious way, and by his commitment to the formation of a state ruled by Islamic law. As early as 1964, Gumi teamed up with Ahmadu Bello, then leader of northern Nigeria, to form the *Jama'at Nasrul Islam* (JNI, Society for

---

[25] Kane, *Muslim Modernity in Postcolonial Nigeria*, p. 116.

the Victory of Islam). Funded largely by monies from Saudi Arabia, the JNI was an umbrella organization aimed at the propagation of Islam, and its initial efforts were geared largely towards converting pagan peoples from the Middle Belt of Nigeria to Islam. This was a direct response to the success of Christian missionization that threatened the Islamic claim to religious homogeneity in the north, and set off a 'race' to see who could convert pagans first — Muslims or Christians. This was famously part of a much larger electoral strategy of Ahmadu Bello, the northern leader, to represent himself as a religious as well as a political leader, to his electoral base.

With its ostensibly anti-Christian agenda, combined with its close ties to the northern political elite, the JNI was the first explicitly religious political institution in Nigeria . Unlike southern nationalist leaders such as Azikwe or Awolowo, who tended to separate their Christianity from their political identities, in the north the two were always intertwined. Enwerem, in his study of the rise of the Christian Association of Nigeria, refers to the JNI as a 'political organ wearing a religious garb for a political purpose' and as a key factor in provoking Christians into more explicitly political engagement.[26] Ahmadu Bello courted support from Saudi Arabia and the Gulf at the same time as those states were worried about the prestige and influence of Nasser's Egypt. Bello himself had flirted with Nasser, travelling to Egypt several times as a representative of the largest Muslim region in sub-Saharan Africa, but he was brought round to the Saudis when they made him vice-President of the World Muslim League, a forerunner of the Organization of Islamic Countries. In his trips to the Gulf, Abubakar Gumi served as his translator and religious adviser, cementing not only his commitment to a Salafi theology, but his social and religious connections to the highest echelons of the Saudi state, at a time when that state was embarking on an ambitious program of expansion to establish its suzerainty in the Islamic world. (This campaign was extended by the success of the Iranian revolution which, like Nasser previously, offered Muslims around the world a powerful alternative to Saudi authority).

The consequence of the rise of Islamism has been an intensification in the trafficking of religious ideas, money, people and organizations between Nigeria and Saudi Arabia. The figure of Gumi, along with other Izala leaders such as Sanusi Gumbi, is important, as is the *Da'wa* propagation movement of the Kano sheikh, Aminudeen. Other Islamists, such as Sheikh El-Zakzaky and Abubakar Tureta, turned

---

[26] Iheanyi M. Enwerem, *A Dangerous Awakening: The Politicisation of Religion in Nigeria* (Ibadan: IFRA Press, 1995), p. 55.

instead to Iran after the 1979 revolution, drawing upon the revolutionary ideology of Shi'ism and the material support of the Iranian government. This demonstrates a dual theological and material movement that is common to many religions in Nigeria, from Sufism to Catholicism to Pentecostalism. Nigerian scholars claim authority by representing a religious training and network that derive from foreign religious centers, and then act as mediators between Nigeria and that religious center, thereby gaining prestige and economic support in the process.[27]

Ousmane Kane has written incisively on the way Islamist movements attracted 'economic and political entrepreneurs' who supported Izala as a means of advancing their interests, and recognized the tight link between religion and economic success. One of the basic features of Izala was an attack on the wealth and perceived greed of Sufi Sheikhs who 'dressed like Saudis' and drove new, expensive Mercedes-Benz. Some in Izala, Gumi in particular, stressed a more ascetic, restrained lifestyle, while other Islamists such as Aminudeen in Kano were famous for their extremely wealthy following. What is clear is that whatever the personal lifestyle of the sheikh, the rise of Islamism paralleled the reorienting of northern Nigeria's economy towards new economic entrepôts in the Middle East, especially Jeddah, Beirut and Dubai. Islamism, rather than being attached to the past, was modern because of its support within the modern sector of the post-colonial bureaucracy, and because it offered new forms of economic advancement. Writing about Sheikh Aminudeen, Kane points out that 'like Sheikh Gumi he is said to have been in a position to recommend economic entrepreneurs for obtaining visas at the Saudi consulate and, likewise, to introduce Kano businessmen to partners in Saudi Arabia and other countries in the Gulf'.[28] The dynamism of new religious movements in Africa, whether Christian or Muslim, lies not just in the ability to provide a hermeneutics of the economic situation Africans find themselves in — to 'moralize political economy' as Ruth Marshall-Fratani puts it in a different context — but also in providing the networks and infrastructures that allow individuals to negotiate the material anxieties of living in uncertain economic times.

---

[27] Gumi's mosque in Kaduna was built with Saudi and Kuwaiti money; Saudis funded the construction of Aminudeen's mosque in Kano; Gumbi and Zakzaky were trained in Saudi Arabia and Iran respectively, and after returning to Nigeria continued to maintain close religious and economic ties with those centers.

[28] Kane, *Muslim Modernity in Postcolonial Nigeria*, p. 80.

Conclusion: the mirroring of Pentecostalism and Islamism

When Izala embarked on a campaign of winning converts it divided the country into different regions and organized preaching sessions. Known as *'wa'azi'*, preachers at these meetings would recite from the Qur'an to demonstrate the backsliding, non-Islamic ways of Sufi sheikhs and to admonish listeners to reform their behavior. At the national meetings where attendance was numbered in thousands, it would choose a region months in advance and then advertise the event heavily on the radio to make people aware of it. The event was then tape-recorded, duplicated and sold in markets all around Nigeria and the surrounding countries. This mode of proselytizing, central to the rise of the Islamist mass movement, borrowed heavily from the tactics of Pentecostal crusades and is a clear marker of the integration of Christian religious/political tactics into the heart of Islamism.

In contrast, the increased participation of Christians in the political process — putting pressure on the state, demanding that one vote as a Christian, or as a Pentecostal — is an indicator of the induction of Islamic religio-political organization into Christian practice. The Catholic priest and scholar Matthew Kukah writes that the success of Islam in the political arena has forced Christians to come to the conclusion that 'it has become imperative for Christians now to *use* religion for achieving their socio-political activity and the place of religion in the political process'.[29] Enwerem, in his study of the Christian Association of Nigeria, argues that the politicization of Christianity in Nigeria came about in response to three main events — the formation of the JNI and the Sardauna's conversion campaign, the first debates around the imposition of Shari'a law, and the entry of Nigeria, under Babangida, into the Organization of Islamic Countries (OIC) — all of which concern the relationship between Christianity and Islam rather than events internal to Christianity itself.

In our view, the striking similarities between Pentecostal-charismatic and Islamist movements — concerning the rejection of traditional culture, new ways of being modern in a religious idiom and a global orientation — are not coincidental. In part, these similarities can be explained by reference to structural economic and social factors that make African societies basically face the same predicaments: disillusionment and disappointment with the state as the harbinger of development, and a desperate search for new avenues of success.

---

[29] Kukah, *Religion, Politics and Power in Northern Nigeria*, p. x

Experiences of being increasingly disconnected instigate the search for new strategies of extraversion which tend to bypass the state and appropriate new matters through external links. Both Pentecostalism and Islam play a key role in this process, as they offer the possibility for believers not only to dissociate themselves, albeit symbolically, from their extended family and generate new notions of the self, but also to present religion as an access point to global circuits — the West in the case of Pentecostalism, the Middle East in the case of Islam. While there are important differences between the Prosperity Gospel and Islamism's Salafi orthodoxy, it is nevertheless clear that both movements mediate a particular kind of religious modernity in which morality is brought to bear on the question of the achievement and distribution of wealth. Both provide members with a secure moral and religious position from which to renegotiate obligations to their kin groups and communities, and distinguish themselves with this new lifestyle. What is at stake here is the genesis of a religious imaginary which affirms a distinctly religious conception of the moral order of society.

Such a turn to religion, we would like to stress, should be seen not as a mere return to the purity of a religious past that became increasingly degenerated (as is often argued with regard to the attraction of Islamist revival movements or in Pentecostal talk about the need to convert so-called 'nominal' Christians), but rather as bringing about particular, new possibilities of 'worlding' and hence situating religion in a new context. The point is that Pentecostal-charismatic and Islamist movements, while presenting themselves as transnational, tend to stand in a particular relation to the post-colonial state. It is no accident that the rise of Islamism and Pentecostalism took place under military rule. Both religions enabled the articulation of political protest under the banner of religion during a time of intense repression. Both also emerged in the wake of the failure of socialism and communism as viable mass movements in West Africa. The egalitarianism present in both Pentecostalism and Islamism was successful in drawing on nascent class protest and rearticulating political movements based on class, to religious ones based on religious belonging.

Certainly after the 'return' to democracy in Nigeria and Ghana under conditions of neo-liberal capitalism in the mid-1990s, the relations between religion and the state have been significantly reconfigured. After the end of military rule, with the liberalization of the media and the guarantee of religious freedom as a constitutional right in both Nigeria and Ghana, religion started to play an increasingly important and new role in the public sphere. In Ghana, it was, above all, the Pentecostal-charismatic churches that ventured into TV and radio and made their message heard and seen by the nation, whereas the mainline churches still tended to see the church as the appropriate space to address and bind the congregation. In Nigeria, too, Pentecostal-charismatic churches have adopted new electronic media technologies — of course, a sign of the successful mastery of modernity — and have become a major voice in the public sphere of the Christian South. Media proficiency is indispensable in Pentecostal-charismatic campaigns dedicated to 'winning Nigeria for Jesus' with, as its flipside, a demonization of Islam which is intended to counter the 'Islamization' of the nation. In the north of Nigeria the situation is different because religion has never been something outside of state structures, but is profoundly intertwined with them. The need for major preachers to have their own media outlets is less because both military and civilian administrations have been wide open to the religious use of government media.

Thus, democracy has made it increasingly difficult for the state to contain religion within the private sphere. In many respects, Pentecostal-charismatic and Islamist movements offer alternative imaginations of community and religiously informed visions of the nation. Yet it would be too simple to state that these religious movements 'counter' or offer a full 'alternative' to, the post-colonial state, as both Pentecostalism and Islamism issue claims upon the state and, at times, are happy to be co-opted within its ambitions (for instance, the Ghanaian charismatic pastor Mensa Otabil, once a fierce critic of the Rawlings regime, took a seat in the National Commission of Culture). Emphasizing transnational loyalties and connections can often be nothing more than a means of putting pressure on the state, brokering for position, and thus intimately tied to the state rather than separate from it.

In sum, in this chapter we have tried to highlight that, as a result of similar structural factors and actual processes of mutual observation and mirroring, Pentecostal-charismatic and Islamist movements have much more in common than the respective discourses about one another would suggest. It appears that there has evolved a particular kind of 'postnational religious identity',[30] characterized by distinct ways of speaking to the nation-state from a transnational perspective, granting access to global infrastructures and tying members into a new religious regime thriving on new forms of subjectivation. If the sincerity of self-formation seems to resonate with Protestant modes of conduct so as to (re)model the inner self of the individual believer, the drive into politics and the public sphere seems to echo Islam's blurring of modernist boundaries between the secular — as the sphere of politics — and the

[30] Marshall-Fratani, 'Mediating the Global and the Local', p.104.

private as the sphere of religion. This chapter calls not only for more comparative work on contemporary Pentecostal-charismatic and Islamist movements with attention paid to both similarities and differences, but also for further exploration of the relationship between religion and the post-colonial African state in the era of globalization, in which the politics of identity and processes of subjectivation exceed old boundaries (such as the nation-state), yet also produce new forms of closure (such as insisting on religious difference).

Recommended Reading

Pentecostalism

Corten, André and Ruth Marshall-Fratani (eds) (2001) *Between Babel and Pentecost: Transnational Pentecostalism in Latin America and Africa* (Bloomington, IN: Indiana University Press).

Enwerem, Iheanyi M.O.P. (1995) *A Dangerous Awakening: The Politicisation of Religion in Nigeria* (Ibadan: IFRA Press).

Gifford, Paul (1998) *African Christianity. Its Public Role* (London: Hurst).

—— (2004) *Ghana's New Christianity: Pentecostalism in a Globalising African Economy* (London: Hurst).

Kukah, Rev Fr. Matthew Hassan (1993) *Religion, Politics and Power in Northern Nigeria* (Ibadan: Spectrum Books).

Hackett, R. I. J. (1998) 'Charismatic/Pentecostal Appropriation of Media Technologies in Nigeria and Ghana', *Journal of Religion in Africa* XXVIII (3), pp. 1–19.

Marshall-Fratani, Ruth (1998) 'God is not a democrat: Pentecostalism and democratization in Nigeria', in P. Gifford (ed.), *The Christian Churches and the Democratisation of Africa* (New York: Brill), pp. 139–60.

Martin, David (2002) *Pentecostalism: The World Their Parish.* (Oxford: Blackwell).

Meyer, Birgit (1999) *Translating the Devil. Religion and Modernity Among the Ewe in Ghana* (Edinburgh: Edinburgh University Press).

—— (2004) 'African Independent Churches/Pentecostal-Charismatic Churches in Africa', *Annual Review of Anthropology*, 33, pp. 447–74.

Van Dijk, Rijk (2002) 'The Soul is the Stranger: Ghanaian Pentecostalism and the Diasporic Contestation of "Flow" and "Individuality"', *Culture and Religion* 3 (1), pp. 49–66.

Witte, Marleen de (2003) 'Altar Media's *Living Word*: televised charismatic Christianity in Ghana', *Journal of Religion in Africa* 33 (2), pp. 172–202.

Islamism

Brenner, Louis (ed.) (1993) *Muslim Identity and Social Change in Sub-Saharan Africa* (Bloomington: Indiana University Press).
Gumi, Abubakar with Ismaila Tsiga (1992) *Where I Stand* (Ibadan: Spectrum Books).
Kane, Ousmane (2003) *Muslim Modernity in Postcolonial Nigeria. A Study of the Society for the Removal of Tradition and Reinstatement of Tradition* (Leiden: Brill).
Loimeier, Roman (1997) *Islamic Reform and Political Change in Northern Nigeria* (Evanston, IL: Northwestern University Press).
Umar, Muhammad Sani (1993) 'Changing Islamic Identity in Nigeria from the 1960s to the 1980s: From Sufism to Anti-Sufism', in Brenner (ed.) *Muslim Identity and Social Change in Sub-Saharan Africa*, pp. 154–178.
Schulz, D. (2003) 'Charisma and Brotherhood Revisited: Mass-mediated forms of Spirituality in Urban Mali', *Journal of Religion in Africa* 33 (2), pp. 146–71.
Westerlund, David and Eve Rosander (eds) (1997) *African Islam and Islam in Africa. Encounters Between Sufis and Islamists* (London: Hurst).

Violence, politics and economy

Bayart Jean-François (2000) 'Africa in the World: A History of Extraversion', *African Affairs* 99, pp. 217–67.
Bayart, Jean-François, Stephen Ellis and Beatrice Hibou (1999) *The Criminalization of the State in Africa* (Oxford: James Currey).
Falola, Toyin (2001) *Violence in Nigeria: The Crisis of Religious Politics and Secular Ideologies* (Rochester, NY: University of Rochester Press).
Ibrahim, Jibrin (1989) 'The Politics of Religion in Nigeria: The Parameters of the 1987 Crisis in Kaduna State', *Review of African Political Economy* 45/46, pp. 65–82.
Haynes, Jeff (1996) *Religion and Politics in Africa* (London: Zed Books).
Simone, Abdoumaliq (2002) 'On The Worlding of African Cities', *African Studies Review* 44 (2), pp. 15–41.

Index

Index

Index

Index

Index

Index

Index

Index

Index

Index